ALESSANDRO GRAHELI

HISTORY AND TRANSMISSION OF THE NYĀYAMAÑJARĪ

Critical Edition of the Section on the Sphoṭa

ÖSTERREICHISCHE AKADEMIE DER WISSENSCHAFTEN

PHILOSOPHISCH-HISTORISCHE KLASSE
SITZUNGSBERICHTE, 870. BAND

BEITRÄGE ZUR KULTUR- UND
GEISTESGESCHICHTE ASIENS, NR. 91

History and Transmission of the Nyāyamañjarī

Critical Edition of the Section on the Sphoṭa

Alessandro Graheli

VERLAG DER
ÖSTERREICHISCHEN
AKADEMIE DER
WISSENSCHAFTEN

Vorgelegt von w. M. Ernst Steinkellner in der Sitzung vom 3. Juli 2015

Diese Publikation wurde einem anonymen, internationalen Peer-Review-Verfahren unterzogen.
This publication has undergone the process of anonymous, international peer review.

Die verwendete Papiersorte ist aus chlorfrei gebleichtem Zellstoff hergestellt, frei von säurebildenden Bestandteilen und alterungsbeständig.

ISBN 978-3-7001-7746-3

Druck und Bindung: Sowa Sp. z o.o.
Printed and bound in the EU

http://epub.oeaw.ac.at/7746-3
http://verlag.oeaw.ac.at

Contents

Acknowledgements

This book is the culmination of project M-1160 G-15 (July 2009 – June 2011), financed by the FWF (Fonds zur Förderung der wissenschaftlichen Forschung) and based at the ISTB (Institut für Südasien-, Tibet- und Buddhismuskunde), University of Vienna.

Credits are due to the repositories where the manuscripts used for this edition are preserved:

- Allahabad, Shri Ganganath Jha Campus (Deemed University)
- Chennai, The Adyar Library and Research Center, Theosophical Society
- Chennai, Government Oriental Manuscript Library, Madras University Library (Chepauk Campus)
- Jaisalmer, Jñānabhaṇḍāra (Baḍā Bhaṇḍāra), Jaisalmer Fort, Jaisalmer Lodrapur Parshvanath Jain Trust
- Kolkata, The Asiatic Society
- Mysore, Oriental Research Institute, University of Mysore
- Pune, Anandashram
- Pune, Bhandarkar Oriental Research Institute
- Pune, Deccan College
- Srinagar, Oriental Research Institute Library
- Kozhicode (Thenhipalam), Malayalam Department of the University of Calicut
- Varanasi, Sampurnanand Sanskrit Vishwavidyalaya

Most of the copies of manuscripts were acquired and archived at the ISTB in the course of FWF Projects P-17244, P-19328 and P-24388. Additional copies were shared by Dominic Goodall, Kei Kataoka, Yasutaka Muroya, Hiroshi Marui, T. Ono, Karin Preisendanz, Taisei

Shida, Raffaele Torella, and Alex Watson.

The contents of this book result from exchanges with many colleagues. First of all, my gratitude goes to Elisa Freschi. Her commitment to philosophy, her intellectual integrity and her enthusiasm for debate have been a constant source of inspiration throughout the years. She went through many sections of this publication more than once and helped me correcting countless errors. The Sanskrit part was further enhanced by the insightful remarks suggested by both Hugo David and Elisa Freschi, with whom we recently read the critically edited text once more. Also Kei Kataoka improved specific passages of the Sanskrit text and contributed important remarks, besides being an invaluable source of knowledge through his writings on Jayanta. Yasutaka Muroya enriched my knowledge of the manuscript tradition of the *Nyāyamañjarī* by sharing thoughts, discussing crucial topics, and providing material and information otherwise unavailable to me. I am thankful to Cristina Pecchia, Philipp Maas and Dominik Wujastyk for engaging in debates on various aspects of textual criticism in the last few years. Furthermore, Dominik Wujastyk's TeX savvy is behind some key choices in this publication.I also want to acknowledge other countless TeX and LaTeX stalwarts who make the typesetting of publications such as this one possible. I am grateful to Oliver Frey for his feedback on typographical and aesthetic issues, as well as for his contagious approach to problem solving. Other friends and colleagues who helped me throughout the years are Daniele Cuneo, Christian Ferstl, Camillo Formigatti, Dennis Johnson, Toshikazu Watanabe, Erika Wieder and Dagmar Wujastyk.

I am indebted to my Vyākaraṇa and Nyāya teachers, Shri Haridas Shastri, Shyamasharan Swami and Satya Narayana Das Babaji; to Raffaele Torella and Raniero Gnoli, with whom I discovered Bhaṭṭa Jayanta and the *Nyāyamañjarī*; to Karin Preisendanz, who gave a decisive impetus to this enterprise, first by endorsing my FWF project and later by welcoming me in the *Nyāyabhāṣya* project where I could deepen my knowledge of the history of Nyāya and refine my philological method. And I am deeply grateful to Ernst Steinkellner for his pragmatic advices and for submitting this book to the Austrian Academy of Sciences.

Introduction

Bhaṭṭa Jayanta's *Nyāyamañjarī* (henceforth NM) is a rich compendium of ontological, epistemological and linguistic issues. Due to its clear prose and thorough exposition, it is an invaluable tool to reconstruct the history of ideas of Nyāya, Mīmāṃsā, Vyākaraṇa and other traditions, and as such it has become one of the most quoted and studied Sanskrit philosophical works.

Why a new edition of the Nyāyamañjarī (NM)?

The NM has been edited and studied in multiple forms. Most importantly, the two editions based on manuscript sources are those by Gangadhara Shastri Tailanga and K.S. Varadacarya. These pioneering works are both extremely valuable and deserve utmost respect, since they paved the way for most later researches on the NM, including the present one. Yet, these two editors obviously worked with a restricted number of manuscripts and could not avail themselves of the present technology. Moreover, neither of them appears to have followed a consistent editorial method, so there is still room for improvement on their work.

Gangadhara mostly based his edition on a single manuscript, with the sporadic assistance of a second one. Varadacharya improved Gangadhara's edition by means of some additional manuscripts and was capable of reconstructing a much more complete text. In both editions, however, the manuscripts are barely mentioned and not described in any detail. Also, neither editor clarified the criteria used in the editorial choices.

The impact of Nagin J. Shah's writings on the present edition should be mentioned. He edited the only extant commentary of the NM, the *Nyāyamañjarīgranthibhaṅga,* with remarkable accuracy, lucidity, and historical perspective. Furthermore, he contributed important studies on the NM itself, besides editing and translating the NM into Gujarati.

In the last decade, Kei Kataoka has edited thematic passages of the NM on the basis of previously unedited manuscripts, thus improving the quality of the text and in the process shedding further light on the NM manuscripts and editions. His editorial work, however, has so far not covered any part of the sixth *āhnika* of the NM, which is the target of the present book.

In general, there is no NM edition based on a genealogical study of the sources and with a focus on the history of the transmission. Notwithstanding the intellectual debt to all the scholars who have previously worked on the NM, the intention is to contribute here in the following areas:

- identification, location and detailed description of all the witnesses;
- collation of all the relevant witnesses, including some previously never used ones;
- study of the genealogy of the sources, culminating in a *stemma codicum*;
- elimination of apographs (*codices descriptii*);
- elaboration of a pragmatic editorial strategy;
- documentation of all the substantive variants;
- improvement of the text on the basis of the *stemma codicum* and, when needed, of internal criteria;
- study of the indirect transmission (secondary testimonia).

Reasons for the choice of NM 6

The sixth *āhnika* of the NM (NM 6) is structured in three conceptually independent sections, dealing, respectively, with the object of words (*padārtha*), the object of sentences (*vākyārtha*), and the object of the Veda (*vedārtha*).

The first of these three sections was the topic of my *Laurea* (MA) thesis at the University of Rome "Sapienza" (Graheli, 2003). At that time my research was limited to the printed editions, in which I found some passages that were difficult to interpret on the basis of the printed texts alone. At that time I began to sketch a survey of the known manuscripts of the NM and to gradually realize the importance of building an accurate inventory and description of both the printed and manuscript sources. Once accomplished a fairly exhaustive version of this survey (see Graheli, 2012a), it dawned to me that some crucial yet mutilated manuscripts covered NM 6 but lacked other chapters of the NM; for this reason, in order to develop a stemmatic method to edit the NM, the obvious choice was to focus on this very section of Jayanta's work.

In short, the first section of NM 6 is for the present purposes the ideal choice because conceptually self-contained, extensive enough to provide statistically meaningful hypotheses on the genealogy of the manuscripts, and documented in all the key witnesses of the transmission.

The structure of this book

This book is divided into two major parts: the study of the history of the transmission and the critical edition of the *padārtha* section of NM 6.

The first part includes all the propaedeutic steps in view of the critical edition. Briefly said, it consists of the *recensio* of the NM sources, including their inventory, description, collation of their variants, and study of their genealogy. The sequence of the chapters largely conforms to the method and the heuristic process followed in the course of the research. This part begins with a general presentation of the NM and its author, about whom there is, in comparison to many other Indian works and authors, a more extensive amount of historical and chronological information. There is here a deliberate choice to pay full attention to the printed sources as well, to facilitate an evaluation of their respective merits and to further clarify the needs of better editions. Hence, the survey of the editions precedes that of the manuscripts. This part continues with a detailed study of the genealogy of the editions only after the description of the manuscripts, because the assessment of the relation among the editions is better understood in the context of the number and quality of the manuscripts on which the editions are based. The genealogy of the manuscripts is then studied on the ground of the collation of NM 6, resulting in the *stemma codicum* on which the choice of the variant readings has been largely based during the editing process.

The second part of this book contains the edition of the first third of NM 6, which concerns a presentation and rebuttal of the *sphoṭa* theory of word-meaning. The decision to publish this part separately from the two other sections of NM 6 is eminently pragmatic, since it is extensive enough to allow for statistically meaningful considerations, but also short enough to be single-handedly manageable in the present publication. The publication of the complete NM 6 would have been difficult to manage in a single book; thus the decision to divide it into three segments according to its natural division in the three section of *padārtha*, *vākyārtha* and *vedārtha*. One of the main goals of this research was to devise a method to edit NM passages that could be feasible for individual enterprises, without the demand of formidable resources in terms of time, man-power, and funds.

The plan is to complete the edition of NM 6 in two more volumes, on the strength of the method and the editorial principles established in the present publication.

The choice of Devanāgarī

The present edition is typeset in Devanāgarī characters. There are two reasons behind this choice: the first is pragmatic, related to aspects of dissemination, and the second heuristic, related to a personal approach to stemmatics and critical editing.

The advantage of Devanāgarī characters is that it makes the book widely accessible to Indian scholarship. In fact, while most seasoned Sanskritists in the West are accustomed to read Sanskrit in either Devanāgarī or Roman transcription, Indian scholars who are comfortable with romanized Sanskrit are comparatively rare.

Furthermore, the study of the history of the transmission and of the genealogy of the sources is a central aspect of the present research. During the editorial processes I found that studying the NM in Roman characters was a step away from the linguistic universe of Jayanta, Cakradhara, the scribes, and the Indian editors: even if some of these personalities wrote in other Indic scripts, all of them reasoned in terms of *akṣara*-s, or *abugida* scripts, rather than Roman letters. Though Devanāgarī is in a sense also an arbitrary choice, I found that this script was more conducive to my inferences about the genealogy of errors, and thus heuristically productive in terms of stemmatic hypotheses, because its visual representation helped my judgement on the weight of variants, on specific typologies of errors such as dittography and haplography, on the likelihood for errors to be genetically or polygenetically derived, etc.

The Romanization of Sanskrit offers the advantage of facilitating a more detailed analysis of the text, due to the graphical division of vowels and consonants and to a more frequent separation of words. Moreover, machine-readable texts are certainly more useful in Roman Unicode characters, rather than in Devanāgarī ones. For such purposes the interested reader can profit from the full documentation, in Roman characters, of the collated variants on which this edition is based and that has been made available online, presently at http://homepage.univie.ac.at/alessandro.graheli.

Part I

The history of the transmission

1 Bhaṭṭa Jayanta

1.1 His life

Bhaṭṭa Jayanta flourished in Kashmir, in the last quarter of the 9th century, under the rule of king Śaṅkaravarman (r. 883–902 CE) of the Utpala dynasty.

Jayanta was a Śaiva and a brahmin of the Bhāradvāja *gotra*. His ancestor, Śakti, migrated six generations before from Gauḍa, probably Bengal, to Darvābhisāra (South-West of the Kashmir valley). There are also textual passages that connect Jayanta and his family to Gauramūlaka, a village that may have also been in Darvābhisāra.

Biographical sketches have already been written,[1] so the following paragraphs are mostly devoted to some problematic aspects.

Jayanta's son, Abhinanda, mentioned his father both in the colophon and the introductory verses of KKS.[2] In the colophon Abhinanda refers to himself as the "son of Bhaṭṭa Jayanta, the emperor of savants",[3] and in the introductory verses he describes him in the

[1] See, in particular, ĀḌ^{Ra}, Introduction, Hegde, 1983, ĀḌ^{De}, Introduction, and Slaje, 2012. The introduction in ĀḌ^{De} and its online version (Dezső, 2004) are rich in insight into Jayanta's personality, and Slaje, 2012 addresses important historical and chronological aspects. Further evidence about the date and other biographical information can be found in Frauwallner, 1936, 267–8; Hacker, 1951; Oberhammer, 1962, 146; Gupta, 1963, 9–12; Matilal, 1977, 92–4; Potter, 1977, 345–6; Slaje, 1986, 245 *et passim*; Kataoka, 2007b.

[2] According to Raghavan, 1980, 83, in the DhV, 142,23–24, Abhinava Gupta seems to ascribe the KKS to Bhaṭṭa Jayanta: *kathātātparye sargabandho yathā bhaṭṭajayantakasya kādambarīkathāsāram*. But, as acknowledged by Raghavan himself, one could interpret the *ka* suffix in *bhaṭṭajayantakasya* as a diminutive, thus referring to Bhaṭṭa Jayanta's son.

[3] *iti śrīsakalavipaściccakravartiśrībhaṭṭajayantasūnor abhinandasya* [...]

context of his family lineage:[4]

(5) Once upon a time there was a *gauḍa* brahmin of the Bhāradvāja clan, Śakti, who married after settling in Dārvābhisāra.
(6) His son was called Mitra ("sun"), a treasure of brilliant qualities, whose birth was saluted by those who were awake after darkness.
(7) He (Mitra) begot a well-educated son, Śaktisvāmin, the minister of king Muktāpīḍa of the Karkoṭa dynasty.
(8) His son, called Kalyānasvāmin, became like Yājñavalkya, who had shaken off the impurity of existence by the power of pure yoga.
(9) From him, who had a profound mind, a beloved son, Candra ("moon"), the ornament of Parameśvara (Śiva), was born, as if from the ocean of milk.[5]
(10) He generated a son, Jayanta, who made everyone's happiness. His poetry and eloquence were the embodiment of the Goddess of Speech.
(11) He was known by a second name, "the commentator" (Vṛttikāra), was well versed in the Veda and its accessory disciplines, and was capable of debating topics in every discipline.
(12) From the wise Jayanta a son, well-read in the essence of belles lettres and known as Abhinanda, was born.[6]

---

[4]In this book Sanskrit terms and passages are in general hyphenated according to Sanskrit prosodic rules, i.e., by *akṣara*-s, defined as either a vowel at the beginning of a word or a consonant, or a consonants' cluster ending with a vowel.

[5]Here the editor of KKS, verse 9, p. 2, as well as Borsani Scalabrino, 1962, 150, interpreted Kānta, and not Candra, as Jayanta's father's name. But Jayanta himself, in NM^{Va}, II 718,7, NM 12, explicitly describes himself as "the son of Candra, whose fame is all-pervading" (*sūnur vyāptadigantarasya yaśasā candrasya*).

[6]*śaktināmābhavad gauḍo bhāradvājakule dvijaḥ / dārvābhisāram āsādya kṛta-dāraparigrahaḥ //5// tasya mitrābhidhāno 'bhūd ātmajas tejasāṃ nidhiḥ / janena doṣoparamaprabuddhenārcitodayaḥ //6// sa śaktisvāminaṃ putram avāpa śrutaśālinam / rājñaḥ karkoṭavaṃśasya muktāpīḍasya mantriṇam //7// kalyāṇasvāmināmāsya yājñavalkya ivābhavat / tanayaḥ śuddhayogarddhinirdhūtabhavakalmaṣaḥ //8// agādhahṛdayāt tasmāt parameśvaramaṇḍanam / ajāyata sutaḥ kāntaś candro dugdhodadher iva //9// putraṃ kṛtajanānandaṃ sa jayantam ajījanat / āsīt kavitvavaktṛtvaphalā yasya sarasvatī //10// vṛttikāra iti vyaktaṃ dvitīyaṃ nāma bibhrataḥ / vedavedāṅgaviduṣaḥ sarvaśāstrārthavādinaḥ //11// jayantanāmnaḥ sudhiyaḥ sādhusāhityatattvavit / sūnuḥ samudabhūt tasmād abhinanda iti śrutaḥ //12//* A slightly different translation of these verses with a discussion on some subtler nuances can be found in Dezső, 2004, Introduction, 5.

To better understand Jayanta's ancestry it is important to extract from these verses the historical and geographical coordinates. In this connection, one must keep in mind that the value of this testimony may be conditioned by the fact that the KKS is not a critical edition and is thus not necessarily reliable, as noted by Slaje (2012, 121).

Slaje (2012, 123) assumes that Śakti may plausibly have settled in Darvābhisāra at the time of the surge to power of the Kārkoṭa dynasty, i.e., in the first half of the 7th century. His reasoning is based on Jayanta's link with king Śaṅkaravarman, who is known to have ruled from 883 to 902 CE, and on Śaktisvāmin's one with king Muktāpīḍa, as mentioned in verse 7 above.

Slaje also suggests that Śakti might have settled in Darvābhisāra at the dawn of the Karkoṭa dynasty (ca. 650 CE). In Cat. Stein 1894, Introduction, xix, Stein had noticed how another manuscript ("MS. 304") of the KKS reads *candrāpīḍasya* in place of *muktāpīḍasya*, in verse 7. Slaje (2012, 123) favours the *candrāpīḍasya* reading, arguing with good reason that a corruption of the text from the famous Muktāpīḍa to the relatively unknown Candrāpīḍa is less likely than the reverse. One may add that a mechanical error causing a shift from *mu* to *ca*, in Śāradā script, is not unlikely, but a mistake from *kta* to *ndra* seems far-fetched, so the *candrāpīḍasya* reading would indeed seem the original one. As for the dates of these two kings, Candrāpīḍa and Muktāpīḍa ruled in 713–720 and 724–760, respectively.[7]

While Slaje's reasoning has philological merit, it is chronologically difficult to explain Śaktisvāmin as a minister of Candrāpīḍa, while the date of Muktāpīḍa's reign better fits the genealogy given by Abhinanda. Slaje tries to find a consistent explanation by calculating an average of about 44 years per generation, obtained after dividing by the number of generations (4) the longest (189 years) and short-

[7]The chronologies of the Karkoṭa kings are obtained by Stein after adding a correction of 25 years to Kalhaṇa's chronology on the basis of Chinese records (Stein, 1989a, Introduction, 67, and Book IV, 125, fn. 45, and 131, fn. 126). The necessity of a correction was originally noticed by Alexander Cunningham (see Cunningham, 1871, 91), and endorsed in Cat. Report 1875, 43, 55. For an explanation of the 25 years correction, see also Witzel, 1990, 51, fn. 103, quoted in Slaje, 2012, 123, fn. 12.

est (163 years) possible lapses from Candrāpīḍa's reign (713–720) to Śaṅkaravarman's (883–902):

$$(189 / 4 + 163 / 4) / 2 = 44$$

Following Slaje's reasoning, it would indeed be possible that Śakti settled in Darvābhisāra around 650 CE, close to the rise of the Karkoṭa dynasty. Yet, this is inconsistent with Śaktisvāmin's ministry under Candrāpīḍa as early as in 720. The fixed point from which the calculation starts is 883–902, let's say 890, when we assume that Jayanta, as a mature adult, was writing the NM and was an advisor of Śaṅkaravarman. There seems to be a problem in Slaje's calculation: if we start from 890 and move back to the time Śaktisvāmin's adulthood, when he would have been a minister of Candrāpīḍa, there are three intervening generations, not four, and therefore instead of 44 years we would obtain an average of 57 years per generation:

$$(189 / 3 + 163 / 3) / 2 = 57$$

Therefore, only by 57-years intervals it would have been possible for Śaktisvāmin to be a minister of Candrāpīḍa, as argued by Slaje, but by the same logic Śakti would have then been an adult in 605 CE, before the rise of the Karkoṭas. Now, an average interval of 44 years across six generations in a patrilineage, although not impossible, would be surprisingly long, while an average of 57 years would be close to impossible. A likely average of patrilinear generations could be, instead, of 35 years.[8]

The chronologies shown in Fig. 1.2 can be sketched by applying, respectively, the hypotheses of spans of 57, 44, and 35 years. The assumption is that Jayanta was an adult in 883–902, since he is repeatedly referring to Śaṅkaravarman in the NM, his mature work. 890 CE, the middle of Śaṅkaravarman's reign, is chosen as the starting point of the calculation from Jayanta back to his ancestors. To

[8]A well known example is the patrilineage of Elizabeth II, present Queen of England, that can be traced back to Theodoric I (c. 916 – c. 976), lasting one thousand years across thirty patrilinear generations.

have Śaktisvāmin as a minister of Candrāpīḍa, the 57-year span of generations should be adopted. With the span of 44 years per generation, applying Slaje's argument with the correct divider of three intervals from Jayanta back to Śaktisvāmin, the latter would be linked to last years of Muktāpīḍa's reign. With the more plausible span of 35 years per generation, however, Śaktisvāmin would have lived during Jayāpīḍa's reign (773–806), thus conflicting with Abhinanda's narration. There are no other names of Karkoṭa kings that can be associated with either "Candrāpīḍa" or "Muktāpīḍa" found in the manuscripts of Abhinanda's work (see Fig. 1.1).

Hegde (1983, 15) is apparently unaware of the *candrāpīḍasya* variant in ms. 304. He does an inverse calculation, from the starting point of 760 CE, the latest time in which Śaktisvāmin could have been a minister of Muktāpīḍa (also known as Lalitāditya):

> If Kalyānasvāmin took birth in 760 A.D. by the time Śaktisvāmin became the minister of Lalitāditya, then 790 may be the probable date of Candra's birth. Consequently Jayanta might have been born in 820 A.D. [...] Thus the date of Bhaṭṭa Jayanta falls, beyond any doubt, between 820 A.D. and 900 A.D.

To conclude, there is no easy solution to account for the connection of Śaktisvāmin with either Candrāpīḍa or Muktāpīḍa. In any case, common sense dictates that family memories beyond one's great-grandfather's times are not always accurate, so in principle the historicity of Abhinanda's notions about the early stages of his patrilineage should be cautiously evaluated and confirmed by external evidence, as far as possible.

From Abhinanda's verses some information about the geographical roots of Jayanta's family can also be derived, starting from the mention of Darvābhisāra, where Śakti settled after his marriage, in KKS, verse 5. Darvābhisāra is the region "between the Vitastā and the Candrabhāgā" (Stein, 1989a, vol. I, 32, n. 180), i.e., the Jhelum and the Chenab rivers, separated by the Pir Panjal range from the Kashmir valley. Furthermore, Jayanta himself mentions the homeland of his ancestors in the NM^{Va}, I 653,10–12, NM 4. In a discussion about

Figure 1.1: Karkoṭa and Utpala dynasties up to Jayanta's time, following Stein's reconstruction

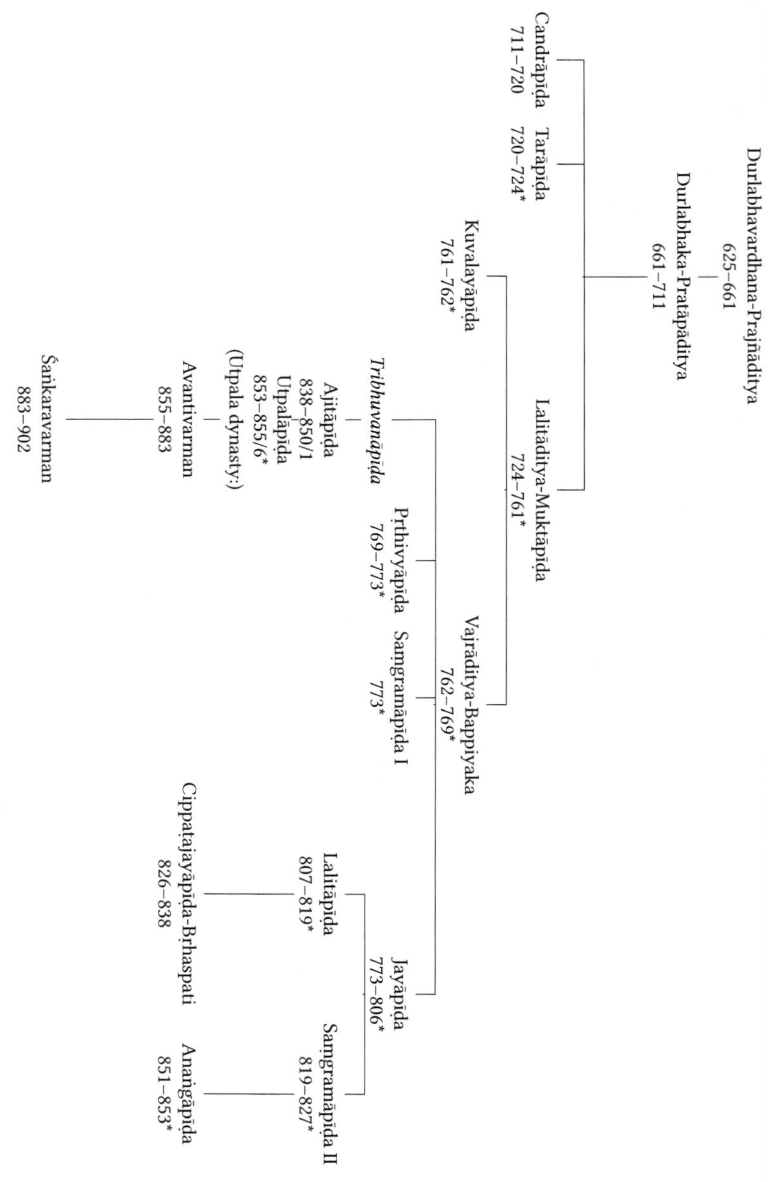

Figure 1.2: Hypothetical chronologies of Jayanta's patrilineage

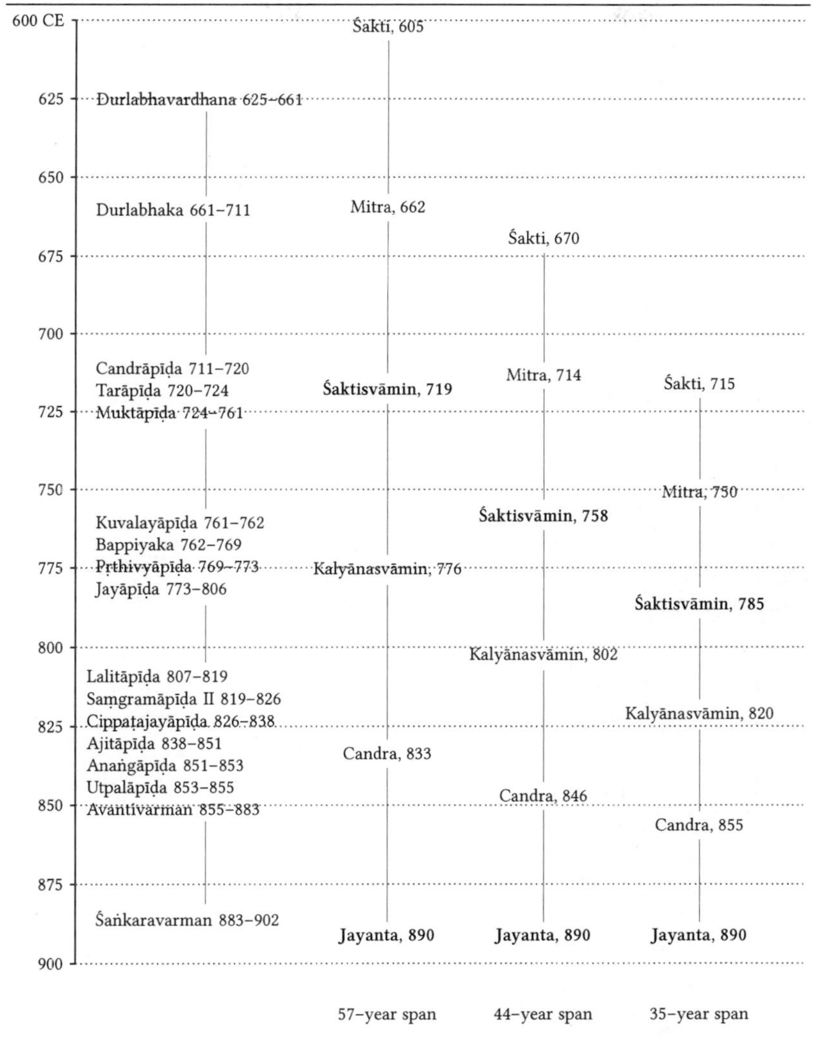

the likelihood of achieving the result of a sacrifice right after its performance, he tells a personal anecdote:

> My grandfather, who desired a village, performed a Sāṃgrahaṇī sacrifice.[9] He obtained the Gauramūlaka village right after the end of the sacrifice.[10]

Moreover, Gauramūlaka also occurs in examples made by Jayanta in two distinct philosophical contexts: on *abhāva* (NM^{Va}, I 132,2–4, 142,4, 142,10, 143,11, NM 1), and on the ontology of *śabda*, specifically in relation to the absurdity of a sound pronounced in Kanyakubja and heard in a distant place such as Gauramūlaka (NM^{Va}, I 536,4, NM 3). In Stein, 1989a, 8.1861, a Ghoramūlaka site in the Rajauri (Rājapurī) area, i.e., in Darvābhisāra, is mentioned. Stein connected it with the Gauramūlaka of the NM, although he was unable to positively locate the place.

At the time of the composition of the NM the ruler was Śaṅkaravarman (883–902, see Stein, 1989a, 202ff.) of the Utpala dynasty, as we know from direct references to the king in the NM and in the *Āgamāḍambara*, where he is also called Yaśovarman.[11] Jayanta (NM^{Va}, I 388,25–26, NM 2; I 649,6–7, NM 4) writes of him as "King Śaṅkaravarman, knower of dharma" (*dharmatattvajñaḥ rājā śaṅkaravarmā*). There and elsewhere Jayanta refers to the king in flattering terms, in stark contrast to the criticism of Śaṅkaravarman's rule found in the RT. Kalhaṇa reports that Śaṅkaravarman's greedy and oppressive policies gradually increased with time.[12] In the NM (NM^{Va}, II 199,9–10, NM 6), however, there is also a passage in which Jayanta reveals that he was imprisoned, exiled, or for whatever reason was living in some sort of isolation, under the king's order.[13] One may

[9] Cf. *Baudhāyanaśrautasūtra*, Ch. 13, Par. 30, Verse 140.8, *vaiśvadevîṁ sāṃgrahaṇîṃ nírvaped grā̆makāmaḥ.*

[10] *asmatpitāmaha eva grāmakāmaḥ sāṃgrahaṇīṃ kṛtavān sa iṣṭisamāptisamanantaram eva gauramūlakaṃ grāmam avāpa.*

[11] See ĀḌ^{De}, Act IV, p. 204,3. See also Kavi, 1940.

[12] *atha krameṇa nṛpatir lobhābhyāsena bhūyasā / ādhīyamānacitto 'bhut prajāpīḍanapaṇḍitaḥ* (RT, V.165).

[13] For a discussion of this passage, see Slaje, 2012, 128 *et passim.*

speculate that Jayanta's positive remarks were written in the early period of Śaṅkaravarman's rule, when the king had not yet revealed his uglier side, or that for political opportunity he preferred to refrain from criticizing him in his writings.

As for Jayanta's religious affiliation, from the benedictory verses of the NM it appears that he was a Śaiva, as was probably his father (see KKS, verse 7, quoted above). In NM 4 he defends the authority of the *Atharvaveda* and even hints at its primacy as the main Veda (NM^{Va}, II 626,14–15, NM 11). Thus Raghavan and Thakur (ĀḌ^{Ra}, Introduction, iii) have suggested that he belonged to the Atharvaveda school. More specifically, Kataoka (2007b) argued that he must have been a Paippalādin brahmin.

From the *Āgamaḍambara* one can gather that he was a respected teacher,[14] and that he may have been a disciple of Bhaṭṭa Sāhata, also known as Dhairyaraśi.[15]

1.2 His works

Bhaṭṭa Jayanta is mostly known as the author of the NM and is consequently characterized as a Naiyāyika. In the NM, however, he shines as a well-rounded and eclectic author, well versed in *śāstra*-s such as Mīmāṃsā and Vyākaraṇa, and gifted with an uncommon literary skill. He reportedly wrote a lost commentary on grammar as a child prodigy, and he composed a philosophical play, the *Āgamaḍambara*. Two further Nyāya works have been ascribed to him, the *Nyāyakalikā* and the *Nyāyapallava*.

Jayanta was also known as "Vṛttikāra", or "Navavṛttikāra", as we know from the KKS, verse 11, quoted above, and from NM^{Va}, II 718,6, NM 12. Different hypotheses have been put forward about the nature of the *Vṛtti* in question (see Raghavan, 1960): some have suggested that it could have referred to the NM itself (Gopinath Kaviraj), or even the *Kāśikāvṛtti* (Stein). It is clear, however, that it was a commentary on grammar written by Jayanta in his tender age, as ex-

[14] See ĀḌ^{De}, Prologue, p. 32,15, *bhaṭṭajayantasya śiṣyapariṣad aham ajñāptaḥ, yathā asmadguroḥ kṛtir* [...].

[15] See Thakur, 1955, 508.

plicitly stated by himself in ĀḌ^{De}, Prologue, p. 32,13–14: *śaiśava eva vyākaraṇavivaraṇakaraṇād vṛttikāra iti prathitāparanāmno* [...].

The *Nyāyakalikā* is a primer on Nyāya. It was originally edited in (1925) and a new edition is presently in progress, with the first part recently published (NKa^{Ka}). As for its contents, Kataoka (NKa^{Ka}, 1) writes:

> The *Nyāyakalikā* [...] explains the sixteen *padārthas* and their subdivisional items [...] This work simply explains basic Naiyāyika concepts for the sake of understanding of beginners (*bālavyutpattaye*). It is one of the earliest extant examples of works in the Nyāya tradition that intends to be a concise textbook for students.

According to Marui (2000, 2008) and Kataoka (NKa^{Ka}, 1), it is Jayanta's work without reasonable doubt. The contents and the formulation of the technical passages matches those of the NM very closely, often mirroring them *verbatim*. My impression is that of an abridgement of the NM, written by Jayanta or some later student of the NM, although Raghavan and Thakur (ĀḌ^{Ra}, Introduction, v) thought that it was written before the NM. On the issue of Jayanta's authorship and the relation to the NM, however, it is difficult to express a conclusive judgement on the basis of the *editio princeps* (NKa^{Jha}) alone, since there the text seems to be incomplete and faulty in some passages. A better assessment will probably be possible with Kataoka's new edition, together with a detailed comparison of the parallel passages in their respective contexts.

Raghavan and Thakur (ĀḌ^{Ra}, Introduction, v) inferred that Jayanta also wrote "the *Nyāyapallava*, a moderately sized metrical gloss on Gautama". As far as I can see Raghavan's assumption is based on three explicit mentions of the *Pallava* found in Vādideva Sūri's *Syādvādaratnākara.*

The first mention is *tathā ca samācaṣṭa bhaṭṭajayantaḥ pallave* (SVR, 64,1), which introduces a string of seven stanzas devoted to topics discussed in NM I 31–40. The second is *tad api cātra plavate yad ajalpi jayantena pallave* (SVR, 302,13), which introduces another group of stanzas; one of these, *svarūpād udbhavāt kāryaṃ sahakāryupabṛṃhitāt / na hi kalpayituṃ śaktaṃ śaktim anyām atīndriyām,* is found also in the NM (NM^{Va}, I 107,10–11, NM 1), while the others seem to condense in metrical form the topics discussed in that very section of the NM. The third is *tad uktaṃ bhaṭṭajayantena pallave* (SVR, 780,7–8), which introduces a stanza, not found in the NM, concerning the refutation of the Buddhist theory of momentariness; the theory is presented and refuted in NM^{Va}, II 299–247, NM 7, but in this case there is no obvious correlation between the NM and in the SVR.

The editor of the SVR, Motilal Ladhaji, thought that by *pallava* Vādideva actually referred to the very NM, although he was aware, as acknowledged in a footnote, that these passages are not found in the NM in the same form.[16] In support of Ladhaji's interpretation, in the SVR there are several other passages which are apparently re-used from the NM. These re-uses are introduced by formulas such as *ucyate jayantena* (SVR, 336,18), before quoting NM^{Va}, I 536,16–537,10, NM 3, *agādi jayantena* (SVR, 976,19), before quoting NM^{Va}, I 29,1–4, NM 1, *jayanto 'py ajalpayat* (SVR, 1097,15), before quoting NM^{Va}, II 356,13–14, NM 7 and other stanzas in that very context; or, they are produced without credits (SVR, 1231,13–14), before re-using NM^{Va}, II 592,11–12, NM 11. Conversely, in my knowledge, there are not any direct mentions of *nyāyamañjarī* or *mañjarī* in connection to such NM re-uses.

A verdict about the existence of an independent work called *Pallava* would require further evidence, in addition to these passages of the SVR; but if Raghavan's intuition proves right, there might have been a trilogy of Nyāya works (ĀḌ^{Ra}, Introduction, v) growing from a *kalikā* (bud), to a *pallava* ("twig with leaves"), and to a *mañjarī* ("twig with flowers").[17]

Jayanta's literary vein found expression also in a philosophical drama, the ĀḌ^{Ra}. The play is rich in clues about Jayanta's time and personality, as eloquently discussed in the introduction to the edition and translation by Csaba Dezső (2005).

---

[16] *adhunā mudritāyāṃ nyāyamañjaryām idaṃ nopalabhyate / nyāyamañjary eva pallavasaṃjñayā śrīvādidevasūribhiḥ saṃmanyate* (SVR, 64, fn. 1).

[17] Cf. *Amarakośa*, vanauṣadhivarga 13, 14, 16, p. 55 *vallarir mañjarī striyau, pallavo 'strī kisalayaṃ, kalikā korakaḥ pumān*, where the synonyms of *kalikā*, *pallava* and *mañjarī* appear to be listed in stages of blossoming.

1.3 The contents of the NM

The NM is a large treatise unfolding in twelve books (*āhnika*-s, lit. "daily lessons"). At the very outset (NM^{Va}, I 2–3), Jayanta introduces the work as a mere rearrangement of former Nyāya ideas. Jayanta also explains (NM^{Va}, I 30,9, NM 1) how the NM is devoted to those aphorisms of the *Nyāyasūtra* that contain classifications (*nirdeśa*) and definitions (*lakṣaṇa*) of the Nyāya categories (*padārtha*). The bulk of the *Nyāyasūtra* is constituted of aphorisms meant to test (*parīkṣā*) those classifications and definitions. Yet, such *parīkṣā* aphorisms are only occasionally discussed in the NM.

The NM is organized in two major divisions: the first (NM 1–6) treats means of knowledge (*pramāṇa*), while the second (NM 7–12) discusses objects of knowledge (*prameya*) and the other fourteen categories listed in NSū 1.1.1. An overview of the work can be found in Table 1.1. This table also reveals, in a rough calculation, the length of the whole work, altogether more than thirteen thousand *śloka*-s.

The very structure of the NM confirms the main interests of Jayanta and perhaps of the whole Nyāya tradition at his time, namely epistemology. In particular, among the four means of knowledge accepted in Nyāya verbal testimony (*śabdapramāṇa*) is Jayanta's focus. It is the subject matter of NM 3 to 6. The centrality of *śabdapramāṇa* can be appreciated in Table 1.1, which shows how almost half of the work is devoted to this topic. In NM 1 to 6 each *sūtra* is commented and debated very extensively, while in the rest of the NM an increasing amount of *sūtra*-s is found, along with a decreasing extent of the commentary. In other words, Jayanta has much more to say on *śabda* and on the other *pramāṇa*-s than on the other fourteen categories of the old Nyāya school. In the present context it is important to notice how the text of NM 6 is not a commentary of any *sūtra*, but rather Jayanta's own elaboration on the some issues around *śabdapramāṇa*.

The following list is a table of contents of each *āhnika*, with a reference to the commented *Nyāyasūtra*-s:[18]

NM 1 Propitiatory and introductory verses. Discussion of the Nyāya

[18] See Section 14 for a full list of commented *sūtra*-s.

classification into sixteen fundamental categories. Discussion of the first of these, "means of knowledge" (*pramāṇa*). Discussion of the sub-classification of means of knowledge into four types: perception (*pratyakṣa*), inference (*anumāna*), inferential analogy (*upamāna*), and verbal testimony (*śabda*) (NSū, 1.1.1, 1.1.3–4).

NM 2 Discussion of the first three means of knowledge: perception (*pratyakṣa*), inference (*anumāna*), and analogy (*upamāna*) (NSū, 1.1.5–6).

NM 3 Beginning of the discussion of verbal testimony (*śabda*). Definition of verbal testimony based on the trustworthiness of the source (NSū, 1.1.7).

NM 4 Discussion of the epistemic authority of Vedic scriptures, as well as other authoritative scriptures, and of common language (NSū, 1.1.8).

NM 5 Discussion of the types of objects of knowledge (*artha*) knowable by means of verbal testimony, beginning from the threefold classification into particulars (*vyakti*), universals (*jāti*) and shapes (*ākṛti*) (NSū, 2.2.66).

NM 6 Discussion of the aetiology of knowledge from words, first through a presentation and refutation of the Vaiyākaraṇas's holistic view on word- and sentence-meaning, then through a discussion of the Mīmāṃsakas's views on sentence-meaning, and finally by linking the purpose of studying grammar with the object of the Veda.

NM 7 Introduction on the "objects of knowledge" (*prameya*), i.e., the second of the sixteen categories listed in NSū, 1.1.1. Discussion of the classification into twelve objects of knowledge: self (*ātman*), body (*śarīra*), sense-organs (*indriya*), sense-objects (*artha*), intellect (*buddhi*), mind (*manas*), activity (*pravṛtti*), defects (*doṣa*), rebirth (*pretyabhāva*), result (*phala*), distress (*duḥkha*), and salvation (*apavarga*). Elaboration on the first of these, the self (*ātman*) (NSū, 1.1.9–10).

NM 8 Elaboration on the next ten objects of knowledge, beginning from the body (*śarīra*) and up to distress (*duḥkha*) (NSū, 1.1.11–21).

NM 9 Elaboration on the twelfth object of knowledge, salvation (NSū, 1.1.2, 1.1.22).

NM 10 Discussion of the next five of the sixteen categories listed in *sūtra* 1.1.1: (3) doubt (*saṃśaya*), (4) purpose (*prayojana*), (5) illustration (*dṛṣṭānta*), (6) tenets (*siddhānta*), and (7) components of inferences (*avayava*) (NSū, 1.1.23–39).

NM 11 Discussion of the next seven categories listed in *sūtra* 1.1.1: (8) hypothesis (*tarka*), (9) judgement (*nirṇaya*), (10) debate (*vāda*), (11) sophistic debate (*jalpa*), (12) one-sided debate (*vitaṇḍā*), (13) pseudo-logical reasons (*hetvabhāsa*), and (14) deceitful arguments (*chala*) (NSū, 1.1.40–41, 1.2.1–17).

NM 12 Discussion of the last two categories listed in *sūtra* 1.1.1: (15) strategies of generalization (*jāti*) and (16) weak spots in arguments (*nigrahasthāna*) (NSū, 1.2.18, 5.1.1–43, 1.2.19, 5.2.1–22).

Table 1.1: Structure and length of the NM

	NM	NSū	char.	akṣ.	śl.
(*pramāṇa* section)					
pramāṇa-s	1	1.1.1, 3–4	100.100	37.070	1158
pratyakṣa, anumāna, upamāna	2	1.1.5–6	138.600	51.330	1604
śabda	3	1.1.7	136.400	50.520	1579
	4	1.1.8	112.500	41.670	1302
	5	2.2.66	120.000	44.440	1389
	6	none	114.600	42.440	1326
(*prameya* section)					
ātman	7	1.1.9–10	78.700	29.150	911
śarīra–duḥkha	8	1.1.11–21	63.800	23.630	738
apavarga	9	1.1.2, 22	81.000	30.000	937
saṃśaya–avayava	10	1.1.23–39	58.900	21.830	682
tarka–hetvābhāsa	11	1.1.40–2.17	60.100	22.260	696
jāti, nigrahasthāna	12	1.2.18–19, 5.1.1–2.22	74.300	27.520	860
			1.139.000	421.860	13.182

Characters are rounded to hundreds; *akṣara*-s are calculated at a ratio of 2.7 characters (an average of random samples of the text) and rounded to tens; *śloka*-s are intended as units of 32 *akṣara*-s.

2 Survey and description of the NM editions

There are already many printed editions of the NM. Most of them have some intrinsic value that should not be ignored, especially because they constitute the basis of later researches on the NM, including the present one. It is important to list and describe the previous editions, both to underline their merits and to clarify the reasons for further editions. Actually a careful evaluation of the NM editions serves even more purposes:

- The description and the genealogy of the editions are necessary to clarify the criteria adopted in the collation of their readings and, conversely, to explain why they have been discarded from the collation.
- The accurate description of the printed sources indicates their weaknesses and strengths, so it enables the reader to assess the merits of each edition and to choose the best one for a given purpose.
- There has been some confusion in the identification of certain editions, so an unambiguous description of each of them helps to dispel doubts on such matters.[1]
- The unambiguous identification of the exact copies of each edition used in the present bibliography may also prove useful: in a typography of movable characters, particularly, as it is the case with the early editions of the NM, every copy can in principle contain dis-

[1] E.g., see the case of NM^{Ga}, NM^{Shu} and NM^{Ma} below: their unambiguous distinction is needed to identify the source of NM^{Va}.

tinctive peculiarities.

- Some printed sources, such as the *editio princeps* of the NM, were produced when manuscripts were still the most popular instrument for the transmission of texts in India. Probably, in the intention of early Indian editors, printed editions were akin to manuscripts in many respects and they deserve to be treated with at least the same attention deserved by late, 19th-century manuscripts.[2]
- The advent of the press in Devanāgarī characters is a quite late phenomenon (early 19th century), so early editions have a historical interest for a reconstruction of the evolution of Indian typography.

More in general, an accurate description of the printed sources is an important tool in the study of the textual transmission of the work, which is the main focus of this book. These aims are best achieved by adopting some of the established descriptive criteria of bibliography.[3]

Each of the next sections is a description of a NM edition. The editions are sorted in chronological order, with the editor's name and year of publication mentioned in the heading. Complete editions published in more than one volume are described with a specific focus on NM 6, while incomplete editions that do not include NM 6 are not described here and are barely mentioned at the end of this chapter. The descriptions are structured as follows:

Title-pages The relevant title-pages and imprints are transcribed diplomatically.

[2]E.g., in the *editio princeps* of the *Nyāyabhāṣya* (NBh[Ja]), studied in Graheli, forthcoming(a), a lengthy colophon in Sanskrit stanzas is found, complete with the editor's signature, an eulogy of the editor's lineage and the date, as often seen in Sanskrit manuscripts.

[3]The criteria adopted in the following pages are largely conforming to those set in Gaskell, 1972. In this sense "bibliography" can be defined as "the study of books as material objects" (Gaskell, 1972, 1). As explained therewith by Gaskell, while quoting Walter Greg's words, bibliography can also be defined as "the study of [...] the evolution of particular texts in the process of their production and reproduction".

Size Width × Height.

Signatures The sequence of the signatures is described by means of the formula explained in Gaskell, 1972, 328–332. For instance, the formula "8°: π^{12} 1–27^{4+1} 28–42^{4+1}" should be interpreted as follows: 8° = octavo, π^{12} = an unnumbered signature composed of 12 leaves, 1–27^{4+1} = twenty-seven signatures, numbered from 1 to 27 in the lower margin, of which all are in octavo while the 27th is in quarto, with a single leaf added to it; 28–42^{4+1} = fifteen numbered signatures, numbered from 28 to 42 in the lower margin, of which all are in octavo and the last one is in quart, with a single leaf added at the end.

Pagination The sequence of page numbers. Numbers given in brackets refer to unnumbered pages.

Contents The contents of the book related to the sequence of page numbers and the original table of contents.

Layout A description of the presentation of the contents.

Notes Elaboration of the above items, particularly in relation to historical and prosopographical notions.

2.1 Gangadhara Shastri Tailanga, 1895

Roman title-page

No. 10.] | THE | VIZIANAGRAM SANSKRIT SERIES | UNDER THE SUPERINTENDENCE OF | ARTHUR VENIS M. A. Oxon. | PRINCIPAL, SANSKRIT COLLEGE, BENARES. | THE NYÂYAMAÑJARÎ | OF | JAYANTA BHAṬṬA | EDITED BY | MAHÂMAHOPADHYÂYA GAṄGÂDHARA ŚÂSTRÎ TAILAṄGA | PROFESSOR, SANSKRIT COLLEGE, BENARES. | VOLUME VIII. | PART 1. | [typography logo: woodcut initials E.J.L.] | PRINTED, PUBLISHED AND SOLD BY | E. J. LAZARUS & Co., BENARES. | MAY BE HAD FROM GANESH DAS AND CO., CHOWK, BENARES; | JAYESTHARAM MUKUNDJI AND CO., BOMBAY; | OTTO HARRASSOWITZ AND M. SPIRGATIS LEIPZIG; | LUZAC AND CO., LONDON.| [rule 14 mm.] | 1895. | [Vertically, on the left margin] (ALL RIGHT RESERVED.) Registered under Act XXV of 1867.

Devanāgarī title-page

श्री | न्यायमञ्जरी ।| [ornament] | गौतमसूत्रतात्पर्यविवृतिः | [ornament] | पदवाक्य प्रमाणपारावारपारीण श्रीजयन्तभट्टकृता ।| [ornament] | तत्पूर्वभागः | काशिकराज

कीयसंस्कृतपाठशालायां साहित्यदर्शनाध्यापकेन | महामहोपाध्यायश्रीगङ्गाधरशास्त्रिणा | यथासंभवं ग्रन्थकारनिर्दिष्टप्रमाणान्तर- | स्थलप्रदर्शनपूर्वं संशोधितः | [woodcut logo: initials E.J.L.] | काश्यां | मैडिकलहालनामकयन्त्रालये मुद्रितः | [rule 20 mm.] संवत् १९५१

Size 150 × 230 mm.

Signatures 8°: π^{12} $1–27^{4+1}$ $28–42^{4+1}$

Pagination [2] 1–6, 1–10, [4] 1–2, 1–660

Contents Title-page in Roman [1], title-page in Devanāgarī [3], Preface (*nyāyamañjarībhūmikā*) 1–5, Table of contents (*nyāyamañjaryāḥ sūcīpatram*) 1–10, Index of unidentified quotations (*nyāyamañjaryāmupalabdhānāṃ granthāntaravacanānāmanupalabdhasthalānāṃ vivaraṇam*) [1], Index of quoted works and authors (*nyāyamañjaryāṃ parigṛhītagranthakāranāmāni*) [1], Errata corrige of second part (*nyāyamañjaryā uttarabhāgasya śuddhipatram*) 1, Errata corrige (*nyāyamañjaryāḥ śuddhipatram*) 1–2, Main text (NM 1–12) 1–659.

Layout Except for the beginning of new *āhnika*-s there are no headings. The text mostly continues uninterrupted for pages, with the exception of stanzas, which are set apart from the text-block, and of sparse indentations marking new paragraphs. There are sporadic footnotes.

Notes Signatures are marked in Devanāgarī digits. The book was printed in two distinct parts. This can be inferred from the presence of two distinct *errata*-s, as well as from the composition of the signatures: signature 27, consisting of a quarto and a single leaf, marks the end of the first part, ending with NM 6. NM 7 begins with signature 28. The footnotes are mostly used for bibliographical references to the *Nyāyasūtra* and a few other works; no variant readings are recorded in them. The Devanāgarī font used in this edition is almost identical to the one seen in the early Bibliotheca Indica volumes, i.e., the one used at the Baptist Mission Press in Calcutta and most likely carved by Manohar, Karmakar Panchanan's apprentice at the Baptist Mission in Serampore (see Naik, 1971, vol. I, 276–278). In the Roman title-page almost each line is printed in a different size and at least ten different typefaces can be seen therein, perhaps meant to advertise the typographical range of the press.

Copies IND–B–7742, Frauwallner Collection, Fachbereichsbibliothek Südasien-, Tibet- und Buddhismuskunde, University of Vienna.

2.2 Suryanarayana Shukla, 1936

Roman title-page
THE | KASHI SANSKRIT SERIES | (HARIDĀS SANSKRIT GRANTHA MĀLĀ | (Nyāya Section No. 15) | No. 106 | [ornament] | THE | NYĀYA MAÑJARĪ | of | JAYANTA BHAṬṬA | Edited with notes etc., by | PANDIT ŚRI SŪRYA NÂRÂYANA ŚUKLA | Nyāya Vyākaranachārya | Professor, Govt. Sanskrit College, Benares | [ornament] PUBLISHED BY | JAYA KRISHNA DÂS HARIDÂS GUPTA | The Chowkhamba Sanskrit Series Office. | Benares City | [rule 11 mm.] 1936

Imprint
(All Rights Reserved by the Publisher) | [text-width rule] PUBLISHED BY JAYA KRISHNA DAS HARIDAS GUPTA | The Chowkhamba Sanskrit Series Office | BENARES. | [text width rule] | Printed at the Vidya Vilas Press, Benares | [rule 15 mm.] | 1936

Devanāgarī title-page
हरिदाससंस्कृतग्रन्थमालासमाख्य-- | काशीसंस्कृतसीरिजपुस्तकमालायाः | १०६ | न्यायविभागे (१५) पञ्चदशं पुष्पम् । | [ornament] | *श्री* | न्यायमञ्जरी | गौतमसूत्रतात्पर्यविवृतिः | पदवाक्यप्रमाणपारावारपारीण श्रीजयन्तभट्टकृता । | वाराणसेयराजकीयसंस्कृतपाठशालानव्यप्राच्यन्यायशास्त्राध्यापकेन | न्यायव्याकरणाचार्यसूर्यनारायणशर्मशुक्लेन | विषमस्थल विवरणपूर्वकं सम्पादिता | [ornament] | प्रकाशकः--- | जयकृष्णदास हरिदास गुप्तः--- | चौखम्बा संस्कृत सीरिज् ग्राफिस, | बनारस सिटी | [rule 15 mm.] | सं० १९९२ वै० | [सर्वेऽधिकाराः प्रकाशकेन स्वीयत्तीकृता]

Size 133 × 215 mm.

Signatures 4°: π^8 1–49 1–26 1–4

Pagination and contents Title-pages and imprint [1–4], Table of contents of the first part (*nyāyamañjaryāḥ sūcīpatram / pramāṇaprakaraṇe*) [5–10], Table of contents of the second part (*nyāyamañjaryāṃ uttarārddhe pratipāditānāṃ viṣayāṇāṃ sūcīpatram*) [11–13], Errata corrige of the second part (*nyāyamañjaryā uttarabhāgasya śuddhipatram*) [14], Preface (*bhūmikā*) 1–8, First part, text of NM 1–6 (*pramāṇaprakaraṇam*) 1–392, Second part, text of NM 7–12 (*prameyaprakaraṇam*) 1–208, Complete *Nyāyasūtrapāṭha* (*śrīvācaspatimiśrapraṇīto nyāyasūtroddhāraḥ*) 1–28, Index of authors (*nyāyamañjaryāṃ parigṛhītagranthakāranāmāni*) 29, Index of works (*nyāyamañjaryāṃ parigṛhītagranthanāmāni*) 30, Index of identified quotations (*nyāyamañjaryām upalabdhānāṃ granthāntaravākyānāṃ ṭippaṇyām apradarśitatattadgranthasthalānāṃ tattatsthalavivaraṇam*) 31, Index of unidentified quotations (*nyāyamañjaryām upalabdhānāṃ granthāntaravacananam anupalabdhasthalānāṃ vivaraṇam*) 32.

Notes The text is segmented into thematic paragraphs with headings. There are occasional exegetical notes. Haridas Gupta founded the Chowkhamba Sanskrit Series Office in Varanasi in 1892; his son, Jayakrishnadas Gupta, is mentioned as the publisher in the title-page.

Copies IND–B–1950, Fachbereichsbibliothek Südasien-, Tibet- und Buddhismuskunde, University of Vienna.

2.3 Suryanarayana Shukla, 1969–1971

Devanāgarī title-page of the second part

॥ श्री ॥ | काशी संस्कृत ग्रन्थमाला | १०६ | [ornament] | (न्यायविभागे पञ्चदशं (१५) पुष्पम्) | पदवाक्यप्रमाणपारावारपारीणश्रीजयन्तभट्टप्रणीता । | न्यायमञ्जरी | (गौतमसूत्रतात्पर्यविवृतिः) | विषमस्थलविवरणेन विभूषिता | (प्रमेयप्रकरणादिनिग्रहस्थानप्रकरणान्त- | द्वितीयो भागः) | विवरणकारः | न्यायव्याकरणाचार्यः | पण्डितराजः श्रीसूर्यनारायणशुक्लः | सम्पादकः | तर्कतीर्थ-वेदान्तमीमांसाचार्यः | आद्योपाह्व अ० श्रीमध्वाचार्यः | चौखम्बा संस्कृत सीरिज् आफिस, वाराणसी | १९६९

Roman title-page of the second part

THE | KASHI SANSKRIT SERIES | 106 | (Nyāya Section No. 15) | [ornament] | NYĀYAMAÑJARĪ | of | JAYANTA BHAṬṬA | With notes | by | Pt. SŪRYANĀRĀYAṆA ŚUKLA | Edited by | Pt. A. MADHVĀCĀRYA ĀDYA | (PART II) | THE | CHOWKHAMBA SANSKRIT SERIES OFFICE | VARANASI–1 | 1969

Devanāgarī title-page of the first part

॥ श्री ॥ | काशी संस्कृत ग्रन्थमाला | १०६ | [ornament] | (न्यायविभागे पञ्चदशं (१५) पुष्पम्) | पदवाक्यप्रमाणपारावारपारीण-श्रीजयन्तभट्टप्रणीता । | न्यायमञ्जरी | (गौतमसूत्रतात्पर्यविवृतिः) | विषमस्थलविवरणेन विभूषिता | (षष्ठाह्निकान्तः प्रथमो भागः) |

विवरणकारः । न्याय-व्याकरणाचार्यः । पण्डितराजः श्रीसूर्यनारायणशुक्लः | [publisher's logo] | **चौखम्बा संस्कृत सीरिज् आफिस, वाराणसी** | १९७१

Roman title-page of the first part
THE | KASHI SANSKRIT SERIES | 106 | (Nyāya Section No. 15) | [ornament] | NYĀYAMAÑJARĪ | of | JAYANTA BHAṬṬA | Edited with notes | by | Pt. SŪRYA NĀRĀYAṆA ŚUKLA | (PART I) | THE | CHOWKHAMBA SANSKRIT SERIES OFFICE | VARANASI–1 (India) | 1971

Size 133 × 215 mm.

Signatures 8°: signatures are unmarked.

Pagination and contents, second part Title-pages and imprint 1–4, Foreword (*prākkathanam*) 5–6, Preface (*bhūmikā*) 7, Errata corrige (*śuddhipatram*) 8, Table of contents (*viṣayasūcī*) 9–12, Main text (NM 7–12) 1–208.

Pagination and contents, first part Title-pages, imprint [1–4], Preface (*bhūmikā*) 1–11, Table of contents (*sūcī-patram*) [12–16], Main text (NM 1–6) 1–392, Nyāyasūtra (*nyāyasūtroddhāraḥ*) 393–420, Index of authors (*nyāyamañjaryāṃ parigṛhītagranthakāranāmāni*) 421, Index of works (*nyāyamañjaryāṃ parigṛhītagranthanāmāni*) 422, Index of identified quotations (*nyāyamañjaryām upalabdhānāṃ granthāntaravākyānāṃ ṭippaṇyām apradarśitatattadgranthasthalānāṃ tattatsthalavivaraṇam*) 423, Index of unidentified quotations (*nyāyamañjaryām upalabdhānāṃ granthāntaravacananam anupalabdhasthalānāṃ vivaraṇam*) 424.

Notes The second part was published in 1969 before the first, as evinced from Shukla's preface to the *prameyaprakaraṇa*, *itaḥ paraṃ pramāṇaprakaraṇābhidhaḥ prathamo bhago 'pi jhaṭiti prakāśam eṣyati.*. Madhvacharya Adya signed his own preface in June-July (Gurupūrṇimā) of 1969, before Shukla's (signed in August-September of 1969, Anantacaturdaśī), and motivates the publication on the basis of a need of a text-book for exams on *prācīnanyāya* at the *śāstrī* level (*tatra prameyaprakaraṇaṃ tatra tatra prācīnanyāyaśāstriparikṣāyāṃ tatra tatra viśvavidyālayīyaparīkṣāsu pāṭhyatvena nirdhāritam asti.*). The edition of 1936 was apparently revised by Shukla and by Madhvacharya Adya, also known as Damodara Shastri Gosvami (who appears as co-editor on the title-page), and further proofread by Brahmadatta Mishra. Although the edition was set with new fonts, so that a reprinting through standing types or stereotypes (see Gaskell, 1972, 116–117) can definitely be ruled out, the layout of the 1936 Chowkhamba edition was reproduced almost identically, with rare shifts of single *akṣara*-s from one page to the next. There are corrections of minor mistakes, as well as introductions of new errors. Major changes in layout, however, are visible only on the title-pages, in the prefaces, and in headers and footers. The purpose of the typesetting effort might have been the preservation of the indices's references from the previous edition.

Copies IND–B–9896/1–2, Fachbereichsbibliothek Südasien-, Tibet- und Buddhismuskunde, University of Vienna.

2.4 K.S. Varadacharya, 1969–1983

Roman title-page of the first volume
ORIENTAL RESARCH INSTITUTE SERIES No. 116 | NYĀYAMAÑJARĪ | OF | JAYANTABHAṬṬA | WITH ṬIPPAṆĪ—NYĀYASAURABHA BY THE EDITOR | Vol. I | CRITICALLY EDITED BY | Vidvan, K. S. Varadacharya | Research Assistant | Oriental Research Institute, Mysore | ORIENTAL RESEARCH INSTITUTE, MYSORE | 1969

Devanāgarī title-page of the first volume
प्राच्यविद्यासंशोधनालयग्रन्थमाला ११६ | श्री जयन्तभट्टकृता | न्यायमञ्जरी | संपादकग्रथितन्यायसौरभाख्यटिप्पणीसमन्विता | भाग १ | संपादकः | विद्वान् के॰ एस्॰ वरदाचार्यः, | रिसर्च् अ्सिस्टेण्ट्, प्राच्यविद्यासंशोधनालयः, मैसूरु | प्राच्यविद्यासंशोधनालयः | मैसूरुविश्वविद्यानिलयः | मैसूरु | १९६९

Roman-Devanāgarī title-page of the second volume
मैसूरुविश्वविद्यानिलयः | प्राच्यविद्यासंशोधनालयग्रन्थमाला–१३९ | श्री जयन्तभट्टकृता | न्यायमञ्जरी | संपादकग्रथितन्यायसौरभाख्यटिप्पणीसमन्विता | भाग २ | संपादकः | विद्वान् के॰ एस्॰ वरदाचार्यः, | रिसर्च् अ्सिस्टेण्ट्, प्राच्यविद्यासंशोधनालयः, मैसूरु | CRITICALLY EDITED BY | Vidvan, K. S. Varadacharya | Research Assistant | Oriental Research Institute, Mysore | प्राच्यविद्यासंशोधनालयः | मैसूरुविश्वविद्यानिलयः | मैसूरु | १९८३

Size 137 × 214 mm.

Signatures of the first volume 8°: π^6 A B^4 *1* 2–44 45–47 48^4 χ^6

Signatures of the second volume 8°: π^{10} 46 χ^4 $\mathit{1}^{10}$ 2–45

Pagination and contents, first vol. Title-pages and imprint [i-vi], Preface vii–x, Preface in Sanskrit (*prastāvana*) i–ii, Table of contents (*viṣayānukramaṇikā*) iii–xvii, Errata corrige (*śuddhipatram*) xviii, Commented *Nyāyasūtra* passages (*śrījayantabhaṭṭena vicāritāni nyāyasūtrāṇi*) xix, Abbreviations (*saṅketākṣaravivaraṇam*) xx–xxii, Title [xxiii–xxiv], Main text (NM 1–4) 1–704, Table of contents of indices (*anubandha*) [xxiii-xxvi], Index of authors (*granthakārādisūcī*) 1–2, Index of works (*granthasūcī*) 3–4, Index of epistemic evidence (*pramāṇānukramaṇikā*) 5–18, Index of hemistiches (*ślokārdhānukramaṇikā*) 19–53, Variant readings from the Allahabad manuscript (*pāṭhāntarāṇi*) 1–12.

Pagination and contents, second vol. Title-pages and imprint [i-vi], Preface i–viii, Preface in Sanskrit (*bhūmikā*) i–iv, Main text (NM 5–12) 1–718, Index of *Nyāyasūtra* passages (*sūtrānukramaṇī*) 1–3, Index of authors and works (*granthagranthakārādisūcī*) 4–5, Index of epistemic evidence (*pramāṇānukramaṇī*) 6–9, Index of verses (*ślokānukramaṇī*) 10–37, Errata corrige (*śodhanikā*) 38–39.

Copies IND–B–8199/1–2, Fachbereichsbibliothek Südasien-, Tibet- und Buddhismuskunde, University of Vienna.

2.5 Nagin J. Shah, 1975–1992

Roman title-page of the fifth volume

JAYANTA BHAṬṬA'S | NYĀYAMAÑJARĪ | [ṢAṢTHA-SAPTAMA-AṢṬA MA-NAVAMA ĀHNIKA] | WITH GUJARATI TRANSLATION | [page-width rule] | L.D. SERIES 115 | GENERAL EDITOR | H. C. Bhayani | EDITED AND TRANSLATED BY | NAGIN J. SHAH | [page-width rule] | L. D. INSTITUTE OF INDOLOGY, AHMEDABAD-9

Devanāgarī title-page of the fifth volume

जयन्तभट्टविरचिता | न्यायमञ्जरी | [षष्थ-सप्तम-अ्रष्टम-नवम आह्निक] | गूर्जरभाषानुवादसहिता | [page-width rule] | संपादक--अ्रनुवादक | नगीन् जी॰ शाह | [page-width rule] | प्रकाशकः | लालभाई दलपदभाई भारतीय संस्कृति विद्यामंदिर अ्रहमदाबाद–९

Size 160 × 250 mm.

Pagination and contents Title-pages and imprint [1–4], General editor's foreword in English 5, Preface in Gujarati (*prāstāvika*) 7–9, Table of contents (*viṣayanirdeśa*) 11–23, Main text (NM 6–9) in Devanāgarī with Gujarati translation 1–423.

Notes The text of the NM is printed in Devanāgarī and segmented in sequentially numbered paragraphs, with a new sequence beginning at each *āhnika*. Each paragraph is followed by the Gujarati translation. Groups of paragraphs are gathered in titled sections which are also sequentially numbered. The edition and translation of the NM is published in five volumes: vol. 1, 1975, L.D. Series 48 (NM 1); vol. 2, 1978, L.D. Series 67 (NM 2); vol. 3, 1984, L.D. Series 97 (NM 3); vol. 4, 1989, L.D. Series 108 (NM 4–5); vol. 5, 1992, L.D. Series 115 (NM 6–9). There is no trace of further volumes covering NM 10 to 12, which were probably never published, as it also appears from the publications lists of the Lalbhai Dalpatbhai Institute of Indology (see http://www.ldindology.org).

Copies IND–B–8316/[6–8], Fachbereichsbibliothek Südasien-, Tibet- und Buddhismuskunde, University of Vienna.

2.6 Gaurinatha Shastri, 1982–1984

Roman title-page of the second volume

M. M. ŚIVAKUMĀRAŚĀSTRĪ-GRANTHAMĀLĀ | [Vol. 5] | NYĀYA MAÑJARĪ | OF | JAYANTA BHAṬṬA | [PART TWO] | WITH THE COM MENTARY 'GRANTHIBHAṄGA' | By | CAKRADHARA | EDITED BY | GAURINATH SASTRI | [Publisher's logo] | VARANASI | 1983

Devanāgarī title-page of the second volume

म॰ म॰ शिवकुमारशास्त्रि-ग्रन्थमाला | [पञ्चमं पुष्पम्] | जयन्तभट्टप्रणीता | न्यायमञ्जरी | [द्वितीयो भागः] | चक्रधरविरचितया | ग्रन्थिभङ्गव्याख्यया | संवलिता | सम्पादकः | श्रीगौरिनाथशास्त्री | [Publisher's logo] वाराणस्याम् | २०४०तमे वैक्रमाब्दे १९०४तमे शकाब्दे १९८३तमे खैस्ताब्दे

Size 155 × 242 mm.

Pagination and contents, second vol. Title-pages and imprint [1–4], Preface in Sanskrit (*upodghātaḥ*) 1–12, Preface in English 1–18, Table of contents (*viṣayasūcikā*) 1–8, Main text (NM 6–8) 1–312, Index of technical words (*nyāyamañjaryyāṃ paṭhitā viśiṣṭapāribhāṣikaśabdāḥ*) 313–332, Quoted passages (*atroddhṛtānāṃ śruti-smṛti-sūtravacanāni*) 333–339.

Notes The complete NM edition is published in three volumes: vol. 1, 1982 (NM 1–4); vol. 2, 1983 (NM 5–8); vol. 3, 1984 (NM 9–12).

Copies IND–B–14494/2, Fachbereichsbibliothek Südasien-, Tibet- und Buddhismuskunde, University of Vienna.

2.7 Other partial editions

Panchanana Tarkavagisha's edition in Bengali script (NM^{Pa}), with his Bengali translation and Bengali commentary, was published in 1939. The first volume covers NM 1 and the second NM 2.

Kei Kataoka has critically edited several passages of the NM as independent articles:

- *Vijñānādvaitavāda*, a section of NM 9 (NM^{KKa})
- *Sarvāgamaprāmāṇya*, a section of NM 4 (NM^{KKb})
- *Īśvarasiddhi*, a section of NM 3 (NM^{KKc})
- *Śāstrārambha*, a section of NM 1 (NM^{KKd})
- Kumārila's criticism of *apoha*, a section of NM 5 (NM^{KKe})
- The Buddhist's reaction to Kumārila's criticism of *apoha*, a section of NM 5 (NM^{KKf})
- Jayanta's view on *jāti* and *apoha*, a section of NM 5 (NM^{KKg})
- The Buddhist's refutation of *jāti*, a section of NM 5 (NM^{KKh})

In a PhD thesis submitted in 2006 at the University of Rome "Sapienza", Paola Nardella edited and translated into Italian the third and last portion of NM 6, relying on four manuscripts in addition to the printed editions (Nardella, 2006, Introduzione, x).

A study and translation into German of the section of NM 6 edited in this book is the *Diplomarbeit* submitted to the University of Vienna by Katharina Wieser (Wieser, 1991).

2.8 Sigla of the NM editions

In this book the various editions of the NM are distinguished by the first syllable of their editor's name, e.g., NM^{Ga}, the *editio princeps* by Gangadhara Shastri. In the critical apparatus, as well as in variants documented elsewhere in the book, sigla of manuscripts and editions are often found side by side. This is particularly true for NM^{Ga} and NM^{Va}, the only two editions kept in the critical apparatus. On the one hand there is a need to avoid a confusion among manuscripts and editions, and on the other to refrain from excesses of symbolism. Moreover, in both the critical apparatus and the study of the genealogy of the sources, where several of the collated variants are listed as examples and evidence, brevity becomes important. Therefore, whenever needed, an abridged form of the sigla of the editions, without the redundant "NM" part, has been adopted. The printed editions can still be distinguished from the manuscripts sources, which are indicated by a single capital letter, because they are invariably constituted by an upper case letter followed by one or more lower case letters. For instance NM^{Ga}, Gangadhara's edition, becomes Ga when used in the apparatus of the critical edition and in the documentation of variant readings.

A concordance of the abbreviations used in this book with those used in previous editions can be found in Table 2.1.

Table 2.1: Sigla of the NM editions

Editor	Full sigla	Short sigla	Kataoka	NM^{Va}
Gangadhara Shastri	NM^{Ga}	Ga	V	ख
Suryanarayana Shukla	NM^{Shu}	Shu	S	ख
Suryanarayana Shukla	NM^{Ma}	Ma	S^2	
K.S. Varadacharya	NM^{Va}	Va	M	
Nagin J. Shah	NM^{Sha}	Sha	N	
Gaurinatha Shastri	NM^{Gau}	Gau	G	

3 Survey and description of the NM manuscripts

3.1 Inventory of the NM manuscripts

A survey of the known NM manuscripts has already been published in Graheli, 2012a, where a brief description of all the manuscripts was also provided. Even if that inventory cannot be considered conclusive, since it will always be possible for hitherto hidden NM manuscripts to emerge, it can be considered fairly exhaustive insofar as manuscripts recorded in published catalogues. The inventory was gradually built through the following progressive steps:

1. consultation of meta-catalogues (*catalogi catalogorum*);
2. consultation of individual catalogues;
3. consultation of published and unpublished hand-lists, indices, and registers;
4. concordance of the manuscripts used in printed editions with those listed in catalogues.

The result of the survey is summarized in Table 3.1 below, where the manuscripts covering NM 6 are marked in bold-face. The manuscripts are ordered alphabetically according to the place where they are currently located, as shown in the first column. The second column gives the manuscript identifier prefixed by the acronym of the repository. The third column mentions the script (N = Nāgarī, G= Grantha-Malayālam, Ś = Śāradā).[1] The fourth column indicates the

[1] In this book the term "Devanāgarī" is reserved for the script used in printed sources, i.e., for typographic fonts. For the script of manuscript sources, which in

parts of the NM covered by the manuscript. The fifth column mentions complete editions in which the manuscript has been used.[2]

Table 3.1: Inventory of located NM manuscripts

Place	*Identifier*	*Script*	*Extent*	*Edition*
Allahabad	**GJ 833**	N	NM 1–12	NM^{Va}
Calcutta/Kolkata	**AS G–10991**	N	NM 1–10	None
Göttingen	NSUB MU II 26	Ś	NM 1	None
Göttingen	NSUB MU I 95	Ś	NM 1	None
Kozhicode/Calicut	**MDUC 2606**	G	NM 1–7	None
Lucknow	ASPL 2381	Ś	NM 1–4	None
Madras/Chennai	**AL 70179B**	G	NM 6–12	NM^{Va}
Madras/Chennai	GOML R. 3583	G	NM 7–12	NM^{Va}
Madras/Chennai	GOML R. 3631A	G	NM 7–12	NM^{Va}
Mysore	**ORI C–1374**	N	NM 1–12	NM^{Va}
Pune	**BORI 390/75–6**	Ś	NM 1–12	NM^{Ga}
Pune	DC 10663	N	NM 1–5, 7	None
Pune	**AA 5329**	N	NM 5–7	None
Srinagar	ORL 1088	Ś	NM 1–4	None
Srinagar	**ORL 1933**	Ś	NM 5–8	None
Srinagar	ORL 2179	Ś	NM 3–4	None
Varanasi	**SSV 3465**	N	NM 1–12	NM^{Ga}
Varanasi	BHU C-1015	N	NM 1–5, 8–9	None

Besides these, there are further records of manuscripts that may contain NM 6, though they could not yet be located or disambiguated.

the case of the NM all pre-date the advent of the Devanāgarī typography, the term "Nāgarī" is used.

[2]Partial editions of other section of the NM, outside of NM 6, are not mentioned in the table. For instance, incomplete manuscripts such as MDUC 2606, NSUB MU II 26, NSUB MU I 95, ASPL 2381, GOML R. 3631A and BHU C-1015 have been used by Kei Kataoka in his editions (see Section 2.7).

Three of them are mentioned in the CC and NCC:

- Pheh 14. According to the *legenda* in CC, vol. 1, *Introduction*, v, Pheh refers to the "Pheariçt Saṃskrit ke Pustakon kā [Hindi for "List of Sanskrit Manuscripts"] 16 pages in 8". Biswas (BBC, 220) located this list at the University of Madras, Dept. of Sanskrit. Nothing more is known about this manuscript.
- Radh 13. "Radh" in the CC refers to the "Pustakānāṃ Sūcipatram, 48 pages in 8" (Cat. Radh. 1871), a list apparently describing the collection of Pandit Radhakrishna of Lahore.[3] The list was compiled by a Kashmiri pandit named Rajaram Shastri, as indicated in the colophon: *likhitaṃ paṇḍitarājarāmaśāstriṇā kāśmīrivāsinā*. Biswas (BBC, 237) mentions this collection under Rajaram Shastri's name, without specifying Radhakrishna's, while Janert (ABC, 144) reports the bare information from the CC. The *Pustakānāṃ Sūcipatram*, a copy of which is preserved in Tübingen, records a NM manuscript at p. 13, no. 119. The number 13 in the CC entry probably refers to p. 13 of the *Sūcipatra*.
- Mad. Uni. R.K.S. 543. In the original edition of NCC (1949), xxi, the "Mad. Uni. R.K.S." siglum is described as "[A] hand-list of 577 Sanskrit manuscripts of the late R. Krishnasvami Sastri, Sub Registrar, Tanjore, acquired for the Madras University by R.A. Sastri". The revised edition, NCC1, xiii, adds "[I]n the Sanskrit Dept., University of Madras". The list is still unpublished (BBC, 178).

As for individual catalogues, an non-located NM manuscript is recorded in Cat. LU 1951, 40. There are also clear traces of a NM manuscript at the library of the Benares Hindu University, with the following details mentioned in the catalogue (Cat. BHU 1971): "Ser. No. 3C/2434, Acc. No. C4666 [B 1042], Śāradā, paper, 89 fols, incomplete, 28.5 × 16.6 cm."; however, so far all attempts to retrieve this manuscript failed because it could not be found on shelf by the Library staff.

In NM^{Va}, vol. I, Prastāvanā, i, a further non-located manuscript is mentioned and described as follows:

[3]Described by Bühler as "Mahârâja Ranjit Singh's former Joshî" (Cat. Report 1875, 2).

> While engaged in searching for other documents, we heard that there was one document in the Parakāla Maṭha in Mysore, but [...] we went there to collect it and we found that this document was not available. Still, we have found that there is now a text owned by Atmakuru Diskshacharya which was edited on the basis of that document [...].

In the English preface to the first volume by G. Marulasiddhah (NM^{Va}, vol. I, Preface, vii), Dikshacharya's document is mentioned as "a manuscript". In the English preface to the second volume, however, H.P. Malladevaru writes of "manuscripts" lent by Dikshacharya (NM^{Va}, vol. II, Preface, vii).[4] On the basis of this description, it seems that Dikshacharya's manuscript (ADP) was a transcription of a lost manuscript previously preserved at the Parakāla Maṭha, as suggested also in NM^{KKa}, 117.

Altogether, there are nine NM manuscripts directly relevant in the present edition:

GJ 833	ORI C–1374	ORL 1933
AS G–10991	BORI 390/75–6	MDUC 2606
AL 70179B	AA 5329	SSV 3465

Of these nine manuscripts three have never been used in editions of NM 6: MDUC 2606, AS G–10991 and AA 5329.

The *codex unicus* of the *Nyāyamañjarīgranthibhaṅga* (GBh), JTGB 386, will also be used in this edition to confirm the text of GBh^{Sha} and to corroborate readings of the NM, on the strength of the readings found in the *pratīka*-s of the GBh.

3.2 Sigla of the NM manuscripts

In the apparatuses of this critical edition the sigla of manuscripts and editions have been kept as simple as possible. The principle adopted by Kei Kataoka, to use the initial letter of the city where the manuscript is presently preserved, is also applied here, though

[4]Some information about Dikshacharya and the Parakāla Maṭha can be gathered from http://www.hindu.com/fr/2004/10/29/stories/2004102903371000.htm (accessed 31/1/2015).

my sigla slightly differ from his because a different system to distinguish manuscripts from editions is used here and because more witnesses need to be accommodated.[5] The sigla are listed in Table 3.2, where they can also be compared with those used by Kataoka, Muroya and Varadacharya.[6] In some parts of this book, however, I also referred to NM manuscripts by their repository and shelf-mark, as indicated in the third column of this table.[7]

Table 3.2: Concordance of sigla of NM 6 manuscripts

Place	Siglum	Shelf-mark	Kataoka	Muroya	NM^{Va}
Allahabad	A	GJ 833	A_1	–	च
Calcutta	C	AS G–10991	–	C	–
Kozhicode	K	MDUC 2606	K_1	–	–
Madras	M	AL 70179B	–	–	घ
Mysore	O	ORI C–1374	O_1	–	क
Pune	P	BORI 390/75–6	–	–	–
Pune	Q	AA 5329	–	–	–
Srinagar	S	ORL 1933	Z_1	–	–
Varanasi	V	SSV 3465	–	–	–

3.3 Conventions of the descriptions

The following descriptions are alphabetically ordered according to the present location of the manuscript. The headings mention the city, the repository and the shelf-mark.

The stipulated sigla are placed in margin for quick reference. As explained above, for each manuscript there are two sigla that I am

---

[5](Notably, S and V. "S" and "V" are used by Kataoka to denote editions. "V" is used by Muroya (2009–2010, 228) for a different Varanasi manuscript, BHU C-1015 (see Table 3.1 above).

[6]There is also some deviation from the sigla adopted in Graheli, 2012b and Graheli, 2012a, where they should be adjusted accordingly.

[7]If the brevity required in apparatuses is not a stringent necessity it is advisable to identify manuscripts by means of the shelf-mark of the repository, rather than by arbitrary sigla, as explained and implemented in Graheli, 2012a.

using. One, e.g., GJ 833, is meant to be unambiguous and useful for referencing even beyond the present edition. The other, e.g., A, is more arbitrary and it is used for brevity's sake in the edition's apparatuses, in lists of variants, and in the discussion on the stemma.

Below the heading there is the external and succinct description of the manuscripts, inclusive of the following information: date of the manuscript or other chronological indication, script, support (paper, birch bark, palm leaf), number of leaves, size of leaves (height × width), number of lines per page, and *akṣara*-s per line. I am using the term *akṣara* to indicate the physical appearance of graphical units, i.e., "graphemes": in northern scripts, *akṣara*-s are here counted as units complete with their inherent visarga, anusvāra, vowel-signs, etc., while in southern ones visarga, anusvāra and some vowel-signs are counted as separate units, in conformance to the space they occupy on the leaf. This convention is adopted both in the following manuscript descriptions and in the edition's apparatuses, for instance when there is a need to indicate a number of illegible *akṣara*-s.

In the following description the "extent and conditions" item contains an autopsy of the manuscript, with a focus on the number of extant leaves and eventual missing parts. The foliation and issues related to it are also described here.

The "beginning" and "ending" are then provided. In the appendix, Section 12, the beginnings and ends of each *āhnika* present in the most important manuscripts are also listed. The purpose of such extracts is to facilitate future research by providing a general orientation about the exact extent of the manuscripts. Therefore, the extracts have been to some extent simplified and standardized; in other words, they are not strictly diplomatic transcriptions. Paratextual material such as invocations, benedictions to readers, signatures, colophons, etc., is recorded here, before and after the actual incipit and explicit of the NM text.

"Scribal features" are described next. Some general characteristics such as the use of class nasals, gemination patterns, orthographical peculiarities, etc., which were not collated, are listed here. Methods used for corrections are also described here. In the examples of corrections, deleted text is shown as "⟦text⟧" in double brackets, and inserted text as "⟨text⟩" in angled brackets. In the case of particularly interesting manuscripts, some palaeographic features are also mentioned.

"History" includes prosopographical information, as well as information about previous locations, changes of repositories, shelfmarks, etc.

For practical reasons the present research, including the following descriptions, is based on copies of the manuscripts, not on a direct examination of the originals. The nature of the available surrogates (microfilm, photocopies, digital images) is mentioned under "Copies".

Lastly, under "Bibliography", there are remarks on the nature of the consulted copies and their provenance, as well as bibliographical references to catalogues, editions and articles in which the manuscript is listed or described.

3.4 Description of the NM manuscripts

3.4.1 Allahabad, Shri Ganganath Jha Campus, ms. 833

GJ 833
A

Nāgarī;[8] paper, 660, 105 × 275, 8–9, 32–36

Extent and conditions Contains the complete text. The original foliation is 1–668, with some repetitions and skips. Specifically, numbers 4, 23, 199, 374 and 474 are repeated and 12, 125, 232, 282, 390–399 are skipped, without related loss of text. The foliation is placed at the upper left margin of each verso, in Nāgarī numerals, preceded by the abbreviated title *nyāyamaṃ*.

Beginning *śrīgaṇeśāya namaḥ oṃ namaḥ śāśvatikānaṃda-*

End *-vṛkṣāya śambhave // iti śrījayaṃtabhaṭṭakṛtāyāṃ nyāyamaṃjaryyāṃ dvādaśam āhnikam samāptā ceyaṃ nyāyamaṃjarī śubhaṃ //*

Scribal features The manuscript is carelessly written, abounding in orthographical errors and nonsensical readings. The punctuation is rare and erratic, and sentence-breaks are mostly marked by means

[8] In this book the term "Devanāgarī" is restrictively adopted for printed sources. In relation to manuscript sources, instead, the script is referred to as "Nāgarī".

of blank spaces and dissolved *sandhi*-s. There are random instances of two small oblique marks in the interlinear space.

The following features were ignored in the collation:
- An initial *u* resembling *nu* (337v4 *ucyate*).
- A non-geminated *cha* (337v5 *paricheda*).
- A confusion of *ta/na* or *ca/va*, as well as of *śca/cca* (likely generated by the derivation from a Śāradā ancestor).
- A *dbha* written as *bhda* (338v6 *sānudbhavaṃtī*).
- The homoglyphs *pa* and *ya*.

There are frequent interlinear insertions and correction marks:
- Underlined vowel-signs are meant to be shortened (334v8) ⟦*ā*⟧*atrābhidhīyate*, 335r7 *grām*⟦*o*⟧*e*).
- Crossed vowel-signs are meant to be deleted (337fv5) (see Einicke, 2009, 111, Nag7(1768)_3).
- 3–4 dots above the line are used to delete *akṣara*-s (343r3, 343v2).
- *akṣara*-s unreadable to the scribe are replaced by dots (336r2).
- Some wrong repetitions are enclosed in brackets (337r4).

History The manuscript is preserved at the Shri Ganganath Jha Campus of the Rashtriya Sanskrit Sansthan (Deemed University), Allahabad, formerly Ganganatha Jha Kendriya Sanskrit Vidyapeetha and Ganganatha Jha Research Institute. The age and provenance of the manuscript, before its record in Cat. GJRI 1967, vol. 1, pp. 548–549, are unknown. "The manuscripts section of the library was started in 1943 with barely a few hundreds manuscripts...]" (Cat. GJRI 1967, vol. 1, p. v). The manuscript was used in the two volumes of $\mathrm{NM}^{\mathrm{Va}}$. In the first volume its variants are listed in an appendix, while in the second they are reported in the apparatus under the siglum च (see $\mathrm{NM}^{\mathrm{Va}}$, vol. 1, Prastāvanā, ii). As shown in Section 5.3.1, it is most likely a direct copy of ORI C–1374, described below.

Copies Photocopies, courtesy Shri Ganganath Jha Campus of the Rashtriya Sanskrit Sansthan (Deemed University), Allahabad.

Bibliography Cat. GJRI 1967, 548–549; $\mathrm{NM}^{\mathrm{Va}}$, vol. 1, Prastāvanā, ii; $\mathrm{NM}^{\mathrm{KKa}}$, 118; $\mathrm{NM}^{\mathrm{KKb}}$, 135; $\mathrm{NM}^{\mathrm{KKc}}$, 60; $\mathrm{NM}^{\mathrm{KKd}}$, 129; Graheli, 2012a, § 2.1.

3.4.2 Calcutta/Kolkata, The Asiatic Society, ms. G-10991 AS G–10991 C

Kāśmīrī Nāgarī, paper, 375, 150 × 320 mm., 11, 47–50

Extent and conditions The manuscript covers NM 1 to 10, in 375 leaves numbered 1–375 in the original foliation, which is placed on the upper left and repeated on the lower right of each verso. An additional foliation in western numerals (7a, 7b, 8a, 8b, etc.) is seen in the right margin of each recto and verso. On the margins of the first few folios there are glosses from the GBh (see Muroya, 2009–2010, 226).

Beginning *oṃ śrīgaṇeśāya namaḥ oṃ namaḥ śivāya gurave // oṃ namaḥ śāśvatikānaṃdajñānaiśvaryamayātmane* [...].

End [...] *prāyaiḥ śakyo na pakṣaḥ kṣapa*[275v]*yitum iti hi vyāharad vṛttikāraḥ avayavapadārthaḥ // bhaṭṭajayaṃtakṛtau nyāyamaṃjaryāṃ daśamam āhnikaṃ samāptam //* (NM^{Va}, II 583,4–6)

Scribal features The abbreviated title *nyāyamaṃ* is written above the upper left foliation and the word *rāma* is written above the foliation in the lower right margin. There are no punctuation marks, but breaks are often indicated by narrow spaces (less than or about the width of a letter) as well as by dissolved *sandhi*-s. Only the initial invocation and the *āhnika* divisions are marked by double *daṇḍa*-s (e.g., 42v10).

Dots at head-line height indicate parts that probably appeared unreadable to the scribe (e.g., 89r6, 89v9, and 372v). Marginal corrections are linked to the text by means of carets (239v7 ⟨*yat*⟩). Elisions are marked with two vertical strokes above the interested parts (e.g., 240r1) (see Einicke, 2009, 108, Nag3.2(1393)_2). Small comma-like marks are seen at the end of the lines, seemingly for hyphenation purpose. Interestingly, similar marks are also observed in AA 5329, described below. The *anusvāra*-s used in place of class nasals, even in internal *sandhi*, as well as the lack of a distinction of *ba* from *va*, were ignored in the collation. Some peculiar characters and ligatures are the following ones:

jha[*gity eva*], 261v5; *rū*[*po*], 264r4; *ṛ*[*tāv upeyāt*], 263r1; [*bā*]*ḍha-*, 245r1; [*ta*]*lla*[*kṣaṇe*], 267v5; *cakkre*, 268r11).

There are unequivocal indications of a close derivation from a Śāradā antigraph: some Śāradā *akṣara*-s were inadvertently and intermittently written by the scribe (e.g., 246v10, [*pade*] *rtha*[*pratipādake*]; *ma* and *rtha* are often found, respectively, in place of the expected

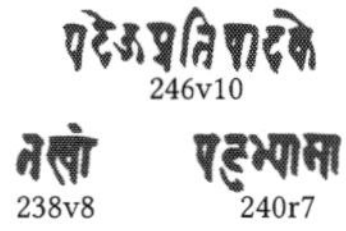

sa and *kṣa*; *ta* is found in place the expected initial *u*, as in *takhām* for *ukham* (238v8), or *tatsīdeyuḥ* for *utsideyuḥ*, *tadāhāri* for *udāhāri*, etc.; the vowel-sign *u* is often found where a Śāradā character easily mistaken for a Śāradā *u* may have been present, as in *paṭu* for *paṭv* (240r7), as well as in *anunura* for *anantara*, *susaṃskāra* for *sa saṃskāra*, etc.; there is often a confusion among *cca* and *śca* (e.g., *anubhavāc ca* for *anubhavāś ca*).

History The copyist was most likely a professional scribe, familiar with both Nāgarī and Śāradā, rather than a scholar, as evinced from the above peculiarities and from the copious orthographical errors.

Copies Microfilm, courtesy of the Asiatic Society, Kolkata, and the ISTB, Nyāya Project, Vienna.

Bibliography Cat. AS 1957, 105–108; Muroya, 2009–2010, 17–18; Graheli, 2012a, § 2.7.

MDUC 2606 K 3.4.3 Kozhicode (Thenhipalam), University of Calicut, ms. 2606

Grantha-Malayālam, palm leaf, 177, 50 × 480, 10, 110

Extent and conditions Contains NM 1–6 and about one third of NM 7. The ms. is protected by thick wooden covers and bound through the left string-hole with a hemp string. The folios are numbered 1–187 in the original foliation, which is placed in the middle-left margin of each recto, in Grantha-Malayālam letter numerals of the *nannādi* system.[9] Despite the original foliation only 177 leaves

[9]See Grünendahl, 2001, 94. In this system the sequence is *na*, *nna*, *nya*, etc., so some authors, like Muroya, 2006, 26 and Esposito, 2012, prefer to use the more logi-

are extant, so some of them seem to be missing. The NM 6 section, however, is complete. The right margin of (recto) folios is damaged, with the occasional loss of a few *akṣara*-s.

Beginning [1r1] *hariḥ oṃ mahāgaṇapataye namaḥ namaś śāsvatikānandajñānaiśvaryamayātmane* [...]

End [187v10] [...] *kiṃ sa evāyaṃ stambha ity ekaṃ jñāna-* (NM^{Va} II 308,10).

Scribal features It is written in Grantha-Malayālam in a single hand.[10] The first folio is foliated with *śrī*, a common feature noticed elsewhere by Muroya, 2006, 26, and Esposito, 2012, 84, and the foliation actually starts from 1 (*na*) with the *nannādi* sequence only from the second folio:

śrī na (1) nna (2) nya (3) ṣkra (4) jhra (5) hā (6) gra (7) pra (8) dre (9)

All folios have 10 lines, except for 164r which has 11 lines. The text is sparsely punctuated by means of dots. Sentence breaks are often indicated by means of dissolved *sandhi*-.

The following features were ignored in the collation:

- The gemination after *repha*, which is remarkably frequent: *rtta* (161r4), *rttha* (161r1), *rgga* (159r5), *rggha* (160r9), *rcca* (160v10), *rppa* (169v6), *rmma* (169v10).
- The gemination of *yya* (172r7 *vāyyākaraṇānāṃ*), *ddhya* (171v7 *sāddhya*) , *ssra* (172v10 *sahassra*), *tssa* (175r10 *jagat ssarggāt*).

---

cal term *nannādi*. In Kerala the system is rather called *nanyādi* (P.L. Shaji, personal communication, October 2014), perhaps for euphonic reasons.

[10] For the label "Grantha-Malayālam", see Grünendahl, 2001; Rath, 2012a. Other scholars, both in India and in the West (Muroya, 2006; Esposito, 2012; Moser, 2012; Rath, 2012a), call this script simply Malayālam. In Kerala is traditionally labelled *ārya eḻuttu*. The geographical distinction by Burnell (1878, 41) into Eastern and Western Grantha, however, may still be the most productive one. In fact, by the use of "Malayālam", either by itself or compounded with "Grantha", there is a confusion among spoken languages and scripts. This problem is noticed by Rath (2012a, 188), who distinguishes scripts and languages by the use of lower- and upper-case letters, respectively.

- The frequent use of class-nasals, which occur even at the end of words (160r10 *buddhin na*).
- The assimilation of *visarga* before sibilant (160v9, 171r3).
- The absence of *visarga* before the medial dot used for punctuation (161r5).
- The assimilation of plosives before homologous plosives (172v1 *tadvārake*, 172v2 *tatva*).

The vowel-sign *au* is mostly written with a single *au* sign, but also with a combination of the *au* sign and the *pṛṣṭhamātra* sign, with no apparent reason for the variation. In 163r3, for instance, *yaugapadya* occurs twice, once with a single *au* and once with the combined form.

163r3, left

163r3, right

History The manuscript is listed in a register of the Library, p. 156, as "No. 2606, Nyāyamañjarī – Nyāyasutravyākhya". On p. 14 of another list, a collection of 191 manuscripts (2603–2793), to which MDUC 2606 belongs, the manuscript is mentioned along with the previous owner, Sri K.V. Ravinamputhiripadu, Killimangalathu Mana, Killimangalam, P.O. Cheruthuruthy (Thrissur District). The Department of Sanskrit of the University of Calicut (founded in 1969) was created in 1977, and the Department of Malayālam in 1971. The latter, according to the website (http://www.universityofcalicut.info, accessed 31/1/2015), takes care of the collection of manuscripts, called Thunchan Manuscript Repository.

Copies Digital photographs dated 2004, courtesy of the Malayalam Department of the University of Calicut, Thenhipalam.

Bibliography NM^{KKb}, 135; NM^{KKc}, 60; NM^{KKd}, 129; Graheli, 2012a, § 2.16.

AL 70179B
M

3.4.4 Madras/Chennai, Adyar Library, ms. 70179b

Grantha-Malayālam, palm leaf, 136, 60 × 480, 10–11, 110–120

Extent and conditions The manuscript covers NM 6–12, although several leaves and parts of leaves are missing due to severe damage. The original foliation is on the middle-left margin of each recto and it is repeated on the right margin. The foliation is in letter numerals of the alphabetical system (Grünendahl, 2001, xiv; see Section 13 below for further details). Apparently, NM 6 originally began on folio *ka* (i.e., 1), ending at *jhau* (i.e., 142). Fols. *ka* (1), *kā* (2), *ghṝ* (56), *ṅā* (66), *ji* (115), and *jī* (116) are not extant. The preserved part begins from fol. 3 (*ki*). Probably the text on *ka* began on the verso side, judging from the extent of text missing at the beginning of NM 6. The foliation is not anymore extant on many leaves, due to the damage of the support, but is nonetheless possible to reconstruct the original sequence. This reconstructed foliation is fully available in Section 13 and is used here and elsewhere in this book.

Beginning [3r1 (*ki*)] *-ntanīyaḥ avyatireke ta eva te varṇā iti kathan na bodhakā* [...] (NM^{Va}, II 147,7; NM 6).

End [142v6 (*jhau*)] *prapannajanasaṃkalpakalpavṛkṣāya śambhave // iti bhaṭṭajayantakṛtau nyāyamañjaryān dvādaśam āhnikam // nyāyamañjarī samāptā // hariḥ namaś śivāya //*

Scribal features The script has angular features, perhaps representing a transitional stage from the older Eastern Grantha described by Burnell (1878, 41). The punctuation is almost absent, except for the rare use of dots and blanks, and for dissolved *sandhi*-s. Also the ends of stanzas are in some cases punctuated with dots. Some traces of thematic headings are still visible above the foliation of the badly damaged right margin, e.g., *vākyārtha* (*kaḥ*, 16r), *vyā+raṇa pra+++* (*khe*, 27r).

The following features were ignored in the collation:

- The gemination of *ta* after *repha.*
- The gemination of *na* after *repha,* even when *na* is at the beginning of a word (21v7 *siddher nnetara*).
- The de-gemination of *ttva* into *tva.*
- The frequent use of class nasals even at the end of words (*kathan na, evan tāvat*).
- The assimilation of *visarga* before sibilants.

As for corrections, missing or wrong *akṣara*-s are frequently integrated or replaced below the line by the same hand, with a cross above the line to indicate the place of insertion: e.g., 23r2,

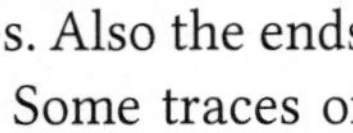
23r2

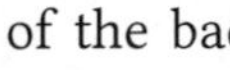
16v5

vidhā⟨ta⟩vyaḥ. The deletion of *akṣara*-s is marked by a horizontal stroke (see Einicke, 2009, 97, Gra4(1717)_14) above the concerned letters: e.g., 16v5, ⟦*dve*⟧ *gau*. The original extent of the corrections cannot be determined, because the original margins are largely lost.

History The scribe appears to have used an antigraph with about 120 *akṣara*-s per line, as assumed from the length of its omissions (e.g., 7r5, the omission of *saṃskārāt ... saṃskārotpattir*, likely to be a skip of a full line); this may have been a palm-leaf manuscript in a southern script, since northern manuscripts rarely have lines of such a length.

The first catalogue record of this manuscript is found in Cat. AL 1911, 182, where it is mentioned without any manuscript number, as follows: "*Nyāyamañjarī* by Jayantabhaṭṭa; No. of copies: 1; Character: Malayālam". It is later recorded in Cat. AL 1928, 98 as "24 C 16 *ke* 280 (*atiśithilā*)" (i.e., shelf 24, row C, manuscript no. 16, leaves 280), "very brittle". A new manuscript number, which is still used at the present day, was assigned to it in the next catalogue, Cat. AL 1972, 82–83: Acc. No. 70179(b). Although the number of folios given in the two catalogues differs (280 in the former, 140 in the latter), this may be due to a reference to the number of pages and leaves, respectively. The bundle 70179 also comprises the *Jayamaṅgalāvyākhyā* ad *Kāmasūtra* (70179a) and an unidentified commentary of the *Tārkikarakṣāsaṅgrahasāra* of Varadarāja (70179c). The *Jayamaṅgalāvyākhyā* part is incomplete. It starts with fol. 4r (*-śada* [*ṇḍabala + taḥ sa cārttha iti*]) corresponding to Dwivedi, 2004, 1.2.15, p. 28, and ends with fol. 85v (the foliation is not visible, but it can be inferred) (*jātaparicayā svayam eva pravekṣyati*), corresponding to Dwivedi, 2004, 5.5.24, p. 438. The manuscript includes readings not present in the printed editions (Dwivedi, 2004, Devdutt Shastri, 1992), so it may prove to be of interest for the improvement of that text. An analysis of the images of 70179a and 70179c has confirmed that there are no scattered NM leaves in those parts of the bundle, although in the NM portion of the bundle there are several misplaced leaves. This shuffle of leaves must have occurred rather recently, because leaves that are found quite apart in the present sequence and that were original adjacent are damaged in the same areas, with coinciding worm-holes, broken margins, etc.

The manuscript was used by Varadacharya under the siglum घ (see NM^{Va}, vol. 2, Bhūmikā, viii). This identity is confirmed both by the extent of the manuscript and by the direct evidence of the collated variants. When consulted by Varadacharya the manuscript may have been in a better condition, since some variants recorded by him with this siglum occur in portions of the text that are presently lost in AL 70179B. In the apparatus of NM^{Va}, however, there is some confusion among sigla: frequent instances of a wrong attribution of variants were spotted in the course of the collation for the present edition.[11]

Copies Digital photographs dated 2006 and 2007, courtesy of The Adyar Library and Research Center, Theosophical Society, Chennai, and of Taishei Shida.

Bibliography Cat. AL 1911, 182; Cat. AL 1972, 82–83; NM^{Va}, vol. 2, Bhūmikā, viii; Graheli, 2012a, § 2.2.

3.4.5 Mysore, Oriental Research Institute, ms. C–1374

ORI C–1374
O

Kāśmīrī Nāgarī, paper, 292, 155 × 330, 16, 50

Condition and extent The manuscript covers the complete NM in 292 leaves, foliated 1 to 291 in the upper left margin of each verso. The foliation numbers are preceded by the abbreviated title *nyā. maṃ* and repeated in the lower right margin. Fol. 170 is skipped, but without loss of text.

Beginning [1v1] *oṃ śrīgaṇeśāya namaḥ oṃ śrīśārikābhagavatyai oṃ śrīgurucaraṇakamalaparāga(puṃje)bhyo namaḥ oṃ namaḥ śāśvatikānaṃdajñānaiśvaryamayātmane* [...]

End [291v13] *prapannajanasaṃkalpakalpavṛkṣāya śaṃbhave // iti śrījayaṃtabhaṭṭakṛtāyāṃ nyāyamaṃjaryyāṃ dvādaśam āhnikam samā*[291v14]*ptā ceyaṃ nyāyamaṃjarī śubhaṃ*

Scribal features It is written in a regular and calligraphic ductus. The scribe used a broad nib, which yielded a sharp modulation. Ends

[11] These instances of confused sigla in NM^{Va} have been exhaustively recorded in the documentation of the collated variants, available at homepage.univie.ac.at/alessandro.graheli.

of chapters are rubricated (i.e., the black text is highlighted with a red substance), and so are the quoted passages from the *Nyāyasūtra*. Punctuation marks are not used, but breaks are frequently indicated by blank spaces and dissolved *sandhi*-s. Some punctuation marks are also visible above lines, perhaps added by a second hand. Medial dots are used at the end of lines to fill empty spaces (e.g., 161v9). Dots at the head-line are used for *akṣara*-s that presumably appeared unreadable to the scribe (161v15).

The following features were not independently collated: the confusion of *ba/va* (161v3, 168v9), *ra/da*, *ta/na*, *ddha/ccha* (163v15), *pa/ya*, *ca/va*, *ya/gha* (171v7 *vighāta*); the *sta* and *sna* written as homoglyphs, e.g., 168v10, *nāsti*; the inversion *dhba*, used in place of *bdha*, e.g., 171v1, *labdha*. Some peculiarly written and potentially misleading ligatures are *ddha*, e.g., 158r15, *tad dhi*, *kṣa*, e.g., 158r9, and *jjha*, e.g., 185r12, *-pojjhati*.

There are interlinear corrections, seemingly by the same hand, and marginal additions, seemingly by a second hand (e.g., 160r). Additions and emendations are done as follows:

- Wrong *akṣara*-s or parts of *akṣara*-s are cancelled with yellow paste (159v5, 159v6).
- Marginal additions are coordinated to the text by means of the line number and carets at the insertion place.
- Short vowels are elongated with a wavy sign above the line, as in 172v13 (see Einicke, 2009, 113, Nag9(1794)_1).

There are clear traces of a relation with the Śāradā script: the ligatures *śca* and *cca* are often confused; the *u* vowel-sign under *ya* is written as a straight horizontal stroke, e.g., 161v13, *yuktaṃ*; *ku* looks like its Śāradā counterpart, e.g., 162v1, *kutastyaṃ*; the ligature *tta* is often seen in place of *tu*: e.g., 168v11, *bhavittam arhati*, where the *rū*-like *bha* mirrors a Śāradā *bha*.

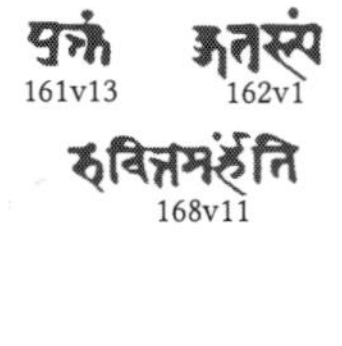

History The manuscript is probably the main manuscript source used in NM^{Va}, where it is given the siglum क. Varadacharya (NM^{Va}, vol. 1, Prastāvanā, ii) describes it as "a paper manuscript located at the [Mysore] Research Library" (*etatsaṃśodhanālayasthaḥ kāgada-patrātmakaḥ kośaḥ* [...]), without a more precise identification; the collation of NM 6, however, confirmed the identity without doubt. The ductus is very similar to that of SSV 3465 (see Section 3.4.10 below), which is dated 1737 CE. By analogy, ORI C–1374 may also be assigned to the early 18th century. The calligraphic and consistent ductus suggests that the copyist was a professional scribe, rather than a scholarly one, as indicated also by the presence of copious Sanskrit errors. The manuscript betrays a close connection to the Śāradā script, and thus to Kashmir.

Copies The digital photographs are dated 2002, courtesy of the Oriental Research Institute, University of Mysore, and of the ISTB, Nyāya Project, Vienna.

Bibliography Cat. GOL 1922, 392; NM^{Va}, vol. 1, Prastāvanā, ii; Graheli, 2012a, § 2.9.

3.4.6 Pune, Bhandarkar Oriental Research Institute, ms. 390 of 1875–1876

BORI 390/75–6
P

1472 CE, Śāradā, birch bark, 432, 130 × 130, 16–21, 30

Extent and conditions The manuscript is a composite codex of 432 leaves (435 according to Cat. Report 1875, xxv), containing the complete NM, an unidentified Vaiśeṣika work and a portion of Kālidāsa's *Raghuvaṃśa*. The original foliation unfolds as follows: 2–149 (NM 1–3) + 1–270 (NM 4–12) + 982–986 (Vaiśeṣika work) + 1–7 (*Raghuvaṃśa* 15.11–78 *passim*). The NM portion is thus divided in two parts, with the foliation started anew from the beginning of NM 4. The NM text, altogether covered in 149 + 271 leaves, is thus complete except for few lost leaves (i.1, i.47; ii.1, ii.69, ii.89, ii.154, ii.211).[12]

[12] This edition concerns exclusively NM 6, which occurs in the second part of the codex. References to the folios of BORI 390/75–6 are all to the second part, so outside of this description the roman number indicating the part will not be repeated.

Folio ii.223 is wrongly placed between ii.153 and ii.155, and bound at the wrong margin with a resulting recto-verso inversion. The foliation i.145 is repeated twice. Original folio numbers are given in Śāradā numerals on the lower left margin of verso folios and are frequently lost due to the damaged support. The last four lines of the NM portion occur on the *recto* of an unnumbered leaf which follows fol. ii.270. After these last four lines, the unidentified Vaiśeṣika text begins. This unnumbered leaf is followed by fols. 982–986 (foliated in the lower verso margins), where the Vaiśeṣika text continues and ends on a badly damaged leaf, supposedly 986r. At a first observation this Vaiśeṣika text does not appear to be complete. It is followed by seven unnumbered leaves where a sequence of numbered verses of the *Raghuvaṃśa*, *sarga* 15 (vv. 11–21a-c, 65, 69–78, 40–49, and 21d-37), is found. Many of the preserved leaves have broken and missing fragments. Large parts of fols. ii.108v–109r are unreadable due to fading, and so are the first four lines of 101r. There were attempts to contain and prevent further damage: several leaves were framed by means of a white strip and in some cases laminated with paper tissue. The strip covers parts of the marginalia and of the foliation. Other marginalia are lost because the margins were trimmed at some point, possibly at the time of the modern binding.

Beginning [i.2r] *-lāviharaṇodyataiḥ* [...] ($\mathrm{NM}^{\mathrm{Va}}$, I 3,9).

End [ii.270v17] *-kalpavṛkṣāya s̆ambhave* // ($\mathrm{NM}^{\mathrm{Va}}$, II 718,10) *ity ācāryārjunasvāmiputraśitikaṇṭhasvāmilikhitāyāṃ bhaṭṭajayantasya kṛtau nyāyamaṃjaryām dvādaśam āhnikam // samāptā ce* [19] *yaṃ nyāyamaṃjarī // śiṣyān adhyāpayituṃ śitikaṇṭhasvāminā guruṇā*[1] *gautamamatatattvavidā* (*tva*)*ritaṃ śrīnyāyamañjarī likhitā // oṃ namaś śrī*[2]*śāradāyai // oṃ namo mahāgaṇapataye // iti śubham astu lekha*[3]*kapāṭhakayoḥ // śāke* 1394 *āśva śuti* 10 //

Scribal features The manuscript is written in Śāradā script by a single hand, with a distinctively cursive ductus. The following orthographical peculiarities were noticed: *visarga*-s are consistently replaced by sibilants before sibilants, except when a sentence break is intended; there are occurances of *pṛṣṭhamātra* for the vowel-signs *o* and *e*, especially in cases of tight interlinear space: e.g., 91v21, *kesara*.

ii.91v21

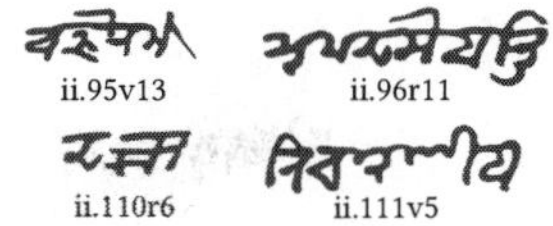
ii.95v13 ii.96r11 ii.110r6 ii.111v5

Occasionally, the *repha* preceding a consonant is written above the head-line and can be easily mistaken for an *e* vowel-sign: e.g., 95v13, *varjanam*, and 96r11, *-m upadarśayanti*; more often, however, it is written in ligature below the head-line, e.g., 110r6, *darśana*; the ligature *rdh* is peculiarly similar to a *va*: 93r10,*nirdhāraṇīya-*.

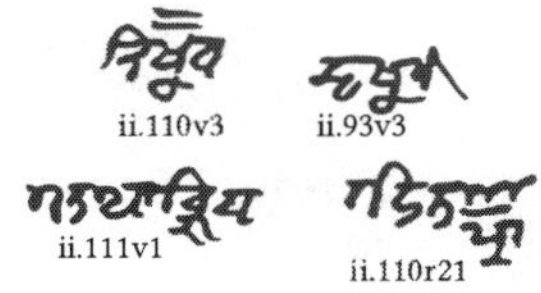
ii.110v3 ii.93v3 ii.111v1 ii.110r21

The *ṣṭa* and *ṣṭha* ligatures are homoglyphs, e.g., 110v3, *niṣṭhaiva*), and 93v3, *dṛṣṭam*; there is a consistent use of *jīhva-mūlīya* and *upadhmānīya* in appropriate places, e.g., 111v1, *gatayaẖ kri-*, and 110r21, *rahitaḫ prā-*.

ii.93r10 ii.90v5

The text is punctuated with *daṇḍa*-s, double *daṇḍa*-s, and peculiar wedge-shaped signs separated by a blank, apparently analogous to *daṇḍa*-s: e.g., 93r10. Such wedges are often used to mark the beginning and the ending of metrical passages, while *daṇḍa*-s generally mark structural parts of the argumentation. There are several smaller *daṇḍa*-s, probably added in a second moment. These are positioned below the line and often in narrow spots, so they do not seem to have been planned at the time of copying. They are used to tag not only clauses, but even single words. Sentence breaks are also indicated by blanks and dissolved *sandhi*-s. The margins have been used to provide several corrections by different hands. These marginalia were written at different times, judging from the varied degrees of fading, from the thickness of the trait and from the different ductus. They are linked to the text by crosses above and/or below the line, e.g., 90v5. Some of the marginalia are written in modern Śāradā, repeat the main text without changes and were probably meant to clarify ambiguously or unfamiliarly written *akṣara*-s. Interlinear corrections are also observed; as in the case of the marginalia, they are both insertions of skipped *akṣara*-s (90v3) and clarifications of ambiguous *akṣara*-s (91v17). Many of these are written by a second hand in smaller and thin *akṣara*-s, immediately above the line.

Right above the folio number, on the external margin, the abbreviation of the work (*nyā*) and the syllable *śrī* are consistently present. The *āhnika*-s end with a statement containing the copyist's signature, e.g., at the end of NM 6 [129r4], [...] *sidhyanti sarve puruṣārthasārthāḥ // ity ācāryaśitikaṇṭhasvāmilikhitāyāṃ bhaṭṭajayantasya kṛtau nyāyamaṃjaryāṃ ṣaṣṭham āhnikam // oṃ namaś śrīmahāgaṇapataye bhīmasvāmine //*

The digits indicating the year and the lunar day in the colophon are curiously written in Nāgarī numerals.

History According to the colophon, the manuscript was completed in Kashmir on the tenth day of the bright half of the Āśvina month, in the year 1394 of the *śāka* era. This date corresponds to Saturday, September 12, 1472.[13] The manuscript was copied and signed by Ācārya Śitikaṇṭhasvāmin, son of Arjunasvāmin. As rightly assumed by Muroya (2009–2010, § 3.5), Śitikaṇṭha was also the author of a commentary (*Nyāsa*) to Jagaddhara's (14th c.) grammatical work *Kātantrabālabodhinī*.[14]

It is one of the two manuscripts utilized in the *editio princeps* (see Section 2.1). It was acquired by Georg Bühler during his journey to Kashmir as an envoy of the Bombay Presidency. In 1888 it was listed with the same number (390) among the manuscripts about to be moved from the Elphinstone College in Bombay to the Deccan College in Pune. The collection was then shifted in 1918 to the newly founded BORI Institute:

[13]Calculated with the online *pañcāṅga* by Michio Yano, www.cc.kyoto-su.ac.jp/~yanom/pancanga/index.html, accessed 31/1/2015.

[14]On Jagaddhara's work, see Potter, 1977, 486 and NCC3, 317. Muroya (2009–2010, 41) noticed how Śitikaṇṭhācārya is evoked as an authority on a grammatical issue in a marginal note to the NM: *ity asya prapañcas tu śitikaṇṭhācāryaviracite bālabodhinīnyāse draṣṭavyaḥ*. Muroya's assumption is confirmed by the identical signature found in a manuscript of the *Nyāsa* (Cat. VOHD 2010, 111), *ity ācāryārjunasvāmiputraśitikaṇṭhasvāmi-* [...] (Graheli, 2015a), as well as by the date of this manuscript, which in Cat. VOHD 2010 is reported as Śāka 1393, the year before BORI 390/75–6 was written. A manuscript of the *Tantrasārapadapañjīkā* signed by Śitikaṇṭha is preserved at the National Library, Vienna (Cat. ÖNB 1990, 87). A *Nyāyasiddhāntamañjarīdīpikā* is also ascribed to Śitikaṇṭha in Cat. BORI 1955, 41, but the identity of these two Śitikaṇṭha-s with the NM copyist is not yet confirmed.

> In 1868 the then Government of Bombay Presidency appointed Georg Bühler and Franz Kielhorn to search for and collect manuscripts from the Presidency and other areas [...] The manuscripts had been initially deposited in the Elphinstone College of Bombay, and subsequently the whole collection was shifted to the Deccan College, Pune in 1878. When the Bhandarkar Oriental Institute of Pune was established, the collection of some 20,000 manuscripts, known as the Government Collection, was shifted to the Institute [...][15]

The age of the present binding is not known. It is likely not original, as indicated by the misplacement and wrong orientation of some leaves. Moreover, the loss of fol. ii.1 suggests the possibility that the two parts of the NM, besides being separately foliated, had also been separately bound.

The BORI images provided by BORI and preserved at the Nyāya Archive, Vienna, include a white sticker with a sequential pagination, following the sequence of the presently bound codex, with a total of 840 pages, including the annexed work and verses in the appendix. The same images are digitally labelled sequentially, according to leaves, with recto and verso named A and B respectively, amounting to 421 photographed leaves. So the fragment of the last preserved folio has the label 840 and the digital label 421b.

Copies Digital photographs dated 2005, 2006 and 2007, courtesy of the Bhandarkar Oriental Research Institute, Pune, and the ISTB, Nyāya Project, Vienna.

Bibliography Cat. Report 1875, xxv; Cat. DC 1888, 95; NM^{Ga}, Bhūmikā, 5; Muroya, 2009–2010, § 3.5; Graheli, 2012a, § 2.11.

3.4.7 Pune, Anandashram, ms. 5329 AA 5329 Q

Nāgarī, paper, 64, 155 × 330, 11, 35

Extent and conditions The manuscript is incomplete and contains parts of NM 5–7. It is foliated from 238 to 303, in Nāgarī digits, on the lower right margin of each verso. It begins with the last third

[15] See http://www.namami.org/historyofcataloguing.html, accessed 31/1/2015, where also further information on these institutions can be found.

of NM 5 with 238r and ends with 303v. The first two folios of NM 6, i.e., 248 and 249, are missing, as well as fol. 265. In most cases these folio numbers need to be inferred, because margins of the photocopies were trimmed and the foliation, as well as some marginalia, were consequently cut off. However, this foliation is easily reconstructed because AA 5329 was originally part of DC 10663, described below, in which the folio numbers are clearly visible. DC 10663, indeed, is written by the same scribe and has a gap from 238r to 303v, where exactly the same NM portion covered by AA 5329 is missing.

Beginning [204r1] *-stīti tataś ca hananasya* [...] (NM^{Va}, II 112,12; NM 5).

End [247v6] *-ty akaluṣaṃ prāmāṇyam asya sthitaṃ // iti śrījabhaṭṭajayaṃtakṛtau nyāyamaṃjaryāṃ pañcamam āhnikaṃ //* (NM^{Va}, II 142,19–20; NM 7).

Scribal features Letters are slanted clockwise to the right. Above the foliation, in the top left margin, there is the word *rāma* and the abbreviated title *nyā. ma.* The manuscript is quite correct. The rare scribal errors are emended by the same hand.

The following features were ignored in the collation: the gemination of *ta* after *repha*; the confusion among *ya/pa*, *ṭu/du* and *va/ba*; the use of *anusvāra*-s in place of class-nasals in internal *sandhi*-s.

History AA 5329 is the part of NM 5–7 which was displaced and is missing in DC 10663. The reasons and the time of the displacement is unknown. In the undated and unpublished hand-list of the Anandashram library the manuscript is listed as "Ms. No. 5329 (B 0837). Devanāgarī, paper, 63 fols., incomplete, *nyāyamañjarī vyākhyā*".

Copies Photocopies, dated 4.3.2004 (see 303v), courtesy of the Anandashram, Pune, Yasutaka Muroya, and T. Ono.

Bibliography A Hand List of 8518 Manuscripts in the Anandashram, Pune (unpublished); Graheli, 2012a, § 2.10.

DC 10663
3.4.8 Pune, Deccan College, ms. 10663

Nāgarī, paper, 372, 155 × 330, 11, 35

Extent and conditions The manuscript is incomplete. It contains NM 1–5 and part of NM 7. Fols. 1–195, 204–237, 304–327 are preserved. NM 1–4 are almost complete, except for a couple of leaves missing at the end of NM 4. The foliation sequence is inconsistent, with occasional skips (e.g., 171–172). Fol. 210, as well as fols. 196–203 —probably the last two of NM 4 and the first five of NM 5— are lost.

Beginning [1v1] *oṃ svasty astu // śrī gaṇeśāya namaḥ // namaḥ śāsvatikānāṃdajñānaiśvaryamayātmane* [...].

End [195v11] *-ṣprayojanatvāt kāryaparād api śabdād vyutpattir bhavaṃtī na vākyārthamātraparyavasāyinī bhavati kiṃ tv ekaikapadāvāpo-* (NM^{Va}, II 693,8–10; NM 7).

Scribal features See AA 5329 above.

Copies Photocopies, courtesy of the Deccan College, Pune, and Raffaele Torella.

History The only information with an identification number comes from the flyleaf, which reads "Nyāyamañjarī | First 7 Ahnikas | Acc. No. 10663 | Deccan College | Pune | 33 × 15.5 cm | Line = 11 | Folios = 372 c | Letters 45".

Bibliography Graheli, 2012a, § 2.12.

3.4.9 Srinagar, Oriental Research Library, ms. 1933 ORL 1933 S

Śāradā, paper, 99, 150 × 240, 14–19, 30–45

Extent and conditions The manuscript contains parts of NM 5–8. There are altogether 99 leaves, fols. 210–309 in the original foliation. In NM 5 the first folios are missing. NM 6 is complete. In NM 7 fols. 190–193 (NM^{Va}, II 336,3–357.14) are either lost or missing in the images, and the last folio (294r) is written by a different hand with fewer and shorter lines; 294v is blank. NM 8 is also incomplete, missing about one fourth of the *āhnika* at the end. Within NM 6, which starts on 239r10 and ends on 272r16, there are two folios numbered 260 (260A and 260B in my numbering). The original foliation is placed on the bottom left margin of each verso, after the abbreviated title *nyā. ma* or, in a few cases, *nyā. ya. ma.* There is an additional foliation in Nāgarī numerals, repeated twice on the upper and lower left margin of 258v, where there is a shift from Śāradā to Nāgarī in the text as well; the lower number reads 256 and the upper one, faithful to the actual sequence, 258. There is a minor loss of support on the right edge of some folios, where few *akṣara*-s are lost. A few lines have faded on the bottom left of fol. 259r.

Beginning *kalpitaṃ tu tat vaktum aśakyaṃ kalpanayaiva* [...] ($\mathrm{NM}^{\mathrm{Va}}$, II 20,12; NM 5).

End [...] *iti coditaṃ parihṛtaṃ tad bhāṣyakāreṇa* ($\mathrm{NM}^{\mathrm{Va}}$, II 405,14; NM 8).

Scribal features Despite its *pothi* shape, the manuscript was written and is read by turning the leaves on their vertical axis, while *pothi*-s are generally turned horizontally, with the turning edge coinciding with the top margin of the recto and the bottom of the verso. The manuscript may have even been bound at some point, with the spine on the left margin of the recto and the right margin of the verso, since this margin is much more worn than the other three. At least five changes of hand can be detected:

[First hand] The first part of NM 6, continuing from the previous *āhnika* (fols. 239v-250v4), has a calligraphic appearance with 17–19 lines on each side. The same ductus reappears, after two and half folios written by a second hand and a third hand, from 253r on. This first scribe uses intermittently two different *o* vowel-signs: one is wavy, as in 246r9, *śloka*, while the other is not, as in 246r9, *loka*. The same scribe shifts to Nāgarī, beginning from 258r17 and throughout 258v. Śāradā characteristics such as the *e* and *o* vowel-signs, however, are still clearly visible, even in the Nāgarī passage, as in 246r9, *vyāpriyattenā*. On this Nāgarī folio the number of lines (17) remains the same. The darkness, thickness and style of the ductus are also identical to the previous and following Śāradā portions. From 259r onwards the same hand reverts to Śāradā again. The punctuation is sparse, with mostly single *daṇḍa*-s and rare double ones (249r18). The latter ones may have been added in a second moment, since they occur below the line (e.g., 246r11). There are *avagraha*-s placed below the line (e.g., 248v15, 246r4). On 245v there are three blank lines with a corresponding omission of text.

246r16 255r2 245v15 246v3 240v13

There are several interlinear and marginal emendations, apparently by the same hand: short dashes at the head-line height indicate lacunae, possibly *akṣara*-s unreadable to the scribe, e.g., 246r16; ; the elongation of vowels is marked by a small crescent, joined to the affected *akṣara* and placed above the line, as in 255r2, ⟦*śa*⟧⟨*śā*⟩*ntiḥ*; words, *akṣara*-s or parts of *akṣara*-s are elided by thin strokes (one or two) above the line, e.g., 245v15, ⟦*ti*⟧⟨*ta*⟩*eva*; there are insertions of *akṣara*-s above lines, sometimes with a caret below the line, e.g., 246r3; the integration of omissions in margins is also linked to the main text by means of carets below the line, e.g., 240v13.

[Second hand] A second scribe wrote fol. 250, which is written in a more angular, less calligraphic hand, along with a reduction from 17 to 14 lines per page.

[Third hand] A third scribe takes over in fol. 251r. This same hand is seen in fols. 263r and 268r. Here the ductus is tighter, narrower, and slightly slanted, again with 16–17 lines, but characterized by peculiar *o* and *ṛ* vowel signs, as well as by a punctuation with frequent double *daṇḍa*-s. The lower part of vertical strokes is often so thick that in some cases it is hard to assess the presence or absence of the *u* vowel-sign (e.g., 267r15 *anupapanna*). It is also difficult to distinguish *rva* from *va* (e.g., 267r15 *durvyavasthita*).

[Fourth hand] A fourth scribe wrote 267v. In stark contrast with the other hands, here the *akṣara*-s are much bigger and the ductus distinctly cursive. From 268r the third hand takes over again.

269r4

[Fifth hand] A fifth change of hand occurs at fol. 269r. This scribe continues up to the end of the sixth *āhnika* (272r15). The lay-out of 16–17 lines is kept also here and this hand resembles that of the third scribe. The ductus, in fact, has the same thickness and darkness. The *o* vowel-sign, however, is quite different. The habit of writing the *upadhmānīya* above the head-line is a peculiarity of this hand, as in 269r4. The *akṣara*-s *ya* and *va* are here almost indistinguishable (e.g., 269v4 *prayojya*). There are also homoglyph pairs such as *rna* and *nna* (e.g., 270v9 *sādhubhir nety*), *ṣṭha* and *ṣṭa* (e.g, 270v10 *pratiṣṭhānāṃ* and 270v12 *dṛṣṭā*). A metathesis at fol. 271r6 is emended by this scribe with the numbers 2 and 1 above the two concerned words, to reinstate the right order.

History Śitikaṇṭha's chapter-endings with his signature (see BORI 390/75–6 above) were copied and later crossed out at the end of NM 6 and of NM 7. Since this can not plausibly be a manuscript from the 15th century, it is an unquestionable evidence of a derivation from BORI 390/75–6. In the study of the genealogy (see Section 5.4.5 below) a shift of exemplar was detected in correspondence with the change of hand in fol. 269r; from that point on, indeed, ORL 1933 is considered a *descriptus* of BORI 390/75–6.

Copies Digital photographs dated 2005, courtesy of the Oriental Research Library, University of Kashmir, Srinagar.

Bibliography Cat. SORL 1989, 94, 220; Graheli, 2012a, § 2.15.

SSV 3465 V 3.4.10 Varanasi, Sampurnanand Sanskrit Vishwavidyalaya, ms. 3465

1737 CE, Kāśmīrī Nāgarī, paper, 320, 130 × 240, 14, 55

Extent and conditions The manuscript contains the complete NM. There are 320 leaves, numbered 1 to 320 in the original foliation. The foliation is on the verso, at the top left margin below the abbreviation *oṃ nyā* and in the lower right margin below the word *rāma*, so that each verso factually begins with *oṃ* and ends with *rāma*. Fol. 320r, where the text ends, is also numbered, despite being a recto side. The manuscript is not easily readable, due to the transparency of the paper that reveals the ink of the back side, hiding or confusing, particularly, the copious and tiny corrections.

Beginning *śrīgaṇeśāya namaḥ oṃ svasti oṃ namaḥ śāsvatikānandajñānaiśvaryamayātmane* [...]

End [320v7] *prapannajanasaṃkalpakalpavṛkṣāya śaṃbhave //* [8] *iti śrījayaṃtabhaṭṭakṛtāyāṃ nyāyamaṃjaryāṃ dvādaśam āhnikam // samāptā ceyaṃ nyāyamaṃjarī // śubham astu sarveṣāṃ lekhakā+ saṃvat 1794 mārgaśīra (śu) 4 amā (tyavāda) pure++++.*

Scribal features The ductus is very similar to that of ORI C–1374 (see Section 3.4.5 above). The word *saṃvat* in the colophon and, less obviously, also the rest of the date might have been written by a different hand. There is no punctuation, not even for verses or between prose and verses, although some breaks are marked by blanks and dissolved *sandhi*-s. The rare *avagraha*-s were added later, below the lines.

The manuscript contains several emendations that seem the work of different hands. At least two typologies of corrections are distinguishable: in one case the trait is thicker and the corrections are in the margins; in the other, the marks are sharp, tiny and often interlinear. Many of these corrections are hardly visible due to the transparency of the paper and to the poor quality of the photocopies. In some cases, carets are visible above (194r4) or below (194r7) the lines, while no related correction or insertion can be detected.

- A short vowel is elongated with a wavy mark above (194r2 *avānta⟦ra⟧⟨rā⟩pūrva*) (see Einicke, 2009, 113, Nag9(1794)_1).
- An *akṣara* is marked for replacement by a horizontal sign above it (193v2, ⟦*spha*⟧⟨*spho*⟩).
- A *visarga* is added above or below the line and with a mark below or above the line, respectively (196r12 *upapatti⟨ḥ⟩*, 196v3 *visarjaniyā⟨ḥ⟩*).
- An *akṣara* is deleted by two vertical strokes above it (193v5, *satya⟦m⟧*).
- A vowel-sign is deleted by one or two vertical or oblique strokes (193v2, 193v10).
- Words are deleted by underlining them (206v6 ⟦*tathāpi na*⟧).
- A metathesis is emended by numbers above the *akṣara*-s, inverting their order (194r10, *vi⟦śvana⟧⟨naśva⟩reṣu*).

History In Cat. SC 1902, 14, the manuscript is described as follows: "Devanāgarī script on paper, fols. 320, Saṃvat 1794 (CE 1736–1737)". This catalogue also mentions that the manuscript was used as the source of the *editio princeps*: *idaṃ tad evādarśapustakaṃ yasmād vijayanagarasaṃskṛtasīrījasañjñikāyāṃ pustakaśreṇyāṃ nyāyamañjarīpustakaṃ mudritam.* The editor of the *editio princeps* writes (NM^{Ga}, Bhūmikā, 5) that the manuscript was made available by Arthur Venis. In Cat. SBhL 1962, the same manuscript is listed under serial no. 33668 and with the same access no., i.e., 3465.

According to the date in the colophon, the manuscript was completed in Vikrama Saṃvat 1794, on the fourth lunar day of the bright half of the Mārgaśira month, i.e., November 26, Tuesday, 1737 CE.[16] However, the date appears to be written by a different hand and some *akṣara*-s are illegible. It is possible that the date was not written by the scribe, but rather by a patron or a purchaser, or that the scribe wrote only the year and that a second person integrated it with the details of month and day, since the ductus of the portion *saṃvat 1794* is more similar to the scribe's, judging from the thickness of the stroke and intensity of the colour. In any case, since there are is no evidence against this chronology and since the characteristics of the whole manuscript are congruous with this date, it may be accepted as genuine.

Many emendations match the readings of BORI 390/75–6 and could be Gangadhara's own.

Copies Photocopies, courtesy Sampurnanand Sanskrit *Vishwavidyalaya* (previously Government Sanskrit College), and of the ISTB, Nyāya Project, Vienna.

Bibliography Cat. SC 1902, 14; Cat. SBhL 1962; NM^{Ga}, Bhūmikā, 5; Graheli, 2012a, § 2.18.

3.5 Description of the GBh manuscript

JTGB 386 J

3.5.1 Jaisalmer, Jinabhadrasūri Tāḍaprakriya Grantha Bhaṇḍāra, ms. 386

Jaina Nāgarī, palm leaf, 186, 327 × 625, 5–6, 60

Extent and conditions The manuscript contains the *Granthibhaṅga* commentary to NM 1–6. In the digital copy available for the present book 186 leaves appear, plus some fragments of leaves. The original foliation, in Nāgarī figures, is placed on the left margin of

[16] Calculated with the online *pañcāṅga* by Michio Yano, www.cc.kyoto-su.ac.jp/~yanom/pancanga/index.html, accessed 31/1/2015.

each verso. Above the figures there are also letter numerals.[17] A modern foliation in Arabic figures has been added below the string holes of each verso, matching the foliation recorded in Shah's edition (GBh^{Sha}). In this book and in this description, however, I will refer to the original foliation.

The edges of most leaves are damaged and in some instances portions of text have been lost, e.g. in fols. 6 and 28. The preserved text, however, is perfectly readable, except for some partially blurred parts (e.g., 21r, 49r3, 60r). Some of the illegible parts might have been erased on purpose, as in 20v3–5.

Shah (GBh^{Sha}, 1) found 18 folios missing or broken. In my count, however, there are more than those: fols. 3–5, 11, 33, 34, 98, 103, 105, 110, 115, 122, 130–136, 138, 168–170, 173, and 181 are all missing. The extant sequence of the folios is the following one: 1–2, 6–10, 12–32, 35–83, 84r, 85–97, 99–102, 104, 106–109, 111–114, 116–121, 123–129, 137, 139–167, 171–172, 174–180, 182–186. Some further anomalies are that fol. 2 is foliated 175, fol. 82r is foliated 85A, fol. 171 is misplaced, fols. 2, 161, and 178 are preserved only in fragments (cf. the description in Muroya, 2009–2010, § 2.1, particularly fn. 26).

There are further fragments of about fifteen folios. Due to the fact that there is no other manuscript of the first half of the GBh and that these fragments do not include clear hints such as catchwords (*pratīka*-s) linked to the commented NM passages, an assessment of their correct position is a demanding task.

Beginning [1v1] ++ *namaḥ śivāya // namo navasitāsaktacitkriyāśaktisaṃpade* [...]

End [186v3] [...] *bhartṛhariprabhṛtayaḥ āryā iti bhadram // bhaṭṭaśrīśaṃkarātmajacakradharakṛte nyāyamañjarīgranthibhaṅge ṣaṣṭham āhnikaṃ samāptam // oṃ jayaty ekaśarāghātavidāritapuratrayaḥ / dhanurddharāṇāṃ dhaureya pinākī bhuvanatraye //*

Scribal features The manuscript is the remarkable handicraft of a skilful Jaina scribe. It is elegantly written and artistically decorated,

[17] Kapadia distinguishes among *aṅkapalli* on one side, denoting the system of numerals in figures, and *aṅkalipi*, as synonym of *akṣarapalli*, on the other, denoting letter numerals (see Kapadia, 1937, 185–186 and Tripathi, 1975, 24).

and at the same time it is quite correct and reliable. It is regularly punctuated by both single and double *daṇḍa*-s. The written area is divided into two blocks by a decorated square resembling a string hole. On some folios (79v, 80v, 123v, 124v, 185v and 186v) an ornamental *maṇḍala* divides the text further into three blocks. These geometrical *maṇḍala* ornaments were probably drawn with stencils, or perhaps with a pair of compasses. The colophons are decorated with patterns of *daṇḍa*-s and ornamental *akṣara*-s. The stanzas at the end of *āhnika*-s were in most cases edited at the beginning of the succeeding *āhnika*-s in Shah's edition. According to their position in the manuscript, however, they seem to be rather meant to close *āhnika*-s. Whenever an *āhnika* ends on the verso of a folio the following recto is left blank.

The letter numerals used for the foliation are akin to those described by Kapadia (1937, Plate I and p. 184), with some variations: 1, 2 and 3 are always in Nāgarī figures and are followed by *rṇka* (4), *rtṛ* (5), *rphu* (6) (and not *rphru*, *rgrā* (7), *rhā* (8) (and not *hra*), *oṃ* (9), *rḷ* (10), etc.

(1) (2) (3) rṅka (4) rtṛ (5) rphu (6) rgrā (7) rhā (8) oṃ (9) rḷ (10)

The following features were ignored in the collation: the gemination of consonants after *repha*; the ambiguous use of *śa* and *sa*; the use of *anusvāra*, rather than class-nasals, except for the *nta* ligature.

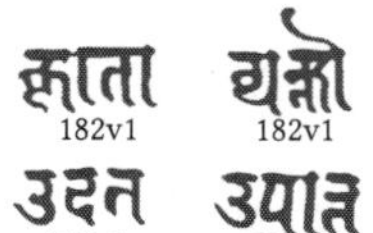

The *e* and *o* vowel-signs are written as *pṛṣṭha-mātra*-s,e.g., 182v1, *kṛto*, except when occurring in the first line or in corrections, e.g., 182v1, *vyakto* . The geometrical appearance of the text block was clearly a priority of the scribe, who copiously adopted line-filling *daṇḍa*-s in the vicinity of the string-holes and at the end of lines, and wrote even *visarga*-s on a new line, separating them from the preceding *akṣara*, in order to have an evenly formed margin (e.g., 158v3–4). Homograph *akṣara*-s are *va/ba*, *tta/nta* and *ddha/dva*, and so are the vowels *u* and *o* at the beginning of words, e.g., 176v1 and 176v2, *odana* and *upātta*.

Also *dha* can be easily taken for a *va* or a *ba*, although the head-line of *dha*, *ddha* and *dhva* is usually finer and clearly convex. When *tha* occurs in the ligature *stha* it closely resembles a *cha*.

There are few corrections, most probably by the hand of the original scribe. They are mostly placed in the margins, generally in the lower one. Single skipped *akṣara*-s (e.g., 7r) are linked to the text by carets in the form of little crosses above the line. The line number is also provided next to the correction (see also 12r, 16v). Longer marginal additions are treated analogously (77r, 85r, 89r, 92v). Words, *akṣara*-s or parts of *akṣara*-s are elided by means of small vertical strokes through the head-line, e.g., 7r6, ⟦*ta*⟧ (see Einicke, 2009, 119, NaJ1(1445)_6).

7r6

History The author of the GBh, Cakradhara, was the son of Bhaṭṭa Śaṅkara and the pupil of Bhaṭṭa Śaśāṅkadhara. Muroya (2009–2010, § 1.2) suggests that Cakradhara may have been a contemporary of Kṣirasvāmin, who was also a disciple of Bhaṭṭa Śaśāṅkadhara, in the 11th century. The manuscript is assigned to the first half of the 13th century in Cat. JJBh 1972, 94, and to the 13th century of the Vikrama era by Shah, although no arguments for these dates are given in either sources. The manuscript was probably written before the foundation of the Jaisalmer library by Jinabhadra (1551 CE); Dundas (2002, 83) writes that "many manuscripts from Patan and Cambay were taken there to save them from Muslim depredation".

Copies Digital photographs dated 2007, courtesy of the Śrī Jinabhadrasūri Tāḍapatrīya Jñānabhaṇḍāra, Lodravapur Pārśvanāth Jain Trust, Jaisalmer, and of the ISTB, Nyāya Project, Vienna.

Bibliography Cat. JJBh 1972, 94; Cat. JJBh 1972, 162; GBh^{Sha}, 1; Muroya, 2009–2010.

4 Genealogy of the editions

4.1 Gangadhara's edition, the editio princeps

The first printed version of the NM dates back to 1895 (NM^{Ga}).[1] In the introduction the editor, Gangadhara Shastri,[2] mentions two manuscripts, a Nāgarī one from Varanasi and a Śāradā one from Pune. The Varanasi manuscript was obtained through the agency of "Mr. Arthur Venis, principal of the Government Sanskrit College in Varanasi". Gangadhara describes this manuscript as "written in Saṃvat 1794 [1737 CE], and not particularly correct", and the other, which he borrowed "from the Government Library in Pune" as "written in Śāka 1394 [1473 CE] on birch bark, in Śāradā script".[3] The two manuscripts are without doubt SSV 3465 and BORI 390/75–6, described above.[4] It is unclear why Gangadhara thought of SSV 3465 as "most ancient" (*prācīnatama*), while he was aware that BORI 390/75–6 is much older.

By 1936, when the next NM edition (NM^{Shu}) appeared, the *editio princeps* was probably out of print. Suryanarayana Shukla was commissioned by the head of Chowkhamba, Jayakrishnadas Gupta, to prepare a new edition, as mentioned in the introduction (NM^{Shu}, Bhūmikā, 8). Shukla did not consult fresh manuscript sources, but

[1]For the description, see Section 2.1.

[2]Also known as Gangadhara Shastri Manavalli (NM^{Shu}, Bhūmikā, 8).

[3]*kāśikarājakīyasaṃskṛtapāṭhaśālāpradhānādhyakṣaśrīmad – ārtharavenisa – sāhibamahodayadattaṃ prācīnatamaṃ saṃvat 1794 varṣalikhitaṃ nātiśuddham … puṇyagrāmastharājakīyapustakālayād āgataṃ śāke 1394 bhūrjapatreṣu śāradākṣaralikhitam aparaṃ pustakam* (NM^{Ga}, Bhūmikā, 5).

[4]Sections 3.4.10 and 3.4.6.

improved Gangadhara's work by adding some exegetical notes and structuring the text into thematic paragraphs with headings.[5]

A partial edition in Bengali characters, with the Sanskrit text and a translation in Bengali, was then edited by Panchanana Tarkavagisha Devasharma (NM^{Pa}). The first volume was published in 1939 and the second one in 1941. Panchanana does not mention other sources besides NM^{Ga}. Specifically, in the preface he quotes NM^{Ga} three times and in the acknowledgements he gives credit to the pioneering work of Gangadhara Shastri Tailanga. It seems that he was also aware of the new Chowkhamba edition, since he referred to NM^{Ga} as the "old edition" (*prācīna saṃskāraṇa*) of the NM, but without directly citing NM^{Shu}.[6]

In 1969, at the Sanskrit College in Varanasi, the NM was added to the *prācīnanyāya* curriculum at the *śāstrin* level, so it was needed as a textbook. At first, for curricular reasons, the second part of the 1936 edition was revised and published by Chowkhamba (see NM^{Ma}, Prākkathanam, 5). According to the information that can be gathered from the brief preface by Suryanarayana Shukla (NM^{Ma}, Bhūmikā), this second edition was revised by Shukla himself and by Madhvacharya Adya. The edition was newly typeset in a different font, although the previous layout was mirrored almost identically. The first part of the NM^{Shu} was then reprinted in 1971, without any new preface and without any explicit revision.

Many errors in NM^{Ga} were corrected by Shukla already in 1936. The differences between NM^{Ga}, NM^{Shu} and NM^{Ma}, however, still need to be assessed in detail. Particularly, it is important to keep in mind the difference between the second and the first volumes of NM^{Ma}, because the former (NM 7–12) was more carefully revised than the latter (NM 1–6).[7] As for the NM 6 portion, in NM^{Ma} some glaring errors present in NM^{Shu} were indeed corrected, although new errors were also generated:

- *pratyayanā-*] Ga Shu Gau; *pratyāyanā-* Va Ma (II 145,6)

[5] For the description, see Section 2.2.

[6] See NM^{Pa}, Vol. 1, Bhūmikā, i-ii, and Nivedanam, i.

[7] For some remarks on a specific section of the NM, see NM^{KKa}, 117.

- *pariteṣa-*] Shu; *paritoṣa-* Ga Va Ma Gau (II 151,16)
- *taskārā-*] Shu; *taskarā-* Ga Va Ma Gau (II 152,1)
- *-pratīr*] Shu; *-pratītir* Ga Va Ma (II 152,10)
- *dvidbhaḥ*] Shu; *vidmaḥ* Ma (II 173,12)
- *vākyārthayor* Ga] *vākyavākyārthayor* Shu Ma Va Gau (II 178,7)
- *vinaśyadavastha-* Ga Va Gau] *vinaśyavastha-* Shu; *vinaśyadhasya-* Ma (II 196,14–15)
- *sa sampradānaṃ* Va (II 240,9)] *tat sampradānaṃ* Ga Shu Gau; *sat sampradānaṃ* Ma
- *kārarakāntara-*] Shu; *kārakāntara-* Ma (II 243,7)
- *buddhasaṃskāravihīnavācaḥ* Shu (broken metre)] *prabuddhasaṃskāravihīnavācaḥ* Ma (II 243,7)

4.2 Varadacharya's edition

In 1969, the first of the two volumes of K.S. Varadacharya's edition (NM^{Va}) was published, containing NM 1–4. In the preface (NM^{Va}, vol. 1, Bhūmikā, i), the editor mentioned both the *editio princeps* and the 1936 edition, citing insufficient manuscript sources as the reason of their unreliability, and thus justifying the need of his new, better founded edition. For the first volume, Varadacharya at first relied on two manuscripts, until he acquired a third one from Allahabad; its variant readings were collated in an appendix.

In the second volume, which covers NM 5–12, Varadacharya used three further manuscripts and sporadically referred to the edition of the *Granthibhaṅga* (see NM^{Va}, vol. 2, Bhūmikā, viii).

These are the five manuscript consulted by Varadacharya:
- A complete manuscript from the Oriental Research Institute, Mysore, with the siglum क (*ka*) in his apparatus (NM^{Va}, vol. I, Prastāvanā). My collation work confirms that it is the same as ORI C–1374 above.
- A second source (ADP), with the siglum ग (*ga*), is described by him as follows: "While engaged in searching for other documents, we heard that there was one document in the Parakāla Maṭha in Mysore, but [...] we went there to collect it and we found that this document was not available. Still, we have found that there is now a text owned by Atmakuru Dikshacharya which was edited on the basis of that document, [...]" (NM^{Va}, vol. I, Prastāvanā, i). On the

basis of this description, a possible conjecture is that ADP may have been a transcription of a non-identified manuscript, as presumed in NM^{KKa}, 117. Throughout NM 6, there are only five variants attributed by Varadacharya to ADP.
- A manuscript obtained from the Ganganath Jha Research Institute in Allahabad, labelled च (*ca*), which coincides with GJ 833 above. Variants from this manuscript are listed in an appendix in vol. 1, while in vol. 2 they are found in the regular apparatus.
- A manuscript from the Adyar Library, with the siglum घ (*gha*). Judging from the extent of the manuscript, missing the first five *āhnika*-s, and on the strength of the data collated for the present edition the match with AL 70179B above is confirmed.
- A manuscript from the Government Library, Madras, with the siglum ङ (*ṅa*). It coincides with GOML R. 3631A (see Graheli, 2012a). It was not used for the present edition because it does not cover NM 6.

Two further editions, NM^{Sha} and NM^{Gau}, use both NM^{Ga} and NM^{Shu} without reference to new manuscript sources. The latter, edited by Gaurinatha Shastri, includes the *Granthibhaṅga*, which Gaurinatha derives (see NM^{Gau}, *Introduction*, 1) from the text previously edited by Shah on the basis of the two extant manuscripts (GBh^{Sha}). Shah must have also consulted NM^{Va}, as it can be evinced from many conjunctive readings.

To date, NM^{Va} is the most complete NM edition, since it fills several gaps that Gangadhara had inherited from SSV 3465, and that went unnoticed in NM^{Shu}, e.g.:
- *śabdād* [...] *pratipādakaḥ*] Va Sha (II 148,11–12); *om.* V Ga Shu Gau
- *yamāna- ... lavaṇopa-*] Va Sha (II 226,10–11); *om.* V Ga Shu Gau
- *kārakam iti vakṣyāmaḥ ... saṅkataḥ*] Va Sha (II 240,14–16); *om.* V Ga Shu Gau

In most cases, such omissions are also recorded in the apparatus of NM^{Va} under the siglum *kha*. In connection to this, both of the previous editions are acknowledged by the editor in the preface (NM^{Va}, vol. 1, Bhūmikā, i). It is not clear whether the siglum *kha* introduced in the next page (*mudritakośa eva tulanātmakasaṃśod-*

hanopayogārthaṃ 'kha' saṃjñayā yogitaḥ) and adopted in the footnotes was meant to indicate both or one of them specifically. In NM 6 there are conjunctive readings that suggest how Varadacharya adopted NM^{Shu} as his text of choice and how, incidentally, NM^{Gau} used instead the *editio princeps* readings in those very passages, e.g.:

- *śravaṇe ca*] Ga Gau, *śravaṇe* Shu Va (NM II 143,4)
- *eva*] Ga Gau, *iva* Shu Va (NM II 153,2) (In this case, interestingly, the archetypical reading is assumed to be *iva*, which was possibly conjectured in Shu although its sole exemplar, i.e., the *editio princeps*, had *eva*)
- *pānakaṃ*] Ga Gau, *pānakaḥ* Shu Va (NM II 154,4)
- *maricādibhyo*] Ga Gau, *marīcyādibhyo* Shu Va (NM II 154,5)
- *tadartha-*] Ga Gau, *artha-* Shu Va (NM II 155,6)

When Varadacharya directly refers to *kha* in the footnotes, however, the readings match those of NM^{Ga}:

- *mām ayaṃ*] Va Shu Gau (I 6,4); *mamāyaṃ* Ga Va^{kha}
- *varttaika*] Ga Va^{kha}Gau; *vattaka* Shu; *varttaiva* Va (I 91,6)
- *dīpra*] Ga Va^{kha}; *dīpa* Shu Va Gau (I 169,5)
- *pratyāyavatvopādhi-*] Ga Va (II 152,9); *pratyāyatvopādhi-* Shu
- *padapadārtha-*] Shu Ma Gau Va (II 203,9); *padārtha-* Ga Va^{kha}
- *niḥśreyasādhigama*] Shu Ma Gau Va (II 231,11); *niḥśreyasāvagama* Ga Va^{kha}
- *kārakam* Va (II 241,13)] *kāraṇam* Ga Va^{kha}; *adhikaraṇam* ShuMaGau

Consequently, I am assuming that Varadacharya built his edition from NM^{Shu} as his text of choice, perhaps under the impression that it was an improved edition of NM^{Ga}, and recorded the latter's readings as *kha* in the apparatus, when they diverged from the former's ones.

4.3 Shah's and Gaurinatha's editions

By the examples cited above, the relation of NM^{Sha} and NM^{Gau} with the previous editions can also be inferred. Shah aptly adopted the more complete text edited in NM^{Va}:

- *śabdād* [...] *pratipādakaḥ*] Va Sha (II 148,11–12); *om.* V Ga Shu Gau
- *yamāna-* ... *lavaṇopa-*] Va Sha (II 226,10–11); *om.* V Ga Shu Gau
- *kārakam iti vakṣyāmaḥ* ... *saṅkataḥ*] Va Sha (II 240,14–16); *om.* V Ga Shu Gau

The readings in NM^{Gau} match the two previous Chowkhamba editions, as evident from the segmentation of paragraphs, which is very close to that of NM^{Shu} and which was reproduced in NM^{Ma}. Yet, in some cases Gaurinatha probably went back to the *editio princeps* to correct faulty readings which had crept into the Chowkhamba text:

- *ekākṣarānugame* Ga Va (II 154,10)] *ekākṣarānanugame* ShuMaGau
- *padena tu* Ga Va (II 158,15)] *padena* Shu Ma Gau
- *kramabhāvināpi* Shu Ma] *kramabhāvinām api* Ga Va Gau (II 159,13)
- *-kriyākṣāṇānām* Ga Va (II 162,1)] *-kriyālakṣāṇānām* Shu Ma Gau
- *prathamavarṇavyakto* Ga] *prathamavarṇavyaktau* Shu Ma Gau; *prathama* Va (II 167,14)
- *iṣyate* Ga Va (II 169,13)] *iṣyate iti* Shu Ma Gau
- *ye codāhṛtās* Shu Ma] *ye 'trodāhṛtās* Ga Va Gau (II 182,12)
- *avyastatvād* Shu Ma] *abhyastatvād* Ga Va Gau (II 183,8)
- *-tirāhita-* Shu Ma] *-tirohita-* Ga Va Gau (II 189,3)
- *-pratyaye* Ga Va (II 190,5)] *mitaye* Shu Ma Gau
- *vākyasyārtho* Ga Va (II 191,13)] *vākyāsyārtho* Shu Ma Gau
- *ity ādi* Ga Va (II 198,4)] *ity api* Shu Ma Gau
- *anupannā* Shu Ma] *anupapannā* Ga Va Gau (II 198,11)
- *vinihato* Shu Ma] *vinihito* Ga Va Gau (II 199,9)
- *so 'yam abhihitānām* Ga Va (II 204,14)] *so 'yabhihitānām* ShuMaGau
- *-pratiteḥ panthaḥ* Ga Va (II 209,16)] *-panthaḥ* Shu Ma Gau
- *-vācyatā* Ga Va (II 210,14)] *-vācitā* Shu Ma Gau
- *-grahaṇāsambhavāt* Ga Va (II 224,8)] *-grahaṇasambhavāt* ShuMaGau
- *ananusaranta* Va (II 225,7)] *ananuharanta* Ga; *anuharanta* ShuMaGau
- *brūyān* Ga Va (II 225,12)] *atha brūyān* Shu Ma Gau
- *-bhāṣikatvam aprasaṅgāt* Shu Ma] *-bhāṣikatvaprasaṅgāt* Ga Va Gau (II 225,18)
- *kīdṛśo niyamārtha iti kiṃ sādhubhir* Va (II 227,14)] *kīdṛśo niyamārtha kiṃ sādhubhir* Ga; *kīdṛśo kiṃ niyamārtha sādhubhir* Shu Ma Gau
- *uccārayety* Ga Va (II 233,5)] *uccārayed ity* Shu Ma Gau
- *pratipadaṃ vihitān śabdān provāca* Ga Va (II 237,14)] *pratipadoktānāṃ śabdānāṃ pārāyaṇaṃ provāca* Shu Ma Gau
- *kārakam iti cet* Va (II 241,13)] *kāraṇam iti cet* Ga; *adhikaraṇam iti cet* Shu Ma Gau
- *ācāryo 'pi* Ga Va (II 247,13)] *ācāryo* Shu Ma Gau
- *prasaṅgadoṣa-* Ga Va (II 258,13)] *prasadoṣa-* Shu; *prasaktadoṣa-* Ma Gau

4.4 The stemma of the editions

From the evidence gathered above, the genealogical tree represented in Fig. 4.1 can be drawn. The manuscripts used in NM^{Ga} and NM^{Va} are shown on the top and connected to the two editions by dotted lines. The main source of NM^{Va} is NM^{Shu}, but NM^{Ga} was also used by Varadacharya, as shown by the dashed line connecting NM^{Ga} and NM^{Va}. All the other editions descend from these.

Figure 4.1: Genealogy of the editions

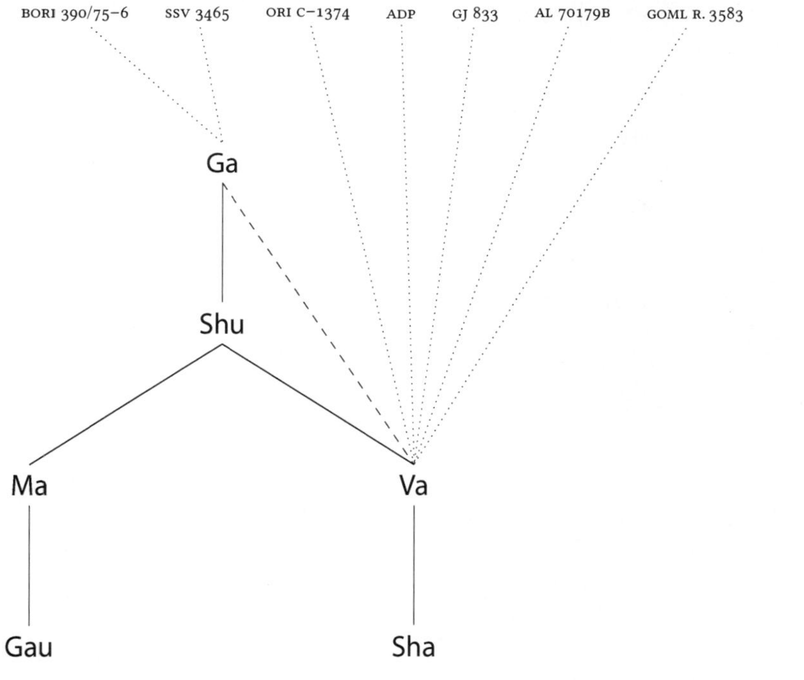

Although all the editions mentioned here have their intrinsic value, to date NM^{Va} remains the most reliable one and as such the best choice for citation purposes. NM^{Ga} and NM^{Shu} can be used to counter-check suspect or faulty readings of NM^{Va}, since Varadacharya built his edition starting from the text of these two.

Shah's edition is also valuable, especially because it was edited with the background of his outstanding edition and study of the GBh.

Lastly, Gaurinatha's edition is the only one with a running *Granthibhaṅga* printed along with the NM text. Yet, since the NM text follows NM^{Ga}, in many cases its readings should be corrected, when disagreeing with NM^{Va}.

5 Genealogy of the manuscripts

5.1 Method and tools

5.1.1 Chronological elements

Bhaṭṭa Jayanta wrote the NM within the last two decades of the 9th century (see Section 1.1). JTGB 386, the oldest extant document preserving NM readings, was probably copied in the 13th century (see Section 3.5.1), and the GBh is obviously older than that. Among the known NM manuscripts, BORI 390/75–6 and SSV 3465 are dated, respectively 1472 and 1736 CE. Furthermore, some historical context is also provided by vestiges of an indirect transmission of the NM.

There are traces of Jayanta's enduring popularity in Kashmir. His son's remarks have been already discussed above (Section 1.1). Jayanta and Abhinanda were also known by Abhinava Gupta, who seems to have inherited the notion of *tātparyaśakti* from the NM.[1] The NM was still studied in Kashmir in 1472 CE, when Śitikaṇṭhācārya was teaching it to his pupils, as stated in the colophon of his personal copy.[2]

Jayanta and the NM were also known to Udayana. In the 11th century,[3], in his commentary to *sūtra* 1.1.6 (NVTP, 215,20, 218,20) he referred to Jayanta as "the old Naiyāyika" (*jarannaiyāyika*), explaining how Vācaspati commented on some of Gautama's *sūtra*-s in the light of Jayanta's views.[4]

[1]A study of the likely relation of Abhinava's ideas to Jayanta's can be found in Graheli, forthcoming(b).

[2]See the description of BORI 390/75–6, Section 3.4.6.

[3]On Udayana's date, see NVTP, Preface, pp. viii–ix.

[4]Apart from this instance, however, there is no definite evidence that proves the

The NM was known beyond the borders of Kashmir already in the 11th century, as proven by the fact that it was very well known to king Bhoja of Dhāra, near Ujjain (presently Dhar, Madhya Pradesh). The ŚPr contains several re-uses of the NM, noticed and listed by Raghavan (1978, 709–711, 741–742). Bhoja never explicitly acknowledges Jayanta or the NM, yet there are several passages from the NM used verbatim in the ŚPr, both in prose and metre.

In 11th-13th century's Gujarat, the NM was studied in Jaina circles as well. Famous Jaina libraries, at the time of the composition of the GBh and the *Nyāyacaturgranthika* manuscripts in Jaina Nāgarī, were located in Patan, Cambay and Bharuch. The Jaisalmer libraries were apparently founded later and many manuscripts were brought there to save them from the Muslim threat (see Dundas, 2002, 83). Incidentally, also the best manuscripts of the *Āgamaḍambara* are preserved in Jaina collections (see Dezső, 2004, Introduction, XXV, LXXII ff.), a further evidence of Jayanta's popularity in the Jaina tradition. As mentioned above (see Section 1.2), several passages from the NM, and, if it existed at all, his lost work, the *Pallava*, are frequently paraphrased, quoted, and refuted in Vādideva Sūri's SVR.[5] The extensive arguments built by Vādideva against Jayanta, moreover, suggest that at that time he and the NM must have been relevant enough to be worthy of being cited.

In the 13th century,[6] also Abhayatilaka refers to views found in the NM a number of times (NĀ, pp. 40, 128, 130, 134). The oldest manuscripts of the *Nyāyacaturgranthikā* date back to Abhayatilaka's time, who must have had some access to the NM as well. Unfortunately there is so far no information of any NM manuscripts reported in the Jaina repositories, but luckily the extremely valuable *codex unicus* of the GBh, JTGB 386 (see Section 3.5.1), has survived. It is a very

relative chronology of Jayanta and Vācaspati, which remains a debated issue, complicated by the existence of another *Nyāyamañjarī* ascribed to Vācaspati's teacher, Trilocana. For some opinions on their relative chronology, see Hegde, 1983, 7–12. On Trilocana's *Nyāyamañjarī*, see Thakur, 1955.

[5] Vādideva was active during the rule of king Jayasiṃha Siddharāja, r. 1094–1143 (Cort, 1998, 91).

[6] On the date and place of Abhayatilaka, see NĀ, Introduction, xxx.

accurately written and correct manuscript, a hint to the relative importance attributed to the work. From the quality of the readings found in the South Indian manuscripts one may assume that the NM must have reached that area quite early. They contain, indeed, several archetypical or original readings, perhaps aided by the relative isolation of this line of transmission from the area of the vulgata.[7]

5.1.2 Software details

The genealogy of the NM manuscripts was here studied on the basis of a collation of the variants of the complete NM 6.[8] The nine available manuscripts (A, K, C, M, O, P, Q, S, and V) and the two relevant editions (Ga and Va) were collated in a Classical Text Editor (CTE)[9] file. The collation work was based on the text of Va, chosen because of its completeness in comparison to Ga. It is indeed more convenient to record omissions, rather than additions, in a variants' apparatus. The collation of the eleven texts of NM 6 resulted in an apparatus containing altogether 7669 variants. Due to the difficulties in building a convincing genealogical hypothesis, mainly because of the many instances of horizontal transmission, the collated data was processed and analysed with the aid of software developed for cladistics. Cladistics is an approach to reconstruct the evolutionary history, or phylogenesis, of organisms, species, etc., originally developed in biology and related disciplines. The CTE has the capacity to export genealogical data in tabular form, suitable to be analysed by cladistic software.

Following the example and ideas developed in the Caraka and Nyāya projects in Vienna (Maas, 2009–2010), themselves inspired by O'Hara and Robinson, 1993 and Robinson and O'Hara, 1996, Paup (version 4.06b10) was used to process the genealogical data and specifically to create a matrix in Nexus blocks and execute it. Paup

[7] On the preservation of ancestral readings in geographically peripheral areas, inherited by philologists from linguistics, see Pasquali, 1988, xvii–xviii and Timpanaro, 2003, 55–56.

[8] Presently available at http://homepage.univie.ac.at/alessandro.graheli

[9] Copyright 1997–2014, Stefan Hagel.

was set to perform a heuristic search for the most parsimonious trees. The processed Nexus file and the resulting trees were then processed by MacClade, a cladistic tool with a better interface for data analysis and tree manipulation.

5.1.3 Terminological clarification

The cladistic approach has been created as a model for biological classification, and as such it is rich in technical terms that, for the present purpose, must be understood and adapted to philological needs. An explanation of the fundamentals of cladistics as applied to philology can already be found elsewhere (e.g., in Maas, 2009–2010), so there is no need to repeat it here. For the sake of completeness, however, I will nonetheless clarify the most recurrent concepts used in this chapter.

One of the main purposes of a cladistic analysis is to find the most parsimonious tree, to explain the evolution of *characters* and *states* in a number of *taxa*. The criteria of parsimony are calculated on the basis of the number of *changes* and *steps*. A change is required whenever a *node* has a different state, in respect to the state of its immediate ancestor. When there are no *homoplasies*, which in the case of a manuscript tradition could be caused either by polygenetic readings or horizontally transmitted readings, the amount of actual changes would equal the minimum number of possible *steps*, which would mean that it would have the highest possible *consistency index*.

The technical terms contained in this description are going to be defined and clarified in the following lines, and a concordance of cladistic and philological terms is provided in Table 5.1 below.

Change "In a most parsimonious reconstruction of character evolution, a change is required whenever a node has a different state from its immediate ancestor" (Maddison and Maddison, 2003, 384).

Characters and states "[A character] can be viewed as a set of alternative conditions, called *character states*, that are considered able to evolve one to another. Thus the character "eye colour" might consist of the states "eyes blue" and "eyes red" [...]" (Maddison and Maddison, 2003, 43).

Consistency index (CI) The CI for a character x is calculated as m_x / s_x, where m = *minimum steps*, s = *reconstructed steps*, according to the particular tree in question. The total CI is the minimum possible treelength divided by the observed treelength. In an ideal situation, when the minimum of possible steps and the reconstructed steps perfectly match, the CI would have a ratio of 1. The CI can be a deceiving indicator, if individual states of taxa are not properly recognized as uninformative by the software, as will be further clarified below. In the philological application of cladistics a low CI is a sign of horizontal transmission (contamination).

Homoplasy "similarity that cannot be directly attributed to common ancestry [...] whenever a character evolved with more changes or some more costly changes (in the sense of "cost" used in a parsimony analysis) than the minimum conceivable, then homoplasy is implied" (Maddison and Maddison, 2003, 43).

Maximum steps In a character, the largest number of steps that could be obtained by rearranging the terminal taxa according to the less parsimonious possible arrangement.

Minimum steps In a character, the smallest number of steps that could be obtained by rearranging the terminal taxa according to the most parsimonious possible arrangement. The total minimum number of steps is "the sum over all characters. This does *not* mean that there exists a tree with this number of steps that could be obtained by rearranging the branches, for the rearrangement required to yield the minimum for one character might not be the same as the minimum required for another" (Maddison and Maddison, 2003, 385).

Node "[T]he point at which a lineage branches or ends" (Maddison and Maddison, 2003, 38). Terminal nodes are "entities (like species) treated as indivisible for the purpose of the analysis". Internal nodes "generally refer to unobserved (hypothetical) lineages, unless a claim is being made that an observed taxon is an actual ancestor". The root node "represents the ancestor of the tree".

Retention index (RI) The RI for a character x is calculated as M_x − s_x / M_x − m_x, where M = *maximum steps*, m = *minimum steps*, s = *reconstructed steps*, according to the particular tree in question. The total RI is the maximum possible treelength minus the observed one, divided by the maximum possible treelength minus the minimum possible one. The RI is particularly useful in the philological application of cladistics, because the unwanted influence on the CI of singular readings has no major impact on the RI.

Step "The number of steps in a character is the summed cost of all changes in a most parsimonious reconstruction [of the tree]" (Maddison and Maddison, 2003, 383).

Taxon An extant and observable entity.

Tree length The sum of the steps over all the characters involved in the elaboration of the tree. If characters are weighed according to their importance, weight is also taken into consideration.

Uninformative character "A character is uninformative if [...] any possible dichotomous tree would require the same number of steps in the character" (Maddison and Maddison, 2003, 285–286). Uninformative characters inflate the CI and they should be ignored in its calculation. If singular readings are not collated as separate characters but as states of other characters, the software cannot recognize such singular readings as uninformative, thus producing a deceivingly high CI. In such a scenario, the RI becomes a more reliable index of the consistency of a tree.

Here and in the following paragraphs I am using "error" to denote any reading that is judged as not archetypical, in other words, any innovation in the transmission of the NM. I will use "reading", instead, to refer to variants that are deemed original or that are not yet assessed as either original or innovative. Expressions such as "conjunctive errors" and "separative errors", versus "conjunctive readings" and "separative readings" should be understood in these sense.

5.2 Phylogenetic tree of all the sources

5.2.1 Experimental tree with the printed editions

The cladistic analysis exclusively concerned the nine available manuscripts (A, K, C, M, O, P, Q, S, and V), since the genealogical relation of the editions with the manuscripts was already known.

Table 5.1: Equivalences of cladistic and philological terms

Cladistic term	Philological equivalent
Taxon	Witness
Character	Lemma, portion of text, reading
State	Variant reading
Synapomorphy	Conjunctive reading or error
Autapomorphy	Separative reading or error
Homoplasy	Contamination *and* polygenesis
Convergence/Parallelism	Polygenesis
Uninformative character	Singular reading
Terminal node	Witness
Internode	Reconstructed ancestor
Internal nodes	Subarchetypes, ancestors
Root node	Archetype, original

Nonetheless, to test the reliability of the process, I began by processing the whole collation, including the two editions. The result is shown in Fig. 5.1.

The consistency index was originally quite high, since it was inflated by a high number of uninformative characters. Once excluded what in MacClade are considered uninformative characters, 2249 "informative" ones remained. "Uninformative" characters are those that do not add any information about the genealogical relation of a taxon, i.e., in the case of manuscripts, readings found in a single witness and not shared by any others. After the exclusion of all the characters recognized by MacClade as uninformative, the CI dropped to 0.81. The software correctly created a family of Ga and Va, since the latter edition largely mirrors the readings of the former. Also, this family of two editions is adjacent to the family composed of V, O, and A, all manuscripts used by the two editors. The reason of the (mis)placement of the editions' family at the centre of the tree is that Ga and Va are "contaminated" by P and M, respectively, and thus this solution is the most parsimonious one. The experiment of the cladis-

Figure 5.1: Paup tree with all the manuscripts and editions

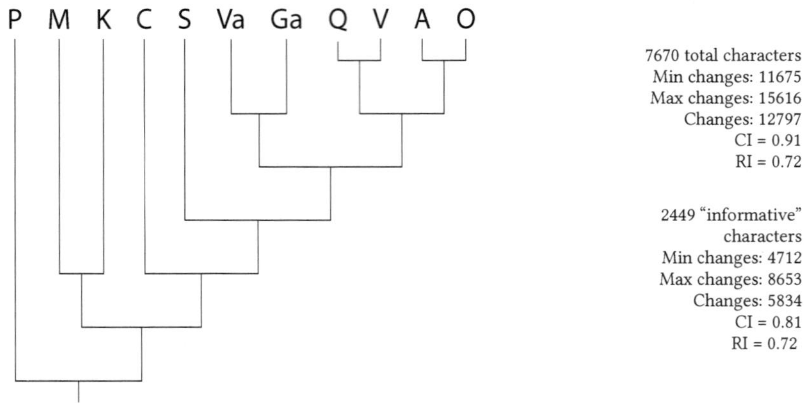

tic analysis with the editions shows a degree of efficiency in pairing closely related witnesses in the terminal branches, while horizontally transmitted readings can produce confusing results in the internodes of the tree.

It is important to be aware of the fact that the cladistic software does not provide any information as to the relationship between ancestors and descendants. Any of the branches in the Paup tree could be taken as the root (i.e., closer to the original ancestor), and the consistency index would not be affected. In other words, Paup traces the most economical relationship among all the taxa, but it is not meant to identify the ancestry of the characters. For instance, one could, paradoxically, reroot the tree from the editions, and the ratio of minimum possible changes and actual changes, i.e., the CI, would remain the same (Fig. 5.2).

5.2.2 Phylogenetic tree of the manuscript sources

Since the genealogy of the editions and their relation to the manuscripts on which they are based are already known, there is no reason to retain the editions in the tree. The tree without the edi-

Figure 5.2: Paradoxical tree, rooted at the editions' node

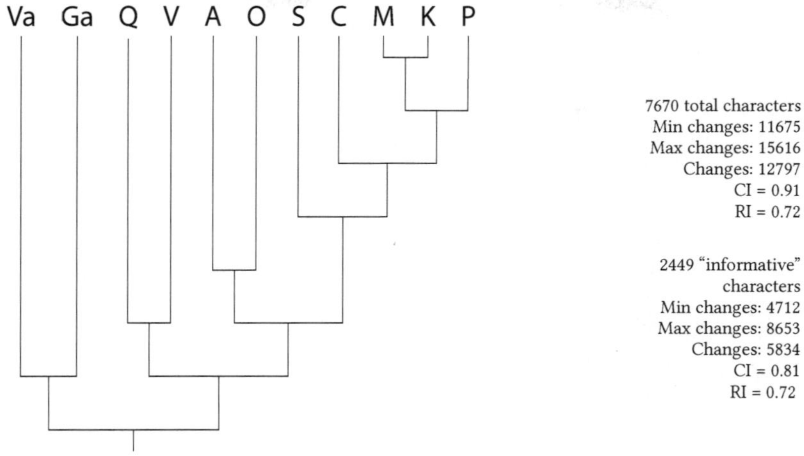

tions is represented in Fig. 5.3. By excluding them a higher CI is obtained, but only because of the homoplasy of many characters related to them. In fact, editions using multiple sources have all the characteristics of other contaminated witnesses.

MacClade can sort characters into informative and uninformative. Upon the exclusion of uninformative characters, 2241 "informative" ones remain. After the exclusion, the CI drops to 0.88. This index, however, is still inflated by many singular readings that the MacClade software cannot detect. The reason lies in the nature of a philological collation, which perhaps cannot be fully adapted to the needs of cladistics, especially when the cladistic analysis is not the only purpose of the collation work, as in the present case.

To elaborate: whenever there is an informative state in a character, uninformative states of single taxa that are associated to that character are also parsed as informative by MacClade. For instance, in NM^{Va}, II 145,16, V, O and A read *kramaparityagād*, C and S *kramāparityagād*, and K *kamāparityagād*. If they are collated by using the

Figure 5.3: Paup tree with all the manuscripts

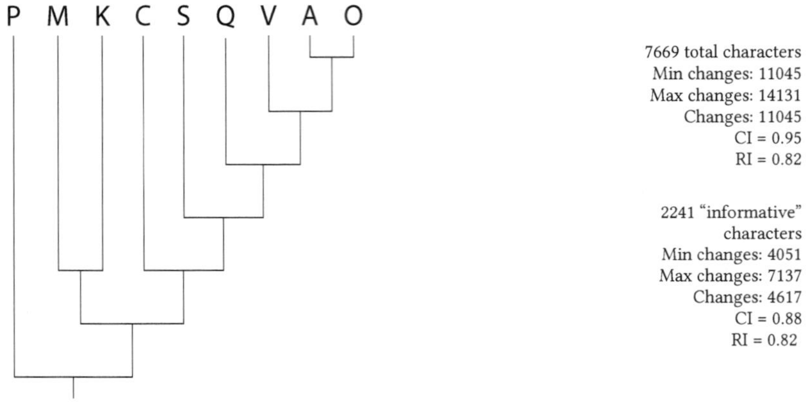

lemma *kramaparityagād*, the reading of K is clearly uninformative, yet it is not discarded by MacClade because the character as a whole is indeed informative; there, the singular reading of K is identified as a state of a character. As the state of a character, it counts as a change in the treelength. Such a singular reading inflates the consistency index, because while the minimum treelength and the observed treelength increase by one, their ratio is altered. For instance, in a tree with 3 minimum changes and 5 observed changes, a further undetected uninformative character would raise the CI from 0.60 to 0.66:

$$3 / 5 = 0.60 \qquad 4 / 6 = 0.66$$

At the time of the collation this problem was not known to me, otherwise I would have collated readings by trying to minimize such occurrences. In this case, for instance, instead of collating the whole word, one could collate a *kra/ka* variant and a *mā/ma* one, thus having two different characters instead of one. The *ka* reading of K would then be correctly excluded as an uninformative character. One could generalize and establish the rule that, for cladistic purposes, the variants should be collated as analytically and atomically as possible. In this way the *eliminatio lectionum singularium* would be largely automatized.[10]

In MacClade there is no way to automatically calculate the amount of such hidden uninformative states, but by counting and filtering changes at terminal nodes of the tree an approximate esteem of these changes can still be obtained. The result is shown in Table 5.2.

Table 5.2: Hidden uninformative changes

P	70
M	236
K	82
C	212
S	90
Q	68
V	142
O	6
A	34
Total:	960

According to this assessment, the collation of NM 6 contains about 960 changes which should not be allowed to inflate the consistency of the tree. By subtracting 960 from the amounts in Fig. 5.3, we would get 4051 – 960 = 3091 minimum changes and 4617 – 960 = 3657 actual changes. Consequently, this corrected consistency index would more faithfully represent the impact of contamination in the tradition:

Automatic CI: 4051 / 4617 = 0.88
Corrected CI: 3091 / 3657 = 0.84

[10] On the codification of the *eliminatio lectionum singularium*, see Maas, 1958, 6, and the words of caution in Timpanaro, 2003, 36. In Maas, 1958 and elsewhere singular readings have been called “peculiar” readings.

Also, it is important to note that the retention index is not affected by the subtraction of the 960 hidden uninformative characters and is therefore less vulnerable to the inconsistencies of a philological collation. In other words, the RI remains stable even after the subtraction of both the explicitly uninformative changes and the hidden ones, so it yields a more faithful representation of the degree of contamination in a genealogy:

Automatic al RI: (7137 - 4617) / (7137 - 4051) = 2520 / 3086 = 0.82
Corrected RI: (6177 - 3657) / (6177 - 3091) = 2520 / 3086 = 0.82

This phylogenetic tree with an RI of 0.82 shows that 82% of its 4617 (or 3657) changes are consistent with the arrangement of the tree, and that 18% of them are homoplasies, i.e., either horizontally transmitted readings or polygenetic occurrences.

The amount of changes relative to each node is shown in Fig. 5.4, where the P node is taken as the root. Such values can give a first impression of possible direct derivations among witnesses. The individuation of apographs is important, because it then becomes possible to get rid of the noise generated by such manuscripts (*eliminatio codicum descriptorum*), and thus to acquire a simplified, clearer picture of the transmission.[11] In the present case, the node with most changes is that of the pair O and A, which is caused by the direct relationship of the two manuscripts, as will be illustrated next.

5.3 Detection of apographs

5.3.1 A is the apograph of O

With the progress of the collation work it appeared more and more vividly that A and O had a direct relation. The 901 changes in Fig. 5.4 reflect their numerous conjunctive errors, which include frequent and lengthy omissions such as that of *lokavyapadeśo ... pramāṇaṃ* (II 171,12–13). The two manuscripts also match each other in scores

[11] On the strategy for the elimination of apographs, see Maas, 1958, 4; on its pitfalls, see Timpanaro, 2003, especially 17 and 127; on the concept of "apograph", "derivative manuscript" and equivalent terms, see Pecchia, 2009–2010, 123.

Figure 5.4: Paup tree with number of changes

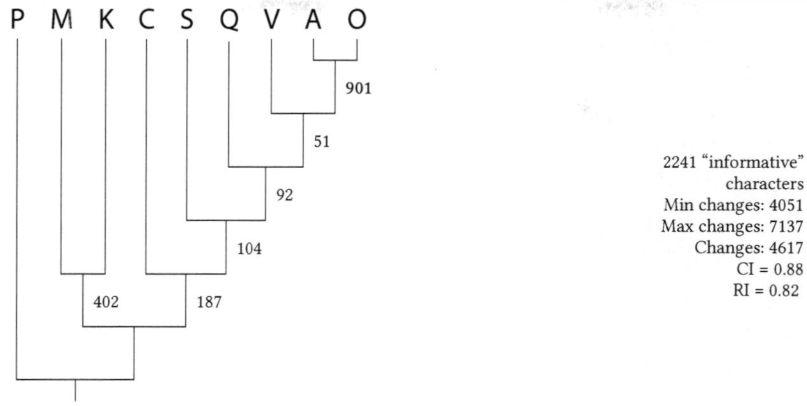

of orthographical mistakes and even in many scribal idiosyncrasies, such as the number of dots at the head-line, probably indicating lacunae or illegible parts in the antigraph.

The possibility that O derives from A can be excluded because of many following separative errors observed in the latter, such as the following omissions not found in O:

- *sā* [...] *kāryeṇa*] *om.* A (II 164,1–3)
- *prasiddhā* [...] *narāvayavās*] *om.* A (II 177,11–13)
- *-rukta-* [...] *ca na*] *om.* A (II 220,6–8)

Conversely, there are no separative errors in O that could exclude its paternity, while there are many pieces of evidence that confirm it. In several cases, exact lines of O are skipped in A:

- *bhūmiḥ* [...] *vāsarā ga-*] *om.* A (II 199,7–10)
- *itaretara-* [...] *dhāvana*] *om.* A (II 230,1–3)
- *iti tad api* [...] *ivādhānaṃ*] *om.* A (II 234,4–6)
- *-vācakatvāt ... guṇa*] *om.* A (II 236,8–10)
- *apaśabdebhyaś ca ... katham*] *om.* A (II 237,16–238.2)
- *-pratipattir ... pratipattis*] *om.* A (II 251,2–3)
- *-vistara ... ākhyāpitaṃ*] *om.* A (II 259,5–7)

There are frequent marginal corrections in O, probably entered by a second hand, and these are not always received in A, so they were either overlooked, for whatever reasons, or integrated in O after A was produced. For instance, *iti / etad api* [...] *-bhihitānvaye* (II 215,16–18) is omitted in the text of O and supplied in margin by a different hand, yet it is omitted in A. The same applies to the omission *dhāraṇe* [...] *sādhutayāva-* (II 254,5–6).

In O there is also a lengthy transposition of a passage of about 500 *akṣara*-s (probably the full side of a leaf), from *mama tv anabhihitatve* to *kiṃ vā* (II 211,2–213.13). The transposition is mirrored exactly in A. Although noticed and marked as erroneous in O, its correction is ignored in A.

Although the present genealogical study is confined to NM 6, on the basis of random tests in other sections of the NM it seems that A can be discarded as an apograph for the whole NM. An evidence that would contradict this hypothesis was given in NM^{KKh}, 11–13. After studying the beginning of NM 5, Kataoka thought it improbable that the two manuscripts have a direct relationship (NM^{KKh}, 11–13). He based his impression on the repetition of *yathāha bhaṭṭaḥ nāniṣpannasya saṃbaṃdho niṣpattau yutasiddhateti yathāha bhaṭṭaḥ nāniṣpannasya saṃbaṃdho niṣpattau yutasiddhateti* in O 127r5–6 (NM^{Va}, II 8a,9), which is not observed in A and would thus count as a separative error. But that repetition is quite noticeable in O and could have been independently spotted and avoided by the A scribe. An error that can have plausibly been corrected by the scribe of the allegedly derivated manuscript cannot be counted as separative (Maas, 1958, Appendix I, 42).

If A were not an apograph of O, indeed, there would be too many inexplicable cases. Just few lines below Kataoka's example, for instance, A (241r2) reads *suśikṣitās tu divacanatvenirūpāṇāṃ* [...] in place of *suśikṣi*[9]*tās tu kramarūpilakṣaṇam ācakṣate jātivyaktyoḥ saṃbaṃdhaṃ so pi nopapadyate rūpaśabdaḥ śuklādivacanaḥ svabhāvavacano vā* [10] *śuklādivacanatvenirūpāṇāṃ* [...] in O 127r8–10, eye-skipping an exact line (*kramarūpilakṣaṇam ācakṣate jātivyaktyoḥ saṃbaṃdhaṃ so pi nopapadyate rūpaśabdaḥ śuklādivacanaḥ svabhāvavacano vā* [10] *śuklā*) of O.

A few lines later, again, O (127r11–12) reads *tā [11] van na pratibhāti*. The scribe of A, in 241r7, copies *tāvan na pratibhā* correctly, but then jumps to *vo hi svabhāvina* at line 11 of O, right above, before realizing the error, enclosing it in brackets, and resuming from *tyuktaṃ vastudharmo* [...]. The slip is probably caused by the aligned two *bhā*-s in O:

O 127r11	*bhede na sva*	*bhāvo hi svabhāvinaḥ* [...]
O 127r12	*van na prati*	*bhātīty uktaṃ vastudharmo* [...]

Such mechanical errors leave little doubt that O was directly present before the A scribe's eyes. Therefore, since A is derived from O, it will be excluded from the following analysis. In Fig. 5.5, the tree is shown and recalculated without A. Once the uninformative characters are excluded, 1357 "informative" ones remain. Notably, without the high amount of characters which built the A-O family and which inflated the consistency of the tree, the impact of homoplasies becomes proportionally greater and the RI drops down to 0.70.

Figure 5.5: Paup tree without A

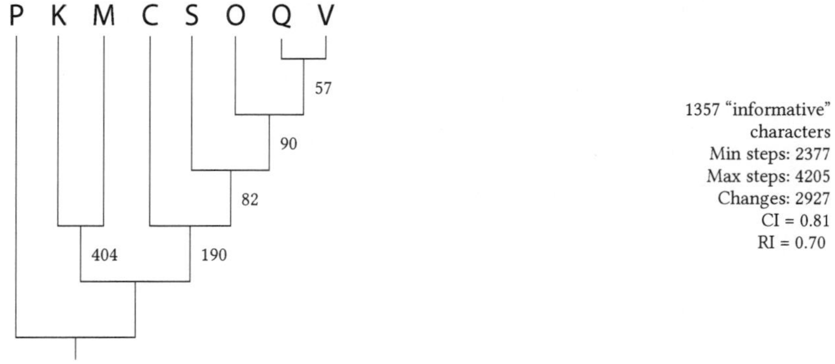

A substantial amount of contamination in the tradition begins to surface, considering that "[i]f the characters in the data matrix are parsimony-informative and perfectly congruent with each other and the tree, RI will have the value of 1. If the data are maximally homoplastic on the tree, RI will have a value of 0" (Maddison and Maddison, 2003, 388). Although, as discussed above (see Section 5.1.3), the term "homoplasy" in cladistics is generically used to describe identical states occurring in unrelated areas of the tree, regardless of the aetiology of the change, in the present collation such "homoplastic" data are mainly caused by contamination, because while collating most cases of polygenetic variants, such as orthographical trivialities, were ignored.

In principle, a polygenesis is always a possible event, even in presence of substantive cases of conjunctive readings. A discussion of the probabilities of polygenesis can be found in D'Arco Avalle, 2002, 78, who proposes a formula for the calculation of such probabilities. According to Inglese, 1999, 131, who elaborates on Avalle's principle,

> [...] we cannot guess an average of errors that a copyist may do [...] and we cannot measure the possible exposure to error of a given textual segment. From the example of the *Favola* [also known as *Belfagor Arcidiavolo*, by Niccolo Machiavelli, exemplified in Inglese, 1999, A.G.] it only follows that, in a text of 30.000 words, the polygenesis of about fifteen coinciding innovations, in two witnesses "of third generation", can be considered plausible [transl. A.G.].[12]

NM 6 is composed of ca. 40.000 *akṣara*-s (see Table 1.1), about two thirds of the length of the text in Inglese's example. I will here adopt a similar principle, i.e., accepting the possibility of polygenesis up to 10 instances for the whole length of NM 6, before considering the hypothesis of a contamination line, provided that such instances can be explained by other factors such as linguistic habits, inter-textual influences, etc., and hence polygenetically plausible.

The following, inspired by Inglese, 1999, 132–137, is a tentative list of errors that are less prone to occur polygenetically and can as such

[12] "[...] noi non sappiamo quanti errori commetta, in media, un copista [...] e non sappiamo misurare l'effettiva esposizione all'errore di ciascun segmento testuale. Dall'esempio della *Favola* ricaviamo soltanto che, dato un testo di 30.000 parole, la poligenesi di una quindicina di innovazioni coincidenti, in due testimoni "di terza generazione", può essere considerata plausibile".

be potentially counted as "typical" of a given witness or family of witnesses:
- Integration of glosses or other marginalia in the text.
- Omission of short words, even meaning-bearing ones such as negations.
- Hurried synthetic reading (e.g. *pratyāyakopādhiḥ* for *pratyāyakatvopādhiḥ*).
- Anticipation or repetition of a syntagm in close areas of the text.
- Repetitions (dittographies) or omissions (aplographies) of *akṣara*-s.

Conversely, there are other types of errors that, although substantive, can be easily produced by parallel thinking of independent scholarly scribes. For instance, a few readings shared by the South-Indian manuscripts are found also in S, but their limited number and their nature induce me to exclude their vertical or horizontal transmission:
- MKS *padārthaṃ*, PCQVO *padārthaṃ ca* (II 185,10)
- MKS *asatī*, PCQVO *asatīyaṃ* (II 194,13)
- MKS *phalasya*, PCQVO *phalasya ca* (II 196,13)
- M*n.a.*KS *pi*, PCQVO *hi* (II 222,7)
- MKS *om.*, PCQVO *śabda* (II 224,3)
- MKS *om.*, PCQVO *ca* (II 224,14)

5.3.2 S is partially derived from P

S cannot be the antigraph of any of the extant manuscripts, because it has omissions that are not found anywhere else:
- *niravayavo 'smabhir ... eva vākyam* (II 153,7–9)] *om.* S (38 *akṣara*-s)
- *saṃskāras* [...] *ceyam a-* (II 165,10–17)] *om.* S (180 *akṣara*-s, three blank lines in place of text)
- *-rahitam avayavi-* [...] *-svarūpopagraha-* (II 174,6–7)] *om.* S (31 *akṣara*-s)
- *-dvārakavyabhicārodbhāvanam* [...] *-paṅkti-* (II 180,13–14)] *om.* S (30 *akṣara*-s)
- *vā vidhīyate* [...] *pratipadaṃ* (II 237,12)] *om.* S (14 *akṣara*-s)
- *kriyārthitayā* [...] *artha-* (II 242,4)] *om.* S (18 *akṣara*-s)
- *tadviparīta-* [...] *sādhutvagrahaṇam*] *om.* S (II 253,2–3) (30 *akṣara*-s)

There are clear indications, instead, that S is derived from P. The most obvious one is that at the end of some *āhnika*-s the scribe of S blindly copied the paratext from P, including the signature of the P copyist, Śitikaṇṭha.[13]

There are also other conjunctive readings shared by S and P, such as the following ones:

- *śabdābhidheyatām* (II 249,17)] *śabdāntarābhidheyatām* PMK S
- *svair*] *svais svair* (II 250,17) PMKS
- *pramāṇaṃ* (II 252,11)] *tāvat pramāṇaṃ* PS
- *pada* (II 252,17)] *śabda* PS
- *saṃskārādi* (II 258,9)] *saṃskāra* PS
- *eva* (II 258,10)] *evātra* PS
- *nipuṇadarśita* (II 259,8)] *nipuṇapradarśibhir darśita* PS
- *matam adhigata-* (II 260,3)] *matam adhigatam adhigata-* PS
- *ihāpy uktam* (II 260,10)] *om.* PS
- *vācaṃ* (II 261,3)] *vedaṃ* PS
- *sulabha-* (II 261,9)] *subhaga* PS

Whether these readings are authentic or innovative needs to be evaluated case by case, since P may well be the vehicle of archetypical readings. What emerges from these examples and from the full list of conjunctive readings (see Section 11.8) is that they all occur, with a few exceptions, in a later part of NM 6. The first convincingly conjunctive reading is found at NM^{Va}, II 249,17. In this context, it should be noticed that Śitikaṇṭha's signature does not appear at the end of NM 5, while it does at the end of NM 7. Thus, it is likely that only from about II 249 the S scribe turned his full attention to P (see Section 5.4.5). Before that, in fact, there are only rare instances that reveal an influence of P on S:

- *cāparo* [or] *ca paro ca tad aparaḥ* (II 184,8)] *punar aparaś* PKS; M*n.a.*
- *ācakṣuḥ* (II 194,13)] *ācakhyuḥ* PMKS
- *paṭutaras* (II 192,8)] *paṭutamas* PS
- *trayo pi ca*] *trayo pi* (II 236,16) PS; M*n.a.*
- *yata iti* (II 239,1)] *yad iti* PS
- *ca nāti* (II 246,4)] *cānati* PS

There are many indications that P could not have been the anti-

[13] See the descriptions in Sections 3.4.9 and 3.4.6.

graph of S. First of all, one of the above-mentioned omissions (II 165,10–17), in which the S scribe leaves three blank lines, cannot derive from the clearly readable text of P (95r16–95v2).

Moreover, there are several singular readings in P that could not have plausibly been emended independently by the S scribe, such as the following ones (for the full list, see Section 11.5):

- *pratibhāsaḥ* (II 175,4)] *śabdapratibhāsaś* P
- *katham* (II 180,6)] *kim* P
- *pratināyakasya* (II 193,14)] *pratirodhakasya* P
- *kalpanāsambhavāt* (II 220,8)] *kalpanā kriyeta* P
- *vyutpattāv* (II 223,5)] *pratipattāv* P
- *nirūpyate* (II 238,10)] *vicaryate* P
- *pratyayayor* (II 245,6)] *prātipadikayor* P

It follows that S should not be eliminated from the picture. It will also not be linked directly to P in the following analysis and diagrams, since the hypothesis of its derivation from P, which will be further discussed below in Section 5.4.5, is limited to the last portion of NM 6.

5.4 From the phylogenetic tree to the stemma

The node based on the highest amount of characters in Fig. 5.5 is that of the K-M family. As in the case of O and A, these two manuscripts are likely to be in a relation of direct derivation. Since the hypothesis of such a relation cannot be fully sustained, however, they will be discussed later (Section 5.4.2).

At this point it should be clear that the two extremes of the tree, namely the positions of P, M and K at the root, and the O and A pair at the terminal branching, are the most reliable outcomes of the cladistic analysis. This is suggested by the configuration of the phylogenetic tree, where the contaminated witnesses tend to be located in the centre, and is corroborated by geographical and historical notions (see Section 5.1.1), as well as by the characteristics of the individual manuscripts (see Sections 3.4.6, 3.4.4, 3.4.3, 3.4.1).

The degree of contamination of the textual tradition is indicated by the RI of 0.70, which would further drop if the conjunctive readings of M and K were excluded from the analysis. The cladistic approach, as far as I can see, does not help to distinguish cases of polygenesis and of horizontal transmission. Moreover, neither Paup nor MacClade are equipped to distinguish cases of vertical and horizontal transmission. Hence, in the present study, the role of cladistics ends here.

It is now time to focus on the quality of the variants and on the available historical information, and to start envisioning the tree from the root, rather than from the terminal nodes. As put by Timpanaro (2003, 138) while discussing bipartitism in stemmata, "the fundamental flaw of all these probabilistic speculations is to start from the 'tail' and not from the 'head' [of the transmission]. One tends to forget that the real, historical process is the proliferation, from one exemplar, of a given number of copies, and then of a given number of sub-copies, and so on [transl. A.G.]".[14]

5.4.1 C, S, Q, V, and O, the γ family

Due to geographical and historical reasons, it seemed quite plausible that most archetypical readings would have been found in P, M, and K, even before their collation. The evaluation of their readings confirms this assumption, as will be hopefully be clearer at the end of this chapter and fully evident upon a perusal of the critical edition and its apparatuses. But the genealogical relationship among these three best manuscripts, as well as their relationship with the other five, C, S, Q, V, and O, still needs to be assessed.

These last five manuscripts have several conjunctive errors.[15] Most importantly, among these errors there are also some major omissions:

- *yad* (II 148,7)] *om.* CSQVO
- *eva* (II 150,10)] *om.* CSQVO
- *hi* (II 190,11)] *om.* CSQVO
- *tadanupadārthajñānaṃ / tato pi tathaiva paṭutaras* (*paṭutamas* P) *saṃskāra*] *om.* CSQVO (II 200,4) (21 *akṣara*-s)

[14]"In realtà, il vizio fondamentale di tutti questi ragionamenti probabilistici è di partire "dalla coda", anziché "dalla testa". Si tende infatti a dimenticare che il processo storico reale è la filiazione di un certo numero di copie da un modello, e poi di un certo numero di sottocopie, e così via".

[15]For the full documentation of their conjunctive errors, see Section 11.1.

- *varṇā eva bhavantv ete ... padasaṃhatiḥ* (II 201,12–13)] *om.* CSQVO (32 *akṣ.*)
- *sarvatra* (II 206,3)] *om.* CSQVO
- *iti* (II 208,3)] *om.* CSQVO
- *tat ... vācyam* (II 223,13)] *om.* CSQVO (23 *akṣ.*)
- *tu* (II 232,5)] *om.* CSQVO
- *tu* (II 235,8)] *om.* CSQVO
- *ca* (II 238,19)] *om.* CSQVO
- *evaṃ* (II 239,3)] *om.* CSQVO

The hypothesis is that the text omitted by these five witnesses was in origin present, and that a common ancestor must have passed down the omissions to them. Rare instances of lack of text are seen in the family of P, M, and K as well:

- *hastinā* (II 156,4)] *om.* PM (K*n.a.*)
- *sādho* (II 156,19)] *om.* PMK
- *iti* (II 157,6)] *om.* PM (K*n.a.*)
- *ca* (II 168,3)] *om.* PMK
- *varṇās* (II 169,15)] *om.* PK (M*n.a.*)
- *ca* (II 170,9)] *om.* PMK
- *atha* (II 170,18)] *om.* PMK
- *tathā* (II 179,15)] *om.* PK (M*n.a.*)
- *pi* (II 183,5)] *om.* PK (M*n.a.*)
- *yad uktam* (II 189,16)] *om.* PMK
- *varṇa* (II 200,3)] *om.* PMK
- *ca* (II 201,1)] *om.* PMK
- *ca* (II 214,10)] *om.* PMK
- *eva* (II 224,18)] *om.* PMK
- *iti* (II 245,15)] *om.* PK (M*n.a.*)

Unlike the previous ones, these "omissions" are rather short and can be explained as archetypical readings which, in the five manuscripts discussed here, resulted in attempts of clarification which produced added text. Hence, the assumption is that C, S, Q, V, and O derive from a common ancestor, γ (Fig. 5.6).

5.4.2 K and M, the β family

K and M are undated, and although M looks older, judging from the features of the script (see Burnell, 1878, 41), the characteristics of the

Figure 5.6: Preliminary stemma: the γ family

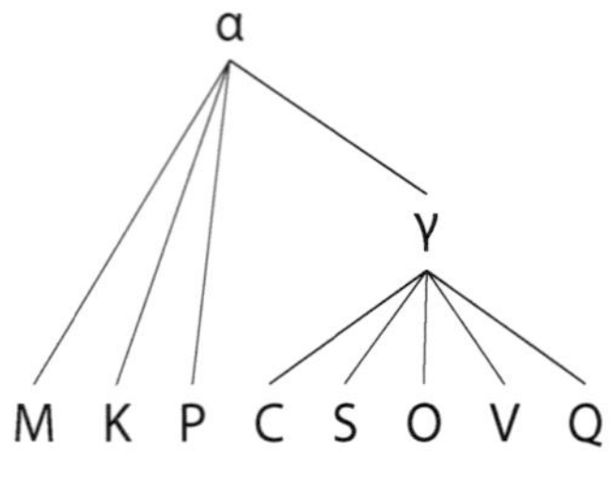

support and the state of preservation, it is difficult to reach a final judgement on their genealogical relation.

The two manuscripts share a high number of conjunctive errors,[16] among which there are more than one hundred omissions, including lengthy ones such as that of *padārtha ... tarhi* (II 193,12–15), about 75 *akṣara*-s of text.

K cannot be the antigraph of M, because it has several separative errors.[17] Most importantly, in K there are the following omissions that could not have been corrected independently in M:

- *om. vākyavākyārthav* [...] *karmāpi* (II 195,14–17) (75 *akṣara*-s, matching almost the full line of M, 13r1)
- *om. anavasthā* [...] *darśanād* (II 246,7–10) (78 *akṣara*-s)
- *om. gavādiśabda-* [...] *śabda na* (II 248,11–15) (78 *akṣara*-s)

Even M has many singular readings,[18] although it is more difficult to detect clearly separative errors among these. Some possible candidates, in which K seems to preserve the archetypical reading along with other manuscripts, are the following ones:

- *hi*] K; *om.* M (II 179,10)
- *padoparāga*] K; *paroparoga* M (II 197,1)

[16] For a full list see Section 11.2.

[17] For a full list see Section 11.3.

[18] For a complete list see Section 11.4.

- *aparaṃ na saṃsarggapratīter* K] *aparaṃ saṃsarggaprīter* M (II 209,18)
- *eva nābhidhīyamānānvayaḥ*] K; *evābhidhīyamānānvayaḥ* M (II 215,5)
- *ca*] K; *om.* M (II 217,11)
- *sāddhyatām iti*] K; *sāddhyatām itaḥ* M (II 232,9)
- *prayojanāntarāṇi*] K; *prayojanād antarāṇi* M (II 233,18)
- *svarūpataś*] K; *rūpātaś* M (II 239,18)
- *kārakasandarbha*] K; *sandarbha* M (II 241,2)
- *śrotrendriya*] K; *śrotriya* M (II 253,7)
- *asādhubhir*] K; *adhātubhir* M (II 255,14)
- *deśādyaśakyatvam*] K; *deśāśakyatvam* M (II 256,3)
- *pavitraṃ*] K; *om. pavitraṃ* M (II 260,6)

Due to the high number of conjunctive readings, a derivation of K from M cannot be ruled out. If K directly derived from M, however, the readings of this last series would have been caused either by contamination or by an independent conjecture of the K scribe. At the present state of knowledge it is safer to assume that K and M descended from a common ancestor.

The ancestor of M and K will be labelled β, as shown in Fig. 5.7. The ancestor β, as can be inferred from the length of the three omissions listed above, must have been a South Indian manuscript. Moreover, in M there is a repetition of a full folio, *ātmakaṃ vākyam anyan nāsti* [...] *bhavantaḥ* (II 188,3–190.4) beginning at M11v5 and ending at M12r5. It is bracketed by the scribe, who must have soon realized the mistake. The repetition gives an indication of the length of folios in the antigraph, showing how M loosely reproduced the layout of β as far as the extent of text per folio, probably with ten lines per page and a similar number of *akṣara*-s per line.

That K comes from a South Indian antigraph is also confirmed by the presence of a frequent confusion of *ha* and *va* (e.g., *bhāhinām* for *bhāvinām* II 159,13), which can be easily mixed up in Grantha-Malayālam.

5.4.3 The polytomy of β, P and γ

In Fig. 5.7 there is a three-branched polytomy, with P and γ in independent branches, stemming directly from α. While a common ancestor of β and γ is ruled out, due to the distinct peculiarities of the

Figure 5.7: Preliminary stemma: the β family

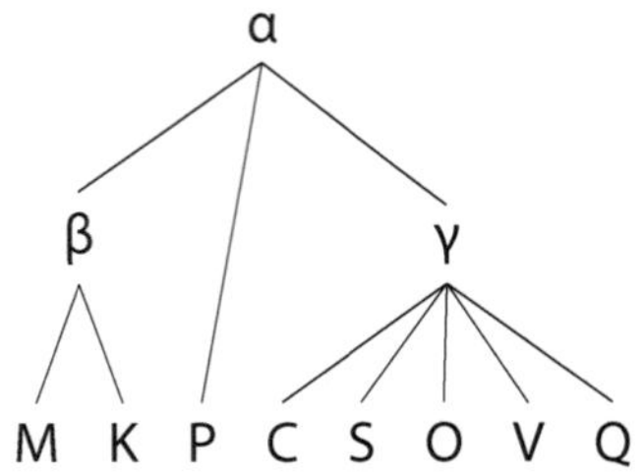

two families, the possibility that either P and β or P and γ derived from a common ancestor is still open.

It can be ruled out that P and β derived from a hyparchetype, and not from the archetype. In fact, if that were the case, there would be a number of archetypical γ readings, but this is not the case.[19] In NM 6.1 no instance of convincingly archetypical reading of γ was found, in respect to the readings shared by P and β.

As from a hyparchetype from which P and γ may have descended, the presence of many omissions characterizing the β family, along with many other conjunctive readings, was already pointed out. If none of those conjunctive readings were archetypical, it would follow that opposing ones would all be so, and in such a case a P-γ family would not be justified because readings associating P and γ would just indicate that they were passed down from the archetype without innovations. The above-mentioned omission of *padārtha ... tarhi* (II 193,12–115), as well as many other readings of β,[20] however, cannot be archetypical, so this first possibility should be ruled out.

If, instead, the β readings are in some cases archetypical and in others innovations, then a P-γ family could be postulated to explain why P and γ share some readings. In other words, at least one con-

[19]See the complete list of γ readings in Section 11.1.

[20]For the complete list see Section 11.2.

vincingly conjunctive error shared by P and γ must be found, in order to justify a P-γ family. The only plausible candidate is found in II 155,12–13, in relation to the following quotation from $\mathrm{VP}^{\mathrm{Iyer}}$, 2.10:

padaṃ kaiścid dvidhā bhinnaṃ caturdhā pañcadhāpi vā /
apoddhṛtyaiva vākyebhyaḥ prakṛtipratyayādivat //

This, with minor variations, is how the quotation is transmitted by P and γ. In β, instead, the first hemistich is omitted. The incomplete quotation is also corroborated by the GBh: *apoddhṛtyaiva vākyebhya iti asya pūrvam ardham / padaṃ kaiścid dvidhā bhinnaṃ caturdhā pañcadhāpi vā iti.* From Cakradhara's integration of the first hemistich in the commentary it is clear that the NM text used by him did not have it. The hypothesis that GBh is itself based on β alone is contradicted by the presence of other readings connecting J, the *codex unicus* of the GBh, with P and γ manuscripts, rather than with β, as in the following instances:

- *vikhara*] *purvikhāra* JP (II 157,9)
- *kleśena samāsa*] *ślokena samāsa* JPCSO (II 236,12–13)

Cakradhara was probably a Kashmiri who lived long before the date of any of the extant NM manuscripts, close to Jayanta's time (see Section 3.5.1). Since the readings of the NM found in the GBh are *pratīka*-s meant to indicate the relation of the commentary to the NM, they are likely to be rather faithful to the NM text. The chronological and geographical proximity, the scholarly quality of the commentary and the accuracy of the J manuscript are all elements that enhance the likelihood of genuinely archetypical readings, barring other irrefutable evidence. It is likely that the original indeed quoted only the second hemistich of $\mathrm{VP}^{\mathrm{Iyer}}$, 2.10, and that the first hemistich was integrated by the tradition.

Moreover, the addition of the first hemistich should not count as a conjunctive error in itself, because it is possible for such a famous passage to be independently integrated by any scholarly copyist or user of manuscripts, such as Śitikaṇṭha.

Therefore, since there is no positive evidence of a common ancestor of P and γ, I assume a trifurcation from the archetype to β, P, and γ (Fig. 5.8).

Figure 5.8: Preliminary stemma: the polytomy of β, P and γ

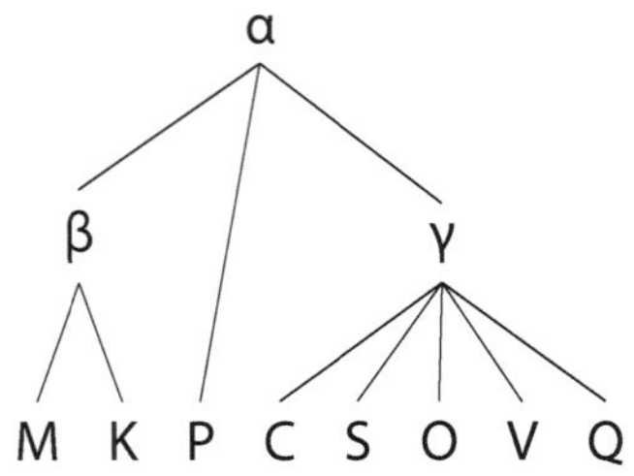

5.4.4 C and the δ family (S, O, Q and V)

Although the position of C as a member of the γ family is well established by the above-discussed evidence (see Section 5.4.1), C also shares a substantial amount of readings with P and β. There are several cases in which P, C and β have conjunctive readings, contrasting with those of the remaining manuscripts, i.e., S, O, Q and V. Most strikingly, there are passages preserved in P, C and β that were omitted in the other manuscripts, such as:

- *paramāṇavo* [...] *bhavitavyaṃ*] *om.* (II 179,11) SQVO
- *saṃskāraḥ* [...] *punaḥ*] *saṃskāra punaḥ* (II 200,3) SQVO
- *sarvāṇy eva* (II 206,4)] *om.* SQVO

Along with β and P, C also preserves the line *tṛtīyapadajñānam ity evaṃ pūrvapadāvacchedo nottarottara* (II 196,11), which is omitted in S, O, Q and V.

The dichotomy is also confirmed by many other conjunctive readings (for the complete list, see Section 11.6):

- *sindūraharitālādi*] βPC; *haritālasindūrādi* SQVO (II 178,1)
- *smaraṇād*] βPC; *smaryamāṇād* SQVO (II 201,7)
- *jñapti*] βPC; *jñāna* SQVO (II 212,6)
- *padārtha*] (II 212,12) βPC; *padāntara* SQVO
- *tad ucyatāṃ*] βPC; *dṛśyatāṃ* SQVO (II 227,7)

There are also cases in which C reads randomly with β or with P, respectively. This pattern would be consistent with the polytomy of β, P and γ. With β, there are cases such as the following ones (for the complete list, see Section 11.7):

- *sa saṃskāra* (II 164,14)] *saṃskāra* βC
- *śabdād artham* (II 171,5)] *śabdārtham* βC
- *hi* (II 187,14)] *om.* βC
- *pada* (II 193,7)] *om.* βC
- *upagamyate*] *upakramyate* (II 251,15) βC
- *roma* (II 252,16)] *gadgadaroma* βC

The few instances in which C reads with either M or K, independently, can easily be explained as polygeneses:

- *vācya* (II 196,4)] *vākya* MC
- *vacaneneva* (II 252,3)] *vacanenaiva* MC
- *arhanti* (II 165,8)] *arhati* KC
- *smaraṇa* (II 192,11)] *om.* KC
- *niyogaḥ* (II 203,7)] *viyogaḥ* KC
- *vyāhatam* (II 228,17)] *vyāhṛtam* KC

As for conjunctive readings shared by P and C, there are several compelling cases, such as the following ones:[21]

- *eva* (II 187,10)] *eva ca* PC
- *viramya* (II 194,6)] *viramyaviramya* PC
- *bhavaty* (II 195,17)] *tadbhavaty* PC
- *na* (II 198,8)] *om.* P^{ac}C
- *paṭhitau* (II 223,15)] *paripaṭhitau* PC

If the hypothesis of a β-P-γ polytomy is correct, it is implied that wherever C confirms the reading of either β or P it is because it preserves the authentic reading of γ, which is most probably the archetypical reading. In fact, it would be unlikely for two out of β, γ and P to accidentally generate the same error (see Maas, 1958, 5).

This behaviour of C can be explained by postulating a sub-family δ composed of S, O, Q and V (Fig. 5.9) in which such archetypical readings preserved in C were lost.

[21] For a complete list see Section 11.7.

Figure 5.9: Preliminary stemma: δ family

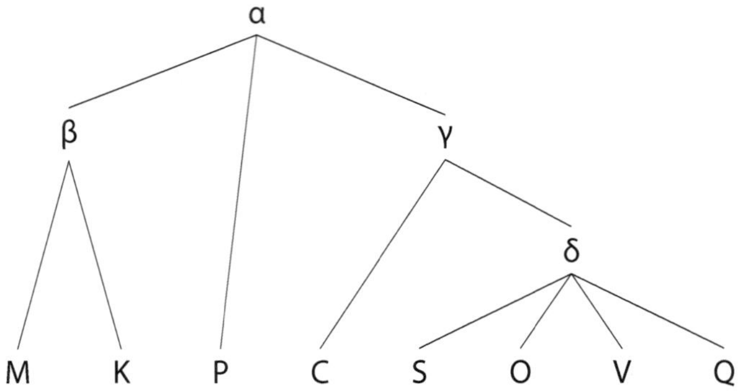

5.4.5 The shift of exemplar in S

In Section 5.3.2 it was already mentioned how S seems to be derived from P in the last part of NM 6. There are no conjunctive readings of the δ family after II 247,3 (see Sections 5.4.4 and 11.6) and, conversely, no conjunctive readings of S with P before II 249,17 (see Section 11.8).

Interestingly, in correspondence to this phenomenon a change of hand can be detected in S, from fol. 269r onwards, corresponding to NM^{Va}, II 249,14.[22] I therefore assume that, from II 143 to II 249,13, S is a descendent of δ, and that from II 249,14 to II 262 it is a direct copy of P (Fig. 5.10). The derivation from δ, i.e., from a lost ancestor, also explains the lacuna of three lines (II 165,10–17), and of other words in the vicinity, that was noticed in S in fol. 245v and that cannot be justified as a derivation from other extant witnesses.

5.4.6 O, V and Q, the ε family

The δ family presents further problems of horizontal transmission. Before studying the possible constellations of its four witnesses, direct derivations need to be ruled out.

[22] As described in Section 3.4.9 above.

Figure 5.10: Preliminary stemma: S shift

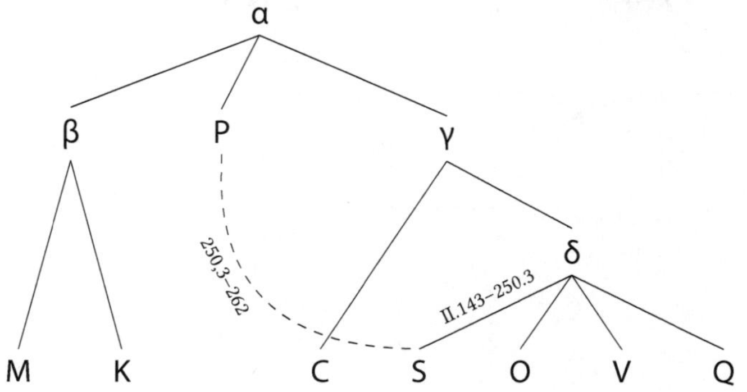

That S cannot be the antigraph of any extant manuscript was already shown in Section 5.3.2. Its direct derivation from P is limited to the last portion of NM 6, and for the rest of the *āhnika* it remains part of the δ family.

O cannot be the antigraph of S, V or Q because of the following separative errors:

- *nirjhara* [...] *kārya*] *om.* O (II 149,5–6) (26 *akṣara*-s)
- *loka ... pramāṇaṃ*] *om.* O (II 171,11–12) (39 *akṣara*-s)
- *tad asatyam* [...] *prayujyate iti*] *om.* O (II 178,13–14) (32 *akṣara*-s)
- *vyākaraṇa-* [...] *paratvāc ca*] *om.* O (II 254,16–17) (33 *akṣara*-s)

V, in turn, cannot be the antigraph of S, O or Q:

- *śabdād* [...] *pratipādakaḥ*] *om.* V (II 148,11–12) (33 *akṣara*-s)
- *varṇebhyas* [...] *dṛśyate*] *om.* V (II 160,16–17) (34 *akṣara*-s)
- *iti vadan* [...] *vyāpārāṇi*] *om.* V (II 190,12–13) (36 *akṣara*-s)
- *saṃghāta* [...] *sarvathā om.* V (II 207,5–7) (40 *akṣara*-s)
- *tulyaṃ* [...] *nvaya ity om.* V (II 211,18–212.2) (38 *akṣara*-s)
- *-vābhihitānvayam* [...] *vākyārthapratītaye cābhi-*] *om.* V (II 216,2–3) (31 *akṣara*-s)
- *sādhvasādhu-* [...] *tāvat*] *om.* V (II 224,3–4) (29 *akṣara*-s)
- *yamāna-* [...] *lavaṇopayogopanīta-*] *om.* V (II 226,10–11) (38 *akṣara*-s)
- *-tipadam* [...] *vidhitsatāṃ*] *om.* V (II 226,17–18) (35 *akṣara*-s)

- *kārakam iti vakṣyāmaḥ* [...] *saṅkataḥ*] *om.* V (II 240,14–16) (38 *akṣara*-s)

V also has a lengthy repetition (ca. 600 *akṣara*-s, 15–16 lines) of *atha nigama-* [...] *vetti vedasya* (II 220,6–221.1). This repetition cannot be directly related to the other manuscripts.

Q, lastly, cannot be the antigraph of one among S, O and V:

- *ratnatattvam*] *om.* Q (II 150,14)
- *āśvinaṃ gṛhnāti*] *om.* Q (II 160,10–11)
- *sambandha-*] *om.* Q (II 173,9)
- *-pratipatti-*] *om.* Q (II 202,13)
- *ayogyatvena saṃsarga*] *om.* Q (II 211,16)
- *kutaś cāsau labhyate*] *om.* Q (II 223,3)
- *vyākaraṇena*] *om.* Q (II 233,14)
- *-nirīkṣaṇa-*] *om.* Q (II 245,11)
- *satyāṃ*] *om.* Q (II 254,11)
- *himavataḥ ā ca*] *om.* Q (II 257,9)

Q, O and V are connected by a significant amount of conjunctive errors such as the following ones:[23]

- *yasyānavayavaḥ*] *yasyāvayavaḥ* QOV^{ac} (II 150,5)
- *ikārokārantayor*] *ikārokārayor* QOV (II 156,10)
- *janmā tu*] *janmāntara* QOV^{ac} (II 163,8)
- *pratyayaviṣayatām*] *pratyayatām* QOV (II 167,4)
- *prātipadikārthasya*] *prātipadikasyārthasya* QOV (II 172,4–5)
- *padārtha*] *pada* QOV (II 176,4)
- *grahaṇādyavasareṣu*] *grahaṇāvasereṣu* QOV (II 179,2)
- *eva hi*] *eva* QOV (II 209,16)
- *saṃsargaviṣaya*] *viṣayasaṃsarga* QOV (II 212,3)
- *vābhihitānvayaḥ*] *vābhir ivānvayaḥ* QOV^{ac} (II 214,14)
- *karaṇa*] *om.* QOV (II 223,10)
- *apramādokta*] *apramādottha* QV, *aprasādottha* O (II 228,9)

In conclusion, it is necessary to postulate a common ancestor of Q, O and V, labelled ε (Fig. 5.11).

5.4.7 O and V, the ζ family

The possible genealogical relations among Q, O and V still remain to be weighed. To begin with, V and Q share two major omissions:

[23]For a complete list see Section 11.9.

Figure 5.11: Preliminary stemma: the ε family

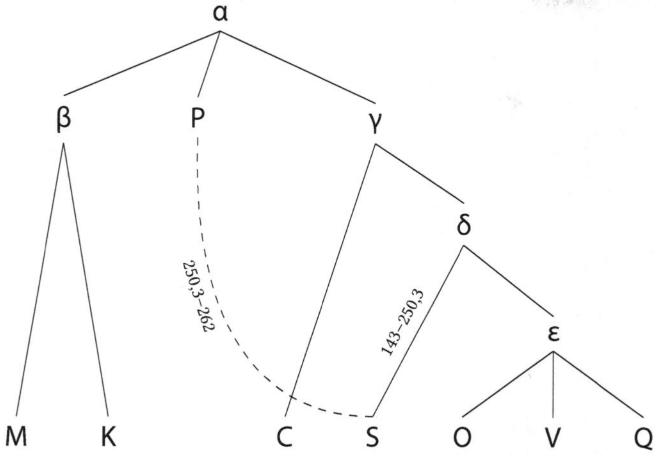

- *ato nupasarge* [...] *bhavatīti*] *om.* VQ (II 238,4–6) (40 *akṣara*-s)
- *śiṣṭā* [...] *śabdāḥ*] *om.* VQ (II 258,10–11) (21 *akṣara*-s)

V and Q also have several other conjunctive errors, such as the following ones:[24]

- *yasya*] *api* QV (II 234,1)
- *parityāgād*] *tyāgād* QV (II 238,17)
- *-kṛt*] *om.* QV (II 246,4)
- *jagat*] *om.* QV (II 247,15)
- *patati*] *patitaḥ* QV (II 249,4)
- *iti anekaśabdavācyas*] *om.* QV^{ac} (II 249,16)
- *nanu*] *om.* QV (II 251,5)
- *trāsa*] *om.* QV (II 252,1)
- *nanu*] *om.* QV (II 254,11)
- *praṇītavān*] *kṛtavān* QV (II 258,17)
- *-ābhiyoga*] *prayoga* QV (II 260,16)
- *lakṣaṇasāmyam*] *lakṣaṇam* QV^{ac} (II 262,4)

[24]For a complete list see Section 11.10.

The number of conjunctive errors of O and V is also high, e.g. (see Section 11.11 for the complete list):
- *maricādibhyo*] *maricādibhyo bhya* V^{ac}O (II 154,5)
- *na*] *om.* VO (II 169,16)
- *grāhyatva*] *grāhitva* V^{ac}O (II 172,8)
- *nāvayaviva na*] *nāvayaviva* VO (II 174,13–14)
- *tena*] *iti* VO (II 178,13)
- *padatāṃ*] *padatvaṃ* V^{ac}O (II 184,7)
- *saṃskāreṇa*] *saṃskāreṇa ca* VO (II 195,6)
- *draṣṭum*] *dṛṣṭaṃ* VO (II 199,4)
- *yadi*] *yadi vākyasya vākyārthe padasya padārthe iti yadi* VO (II 202,9–11)
- *tathāpi na na*] *tathāpi na* V^{ac}O (II 208,8)
- *saṃsargāvagati*] *saṃsargān nāvagati* V^{ac}O (II 217,13)
- *kalañja*] *kalañjasya* VO (II 224,1)
- *tat*] *uta* VO (II 231,9)
- *vācakasyaiko*] *vācakasyai* V^{ac}O (II 250,5)

As for Q and O, however, there are just a few and rather insubstantial shared errors:
- *kalpanikābhāga*] *kalpanikabhāva* QO (II 151,4)
- *na yāvati*] *yāvati* QO (II 160,17)
- *abhāvenā-*] *abhāvena-* QO (II 173,9)
- *na vyavasthitam*] *vyavasthitam* QO (II 173,10)
- *na*] *nā* QO (II 180,11)
- *antya*] *anya* QO (II 201,3)
- *viṣayā*] *viṣaya* QO (II 208,8)
- *rahitaḥ*] *rahitā* QO (II 212,7)
- *avabhotsyāmaha*] *avavotsyāmaha* QO (II 246,6)
- *jaraṭha*] *jaraḍha* QO (II 248,5)

A remarkable aspect in the series of conjunctive errors of the ε family is that in O, V, and Q, after *apramādottha* (II 228,9), there are no further conjunctive errors. In O and V, similarly, there are no shared errors after *uta* (II 231,9), with the exception of a single one (*vācakasyai*, II 250,5), which is corrected in margin in V. In Q and V, before *purā* (II 233,18), there are rare, less evident errors, while from there on the list is much more populated and includes more striking cases. The few errors that Q and O have in common, in the range where the O-V-Q and O-V conjunctive errors are found (i.e., up to II

230), can be easily explained as polygenetic.

From this distribution of errors, the most reasonable assumption is that O and V descended from a common ancestor, ζ (see Fig. 5.12), and that somewhere between II 228,9 and II 231,9 O deviated from ζ. This shift in O provoked a peak of conjunctive errors in the Q-V pair after the shift.

Figure 5.12: Preliminary stemma: the ζ family

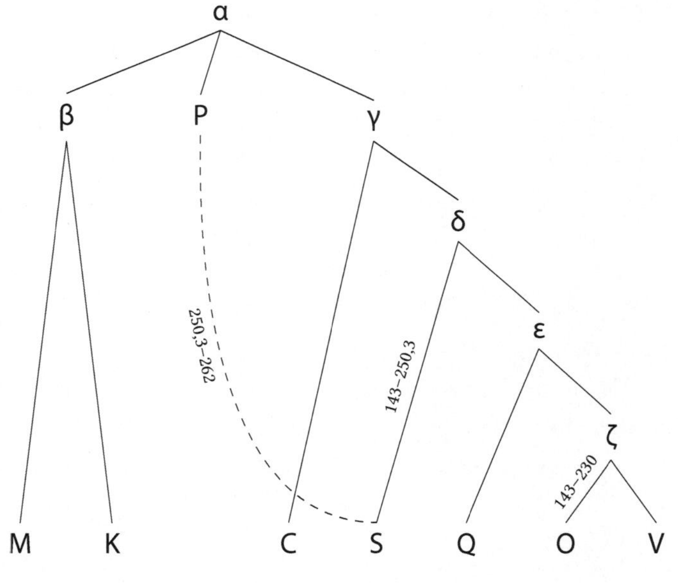

Incidentally, the hypothesis of a shift in O corroborates the δ family, composed of S, Q, V and O. Their last clearly conjunctive error is *dṛśyatāṃ* (II 227,7), before the shift.[25] As for the S-Q-V constellation, no conjunctive errors are found before the shift, except for a couple of insignificant cases, while a convincing series begins with *iti* in II

[25]For the complete list of the δ errors see Section 11.6.

232,6, i.e., after the shift of O:[26]

- *iti*] *om.* VSQ (II 232,6)
- *vyaktikatvam*] *vyaktitvam* VSQ (II 234,11)
- *tathā*] *om.* VSQ (II 236,6)
- *utpadyerān*] VSQ *utpadyerān / samastapakṣe ityādipatitam* (II 239,9)
- *īpsitatamaṃ*] *īpsitam* VSQ (II 242,5)
- *tābhyāṃ*] *om.* VSQ (II 244,10)
- *buddhitaro*] *buddhir* VSQ (II 246,4)
- *prayoga*] *om.* VSQ (II 248,6)
- *viśeṣe tarhi*] *tarhi viśeṣe* VSQ (II 249,5)

These three manuscripts also share the omission (21 *akṣara*-s) of *pratyekam* [...] *pakṣe pi* (II 239,6–7). So even the conjunctive errors of S, Q and V after the shift in O indirectly corroborate the postulation of δ. It is also interesting that the last conjunctive error of the S-Q-V triad is *tarhi viśeṣe* (II 249,5), which supports the hypothesis of the direct derivation of S from P, which was assumed to begin after II 250,3.[27]

5.4.8 The shift of exemplar in O

But what happens to O in the last part of NM 6? It has a relevant amount of conjunctive errors in common with C, including an abnormal number of possibly polygenetic ones. Many of these errors are apparently Śāradā-generated ones, such as the confusion of *sa/ma*, the loss of the *u* vowel-sign and frequent misplacements of the *e* vowel-sign:

- *hetutvāc* (II 155,6)] *hetatvāc* CO
- *grāsānām* (II 162,1)] *grāmānām* CO
- *pratīyeta* (II 203,7)] *pratīyate* CO
- *pramādataḥ* (II 211,9)] *prasādataḥ* CO

After the shift, however, along with further relatively less striking errors, there are also some substantive ones:

- *aparam* (II 232,17)] *om.* CO
- *pratipadaṃ* (II 237,12)] *prapade* C, *prapadaṃ* O
- *atiśaya* (II 241,3)] *atiśayita* CO

---

[26] For a complete list of the S-Q-V errors see Section 11.12.

[27] See Sections 5.3.2 and 5.4.5.

- *adhikaraṇa* (II 241,16)] *api* C O
- *mā ca* [...] *pacatīti* (II 243,1)] *om.* C O
- *akartṛtvaṃ* (II 243,6)] *akartṛkatvaṃ* C O
- *abhiyoga* (II 251,11)] *abhidheyoga* C O
- *api na sāmpratam* (II 257,2)] *apy asat* C O

It is therefore possible that from II 232,17 O followed the ancestor of C, i.e., γ, or a lost descendent of γ. C contains several peculiar, separative errors not observed in O, so it is quite unlikely that O used C directly (Fig. 5.13).

Figure 5.13: Preliminary stemma: O shift

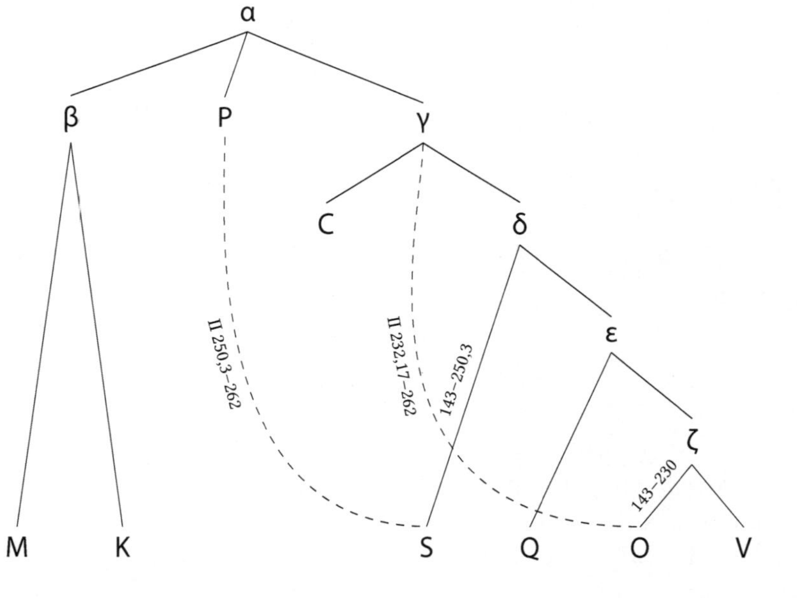

5.5 Traces of horizontal transmission

The genealogy built so far is not free from turbulence caused by horizontally transmitted readings. Traces of horizontal transmission, i.e.,

Figure 5.14: The stemma codicum

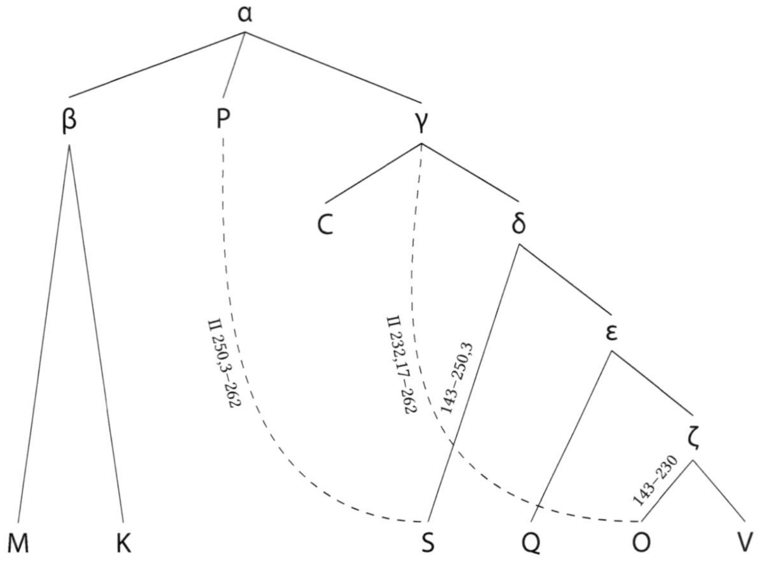

contamination, besides the two shifts of exemplar discussed above, will be shown and discussed next.

The main structure of the stemma was built by keeping in mind that there are certain errors that are much less likely to be produced via horizontal transmission. Major omissions are for this purpose particularly important, as already noticed elsewhere: "[...] while scribes were frequently anxious to copy readings from other MSS into their own, they were apparently unwilling to cancel any line or passage simply because it did not appear in some other version" (Fowler, 1951, 498). In other words, an omission is not likely to be the result of a sporadic contamination.

P, M, V, O and Q show contamination traces to different degrees. Some of these manuscripts contain *variae lectiones* caused by emendations, either interlinear or in the margins, some by the same hand

and others by second ones. It may be productive to distinguish *ante correctionem* and *post correctionem* readings and concord them with the stemma findings.

The clearest evidence of contamination is the presence of emendations or additions derived from other branches of the transmission. Horizontally transmitted readings may originate in various situations:

1. they may be caused by a shift of antigraph, as seen above;
2. in the case of scholarly scribes, they may come from the differently recollected stanzas, etc., i.e., from an oral tradition;
3. they may come from a further exemplar checked by the scribe while revising the text, in which case there is no change of hand;
4. they may come from a further exemplar checked by students of the manuscript at a later time, in which case a change of hand may be detected;
5. the antigraph may already contain contaminated readings in the form of corrections or *variae lectiones*, which are then integrated in the new copy;
6. the antigraph may contain contaminated readings which crept in the tradition through any of the above processes, but are already assimilated in the text.

Different combinations of these are also possible. The fourth type, for instance, may occur when a copyist such as a student writes a first draft on behalf of his teacher, who later corrects the draft either from memory, by conjecture, or on the basis of other exemplars. A different and rather common case is that of a copy commissioned to a professional scribe which is later corrected by scholarly readers.

It seems quite unlikely, in the case of the NM manuscripts studied here, that any of them was an edited version consciously produced on the basis of multiple exemplars.

5.5.1 Corrections in P and possible traces of contamination

In P there are corrections by different hands. Some were added while revising or studying the text and seem to be by Śitikaṇṭha's own pen, with his distinctive handwriting. It is plausible that the manuscript was improved by him during his teaching activity, for which it was intended according to the statement found in the colophon (see Section 3.4.6). One of the correctors also added some rare glosses (e.g., *pārthagarthya* in 122v21, glossed in the lower margin with *pṛthag arthasya bhāvaḥ*). These are additions and corrections, both in margin and between lines, as well as punctuation marks such as half *daṇḍa*-s and *avagraha*-s.

P also contains other emendations, both marginal and interlinear, by second hands. These can be useful to corroborate the genealogy studied so far. Although the sample of NM 6 is rather small to draw conclusions, four things can be learned: (1) many corrections were done by Śitikaṇṭha himself; (2) there is a correspondence of the readings of β and P after the correction, with rare exceptions; (3) some corrections reveal a specific correspondence of S and P; (4) fewer and less substantial corrections may suggest a correspondence of C and P.

There are corrections, both marginal and interlinear, in which the readings before correction are peculiar of P. Some emendations are by Śitikaṇṭha's own hand, which may be instances of errors done while copying the antigraph and corrected later with the very antigraph. In other words, they are not caused by a horizontal transmission:

- *tasmād ... eva śabda*] P^{pc} (II 149,7–9); *om.* P^{ac} (90v5)
- *-rūpaṃ*] P^{pc} (II 178,2); *om.* P^{ac} (99r17)
- *punas tenaiva krameṇa ... saṃskāro janyate*] P^{pc} (II 192,14–16); *om.* P^{ac} (103v16) S
- *adyāvasthāyām*] P^{ac} (116r1); *apy avasthāyām* P^{pc} (II 226,9)
- *kiṃ sādhubhir ... pramādaḥ*] P^{pc} (II 227,15); *om.* P^{ac} (116r21)
- *vyākaraṇādhyayanam ... tasya viśeṣaḥ*] P^{pc} (II 251,12–13); *om.* P^{ac} (125v6)

There are several cases in which the corrections produced conjunctive readings of P and β, with one exception. These are likely to be all by Śitikaṇṭha's hand:

- *śrotragrahaṇāt*] P^{ac}Ω (90v4); *śrotragrahaṇatvāt* P^{pc}K (II 149,6)
- *pi*] P^{ac} (91r4) Ω; *pi hi* P^{pc}K (II 151,6)
- *vyaktyālambane*] P^{ac} (91r18); *vyaktyālambano* P^{pc}K; *vyaktyālamba-*

nato Ω (II 152,7)
- *nirbandhena*] P^{ac} (95r10) Q; *nirbandhena na* P^{pc}MKCS; *nirbandhane na* ΩVO (II 165,4)
- *-viṣayair*] P^{ac} (95r15); *viṣayaiḥ kramabhāvibhir*] P^{pc}Ω (II 165,10)
- *sarvapūrva-*] P^{ac} (103v19); *sarvapūrvapada-* MKP^{pc}; *sarvapada-* CSQVOGaVa (II 192,17)
- *om. kathaṃ na kariṣyate*] P^{ac} (106v17)SQVOGa; *kathaṃ na kariṣyate* MKP^{pc}CVa (II 201,5–6)
- *vākyārtha*] P^{ac} (106v17) M^{ac}CSQVOGa; *vākyavākyārtha-* P^{pc}M^{pc}KVa (II 201,6)
- *vyākaraṇasya*] P^{ac} (117r7)MK; *vyākaraṇasya tu* P^{pc}Ω (II 232,2)
- *kiṃ*] P^{ac} (118r11) CSQVO; kaṃ P^{pc}MK (II 233,4)

There are some further corrections by Śitikaṇṭha that went ignored by the S scribe, who copied the *ante correctionem* text:
- *parivāda*] P^{ac} (125v18) S; *parivādaḥ* P^{pc}Ω (II 252,10)
- *kṛśāṇu-*] P^{ac} (127r10) S; *kṛśānu-* P^{pc}Ω (II 255,18)
- *śabdavat*] P^{ac} (127r2) S; *śabdavit* (II 255,4)
- *kartu*] P^{ac} (128v4) S; *kartuṃ* P^{pc}Ω (II 260,2)

There are then instances in which P was emended and adapted to the vulgata reading by a second hand:
- *yatrābhyaste*] P^{ac} (104r4) MKO; *yatrāpy abhyaste* P^{pc}CSQ VGaVa (II 193,6)
- *nava-*] P^{ac} (109r4)MK; *anyathā nava-* P^{pc}CQVOGaVa; *anyathābhinava-* S (II 208,1)
- *pratipadyate*] P^{ac} (114v7) K; *pratipatsyate* P^{pc}CSQVOGaVa (II 223,5)
- *itara*] P^{ac}MKVa (122v16); *itaravākya-* P^{pc}CSQVOGaVa (II 245,2)

Lastly, there are some corrections that may point to a feeble connection between P and C. Only the first of these appears to be by Śitikaṇṭha's hand:
- *kiñ ca pravara-*] P^{ac} (105v16)C; *kiñ ca na pravara-* P^{pc}Ω (II 198,8)
- *doṣānvitābhidhāne*] P^{ac} (111v9) C; *doṣo 'nvitābhidhāne* P^{pc}Ω (II 215,17)
- *mānasajñānaṃ*] P^{ac} (126r18); *manasajñānaṃ* C; *pānase jñānaṃ* KM; *panasajñānaṃ* P^{pc}SQVOGaVa (II 254,2)
- *gamyāpi*] P^{ac} (126v6) C^{ac}; *gamyādi* P^{pc}C^{pc}Ω (II 254,2)

5.5.2 Traces of contamination in Q

There are some conjunctive readings of Q with P and the β manuscripts:

- *eva*] *iva* (II 153,4) PβQ
- *sa madhyamocyate* / *madhyama socyate*] *sa madhyamety ucyate* (II 157,14) PKQ; M*n.a.*
- *saṃsthānāntarābhyāsaiḥ*] *saṃsthāntarābhyāsaiḥ* (II 167,13) PMKQ
- *ced adṛṣṭatvād*] *cen na adṛṣṭatvād* (II 182,12) PKQ; M*n.a.*
- *pratīto*] *praṇīto* (II 224,9) PMK*n.a.*Q
- *sarasvatīm*] *sārasvatīm* (II 230,11–12) PβQ
- *leśaḥ*] *kleśaḥ* (II 235,14) PβQ
- *tiṅ*] *tiṅaḥ* (II 238,13) PβQ

These cannot be dismissed as polygenetic and are not genealogically explicable with the stemma as presently construed. Therefore, one may assume that they were somehow horizontally transmitted to Q, from either β or P. There are also further traces of contamination linking Q exclusively to the β manuscripts, so one may reduce the contamination source to β only:

- *upayāyāt* (II 149,15)] *upeyāt* KQ; M*n.a.*
- *śrautre* (II 151,17)] *śrotre* KQ; M*n.a.*
- *eva ca* (II 218,3)] *eva* βQ
- *kāraṇaṃ*] *kārakaṃ* (II 241,13) βQ^{ac}
- *so py anyena so py anyena* / *so 'pi tadanyena so 'pi tadanyena* (II 247,14)] *so py anyena* KQ; M*n.a.*
- *vācāṃ* (II 251,1)] *vācāṃ vā* βQ
- *sahaiva* (II 257,13)] *saha* βQ

5.5.3 Traces of contamination in V

There are several emendations by at least two different hands in V, both interlinear and marginal. Most of these corrections are not seen in any other manuscripts, so they may be conjectures by Gangadhara himself, e.g.:

- *na kṛtaśrama-*] *na lokato'vagamyate kṛtaśrama-* GaV^{pc} (II 224,4)
- *dhyetavya iti*] *'dhyeyo jñeyaś ca iti* GaV^{pc} (II 229,15)
- *cet tarhi*] *cet tarhi taddhitasamāsapratipattyoḥ* GaV^{pc} (II 244,10)

There are also several corrections in V reflecting the readings of P, so it is possible that these were collated in the margins of V during the editing work by Gangadhara, who mentions P as his second source.[28]

In V there are also some corrections that do not match P and are rather linking V to β:

- *pari*] *tatpari* (II 151,16) βV^{pc}
- *hetutvaṃ tu* (II 172,7)] *hetutvaṃ* βV
- *ekāctvādupādheḥ* (II 174,11)] *ekājupādheḥ* βV^{pc}
- *śabda* (II 175,9)] *śabdatva* βV^{pc}
- *apekṣyate*] *apekṣyeta* (II 178,12) βV^{pc}
- *padārthaṃ ca* (II 186,4)] *padārthaṃ* M*n.a.*KV
- *padārthasambandhasya* (II 192,15)] *padārthasya* βV^{pc}
- *trayo*] *yathā trayo* (II 206,5) βV^{pc}
- *ata eva*] *ata eva na* (II 207,8) βV^{pc}
- *yugalaka*] *yugala* (II 224,5) βV^{pc}
- *anubhūtāni* (II 225,3)] *ananubhūtāni* βV^{pc}
- *dravyaguṇa*] *dravya* (II 229,8) βV^{pc}
- *etat*] *evaṃ* (II 229,10) βV^{pc}

There is no evidence that Gangadhara had access to the β manuscripts, so either these readings were independently conjectured by Gangadhara and by the copyist of β , as I tend to believe after examining their context and meaning, or some contamination in V occurred before Gangadhara's time.

5.5.4 Traces of contamination in O

The following conjunctive readings shared by O with β were found, too many to be considered polygenetic occurrences. The above-mentioned shift of antigraph in O is not a factor here, as clear from the even distribution of this series throughout NM 6:

- *sphoṭasya ca*] *sphoṭasya* βO (II 144,3)
- *mātra*] *om.* M*n.a.*KO (II 147,4)
- *nirjñāta*] *jñāta* M*n.a.*KO^{ac} (II 147,4)
- *pi*] *om.* M*n.a.*KO (II 150,16)
- *nānākāra*] *nākāra* M*n.a.*KO (II 151,3)
- *karaṇāt*] *kāraṇāt* KO (II 162,3)

[28]Ssee Section 2.1 above and Appendix, Section 11.13 below.

- *sa*] *om.* KO (II 164,1)
- *iha*] *om.* MO (II 170,17)
- *iha*] *ihāpy* M*n.a.*KO (II 177,14)
- *tena*] *na* M*n.a.*KO (II 180,8)
- *sva*] *om.* βO*ac* (II 188,7)
- *tayor*] *om.* βO (II 189,11)
- *vā*] *om.* βO (II 202,9)
- *vṛddhaiḥ*] *vṛddheḥ* M*n.a.*KO (II 210,2)
- *ivainaṃ*] *evainaṃ* M*n.a.*KO (II 216,5)
- *śabdeṣu*] *om.* M*n.a.*KO (II 221,18)
- *na*] *om.* M*n.a.*KO (II 232,11)
- *abhiprīyamāṇasya*] *abhipreyamāṇasya* βO (II 240,12)
- *na samyag*] *asamyag* M*n.a.*KO (II 246,3)
- *karaṇaka*] *kāraṇaka* M*n.a.*KO (II 254,7)

It is worth noticing how in this list β is fully attested only in four cases and how there is a single conjunctive reading of O and M. It thus seem that the contamination came from K to O.

5.6 The stemma codicum

As mentioned above (see Section 5.1.1), there are some landmarks that give us a clearer picture, both geographical and historical, of the transmission of the NM. After the last decades of the 9th century, when Jayanta wrote his work, the NM remained a known and studied work in Kashmir. This is suggested by the traces that we find in Abhinava Gupta's writings and confirmed by the existence of the *codex vetustior* of the NM, which dates back to 1472 CE and was written by Śitikaṇṭhācārya, who declares in his colophon that the codex was meant for teaching purposes. S and the Kāśmīrī Nāgarī manuscripts also corroborate the enduring popularity in Kashmir. Furthermore, the GBh commentary was also most likely composed by a Kashmiri, Cakradhara, in the 11th century.

The NM is at first attested beyond the Kashmir valley in the beginning of the 11th century, in Dhāra, as proven by the abundant re-uses found in Bhoja's ŚPr, and soon after also in Jaina works. The oldest extant document preserving NM readings is the GBh manuscript in Jaina Nāgarī, which dates back to the 13th century (see Section 3.5.1) and is a proof of the interest generated by the NM in among Jaina scholars of that time. This is also confirmed by the copious quotations of Jayanta's work found in the SVR.

From the readings found in the Grantha-Malayālam manuscripts, one is led to think that the NM arrived in South India rather early. These manuscripts, unfortunately undated, cannot be very old, but they still represent an ancestral branch of the transmission. Yet, there is no way to tell when the transcription from that (Jaina?) Nāgarī or Śāradā ancestor into South-Indic scripts occurred, because the preservation of archetypical or original readings has to do with genealogical lines of transmission, not with antiquity. Paraphrasing Pasquali, a more recent age may suggest a higher number of lost links between the archetype and the observed witness, but there is actually no way to tell how ancient the exemplar used by the witness was (*recentiores non deteriores*).[29] It is safe to assume, however, that the ancestor which generated the southern manuscripts represented an early recension of the NM.

The manuscripts of the γ family, which may be called the vulgata, contain more recently developed readings in a Nāgarī recension of the NM. The genealogy reconstructed from the variants suggests that the vulgata was not produced from the Jaina or South Indian manuscripts, but it was rather developed from Śāradā ones. In fact, in most of the extant Nāgarī manuscripts there is some evidence of Śāradā-generated errors. Since the V manuscript is dated 1736 CE, and since the other γ manuscripts do not have characters suggesting a much greater antiquity, one may conclude that the transcription of the Śāradā exemplars of the NM into Nāgarī began quite late.

On the strength of these notions and hypotheses, therefore, the stemma in Fig. 5.15 is proposed, with the witnesses positioned in a tentative chronology.

[29] "Si può ancora obiettare [...] che età più recente fa presumere un numero maggiore di anelli [...] Questa presunzione è tutt'altro che ineccepibile, e proprio le età filologiche hanno prediletto codici antichi" (Pasquali, 1988, 46).

Figure 5.15: The stemma codicum with a tentative chronology

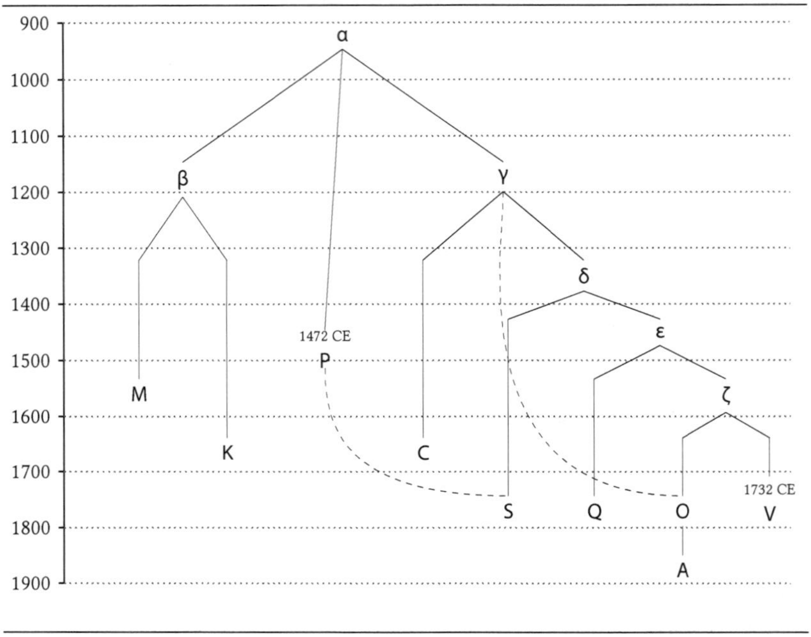

6 Editorial conventions

6.1 The purpose of the critical edition

The primary purpose of the critical edition is to reconstruct the text of α on the basis of the *recensio*, i.e., on the strength of the documentation of variant readings built during the collation phase and of the genealogical study that culminated in the stemmatic hypothesis, substantiated by historical evidence whenever possible. The nature of α, i.e., whether it should be conceived as the original, as the archetype, or as something else, needs to be clearly stated, because only then can the best editorial strategy be adopted. As put by Tanselle (1989, 70), "we must know what stage in the history of the work we wish to reconstruct, or else our emendations will be no more than aimless tamperings".

The concept of "archetype" can be ambiguous. According to Maas (1958, 3), "[t]he exemplar from which the first split originated we call the *archetype*. The text of this archetype is free from all errors arising after the split and is therefore closer to the original than the text of any of the witnesses". For Dain (*Les manuscrits*, Paris 1949, 109, quoted in Pasquali, 1988, 477), it is "le plus ancien témoin de la tradition où le texte d'un auteur se trouve consigné dans la forme qui nous a été transmise". West (1973, 32) echoes Dain, when he suggests that in a closed recension the archetype can be defined as "the lowest common ancestor of the known manuscripts". According to such definitions, indeed, it remains open whether this archetype can be thought of as the author's autograph or not. Some authors, such as Inglese (1999), argue that the existence of an archetype should be positively proven by means of errors present in the archetype that could not have been original ones, otherwise there is no advantage in postulating an archetype different from the original. This notion of an "archetype with variants" (Pasquali, 1988, 195) is commonly applied to the medieval tradition of Byzantine codices, in which witnesses in minuscule Greek are proven to be derived from archetypes in minuscule —thus no older than the 9th century— that for several reasons cannot possibly be identical to the majuscule originals of those works. Yet, the presence or absence of errors cannot be the sole mark of the archetype, since it is often seen that even autographs contain frequent errors (Segre, 1999, 378). In any case the original, as opposed to the archetype, is an often idealized object that as "perfect text" never existed (see D'Arco Avalle, 2002, 33, quoted in Segre, 1999, 379).

In the case of the NM, there is so far no evidence of errors imputable to α which would separate α from the original. There is some considerable distance between Jayanta's and the oldest exemplars' time, and it is plausible that progressive transcriptions from proto-Śāradā to Śāradā, Nāgarī, Grantha, etc., generated their own innovations. The oldest witness, P, dates back to 1472 CE, almost six centuries after Jayanta's time. Yet, it is plausible that Śitikaṇṭha had access to some very old document or in any case to a manuscript that might have been genealogically close to Jayanta's autograph. Also, many readings found in P, M and K are corroborated by the GBh, whose author lived in Kashmir at a time much closer to Jayanta. It is reasonable to claim that α is an approximation of the NM text available to Cakradhara, which may have even been Jayanta's autograph. In this connection, however, it is important to be aware that even Cakradhara betrayed some scepticism about some of the NM readings available to him (see GBh^{Sha}, 13–14).

Accordingly, in the present edition the text of α will be mainly reconstructed on the basis of readings found in β, P and γ, according to the stemma. In most cases, this polytomy allows for a mechanical choice of the most likely reading. When β, P and γ mutually disagree, confirmation can sometimes be found in the GBh. When the concerned passage is not glossed in the GBh, however, internal criteria such as *usus scribendi*, *lectio facilior/difficilior*, etc., will have to be adopted.[1] So far, multiple cases in which the GBh text confirmed either or both the β and P readings were found, but no instances of conjunctive readings of GBh and γ.[2]

The Sanskrit parts of the critical edition are typeset in Devanāgarī. None of the available Devanāgarī fonts fully filled the desired requirements in terms of range of ligatures. Moreover, behind many Devanāgarī fonts there is a certain lack of awareness of the historical relation between typography and the Nāgarī script found in manuscripts.[3] The development of a new font, Manohar.ttf, was thus undertaken for the specific needs of this book. The font is designed in Font Forge (Copyright © 2000–2011 by George Williams). For the shapes of most glyphs, I went back to one of the earliest Devanāgarī fonts, designed by Panchanan and Manohar for the Serampore Baptist Mission in the early 19th century. The design of this font has exercised a major influence on the later history of Devanāgarī typography and was used in the *editio princeps* of the NM in 1895. The inspiration for the design of missing or unsatisfactory ligatures was derived from J and from two Nāgarī manuscripts of the 15th–17th century period.[4] This Manohar font is thus an attempt to reset Devanāgarī typography to an earlier stage, to bridge the gap between the manuscript tradition and modern fonts, and to bring back some of the liveliness of earlier typography, which is often lost in the exactness of Devanāgarī fonts of the computer era.

---

[1]For wise words of caution on the application of internal criteria and on a method for their use, see Pasquali, 1988, 122–126.

[2]A discussion of the best method for the choice of NM readings can also be found in Graheli, 2012b.

[3]I recently became aware of a promising Hindi font designed by John Hudson and Fiona Ross of Tiro Typeworks and commissioned by the Harvard University Press for the upcoming Murty Classical Library (http://www.murtylibrary.com/design-and-typography.php).

[4]Specifically, two *Nyāyabhāṣya* manuscripts: (1) ms. 67, Jñānabhaṇḍār (Baḍā Bhaṇḍār), Jaisalmer Lodrapur Parshvanath Jain Trust, Collection of Jinabhadrasūri (1444 CE), and (2) ms. 1625 of the Ranbir Research Institute, Raghunath Mandir, Jammu (early 17th century).

6.2 The text of the edition

The segmentation of the text into sections and paragraphs as found in any of the previous editions was not fully satisfactory, so a new structure and segmentation of the text is proposed here.[5] The Sanskrit headings are formulated with the intention to capture the gist of the argumentation in the section, using the closest possible wording to Jayanta's own. The headings are enclosed in square brackets, to unambiguously mark their status of para-text. The resulting table of contents is quite detailed, to the extent that it should be possible to follow the main structure of the debate by browsing through it.

The presently edited text was frequently read aloud in reading sessions, so its punctuation largely reflects the sensibility derived by voiced reading.[6]I decided not to use modern punctuation in the form of quotation marks, question marks, etc., to avoid the tautology with Sanskrit *dyotaka*-s such as *iti*, *kim*, *bho*, etc. In the attempt to represent Jayanta's work and its textual transmission as faithfully as possible, but at the same time as intelligibly as possible, I made an extensive use of double *daṇḍa*-s, *daṇḍa*-s, half *daṇḍa*-s, blanks (i.e., graphical separation between letters) and even *sandhi* breaks. These should be understood as increasingly subtler textual separators:

- Double *daṇḍa*-s are used to mark the end of paragraphs before a new line, generally signalling the end of a topic or, in a specific application, separating an objection (*pratipakṣa*) from its re-

[5]Some remarks on the genesis of the structure in printed editions of the NM are provided in Section 2 above.

[6]The passage from the *scriptio continua* to the introduction of textual separators is indeed related to reading practices: "[...] the quicker and more mental the reading, the more analytic the presentation of the text is, requiring an indication of the value of its components" ("[...] quanto più la lettura è mentale e veloce, tanto più si richiede che il testo sia presentato analiticamente, con indicazioni sul valore delle varie parti" Cardona, 1981, 102. "This is because the expert reader does not proceed by spelling letter by letter, syllable by syllable, but is rather accustomed to represent himself blocks of words as organized forms" ("Questo perché il lettore esperto non procede compitando lettera per lettera, sillaba per sillaba, ma è abituato a rappresentarsi i blocchi di parole come forme organizzate [...]" Mortara Garavelli, 2007, 6). See also Svenbro, 1995, 11.

ply (*pakṣa*). Double *daṇḍa*-s are also used to mark the end of metrical passages.

- *daṇḍa*-s are used to punctuate full sentences. A sentence is here meant as a group of words in syntax with a finite verb.
- Half *daṇḍa*-s are used to mark sub-clauses, such as causal ablatives, or to provide some breath in lengthy and cumbersome sentences, for instance by separating long relative clauses. Moreover, they serve the purpose of separating a *pratipakṣa* from the *pakṣa*, whenever a new line for the latter is not suitable (e.g., in the case of a *cet* clause). They are also used to separate expressions such as *nanu, atha vā, api ca* etc., when these mark the beginning an objection (e.g., *nanu etad*, line 7).
- Furthermore, whenever finer subdivisions are needed for clarity's sake I took the liberty to solve *sandhi*-s, mostly to emphasize concepts, to clarify ambiguities, to stress key words and, in general, for readability's sake.[7]

The Romanisation of Sanskrit facilitates a detailed analysis of the text, due to the graphical division of vowels and consonants and to a more frequent separation of words. In many cases a separation of words by means of blank spaces can be achieved in Devanāgarī as well, and in this edition this option is going to be exploited, even at the cost of some degree of inconsistency and graphical oddity that may be considered inelegant. Some examples are the following ones:

- **प्रकृतिप्रत्ययांशवद् असत्य-** (line 178), where the *vatup*-ending word is separated to show that it is not in compound with *asatya*-;
- **प्रत्ययानाम् अस्ति**, where the rhetorical force on the finite verb is stressed by separating it from the preceding word (line 368);
- **कल्पनामात्रं त्वेतद् इयं प्रकृतिरेष प्रत्यय इति** (line 191), where the blank space before *iyam* marks the beginning of the *iti* clause.

[7] In the Vyākaraṇa tradition an explicit license is given in the matter of external *sandhi*-s, e.g., in ŚKau, 1.2, Commentary ad Maheśvarasūtra 1, 40,17–18, *saṃhitaikapade nityā nityā dhātūpasargayoḥ / nityā samāse vākye tu sā vivakṣām apekṣate*, or in HNAV, Saṃjñāsandhi, 43, *sandhir ekapade nityaṃ nityaṃ dhātūpasargayoḥ / anityaṃ sūtranirdeśe 'nyatra cānityamīṣyate*. As often seen even in good manuscripts and editions, many great scholars take their liberty in this respect.

- यदुपजायते तद् अर्थप्रत्यायनाङ्गं भविष्यति, where the blank between *tad* and *artha-* explicitly shows that the two words are interpreted as not being in compound (line 289).

Some examples of unconventional *sandhi* breaks are the following ones:

- to help the reader in the recognition of *iti* clauses, the word *iti* is often separated from the preceding and following words, particularly with long *iti* clauses (e.g., cf. *sphoṭa iti*, line 18, *prasajyata iti*, line 42, *iti ekākārā*, line 138);
- for the same reason, the beginning word of an *iti* clause is also separated from the previous word (e.g., *tathā aindravaṃ gṛhṇāti āśvinaṃ gṛhṇāti iti*, line 261);
- absolutive constructions are separated from preceding or following clauses (e.g., *krame ca sati ekaika-*, line 38);
- participles and gerunds in subordinate clauses are in some cases separated to enhance readability (e.g., *sphoṭātmani tu śabde'rthe pratipādake iśyamāne*, line 89, *ullaṅghya arthapratyaya-*, line 359);
- also other sub-sentential components are in rare instances clarified by *sandhi* breaks, particularly in the case of long *kāraka*-s and *upapada*-s (e.g., *-karaṇatvena arthapratīti-*, line 247).

6.3 The apparatuses

The text is integrated and supported by five apparatuses:

- The *Granthibhaṅga* apparatus.
- The apparatus of the testimonia.
- The apparatus of glosses by previous NM editors.
- The critical apparatus, i.e., the apparatus of variants.
- The apparatus of exegetical notes.

6.3.1 The apparatus of the Granthibhaṅga

This apparatus immediately follows the text of the NM. The NM expressions quoted by Cakradhara (i.e., the *pratīka*-s) are shown in the same font-size as the NM text. Shah's edition of the Gbh has been thoroughly counter-checked with the *codex unicus*, J, and corrected if strictly required. Although Shah's edition is outstanding, in the course of the edition of NM 6.1 rare instances of better readings in JTGB 386 were spotted and implemented in this apparatus. These were mostly cases in which Shah was influenced in his emendations of JTGB 386 by the *vulgata* of the NM text, while the readings in β and P actually confirmed those of JTGB 386 and disproved Shah's emendations. The variant readings, either of J or of $\mathrm{GBh}^{\mathrm{Sha}}$, are shown in the apparatus itself at the end of the GBh text. A separator (three diamond-shaped dots) marks the end of the GBh text.

6.3.2 The apparatus of the testimonia

This apparatus, which contains related readings from other works, has two main functions. On the one hand, it offers additional information for the reconstruction of the textual transmission of the NM by means of parallel readings found elsewhere. On the other, the form and the context of passages re-used by Jayanta assist the interpretation of the contents. With both purposes in mind, passages from works written both before and after the NM have be included.[8] For pragmatic reasons, manuscripts have not been consulted for this apparatus. In the case of more testimonia referring to the same passages, quotations are presented in the accepted chronological order, and separated by a diamond-shaped dot. The text of the printed editions used in this apparatus is reproduced verbatim, without *sandhi* normalization, but the punctuation has been occasionally adjusted.

6.3.3 The apparatus of glosses by previous editors

The third apparatus records exegetical notes found in the printed editions, specifically $\mathrm{NM}^{\mathrm{Shu}}$ and $\mathrm{NM}^{\mathrm{Va}}$ (Shu and Va in the apparatuses) . Some of these were indeed valuable and influenced my editorial choices, so it was important to make them available here. In this apparatus the punctuation is corrected or simplified, odd *sandhi*-s

[8] The legitimacy of having sources (written before the edited work), parallels (instances of the edited work paraphrased or alluded to by other authors), and testimonia (quotations of the edited work) in the same register of the apparatus is discussed in West, 1973, 84. Nuances about re-uses in the NM are discussed in Graheli, 2015b.

are normalized, and glaring orthographical errors are silently corrected. This apparatus should not be considered exhaustive, because no editions published after NM^{Va} were checked for its purpose. The *pratīka*-s in bold-face seen in the notes of NM^{Va} have not been reproduced here, since the notes are here referred to the text by means of lemmata with their respective line-numbers and followed by a separator, as in the other apparatuses.

6.3.4 The critical apparatus

The critical apparatus records only those variant readings which are considered substantive, i.e., those which yield meaning in the immediate context. These have been selected from the full collation, which can be found at http://homepage.univie.ac.at/alessandro.graheli.

Lemmata are built for easy recognition, with focus on the morphological appearance of a word, rather than on semantic considerations. They are followed by a right square bracket and by the sigla of available witnesses that testify to the text of the lemma, if they are outnumbered by the witnesses having variant readings. If lemmata are not complete words (i.e., they are not *pada*-s), or if they are members of compound words, their expectancy to the missing parts is shown by a hyphen. If two or more identical words appear in a given line of the critically edited text, the lemma is specified by a superscript number.

In general, specific orthographical features of the witnesses that reflect individual habits or preferences of the copyists, editors and printers are not considered as variant readings, and thus not included as variants *per se* in this apparatus. Such specificities are dealt with in the descriptions of the manuscripts (see Chapter 3.4). The order of more variant readings under one same lemma, which are separated by a black diamond-shaped dot, is determined by a judgement of their genealogical developments, reflecting as far as possible the stemmatic considerations. In general, only syntactically and semantically acceptable readings have been kept in this apparatus, with rare exceptions meant to show specific genealogical relations.

Omissions or lacunae, even if they result in an unacceptable text, are recorded if there are other lemmata occurring in the lacking portion of text. The witness that has the lacuna is then shown, in the intervening lemmata, as not available (*n.a.*). In this way, the reason of the non-availability should be always explicitly expressed by the larger lemma documenting the lacuna.

When the reconstructed text is uncertain, the lemma in this apparatus is marked by a wavy underline. This indicates that the reading of the archetype could not be identified with reasonable certainty and that there exists an alternative to the chosen reading which could justified on the basis of the stemma or because of other reasons such as better philosophical sense, adherence to internal criteria such as the *usus scribendi*, etc.

This apparatus is a "positive" one in the sense that the lemma and the corresponding variant are explicitly shown, according to the definition of "positive apparatus" found in Malato, 2008, 23. It is not positive, however, in another and perhaps more widely used sense of "positive apparatus" (see Stussi, 1998, 21), because the witnesses testifying to the received text are not always explicitly listed. They are explicitly shown only when the situation calls for it, i.e., when the number of witnesses testifying to the lemma is inferior to that of the witnesses testifying to the variants, because in this case the subtraction of the explicitly mentioned witnesses becomes impractical. For the sake of clarity, the list of all the available witnesses can be found with the ruler separating this apparatus from the previous one, in every page. It is thus implied and easily discernible by the reader that all witnesses but the explicitly mentioned ones agree with the text of the lemma.

Variant readings of the two selected printed editions, NM^{Ga} (Ga) and NM^{Va} (Va), are also found in this apparatus, abiding by the same criteria applied to the choice of variant readings of the manuscripts. The variants given in the footnotes of Va have been discarded, since the sources they were derived from could all be checked and confirmed. There are only rare cases in which Ga and Va do not agree with any manuscripts. This is due to the fact that Ga often uses the emendations in the V manuscript. Va, in turn, largely inherits the Ga readings, either directly or through NM^{Shu}. It is likely that most of the corrections in V were added to the manuscript during the process of production of the *editio princeps*.

The hyparchetypes β and γ were not reconstructed in the apparatus, so these sigla will not be found here. The reason is that I thought it easier for the reader to focus on the individual and extant witnesses, also because of their limited number. All the witnesses represented in the apparatus are listed at every page right above the variant readings, to facilitate the reader's orientation. According to the stemmatic hypothesis built above the reader is invited to pay particular attention to the position of P, M, K and C, as well as to the GBh readings, when available.

6.3.5 The exegetical notes

The edited text is further supplemented by text-critical and exegetical notes in English. These are always found at the bottom of the page and mostly consist of explanations of the choices adopted in the various apparatuses or clarifications about the readings chosen in the reconstructed text. In these notes also cross-references to other part of NM 6.1 can be found.

6.4 Foliation and pagination

The folio changes of the manuscripts and the page changes of the editions have been printed as endnotes (Section 10). An exception is the pagination of Va and Shu, which can be found right in the margin of the edition for easy reference and orientation, since they are the most cited and widespread editions. The folio number refers to the beginning of the folio or the page, e.g., "कश्चि[189v]दस्ति V" means that, in V, 188 recto ends with "कश्चि" and 189 verso begins with "दस्ति".

6.5 Synopsis of symbols and sigla

The following symbols and abbreviations have been used in the apparatuses:

क]	lemma separator in the critical apparatus
क ✱	lemma separator in the other apparatuses
क ◆ ख	separator of multiple elements occurring in a single note, in any apparatus
◆◆◆	separator of *Granthibhaṅga* text from variants, only in the GBh apparatus
क/// ///ख	beginning or end of damaged support
क---ख	missing *akṣara*-s, due to damage of support or other mechanical causes, etc.; the esteemed number of the missing *akṣara*-s is indicated by the number of - signs
कखग	text which may or may not be archetypical
conj.	conjecture
n.a.	unavailable witness
om.	*omittit*, omission
ac	*ante correctionem*, before correction
pc	*post correctionem*, after correction

The sigla of the witnesses used in the various apparatuses are summed up in Table 6.1, along with a concordance of sigla used in the previous editions.

Table 6.1: Sigla of useful witnesses

Siglum	Place	Longer reference	In Kataoka	In NM^{Va}
M	Madras	AL 70179B	n.a.	घ
C	Calcutta	AS G–10991	n.a.	n.a.
O	Mysore	ORI C–1374	O_1	क
P	Pune	BORI 390/75–6	n.a.	n.a.
Q	Pune	AA 5329	n.a.	n.a.
K	Kozhicode	MDUC 2606	K_1	n.a.
V	Varanasi	SSV 3465	n.a.	n.a.
S	Srinagar	ORL 1933	Z_1	n.a.
J	Jaisalmer	JTGB 386	n.a.	n.a.
Ga	Varanasi	NM^{Ga}	V	ख
Shu	Varanasi	NM^{Shu}	S	ख (see Section 4)
Ma	Varanasi	NM^{Ma}	S^2	n.a.
Va	Mysore	NM^{Va}	M	n.a.
Sha	Ahmedabad	NM^{Sha}	N	n.a.
Gau	Varanasi	NM^{Gau}	G	n.a.

Part II

Critical edition

7 [उपोद्घातः]

7.1 [विषयः]

ननु ' नाद्यापि शब्दस्य निरणायि प्रमाणता । NM^Shu, 336
बीजं पदार्थवाक्यार्थबुद्धेर्न हि निरूपितम् ॥ NM^Va, 143

उच्यते ' किमत्र निरूपणीयम् । यदनन्तरं हि यद् भवति तत् तस्य निमित्तम् । पदवाक्यश्रवणे च सति पदार्थवाक्यार्थसम्प्रत्ययो भवतीति ते एवात्र निमित्तम् । किं पुनरिदं पदं नाम किं च वाक्यमित्युक्तमत्र वर्णसमूहः पदं

Granthibhaṅga

2 [156r2]बीजं पदार्थवाक्यार्थबुद्धेः पदवाक्ये ॥

Testimonia

5 किं … नाम ⁕ किं पुनरिदं पदं नाम ? शब्दः (SphS, 73,5)

5–6 वर्णसमूहः … वाक्यम् ⁕ तस्मादेकार्थः पदसमूहो वाक्यम् (ŚBh, 2.1.46, p. 435,4) ◆ पदसमूहो वाक्यमर्थपरिसमाप्ताविति (NBh^Tha, 2.1.55) ◆ पदसमूहप्रतिसन्धानाच्च वाक्यं व्यवस्यति (NBh^Tha, 3.2.58) ◆ पदं पुनर्वर्णसमूहः । पदसमूहाः सूत्रम् । सूत्रसमूहः प्रकरणम् । प्रकरणसमूह आह्निकम् । आह्निकसमूहोऽध्यायः । पञ्चाध्यायी शास्त्रम् । (NV, 1,13–14) ◆ वर्णसमूहपदम्, पदसमूहो वाक्यम्, वाक्यसमूहः प्रकरणम्, प्रकरणसमूहो यथासमयं पादो वाह्निकं वाध्यायो, वा, तत्समूहः शास्त्रमिति (NBhū, 274,20–21) ◆ तस्मात् पदसमूह एव वाक्यमिति स्थितम् (NBhū, 282,10–11) ◆ पदं हि विभक्त्यन्तो वर्णसमुदायः (NM^Va, II 57,1–2, NM 5)

Notes from editions

2 बीजं ⁕ कारणम् । पदस्वरूपस्य, वाक्यस्वरूपस्य, तेषां अर्थप्रत्यायनप्रकारस्य च दुर्निरूपत्वात् शब्दप्रामाण्यं दुरवस्थमेवेत्यर्थः ॥ (NM^Va)

M K P C S O Q V Ga Va

1 ननु] M is not available up to गमयेयुः, line 63, and Q up to च्चपण, line 82

4 च] om. K Va ◆ n.a. M Q

4 एवात्र] एव तत्र V O Ga Va ◆ n.a. M Q

पदसमूहो वाक्यमिति ॥

7.2 [स्फोटपक्षप्रतिज्ञा]

ननु ' एतदेव न क्षमन्ते । न हि वर्णानां समूहः कश्चिदस्ति वास्तवः । तेन कुतस्तत्समूहः पदं भविष्यति । तदभावाच्च नतरां पदसमूहो वाक्यमवकल्पते । न च वर्णानां व्यस्तसमस्तविकल्पोपहतत्वेन वाचकत्वमुपपद्यते ।

Granthibhaṅga

9 ॰व्यस्तसमस्तोपहतत्वेनेति॰ व्यस्तानां प्रत्येकवाचकत्व इतरवर्णोच्चारणवैफल्यप्रसङ्गः । सामस्त्यं तु नास्ति क्रमोपलभ्यमानानामिति वक्ष्यति ॥ ◆◆◆ व्यस्तसमस्तविकल्पोपहतत्वेनेति Sha

Testimonia

7–8 न हि … भविष्यति * कथं पुनः क्षणिकानां वर्णानां समूहः सम्भवति (NBhū, 274,21–22)

9 न च वर्णानां … उपपद्यते * यद्येवम्, अर्थप्रत्ययो नोपपद्यते । कथम् । एकैकाक्षरविज्ञाने ह्यर्थो नोपलभ्यते । न चाक्षरव्यतिरिक्तोऽन्यः कश्चिदस्ति समुदायो नाम, यतोऽर्थप्रतिपत्तिः स्यात् (VKG, 38,6–8) ◆ नैतत्सारम्, प्रत्येकमप्रत्यायकत्वत्, साहित्याभावात्, नियतक्रमवर्तिनामयौगपद्येन संभूयकारित्वानुपपत्तेः, नानावक्तृप्रयुक्तेभ्यश्च प्रत्ययादर्शनात् क्रमविपर्यये यौगपद्ये च । तस्माद् वर्णव्यतिरेकि वर्णेभ्योऽसंभवन्नर्थप्रत्ययः स्वनिमित्तमुपकल्पयति (SphS, 75,10–11) ◆ किञ्च स्फोटाभावेऽर्थप्रतीतिर्न स्यात्, न हि वर्णानां समस्तानां व्यस्तानां वार्थप्रतिपादनसामर्थ्यमस्ति (NBhū, 274,5–6)

M K P C S O Q V Ga Va

7 एतदेव] एतदपि S ◆ n.a. M P Q ◆ P not available from एतदेव upto [निर्ज्ञातसामर्थ्यस्येन्द्रि]येन, line 61

8 नतरां] नितरां V ◆ न नितरां O ◆ n.a. M P Q

---

7 एतदेव * Due to the unavailability of P and M, the stemma is in this section less dependable. In their absence, the most reliable manuscripts are K and C.

8 नतरां * The suffix *tarap* is replaced by *tarām* when affixed to an indeclinable and used adverbially, as prescribed by Pā, 5.4.11. The use of the fourth ending with the root *kṛpū sāmarthye* is enjoined by Kātyāyana ad Pā, 2.3.13–15 (*kḷpi sampadyamāne*). When the cause and the produced effect are identical, however, the second ending should be used, as in *yavāgur mūtraṃ kalpate*, as explained by Nāgeśa (see VMBh^{Bha}, vol. 2, 498b). See also the use of *anavakḷpti*, in the sense of "impossibility", in Pā, 3.3.145.

तस्मादन्य एव स्फोटात्मा शब्दोऽर्थप्रतिपादक इति प्रतिजानते ॥

7.3 [वर्णपक्षप्रतिज्ञा]

ननु ' एवमस्तु । स्फोटोऽन्य एवार्थप्रतिपादको भवतु । का क्षतिर्नैयायिका- NM[Va], 144
नाम् ॥

कथं न क्षतिः । आप्तप्रणीतत्वेन हि शब्दस्य प्रामाण्यं तैरुक्तम् ' स्फोटस्य च नित्यत्वेन नाप्तप्रणीतत्वम् ' अतश्च यस्यानित्यत्वं वर्णात्मनः शब्दस्य साधितं नासावर्थप्रतीतिहेतुः ' अतो न प्रमाणम् ' यश्चार्थप्रतीतिहेतुः स्फोटात्मा शब्दस्तस्य नानित्यत्वं न चाप्तप्रणीतत्वम् ' इत्यस्थाने नैयायिकाः क्लिष्टा भवेयुः । तस्मादनित्यानां वर्णानामेव वाचकत्वं प्रतिष्ठापनीयं पराकरणीयश्च NM[Shu], 337
स्फोट इति तदुच्यते । गकारादिवर्णावगमे सति अर्थप्रतीतेर्भावात्तदभावे चा-

Granthibhaṅga

10 **स्फोटात्मा** अभिव्यञ्जकैर्नादैः स्फुटीक्रियते व्यक्तिं नीयते इति स्फोट इति नाम्ना व्यपदेश्यः ॥

13–14 **स्फोटस्य च नित्यत्वेनेति** । स ह्यक्रमो निरवयवश्च नित्य एव कल्पयितुं शक्यते । अर्थप्रतीत्या हि स कल्प्यते । न चानित्यादर्थप्रतीतिरुपपद्यते ' सङ्केतकालावगतस्येदानींतनस्य चान्यत्वात् । स च स्थित एव केवलमभिव्यज्यते ध्वनिभिरिति ॥

Testimonia

10 तस्माद् … प्रतिजानते ✱ अतो गकारादिव्यतिरिक्तोऽन्यो गोशब्दोऽस्ति, यतोऽर्थप्रतिपत्तिः स्यात् (VKG, 38,9–10) ◆ केचिदत्र ब्रुवते । वर्णव्यतिरिक्ताः पदवाक्यात्मानः शब्दाः सन्ति । यथा स्वमर्थं परिस्फुटयन्तः स्फोटाख्यां लभन्त इति (NBhū, 273,28–274,1)

13 आप्तप्रणीतत्वेन … उक्तम् ✱ आप्तोपदेशः शब्दः (NSū, 1.1.7) ◆ आप्तोपदेशसामर्थ्याच्छब्दादर्थसम्प्रत्ययः (NSū, 2.1.52)

Notes from editions

16–17 नैयायिकाः क्लिष्टा भवेयुः ✱ शब्दनित्यत्ववत् स्फोटनित्यत्वादिकमपि न वेदप्रामाण्योपपादकम् । इतरव्यावृत्तमीश्वरोपदिष्टत्वमेव तदुपपादकं भवेत् । वेदप्रामाण्यसमर्थनमेव हि न्यायशास्त्रस्य परम उद्देशः ॥ NM[Va]

M K P C S O Q V Ga Va

10–11 ऽर्थप्रतिपादक … भवतु] om. K ◆ n.a. M P Q

13 च] om. K O ◆ n.a. M P Q

भावात्तेषामेवार्थप्रत्यायनसामर्थ्यम् । त एव च श्रवणकरणकावगमगोचरतया शब्दव्यपदेशभाज इति न प्रतीत्यनुपारूढः स्फोटो नाम शब्दः कश्चित् प्रत्यक्षानुमानातीतः परिकल्पनीयः ॥

M K P C S O Q V Ga Va

19 सामर्थ्यम्] समद्त्यम् C ◆ n.a. M P Q

19 त] om. K ◆ n.a. M P Q

19 च] om. S ◆ n.a. M P Q

20 इति न] न इति K ◆ n.a. M P Q

21 परि-] om. S ◆ n.a. M P Q

8 [स्फोटवादः]

8.1 [वर्णपक्षनिराकरणम्]

8.1.1 [व्यस्तसमस्तवर्णविकल्पः]

आह ' कथमेवं भविष्यति । दूरापेता इमे मनोरथाः । कुतो वर्णानामर्थप्रत्यायकत्वम् । ते हि वर्णा गकारादयोऽर्थं प्रतिपादयन्तः समस्ताः प्रतिपादयेयुर्व्यस्ता वा ॥

8.1.1.1 [व्यस्तत्वनिराकरणम्]

न तावद् व्यस्ताः ' एकैकवर्णाकर्णने सत्यपि अर्थप्रतीतेरनुत्पादात् ॥

Testimonia

22–24 दूरापेता ... व्यस्ता वा ✱ केवलमेष मनोरथः । क्रमवद्भ्यश्च ध्वनिभ्यः प्रत्येकमप्रतीतेः समुदायाभावाच्चार्थप्रतीतिमन्विच्छन्नेकं शब्दात्मानं प्रकल्पयन्न तत्रावस्थातुमर्हति (SphS, 100,14–16)

25 न ... व्यस्ताः ✱ न तावत् प्रत्येकम्, अनुपलम्भविरोधात्, वर्णान्तरोच्चारणानर्थक्यप्रसङ्गाच्च (TB, 64,10)

M K P C S O Q V Ga Va

22 वर्णानाम्] वर्त्तमानाम् K ◆ n.a. M P Q

23 प्रत्यायकत्वम्] प्रत्यायत्वम् C S ◆ n.a. M P Q

23 प्रतिपादयन्तः] प्रत्यायन्तः K ◆ n.a. M P Q

25 सत्यप्यर्थ-] सत्यर्थ- K ◆ n.a. M P Q

23–24 समस्ताः प्रतिपादयेयुर्व्यस्ता वा ✱ Vācaspati uses respectively *pratyeka* and *milita* to present the same dilemma (TB, 64,9–10), while Maṇḍana uses the words *pratyeka* and *samudāya* (SphS, 100,14–16). The use of the words *vyasta* and *samasta* seems to be specific of the NM.

8.1.1.2 [सामस्त्यनिराकरणम्]

NM^{Va}, 145 सामस्त्यं तु वर्णानां नास्त्येव। तद्धि सत्तामात्रेण वा स्यात् प्रतीयमानत्वेन वा। नैयायिकपक्षे तावत्सत्तया यौगपद्यमविद्यमानम्, आशुविनाशिनः शब्दस्य दर्शितत्वात्। अथापि मीमांसकमतेन नित्यः शब्द इष्यते, तत्रापि सत्तया यौगपद्यस्य सकलवर्णसाधारणत्वात् केन वर्णसमुदायेन कोऽर्थः प्रत्याय्येत इति नावधार्यते॥

अथोच्यते, न चक्षुरादीनामिव वर्णानां कारकत्वम्, येनागृहीतानामेव स-

Granthibhaṅga

31 **न चक्षुरादीनामिव कारकत्वमिति**। चक्षुरादीनि ह्यगृहीतसङ्गतीनि यतः प्रमां जनयन्ति, अतस्तान्यर्थस्य न ज्ञापकानीत्युच्यन्ते, ज्ञापकधर्मविर[156v]हात्। अपि त्वर्थप्रतीतेर्जनकानीति॥

Testimonia

26 सामस्त्यं … एव ✳ नापि मिलिताः, तथा भावाभावात्। (TB, 64,11)

26 तद्धि … सत्तामात्रेण वा ✳ वर्णाः पदानि चास्यावयवाः सत्तामात्रेण अनुभूयमानतया वा भवेयुः (TB, 62,3)

27–28 आशु- … दर्शितत्वात् ✳ NSū, 2.2.13–39 ◆ वर्णानां चाविनाशित्वात् कथमीश्वरकार्यता (NM^{Va}, I 513,8, NM 3) ◆ कृतक इति नयज्ञैर्गृह्यतामेष शब्दः (NM^{Va}, I 572,11, NM 3)

31 न … कारकत्वम् ✳ स्वाभाविके सम्बन्धे सति दीपादिवत् किं तद्व्युत्पत्त्यपेक्षणेनेति चेत् न, शब्दस्य ज्ञापकत्वात् … (NM^{Va}, II 593,2–6, NM 11) ◆ यद् ज्ञापकं तद् ज्ञाप्ये प्रतिपन्नप्रतिबन्धमेव प्रतीतिं उत्पादयति यथा धूमादि। ज्ञापकश्च शब्द इति। चक्षुरादीनां तु कारकत्वाद् युक्तं स्वार्थसम्बन्धग्रहणानपेक्षाणां तदुत्पादकत्वम्। स्वयं हि प्रतीयमानम् अप्रतीतार्थप्रतीतिहेतुर्ज्ञापकमुच्यते … (NKC, vol. 2, p. 541,1–5)

Notes from editions

29 सकलवर्णसाधारणत्वात् ✳ वर्णानां नित्यत्वं सर्वगतत्वं चात्र हेतुः॥ (NM^{Va})

31 कारकत्वम् ✳ अज्ञातत्वेऽपि स्वरूपत एव कार्यनिर्वर्तकत्वम्॥ (NM^{Va})

M K P C S O Q V Ga Va

26 तु] om. V O Ga Va ◆ n.a. M P Q

27 सत्तया … -विद्यमानम्] सत्तायोगपद्यम् विद्यमानम् K ◆ n.a. M P Q

28 सत्तया] सत्ता- K ◆ n.a. M P Q

29 वर्ण] om. S ◆ n.a. M P Q

31 -गृहीतानामेव] -गृहीतानां V O ◆ n.a. M P Q

31–32 सत्ता-] सत्तां V^{pc} ◆ सतां Ga Va ◆ सतो K ◆ n.a. M P Q

त्तायौगपद्यमात्रमर्थप्रत्यायनाङ्गं स्यात् । ज्ञापकत्वात् तु तेषां गृहीतानां सतां धूमादिवत् प्रत्यायकत्वमिति प्रतीतानामेव सामस्त्यमुपयुज्यते ॥

एतदप्यघटमानम् । प्रतीतिसामस्त्यं हि किमेकवक्तृप्रयुक्तानां वर्णानामुत नानापुरुषभाषितानाम् । तत्रानेकपुरुषभाषितानां कोलाहलस्वभावत्वेन स्वरूपभेद एव दुरवगम इति कस्य सामस्त्यमसामस्त्यं वा चिन्त्येत । सत्यपि वा तथाविधे सामस्त्ये नास्त्येवार्थप्रतीतिः । एकवक्तृप्रयुक्तानां तु प्रयत्नस्थानकरणक्रमापरित्यागादवश्यम्भावी क्रमः । क्रमे च सति एकैक-

Testimonia

32 सत्तायौगपद्य- … स्यात् ✻ न सत्तयैव तेऽर्थानामगृहीताः प्रकाशकाः (VP[Rau], 1.57cd) ◆ नेन्द्रियाणां प्रकाश्येऽर्थे स्वरूपं गृह्यते तथा (VP[Rau], 1.56cd) ◆ यौगपद्यागृहीतेश्च समुदायौ न सिध्यतः । न सत्तायौगपद्यस्य व्यवहाराङ्गतेष्यते (ŚV[Dvā], vākya 7cd–8ab)

34–35 किमेक- … -भाषितानाम् ✻ किमियमनानाप्रयोक्तृकतार्थज्ञानाङ्गं न वेति (SphS, 86,10)

35–36 तत्रानेकपुरुष- … दुरवगम इति ✻ यौगपद्यं च शक्यत्वान्नैव तेषामिहाश्रितम् । कर्तृभेदश्च तत्र स्याच्च चैवं दृश्यतेऽभिधा (ŚV[Ra], sphoṭa 72)

37–38 एकवक्तृ- … क्रमः ✻ वक्त्रेकत्वनिमित्ते च क्रमे सति नियामकम् । प्रयुञ्जानस्य यत्पूर्वं वृद्धेभ्यः क्रमदर्शनम् (ŚV[Ra], sphoṭa 71)

Notes from editions

32 ज्ञापकत्वात् ✻ शाब्दबोधस्य ज्ञानरूपस्य ग्रात्ममनस्संयोगादिरेव कारकहेतुः । वर्णास्तु ज्ञातः सन्नेव हेतुः ॥ (NM[Va])

34 प्रतीतिः ✻ वर्णानां ग्रहणम् ॥ (NM[Va])

M K P C S O Q V Ga Va

32 -प्रत्यायनाङ्गं] K Va ◆ -प्रत्ययनाङ्गं S V O Ga ◆ प्रत्यप्रत्ययनांगं C ◆ n.a. M P Q

32 तु] K ◆ om. C S O V ◆ n.a. M P Q

32 तेषां] एषां C ◆ n.a. M P Q

33 प्रतीतानामेव] K ◆ प्रतीतावेव C S O V ◆ n.a. M P Q

33 -मुपयुज्यते] K ◆ -मुपयुज्यते इति C S O V Ga Va ◆ n.a. M P Q

35 तत्रानेक-] तत्र एकदानेक- Va ◆ n.a. M P Q

36 -भेद एव दुरवगम] -भेदस्तावदुरवगम K ◆ n.a. M P Q

36 कस्य] तस्य K ◆ n.a. M P Q

36 सामस्त्यम्] सामस्त्ये वार्थप्रतीतिः O ◆ सामस्त्येनार्थप्रतीतिः Va[घ] ◆ n.a. M P Q

37 वा] om. K ◆ n.a. M P Q

37 सामस्त्ये नास्त्येवार्थप्रतीतिः] प्रतीतिसामस्त्ये वार्त्थप्रतीति K ◆ n.a. M P Q

38 क्रमापरि-] क्रमपरि- V O ◆ n.a. M P Q

38 क्रमे च] क्रमे O ◆ n.a. M P Q

वर्णकरणिकार्थप्रतीतिः प्राप्नोति । न चासौ दृश्यत इति व्यस्तसमस्तविकल्पानुपपत्तेर्न वर्णा वाचकाः ॥

8.1.2 [व्यस्तसमस्तवर्णबुद्धिविकल्पः]

NM^{Va}, 146 वर्णविषया अपि बुद्धयस्तथैव विकल्पनीयाः। ता अपि न युगपत् सम्भवन्ति। क्रमे च सति एकैकवर्णबुद्धेरर्थसम्प्रत्ययः प्रसज्यत इति ॥

8.1.3 [संस्कारान्त्यवर्णपक्षनिराकरणम्]

यदप्युच्यते ' पूर्ववर्णजनितसंस्कारसहितोऽन्त्यो वर्णः प्रत्यायक इति ' तदप्ययुक्तम् । संस्कारो हि नाम यदनुभवजनितस्तद्विषयमेव स्मरणमुपजनयति । न पुनरर्थान्तरविषयं ज्ञानमिति ॥

Testimonia

43 पूर्व … प्रत्यायक ∗ पूर्ववर्णजनितसंस्कारसहितोऽन्त्यो वर्णः प्रत्यायक इत्यदोषः (VKG, 38,13; PrP, 380,3)

M K P C S O Q V Ga Va

39 वर्णकरणिकार्थ-] वर्णाकरणिकार्थ- C ◆ n.a. M P Q
41 अपि बुद्धय-] बुद्धयोऽपि K ◆ n.a. M P Q
41 विकल्पनीयाः] कल्पनीयाः K S ◆ n.a. M P Q
41 न युगपत्] युगपन्न S ◆ n.a. M P Q
42 च] om. O ◆ n.a. M P Q
42 प्रसज्यत] प्रसज्येत S O Va ◆ n.a. M P Q
43 पूर्व-] K ◆ पूर्वपूर्व- C S O V Ga Va ◆ n.a. M P Q
43 ऽन्त्यो] K ◆ न्त्य- C S O V Ga Va ◆ n.a. M P Q
43–44 तदप्ययुक्तम्] तदपि ह्ययुक्तम् S ◆ n.a. M P Q
44 हि] पि K ◆ n.a. M P Q
45 ज्ञानम्] om. S ◆ n.a. M P Q

42 प्रसज्यत ∗ The fluctuation among present tense and optative is rather common in the Śāradā transmission, because of the frequent displacement of the *e* vowel sign (e.g., *prasajyate/prasajyeta*).

44 हि ∗ In this passage M and P are not available, so K becomes the main witness. Here, however, there are two reasons to receive *hi* rather than *pi*: firstly, the exemplar of K was likely in a Grantha-Malayālam script, where the confusion between the two consonants is not far-fetched ; secondly, in the immediate context, *hi* makes more sense.

स्मृतिद्वारेण तर्ह्यर्थप्रत्यायकोऽसौ भविष्यतीति चेत् ' एतदपि नास्ति ' ज्ञानयौगपद्यप्रसङ्गाद् । अन्त्यवर्णज्ञानानन्तरं हि पूर्ववर्णस्मरणमिव समयस्मरणमपि तदैवापतति । ततश्च ज्ञानयौगपद्यम् । न च क्रमोत्पादे किञ्चित् कारणमुत्पश्यामः ॥

अथापि क्रमेण ते स्मरणे भवेतां तथापि तदानीमन्त्यवर्णज्ञानमुपरतमिति कस्य साहायकं पूर्ववर्णस्मृतिर्विदधातीति ॥

एतच्चानेकपूर्ववर्णविषयामेकां स्मृतिमभ्युपगम्योक्तम् । न पुनरेका सर्ववर्णगोचरा स्मृतिः । कुतः ' NM^{Shu}, 338

Granthibhaṅga

50 क्रमेण ते स्मरण इति । एकस्य स्मरणस्योत्पादकाले ज्ञानस्य 'ज्ञानान्तरा'विरोधित्वादन्त्यवर्णज्ञानस्य विनश्यत्ता । द्वितीयस्मरणोत्पादकाले तस्य विनाश इति ॥ ◆◆◆
ज्ञानान्तर- Sha *v.l.*

Testimonia

50 क्रमेण ते स्मरणे … ✱ अन्त्यवर्णेऽपि विज्ञाते पूर्वसंस्कारकारितम् । स्मरणं यौगपद्येन सर्वेष्वन्ये प्रचक्षते ॥ सर्वेषु चैवमर्थेषु मानसं सर्ववादिनाम् । इष्टं समुच्चयज्ञानं क्रमज्ञानेषु सत्स्वपि (ŚV^{Ra}, sphoṭa 112–113) ◆ अपरे तु संस्कारत्रयजन्यां वर्णस्मरणरूपां सङ्कलनात्मिकामिच्छन्तीत्याह अन्त्यवर्णेऽपि विज्ञात इति (ŚVT^{Ra}, sphoṭa 112)

M K P C S O Q V Ga Va

46 स्मृतिद्वारेण] स्मृतिद्वारेण हि S ◆ स्मृतिद्वारेणासौ Va ◆ n.a. MPQ
46 अर्थप्रत्यायकोऽसौ] असावर्थप्रत्यायको S ◆ n.a. MPQ
47 अन्त्यवर्णज्ञानानन्तरं] अन्त्यवर्ण/// अन्तरं K ◆ n.a. MPQ
48 तदैवापतति] तदैव पतति O ◆ n.a. MPQ
50 क्रमेण ते] KGBh ◆ ते क्रमेण CS ◆ तेन क्रमेण VOGa Va ◆ n.a. MPQ
50 तथापि] तथापि ज्ञानयोगि K ◆ n.a. MPQ
51 साहायकं] साहाय्यकं KVa ◆ n.a. MPQ
51 विदधातीति] विधदधीतेति C ◆ विदधितः K ◆ n.a. MPQ
52–53 न पुनरेका सर्ववर्णगोचरा] पुनरेका सर्वगोचरा K ◆ n.a. MPQ

47 अन्त्यवर्णज्ञानानन्तरं ✱ The reading of K is recorded in the apparatus because curiously fol. 152v begins with *antaraṃ* as a separate word, i.e., not in ligature with what precedes it; the margin at the end of 152r is damaged, so the last two syllables are lost.

51 विदधातीति ✱ The dual of the present tense in K could refer to the first two (recollected) phonemes in *g-au-ḥ* word.

भिन्नोपलम्भसम्भूतवासनाभेदनिर्मिताः ।
भवेयुः स्मृतयो भिन्ना न त्वेकानेकगोचराः ॥

8.1.4 [सङ्कलनाज्ञानपक्षनिराकरणम्]

अथ वदेत् ' सङ्कलनाज्ञानमेकं सदसद्वर्णगोचरं भविष्यति ' तदुपारूढाश्च वर्णा

Granthibhaṅga

56 **सङ्कलनाज्ञानमिति ।** क्रमगृहीतानामेकस्मिन्ननन्तरकालभाविज्ञाने सङ्कलितानां समुच्चितानां प्रतिभासनं सङ्कलनाज्ञानम् ' शतादिसमुच्चयज्ञानवत् ॥

Testimonia

56–57 सङ्कलना- … प्रत्याययिष्यन्तीति ∗ यद्वा प्रत्यक्षतः पूर्वं क्रमज्ञातेषु यत् परम् । समस्तवर्णविज्ञानं तदर्थज्ञानकारणम् ॥ तत्र ज्ञाने च वर्णानां यौगपद्यं प्रतीयते । नावश्यं यौगपद्येन प्रत्यक्षत्वेन तद्भवेत् ॥ चित्ररूपां च तां बुद्धिं सदसद्वर्णगोचराम् । केचिदाहुर्यया वर्णा गृह्यतेऽन्त्यः पदे पदे ॥ (ŚV^{Ra}, sphoṭa 109–111) ◆ अपरे तु संस्कारत्रयजन्यां वर्णस्मरणरूपां सङ्कलनात्मिकामिच्छन्तीत्याह (ŚVT^{Ra}, sphoṭa 112)

Notes from editions

54 वासना ∗ संस्कारः । कारणानां संस्काराणामनेकत्वे सति तज्जन्यस्मृतेः एकत्वं कथं संभवेदित्याशयः ॥ (NM^{Va})

56 संकलनाज्ञानम् ∗ तावद्वर्णविषकम् [sic] एकं समूहालम्बनात्मकं, समुच्चयात्मकं वा ज्ञानम् ॥ (NM^{Va})

56 सदसत् ∗ इति तत्कालदृष्ट्या ॥ (NM^{Va})

M K P C S O Q V Ga Va

55 -गोचराः] K S Va ◆ गोचरा C O V Ga ◆ n.a. M P Q

56 सङ्कलना] Ga Va ◆ संकल्पना C V O Va^{क} ◆ सकल्पना S ◆ ----ना K ◆ n.a. M P Q

56 गोचरं] गोचरं चित्राकारं K ◆ n.a. M P Q

56 तदुपारूढाश्च] तद्रूपारूढाश्च V Ga Va ◆ n.a. M P Q

55 -गोचराः ∗ The text in C, O, V and Ga should be understood as *ekā anekāgocarā* [*smṛtiḥ*]. The reading in K and S is more difficult but not impossible, perhaps meant as a *karmadhāraya* compound, *ekā cāsāv anekagocarā ca, tāḥ*.

56 ∗ See ŚV^{Ra}, sphoṭa 114 (*śatādirūpaṃ jāyeta*) for the analogy with the numeric cognition mentioned in the GBh. The feminine ending of *saṅkalanā* may convey a causative sense : *sam* + *kala* + *ñic* + *yuc* (Pā, 3.3.107). The expression is not used by Kumārila, who instead uses *samuccayajñāna*, while it is found in Umveka's commentary, possibly Jayanta's source in this context.

56 गोचरं ∗ Here K may be glossing *sadasadvarṇagocaram* with *citrākāram*, inspired by *citrarūpam* in ŚV^{Ra}, sphoṭa 111.

अर्थं प्रत्याययिष्यन्तीति ॥

तदपि दुराशामात्रम् ' तथाविधज्ञानोत्पत्तौ कारणाभावात् । न चेन्द्रियमतीतवर्णग्रहणसमर्थम् । न संस्कारो वर्तमानग्राही भवति । न च युगपदिन्द्रियं संस्कारश्चेमां बुद्धिं जनयतः ' संस्कारस्य सहचरदर्शनाद्याहितप्रबोधस्य सतः स्मरणमात्रजन्मनि निर्ज्ञातसामर्थ्यस्येन्द्रियेण सह व्यापाराभावात् । तस्माच्च वर्णा वाचकाः ॥

NM^{Va}, 147

8.1.5 [विपरीतक्रमप्रसङ्गः]

अतश्चैवम् ' यदि हि ते वाचका भवेयुर्विपरीतक्रमप्रयुक्ता अप्यर्थं गमयेयुः ।

Notes from editions

63 -र्विपरीतक्रम- ✱ विपरीतेत्यादि---विपरीतक्रमेण वर्णानामुच्चारणेऽपि समूहालम्बनात्मकज्ञाने सर्वेषां वर्णानां विषयत्वात् वाचकत्वापत्तिः ॥ (NM^{Va})

M K P C S O Q V Ga Va

58 ज्ञानोत्पत्तौ] विज्ञानोत्पत्तौ K ◆ n.a. M P Q

58–59 न चेन्द्रिय-] नेन्द्रिय- K ◆ n.a. M P Q

59 -ग्रहणसमर्थम्] ग्रहणमसमर्थन् K ◆ n.a. M P Q

59 वर्तमानग्राही भवति] वर्त्तमानवर्त्त---वति K ◆ n.a. M P Q

60 सहचर-] C S V ◆ सहचरित- K ◆ सहचार O Ga Va ◆ n.a. M P Q

60 -दर्शनाद्याहित] -दर्शनाद्याहिते V^{ac} ◆ -दर्शनाभ्यां हि ते O ◆ n.a. M P Q

61 सतः] मतः O ◆ n.a. M P Q

61 -मात्र-] om. K O ◆ n.a. M P Q

61 निर्ज्ञात-] ज्ञात- KO^{ac} ◆ n.a. M P Q

61 -सामर्थ्य-] C S O Ga Va ◆ -सामस्त्य- K ◆ -सामर्थ- V ◆ n.a. M P Q

61 -स्येन्द्रियेण] ///येण P available from here

61 सह] om. Ga

63 यदि हि ते] P K C ◆ यदि S V O Ga Va ◆ n.a. M Q

63 -प्रयुक्ता] -युक्ता K

63 अप्यर्थं] अपि चार्थं S ◆ n.a. M Q

63 अतश्चैवम् ✱ Here *ataḥ*, “because of this”, refers to what follows as the cause of what precedes. Another instances of this usage can be seen at line 83 below, and in NM I 73,7 and 99,4 ; NM II 7,7, 204,1, 291,12, 325,8 and 355,8).

क्रमश्चेदपेक्ष्यते स व्यतिरिक्ताव्यतिरिक्ततया चिन्तनीयः । अव्यतिरेके त एव ते वर्णा इति कथं न बोधकाः। व्यतिरेके तु किमप्यधिकं वाचकमभ्युपगतं भवति इति मत्पक्षमाजिगमिषति भवान् ॥

8.1.6 [व्युत्पत्तिपक्षेऽनवस्थाप्रसङ्गः]

ननु ' व्युत्पत्तिवशेन शब्दोऽर्थप्रत्यायकतामुपयाति। व्युत्पत्तौ च ये यावन्तो यत्क्रमका वर्णा यमर्थमभिवदन्तो दृष्टाः ' ते तावन्तस्तत्क्रमकास्तमर्थम-

Granthibhaṅga

65 **किमप्यभ्यधिकमिति** । वर्णस्वरूपातिरिक्तश्चेदपेक्ष्यते स एव तर्हि स्फोटः ' सर्वथा स्वरूपमात्रस्यावाचकत्वमायातमिति मत्पक्षाभ्युपगमः ॥

Testimonia

67–69 व्युत्पत्ति … अभिवदिष्यन्ति ⁎ सम्बन्धग्रहणवशेन वर्णानामर्थप्रतिपादकत्वं येषां च यावतां यत्क्रमकाणां च यत्तदस्ति, तत्तेषां तावतामेव तत्क्रमकाणामेकवक्तृप्रयुक्तानां च प्रतिपादकत्वमित्यर्थः (ŚVT[Ra], sphoṭa 69)

M K P C S O Q V Ga Va

64 क्रमश्चेदपेक्ष्यते] M available from here
64–65 त एव ते] ते S ◆ n.a. Q
65 बोधकाः] बोधकः C V^{ac} ◆ n.a. Q
65 तु] च P ◆ n.a. Q
65 -प्यधिकं] -प्यभ्यधिकम् GBh
65 अभ्युपगतं] om. S^{ac} ◆ n.a. Q
66–68 भवति … यत्क्रमका] भ/// ///का M ◆ n.a. Q
66 इति] चेति S ◆ n.a. MQ
66 मत्-] PSVGaVa ◆ सत् CO ◆ /// K ◆ n.a. MQ
66 -पक्षम् … आजिगमिषति] -पक्ष संजिगमिषति C ◆ n.a. MQ
67 वशेन] वदेन O ◆ n.a. MQ
67 शब्दो] शब्दे V ◆ n.a. MQ
67 -प्रत्यायकताम्] -प्रत्यायताम् S ◆ -ग्राहकताम् K ◆ n.a. MQ
67 ये] PK ◆ om. SVOGaVaC ◆ n.a. MQ
67 यावन्तो] यावन् ते C ◆ n.a. MQ
68 -क्रमका] -क्रमा Va ◆ ///का M ◆ n.a. Q
68 यम्] यद् Va ◆ n.a. Q
68 तत्क्रमका-] तावत्क्रमका- K ◆ n.a. Q

भिवदिष्यन्ति इति किं विकल्पमालया । तदुक्तम् '

यावन्तो यादृशा ये च यदर्थप्रतिपादने ।
वर्णाः प्रज्ञातसामर्थ्यास्ते तथैवावबोधकाः ॥ इति ॥

उच्यते ' व्युत्पत्तिरेवेयं विचारणीया वर्तते । परावगतिपूर्विका हि शब्दात् स्वयमवगतिः । परावगतौ च के कियन्तः कथं कमर्थं प्रतिपादयन्तोऽनेन दृष्टा येभ्यस्तथैव तमर्थं प्रतीयाद् इति दुरवगमा हि वर्णवर्तनी । NM^{Va}, 148

यावन्तो यादृशा ये चेत्येवं तावत् प्रभाषसे ।
कियन्तः कीदृशाः के चेत्येवं यावन्न पृच्छ्यसे ॥

तस्मात् सर्वप्रकारमवाचका वर्णाः ॥

Testimonia

70–71 यावन्तो … -बोधकाः ॥ ✳ (ŚV^{Ra}, sphoṭa 69)

Notes from editions

70–71 यावन्तो … -बोधकाः ॥ ✳ श्लोकवार्तिके स्फोटवादे श्लो० ६९ । व्यवहारावगम्यं हि वाचकत्वं नास्मदिच्छाधीनमतो यथादर्शनं तदभ्युपगमाच्च काचिदतिप्रसक्तिरस्तीति भावः । (NM^{Shu})
72–73 परावगति … स्वयमवगतिः ✳ प्रयोज्यवृद्धस्य प्रवृत्तिं पश्यन् बालः तस्य प्रवृत्तिं प्रयोजकवृद्धवाक्यार्थज्ञानमूलिकां जानन् हि व्युत्पद्यते ॥ (NM^{Va})

M K P C S O Q V Ga Va

69 किं] om. K ◆ n.a. Q
69–72 तदुक्तम् … उच्यते] त/// ///ते M ◆ n.a. Q
72 उच्यते] P K C S ◆ तदुच्यते V O Ga Va ◆ ///ते M ◆ n.a. Q
73 स्वयमवगतिः] त्वियमवगतिः M K
73–74 च … दुरवगमा] च/// ///मा M ◆ n.a. Q
74 तथैव] तथैवम् O ◆ n.a. M Q
74 तमर्थं] तमर्थमयं K ◆ n.a. M Q
74 दुरवगमा] P K S ◆ दुरधिगमा C V O Ga Va ◆ n.a. M Q
74 -वर्तनी] -वर्त्तिनी M ◆ n.a. Q
75 प्रभाषसे] प्रभावसे C ◆ n.a. Q
76 कीदृशाः] कीदृशान् C ◆ n.a. Q
76 चेत्येवं] वेत्येवं P ◆ n.a. Q
76 पृच्छ्यसे] पृच्छसे V^{ac} ◆ पृच्छसि O ◆ n.a. Q
77–78 प्रकारम् … चेयम्] प्रका/// ///चेयम् M ◆ n.a. Q

8.2 [स्फोटपक्षः]

8.2.1 [अर्थप्रतीतिकारणत्वात् स्फोटकल्पनोपपत्तिः]

अस्ति चेयं शब्दादुच्चरितात् तदर्थावगतिः । न चेयमकरणिकैव भवितुमर्हति । तद्यदस्याः करणं स्फोट इति कार्यानुमानमिदमस्तु परिशेषानुमानं वार्थापत्तिर्वा । सर्वथा अर्थप्रतीतिलक्षणकार्यवशात् कल्प्यमानं तत् करणं स्फोट इत्युच्यते । स च निरवयवो नित्य एको निष्क्रमक इति न व-

Granthibhaṅga

79 **कार्यानुमानमिदमस्त्विति** । अर्थप्रतिपत्तिलक्षणात् तावत् कार्यमात्रात् तत्कारणमात्रावगमः । तत्र कारणमात्रस्य निर्विशेषस्य गोत्वस्येव ' शबलेयादिविशेषशून्यस्यासम्भवात् वर्णानां च पूर्वनीत्या कारणत्वप्रतिषेधादन्यत्र चाप्रसङ्गात् स्फोटस्यैव कारणत्वकल्पनेति कारणमात्रावगतौ कार्यानुमानम् । ˚कारणविशेषावगमे˚ तु **परिशेषानुमानमिति** । ˚-एवंरूपं˚ च परिशेषानुमानं कार्यानुमानसहितमर्थापत्तितयान्यैर[157r]भिहितम् ' तन्नाम्नो वास्याभिधाने न काचित् क्षतिरिति ॥ ◆◆◆ कारणमविशेषावगमे J ◆ अर्थापत्तिर्वेत्येवंरूपं Sha

81–82 **वर्णपक्षक्षपणक्षमेति** । किमेकैकः प्रत्यायकोऽथ संहता इत्यादि यद्दूषणम् ॥

Testimonia

79 परिशेषानुमानं ✳ शेषवन्नाम परिशेषः । स च प्रसक्तप्रतिषेधेऽन्यत्राप्रसङ्गाच्छिष्यमाणे सम्प्रत्ययः (NBh^{Tha}, 1.1.5)

Notes from editions

79 कार्यानुमानमिदमस्तु ✳ अर्थावगतिरूपात् कार्यात् तत्कारणस्य स्फोटस्यानुमानम् ॥ (NM^{Va})
81–82 वर्ण- … -दूषणपात्रतां ✳ वर्णस्यावगतिहेतुत्वपक्षस्य क्षेपणे—निरसने दक्षाणां दूषणानां पात्रताम् ॥ (NM^{Va})

M K P C S O Q V Ga Va

78 -दुच्चरितात्] P K C Va ◆ -दुच्चारितात् S V O Ga ◆ n.a. M Q
78 चेयमकरणिकैव] चेव सकरणिकैव C ◆ n.a. Q
79 तद्यदस्याः] P M K ◆ तदस्याः C S V O Ga Va ◆ n.a. Q
79 स्फोट] स स्फोट M K ◆ n.a. Q
80–81 प्रतीति- … एको] प्रतीति/// ///एको M ◆ n.a. Q
80 कल्प्यमानं तत्] om. K ◆ n.a. M Q
80 करणं] कारणं K ◆ n.a. M Q
81 निष्क्रमक] निष्क्रम M^{ac} ◆ निष्कारणक O Va ◆ n.a. Q

र्णपन्नन्नपणदन्नदूषणपात्रतां प्रतिपद्यते ॥

8.2.1.1 [शब्दादिति लोकव्यवहारे स्फोटोपपत्तिः]

अतश्च स्फोटोऽर्थप्रतिपादकः ' शब्दादर्थं प्रतिपद्यामह इति व्यवहारात् । भवतां हि वर्णजनितः संस्कारोऽर्थप्रतिपादकः । तत्र शब्दादिति प्रातिपदिकार्थोऽनुपपन्नः ॥

Granthibhaṅga

84–85 प्रातिपदिकार्थोऽनुपपन्नः । संस्कारस्य शब्दशब्दवाच्यत्वाभावात् । विभक्त्यर्थस्त्वेकत्वमेकत्वादुपपद्यते संस्कारस्येति ॥ ◆◆◆ नुपपन्नः] ऽप्युपपन्नः Sha

Testimonia

83 शब्दादर्थं … व्यवहारात् ✱ नन्वेवमपि शब्दादर्थं प्रतिपद्यामह इति लौकिकं वचनमनुपपन्नं स्यात् (VKG, 38,14) शब्दादर्थमतिस्तेन लौकिकैरभिधीयते (ŚV^{Ra}, sphoṭa 116cd)

Notes from editions

85 ऽनुपपन्नः ✱ उपपन्नः । स्फोटस्य शब्दत्वात् । संस्कारस्यार्थप्रतिपादकत्वे त्विदमनुपपन्नमेव ॥ (NM^{Va})

M K P C S O Q V Ga Va

82 -पन्न-] -पन्ने P^{ac} ◆ n.a. Q
82 -न्नपण-] -न्नेपण- Va ◆ Q available from न्नपण-
82 -दन्न-] -न्नम- GBh
82 -दूषणपात्रतां] -दूषणपाततां O ◆ दूषणतां S
82 प्रतिपद्यते] प्रतिपद्येत S
83–84 शब्दाद् … -प्रतिपादकः] om. V Ga
83 शब्दादर्थं] शब्दार्थं K ◆ *n.a.* V Ga
83–85 व्यवहारात् … -प्रातिपदिकार्थो] व्य/// ///तिपदिकार्थो M
84 भवतां] P K ◆ भवतो C S Q O Va ◆ *n.a.* M V Ga
84 -जनितः] -जनित- K ◆ *n.a.* M V Ga
84–85 नुपपन्नः] प्युपपन्नः Ga ◆ विभक्त्यर्थश्च द्वयमनुपपन्नः K M^{ac}

84–85 प्रातिपदिकार्थोऽनुपपन्नः ✱ The interpretation and reconstruction of the passage is corroborated by the GBh, where *tatra* refers to *saṃskāra* in the previous sentence and the addition of *vibhaktyarthaś ca*, observed in K and M^{ac}, is discussed. It cannot be excluded that Cakradhara had the variant reading of K and M before his eyes, or that the M scribe deleted the passage on the strength of the Cakradhara's gloss.

85 ऽनुपपन्नः ✱ The Va note on *nupapannaḥ* seems contradictory. Possibly the first part of the note was written with the Ga text in mind.

NM^{Shu}, 339 ग्रथ ' वर्णाः शब्दशब्देनोच्यन्ते । ते चार्थप्रतिपादकाः ॥ इदं त्वन्यथासिद्धम् । तथापि शब्दादित्येकत्वं विभक्त्यर्थो न सङ्गच्छते । शब्देभ्यः प्रतिपद्यामह इति व्यवहारः स्यात् । स्फोटात्मनि तु शब्देऽर्थप्रति- NM^{Va}, 149 पादक इष्यमाणे शब्दादिति प्रातिपदिकार्थो विभक्त्यर्थश्च द्वयमप्युपपन्नम् ॥

Notes from editions

86 ते ∗ स्मृतिविषयास्सन्तः ते इत्यर्थः ॥ (NM^{Va})
89 द्वयमप्युपपन्नम् ∗ वाक्यस्फोटस्य एकत्वात् ॥ (NM^{Va})

M K P C S O Q V Ga Va

86 शब्दशब्देनोच्यन्ते] शब्देनोच्यते S ◆ ///च्यन्ते M
86 चार्थ-] om. P^{ac} ◆ र्थ- P^{pc}
87 इदं त्वन्यथासिद्धम्] P C Q V^{pc} ◆ इदमन्यथासिद्धम् S O ◆ इति । इदमन्यथासिद्धम् Va ◆ इति M K ◆ om. V^{ac} Ga
87 एकत्वं] एकत्व- M K
88 व्यवहारः स्यात्] व्यवहारस्यार्थं K
88 तु] om. M K
89 द्वयमप्युपपन्नम्] द्वयमुपपन्नम् K ◆ /// M

87 इदं त्वन्यथासिद्धम् ∗ The position of the clause is problematic. It could be part of either the *varṇavādin*'s or the *sphoṭavādin*'s argument. A problem is the anaphor of *idam*, since there is no neuter noun in the vicinity; an implicit *tadbhāvabhāvitvam* is probably referred to (cf., e.g., NM^{Va}, I 133,9 and see line 101 below). The *tu* particle suggests that it is the beginning of the *sphoṭavādin*'s rebuttal, and also the later *anyathāsiddhi* charge (see line 101) against the *varṇavādin* supports this interpretation. Although here the clause appears out of place, and the M and K reading is certainly smoother, it is kept on stemmatic grounds.

8.2.1.2 [अर्थप्रत्यायकत्वमेव शब्दत्वम्]

ननु ' न स्फोटः शब्दशब्देनोच्यते किं तु वर्णा एव। श्रोत्रग्रहणे ह्यर्थे शब्दशब्दः प्रसिद्धः। ते च श्रोत्रग्रहणा इति ॥

नैतदेवम् ' शब्दत्वस्यापि श्रोत्रग्रहणत्वात् ' निर्झरझाङ्काररवप्रभृतीनां च सत्यपि श्रोत्रग्रहणत्वे शब्दकार्यनिर्वर्तकत्वानुपपत्तेः। तस्माद् यतोऽर्थप्रतिपत्तिः स शब्दः। अर्थप्रतिपत्तिश्च स्फोटादेव न वर्णेभ्य इति स्फोट एव शब्दः ॥

Granthibhaṅga

93 **शब्दकार्यनिर्वर्तनानुपपत्तेः।** शब्द्यते कथ्यतेऽनेनार्थ इति शब्दशब्दनिर्वचनसामर्थ्यादर्थप्रतीतिजनक एव शब्दः ॥

Testimonia

90–91 श्रोत्रग्रहणे … प्रसिद्धः ∗ श्रोत्रग्रहणे ह्यर्थे लोके शब्दशब्दः प्रसिद्धः। ते च श्रोत्रग्रहणाः (ŚBh, 1.1.5, 54,8) ◆ श्रोत्रग्रहणे ह्यर्थे लोके शब्दशब्दः (Bṛh, 119,6) ◆ श्रोत्रग्रहणे ह्यर्थे शब्दशब्दः प्रसिद्धः। ते च श्रोत्रग्रहणा (ŚVT^Ra, ad ŚV sphoṭa 2, 442,20–21) ◆ श्रोत्रग्रहणे ह्यर्थे शब्दशब्दः प्रसिद्धः (NM^Va, I 399,5–6, NM 3)

92 नैतदेवम् … -ग्रहणत्वात् ∗ श्रोत्रग्राह्यतापि च सत्त्वगुणत्वशब्दत्ववर्णत्वातिव्यापिनी न शब्दलक्षणम् (SphS, 3cd, 75,2)

Notes from editions

93 शब्दकार्यं ∗ अर्थप्रतीतिः ॥ (NM^Va)

M K P C S O Q V Ga Va

90 ननु] न तु O

90 न] om. V^{pc}O

90 शब्द-¹] om. S

90 वर्णा] वर्णं O ◆ वर्ण Q V^{ac}

90 ह्यर्थे] अर्थे O

91–94 प्रसिद्धः … स शब्दः] प्र/// M

91 ते] त एव Va ◆ n.a. M

92 -ग्रहणत्वात्] P^{pc}K ◆ -ग्रहणात् P^{ac} C V^{ac} S Q ◆ -ग्रहण- O ◆ -ग्रहणत्वे V^{pc} ◆ -ग्रहणात्मनो V^{pc} Ga ◆ ग्रहणात्मनो भावात् Va ◆ n.a. M

92–93 निर्झर- … -कार्य-] om. O

93 निर्वर्तकत्वानु-] निर्वर्तनानु- GBh

93–94 तस्माद् … एव शब्दः] om. P^{ac}

94–96 च स्फोटाद् … वादीः] प्रतिपत्ति/// ///दीः M

8.2.1.3 [लिङ्गादीनामशब्दत्वम्]

ननु ' एवं सति धूमादीनामपि अर्थप्रतिपत्तिहेतुत्वाच्छब्दत्वं प्राप्नोति ॥
मैवं वादीः ' अथ गौरित्यत्र श्रौत्रे प्रतिभासे बहवोऽर्थाः प्रतिभासन्ते । तत्र

Granthibhaṅga

96 **अथ गौरित्यत्र श्रोत्रे प्रतिभास इति** । भाष्यकृता हि अथ गौरित्यत्र कः शब्द इत्युक्तम् । अस्य चार्थः । गौरित्यत्र ज्ञाने ये प्रतिभासन्ते जातिगुणक्रियावर्णस्फोटादयोऽर्थास्तेषु मध्ये कः शब्द इति । गौरिति ज्ञाने वर्णाः ' वर्णाभिव्यङ्ग्यस्फोटः ' तद्वाच्यश्चार्थो जात्यादिः ' तदेकार्थसमवेताश्च गुणक्रियादयः प्रतिभासन्त एवेति ॥

Testimonia

95 ननु एवं … प्राप्नोति ✳ अग्न्यादीन् गमयन्तोऽपि शब्दा धूमादयो न हि (ŚV^{Ra}, sphoṭa 7ab) ◆ यदि तावद् गौरिति श्रोत्रविज्ञानप्रतिभासनिरपेक्षमर्थप्रतिपत्तिहेतुत्वमेव केवलं स्फोटस्य शब्दत्वे कारणम्, ततो धूमादेरपि शब्दत्वप्रसङ्ग इत्याह । अग्न्यादीन् इत्यर्धेन (ŚVT^{Ra}, sphoṭa 7) ◆ नन्वेवं धूमादयोऽपि धूमकेतनादिप्रत्ययोपदर्शितसामर्थ्यातिशयाः शब्दतामश्नुवीरन् (SphS, 3ab, 73,8)

96–97 अथ गौरित्यत्र … इत्युपसंहृते ✳ अथ गौरित्येतस्मिन् विज्ञाने श्रोत्रे बहवोऽर्थाः प्रतिभासन्ते । तत्र कस्तेषां शब्द इत्युपक्रम्य येनोच्चरितेनार्थप्रत्ययो भवति स शब्द इत्युपसंहृतम् (ŚVT^{Ra}, sphoṭa 3)

96 अथ … प्रतिभासन्ते ✳ अथ गौरित्यत्र कः शब्दः । (VKG, 38,3) ◆ न वाऽप्रत्यायकत्वात् स्यादेकवर्णेष्वशब्दता । (ŚV^{Ra}, sphoṭa 7cd) ◆ अथ गौरित्यस्मिन् विज्ञाने श्रौत्रे बहूनां प्रतिभासमानानां यस्यार्थप्रतिपत्तिहेतुत्वं स शब्द इति । ततः गौरित्येकस्मिन् पदे एकैकस्य वर्णस्फोटस्य तन्नास्तीति शब्दत्वं न स्यादित्याह । न चाप्रत्यायकत्वमित्यर्धेन । (ŚVT^{Ra}, sphoṭa 7)

96 अथ गौरित्यत्र ✳ VMBh^{Ki}, vol. 1, p. 1,6

Notes from editions

95 एवं सति ✳ श्रोत्राग्राह्यत्वेऽपि अर्थप्रतीतिजनकत्वमात्रात् "शब्द"पद वाच्यत्वे ॥ (NM^{Va})

M K P C S O Q V Ga Va

95 सति] om. P ◆ n.a. M
95 धूमादीनामपि] धूमादीनां K ◆ M *n.a.*
95 -प्रतिपत्ति-] P K ◆ -प्रतीति- C S Q V O Ga Va ◆ M *n.a.*
96 अथ] अयं Q
96 अत्र] अव V^{ac} ; एव Q O n.a. M
96 श्रौत्रे] P ◆ श्रोत्रे K GBh ◆ श्रोत्र- C S Q V^{ac} O ◆ श्रोत्रज- V^{pc} Ga Va ◆ n.a. M
96 गौः … बहवो] गौ/// /// बहवो M
96–103 प्रतिभासन्ते … -प्रतिपत्तिम्] प्रतिभासन्ते/// ///प्रतिपत्तिम् M

96 श्रौत्रे ✳ The received reading, *śrautre pratibhāse*, is found only in P , though confirmed in ŚVT^{Ra}, sphoṭa 7. At line 133 below, however, the expression *śrautre pratyaye* is supported by

कस्तेषां शब्द इत्युपक्रम्य यतोऽर्थप्रतिपत्तिः स शब्द इत्युपसंहृते कुतो धूमादीनां शब्दत्वशङ्कावकाशः ॥

8.2.1.4 [स्फोटव्यञ्जकत्वम्]

8.2.1.4.1 [वर्णप्रत्यायकत्वेऽन्यथासिद्धत्वम्]

ननु च । इयमर्थप्रतीतिर्वर्णेषु भवत्सु भवन्ती तेष्वभवत्सु चाभवन्ती तानुत्सृज्य कथं स्फोटकार्यतामुपयायात् ॥

उच्यते । अनन्यथासिद्धं हि तद्भावभावित्वं तत्कार्यतामवगमयति । नान्यथा-

Testimonia

99 ननु … चाभवन्ती ✻ न गौणोऽक्षरेषु निमित्तभावः, तद्भावे भावात्तदभावे चाभावात् । (VKG, 40,3)

Notes from editions

97 उपसंहृते ✻ "अथ गौरित्यत्र कः शब्दः? गकारौकारविसर्जनीया इत्युपवर्षः" इति शाबरभाष्यम् ॥ (NM^{Va})

M K P C S O Q V Ga Va

97 इत्युपक्रम्य … स शब्द] om. K ◆ n.a. M
97 इत्युपक्रम्य] P C Q V O Ga Va ◆ इति चोपक्रम्य S ◆ n.a. M K
98 शब्दत्व-] शब्द- O ◆ n.a. M
99 भवत्सु] om. V^{ac} Q ◆ n.a. M
99 चाभवन्ती] अभवन्ती S ◆ n.a. M
99–100 तानुत्सृज्य] तावुत्सृज्य K ◆ n.a. M
100 -कार्यताम्] -कार्यन् ताम् K ◆ n.a. M
100 उपयायात्] उपेयात् K Q ◆ n.a. M
101 हि] om. V Ga Va ;n.a. M

a larger part of the tradition. The reading *śrotre pratibhāse*, preserved in the GBh and in K, seems more difficult to construe and was simplified in C and the rest of the vulgata in two different ways. The GBh reading may imply a nested locative, a synaesthesia of an "image in the ear".

100 -कार्यताम् ✻ The full sentence, in K, would read *tau* [*vartamānāvartamānau varṇau*] *utsrjya katham sphoṭakaryam tām arthapratītim upeyāt.*

NM^Va, 150 सिद्धम् । इदं त्वन्यथासिद्धम् । का पुनरन्यथासिद्धिः । स्फोटव्यञ्जकत्वाद्वर्णानां तदानन्तर्यमर्थप्रतीतेरुपप्लवते । वर्णाभिव्यक्तः स्फोटोऽर्थप्रतिपत्तिमादधाति । भ्राम्यति जनो वर्णैरियमर्थप्रतीतिरुत्पादितेति ॥

8.2.1.4.2 [वर्णानां स्फोटव्यञ्जकत्वे कल्पनाद्वैविध्यम्]

ननु ' स्फोटव्यक्तावपीदानीं वर्णानां क्व गतास्ते व्यस्तसमस्तविकल्पाः । आह

Testimonia

102 इदं त्वन्यथासिद्धम् ✱ गौणोऽन्यथाप्रसिद्धो वा प्रयुज्येतान्यथा यदि । (ŚV^Ra, sphoṭa 123ab)

105 ननु … -विकल्पाः ✱ नन्वर्थाभिव्यक्ताविव शब्दाभिव्यक्तावपि तुल्यः प्रसङ्गः सर्वः । तदुक्तम् । यस्यानवयवः … (SphS, 17, 88.3) ◆ यश्चायमर्थप्रतिपत्तौ वर्णानां पर्यनुयोगेन उक्तः, नैकैकस्य, नापि संभूय युगपत् क्रमेण वा इत्यादि, स पदस्फोटाभिव्यक्तावपि भवत्पक्षे ध्वनीनां वर्णानां वा तुल्य इत्याह । यस्येति (ŚVT^Ra, sphoṭa 91) ◆ तद्व्यञ्जकत्वान्न वैयर्थ्यमिति चेत्, न, समानदोषत्वात् । ये दोषा अर्थव्यञ्जकत्वे वर्णानाम्, स्फोटव्यञ्जकत्वे कथं न ? (NBhū, 274.12–13)

Notes from editions

102 इदं ✱ वर्णानां अर्थप्रत्यायकत्वम् ॥ (NM^Va)

M K P C S O Q V Ga Va

102 इदं त्वन्यथासिद्धम्] om. P ◆ n.a. M
102 पुनरन्यथासिद्धिः] पुनरस्यान्यथसिद्धिः P ◆ n.a. M
103 -प्रतीते-] -प्रतीति- O ◆ n.a. M
103 -रुपप्लवते] -रुपपत्तेः K ◆ n.a. M
103 वर्णाभिव्यक्तः] वर्णाभिव्यक्ते स्फोटे K ◆ n.a. M
103 र्थ-] P K Ga Va ◆ र्थे C S Q O ◆ र्थो V ◆ n.a. M
103 आदधाति] S Q V O Ga Va ◆ ///दधाति P ◆ आदधति M K C
104–107 जनो … स्फोटो] जनो/// /// स्फोटो M
104 अर्थप्रतीतिरुत्पादिता] उत्पादिता K ◆ n.a. M
105 स्फोट-] स्फोटार्त्थ- K ◆ n.a. M
105 वर्णानां] om. S ◆ n.a. M
105 गतास्ते] यतास्ते V ◆ n.a. M

103 आदधाति ✱ In the K and M reading the implicit grammatical subject would be *varṇāḥ*, so the plural *ādadhati* seems legitimate. The full sentence of K runs as follows: *sphoṭavyañjakatvād varṇānāṃ tadānantaryam arthapratīter upapatter varṇābhivyakte sphoṭe'rthapratipattim ādadhati / bhramyati jano varṇair iyam utpāditeti.*

105 स्फोट- ✱ With *sphotārttha*, K may be influenced by SphS, 3ab, 73,8, quoted above.

च भट्टः '

यस्यानवयवः स्फोटो व्यज्यते वर्णबुद्धिभिः ।
सोऽपि पर्यनुयोगेन नैवानेन विमुच्यते ॥ इति ॥

भाष्यकृतापि ' ननु संस्कारकल्पनायामदृष्टकल्पना इत्याशङ्क्य प्रतिविहितं NMShu, 340

Granthibhaṅga

109 संस्कारकल्पनायामदृष्टकल्पनेति । बहुभिर्ज्ञानैरेकस्य प्रसिद्धस्मरणरूपकार्यपरिहा[157v]रेणार्थप्रतिपत्तिजनकस्य जननं संस्कारस्येति कल्पना ॥

Testimonia

107–108 यस्यानवयवः … विमुच्यते ∗ ŚVRa, sphoṭa 91

109–110 ननु … शब्दकल्पना च ∗ ननु संस्कारकल्पनायामपि ग्रदृष्टकल्पना । उच्यते । शब्दकल्पनायां सा च शब्दकल्पना च ॥ (VKG, 40,11) ◆ तेन संस्कारसद्भावो नानेनैवं प्रकल्प्यते । तस्यार्थबुद्धिहेतुत्वमदृष्टं केवलं कृतम् ॥ शब्दपक्षेऽपि तच्चैतददृष्टत्वान्न मुच्यते । कार्यबोधनशक्तत्वं तुल्यं संस्कारशब्दयोः ॥ (ŚVRa, sphoṭa 103–104) ◆ ननु स्मरणान्यथानुपपत्तिकल्पितस्य संस्कारस्यार्थप्रतिपत्त्यन्यथानुपपत्त्या शक्तिकल्पनायां स्फोटकल्पनैव वरमित्याशङ्क्याह । तेन संस्कारसद्भावः इति । मम वर्णस्मरणान्यथानुपपत्त्यावगत एव संस्कारात्मके धर्मिणि शक्तिमात्रकल्पना । तव त्वर्थप्रतिपत्त्यन्यथानुपपत्त्या धर्मिणोऽपि स्फोटास्य कल्पनेति विशेषः ॥ सा च संस्कारस्य शक्तिः कल्पयित्वापि स्फोटं भवत्पक्षे स्फोटाभिव्यक्तौ परिकल्पनीयैवेति कल्पनागौरवमित्याशङ्क्याह । शब्दपक्षेऽपीति ॥ (ŚVTRa, sphoṭa 103–104)

Notes from editions

107–108 यस्यानवयवः … विमुच्यते ∗ श्लोकवार्तिके स्फोटवादे श्लो० ९१ । यच्च वर्णानां प्रत्येकं न वाचकत्वमितरवर्णोच्चारणवैयर्थ्यापत्तेः न वा समस्तानां वर्णानामुच्चरितप्रध्वंसितया समुदायासम्भवात् इति वर्णानाम् ग्रर्थबोधकत्वे यद् दूषणं तत्स्फोटवादिमतेऽपि समानम् तथाहि प्रत्येकं वर्णा न स्फोटव्यञ्जका इतरवर्णोच्चारणवैयर्थ्यात् न समुदिताः तेषां उच्चरितप्रध्वंसितया समुदायायोगादित्यर्थः । (NMShu)

109–110 ननु … शब्दकल्पना च ∗ शाबरभाष्ये ग्र० १ पा० १ सू० ५ । शब्दकल्पनायां वर्णातिरिक्तस्फोटरूपशब्दकल्पनायां सा स्फोटाभिव्यक्तये संस्कारकल्पना ग्रतिरिक्तस्फोटरूपशब्दकल्पना चेत्यर्थः । (NMShu) ◆ पदस्फोटवाक्यस्फोटाद्यभिव्यक्त्यर्थं श्रुतचराणां तेषां संस्कारस्य हेतुत्वं कल्पनीयम् । पुनस्तैः स्फोटः, ततः शब्दबोधः । एवं चेत् संस्कारा एव शब्दबोधजनिका भवन्तु, "तद्धेतोरेव तद्धेतुत्वे मध्ये किं तेन" इति न्यायात् ॥ (NMVa)

M K P C S O Q V Ga Va

107 व्यज्यते] व्यज्यतो V^{ac} S

108 पर्यनुयोगेन नैवानेन] पर्यनुयोगे नैवानेन V^{pc}O

109–110 -दृष्टकल्पना … स्फोटव्यक्तौ] -दृष्टकल्प/// ///तस्य व्यक्तौ M

शब्दकल्पनायां सा च शब्दकल्पना च इति, नैष दोषः। न स्फोटव्यक्तौ ते विकल्पाः प्रभवन्ति ॥

कुतः ॥

8.2.1.4.3 [वर्णानां स्फोटव्यञ्जकत्वम्]

एके तावदाचक्षते, प्रथमवर्णश्रवणवेलायामेव स्फोटोऽभिव्यक्तः। न च द्वितीयादिवर्णवैफल्यं, तदवगतेरेवातिशयकरणात्। यथा रत्नपरीक्षकाणां

Granthibhaṅga

110 **सा च शब्दकल्पना चेति**। सा च संस्कारकल्पना च, तथाविधसंस्कारकल्पनां विना क्रमभाविभिर्वर्णैः स्फोटस्याभिव्यङ्क्तुमशक्यत्वात्। शब्दस्य च निरवयवस्यैकस्याक्रमस्यानुपलभ्यमानस्य कल्पना ॥

Testimonia

114–116 यथा … तत्त्वम् ∗ यथा रत्नपरीक्षिणः परीक्षमाणस्य प्रथमसमधिगमानुपाख्यातमनुपाख्येयरूपप्रत्ययोपाहितसंस्काररूपाहितविशेषायां बुद्धौ क्रमेण चरमे चेतसि चकास्ति रत्नतत्त्वम् ॥ (SphS, 98,4–6) ◆ तद् यथा रत्नपरीक्षिणः पुनः पुना रत्नतत्त्वमीक्षमाणस्य रत्नदर्शनानि प्रत्येकं रत्नस्वरूपम् अवगाहमानान्यपि सहसैव न समानासमानजातीयव्यावृत्तं रत्नतत्त्वमवभासयन्ति, किन्तु पञ्चषदर्शनजनितभावनासचिवचेतोलब्धजन्मनि चरमे चेतसि चकास्ति रत्नतत्त्वम्। (TB, 63,12–15)

Notes from editions

113 स्फोटोऽभिव्यक्तो भवति ∗ स्फोटस्य अखण्डत्वात् प्रथममेवाभिव्यज्यते ॥ (NM[Va])

M K P C S O Q V Ga Va

110 न] ननु K ◆ n.a. M

110 स्फोट-] स्फोटस्य M K

110 ते] P M K ◆ om. C S Q V O Ga Va

112 कुतः] om. K

113 वेलायामेव] P M K Va ◆ वेलायां C S Q V O Ga

113 भिव्यक्तः] ऽभिव्यक्तो भवति V^{pc} Ga Va

114 तदवगते-] P M K V^{pc} Ga Va ◆ तदनुगते- C S Q O V^{ac}

114–115 तदवगते- … -दर्शने] तदवग/// ///ने M

114 -करणात्] -कारणात् K ◆ n.a. M

114 रत्नपरीक्षकाणां] P C S V O Q Va Ga ◆ रत्न---आकाले विचारचतुराणां K ◆ n.a. M

113 एके ∗ Here the view attributed to *eke* reflects Maṇḍanamiśra's, though no parallel passages are found in the SphS.

114–116 यथा … तत्त्वम् ∗ The example of the gem can also be seen in VP[Rau], 1.35, where Bhartṛhari seems to use it to argue for repeated practice, which cannot be always replaced by logic rationality.

प्रथमदर्शने रत्नरूपममलं प्रकाशमानमपि पुनः पुनः परीक्षमाणानां चरमे चेतसि चकास्ति निरवद्यं रत्नतत्त्वं । एवमिहापि प्रथमवर्णश्रुत्या व्यक्तेऽपि स्फोटे स्फुटतरप्रतीत्यैव वर्णान्तराणि प्रयोक्ष्यन्त इति ॥

8.2.1.4.4 [ध्वनीनां स्फोटव्यञ्जकत्वम्]

अपरे तु वदन्ति । ध्वनय एव स्फोटस्य व्यञ्जकाः । NM^{Va}, 151

Granthibhaṅga

118 अपरे तु वदन्तीत्यादिना वर्णा एव पारमार्थिका न सन्ति । कुतस्तेषां क्रमेण सामस्त्येन वा स्फोटाभिव्यक्तौ व्यापारः ॥

Testimonia

118 ध्वनय … व्यञ्जकाः ∗ इन्द्रियस्यैव संस्कारः शब्दस्यैवोभयस्य वा । क्रियते ध्वनिभिर्वादास्त्रयोऽभिव्यक्तिवादिनाम् ॥ (VP^{Rau}, 1.80) ◆ ध्वनयो हि नाम संयोगविभागविशेषिता वायवः वायुवृत्तयो वा संयोगविभागाः (NM^{Va}, NM 4, I 527,16)

Notes from editions

118 स्फोटस्य च ∗ चकारात् वर्णपरिग्रहः । परन्तु वर्णाः अपरमार्थाः, स्फोटस्तु परमार्थः । मणिकृपाणाद्यभिव्यङ्ग्ये मुखे सत्यत्वं, श्यामदीर्घतादावसत्यत्वमिति एकाभिव्यञ्जकव्यङ्ग्यत्वेऽपि विशेषः स्पष्टः ॥ (NM^{Va})

M K P C S O Q V Ga Va

115 -दर्शने] दर्शनेन P
115 रत्न-] om. P^{ac}
115 -रूपममलं] -रूपमलं K
115 प्रकाशमान-] अप्रकाशमान- Ga Va
115 परीक्षमाणानां] परीक्षकाणां P^{ac}
115 चरमे] चरम- M K ◆ चरमं Q
116–118 -श्रुत्या … ध्वनय] -श्रुत्या /// ///ध्वनय M
116 पि] om. K O ◆ n.a. M
117 -प्रतीत्यैव] P C S Q V O ◆ -प्रतीत्यै Ga Va ◆ n.a. M
117 प्रयोक्ष्यन्त] प्रयोज्यन्ते O ◆ n.a. M
118 स्फोटस्य] P M K C S ◆ स्फोटस्य च Q V O Ga Va

118 अपरे तु ∗ Here the view attributed to *apare* seems to reflect Bhartṛhari's.

118 ध्वनय … व्यञ्जकाः ∗ Bhartṛhari (VP^{Rau}, 1.77–81) mentions three versions of the process of manifestation of the *sphoṭa* by physical sounds, along with mental dispositions : (a) sounds produce a mental disposition in the hearing faculty ; (b) the disposition is already present in sounds ; (c) the disposition belongs to both sounds and hearing faculty. Jayanta, however, does not elaborate on the role of dispositions in relation to *dhvani*-s.

तैश्च मरुद्भिरनवयव एष स्फोटोऽभिव्यज्यमानस्ताल्वादिस्थानकरणसंयोगोपाधिवशोपप्लवमाननानाकारगकारादिभागयोगीव प्रतिभासते । मरुतां चञ्चलत्वादुच्चरितप्रध्वंसिनस्ते काल्पनिका भागा भासन्ते । दृष्टं चोपाधिवशादसत्यमपि रूपमवभासमानम् ' यथा कृपाणमणिदर्पणादिव्यञ्जकभेदेन

Granthibhaṅga

119 ननु ध्वनयोऽपि स्फोटस्य ध्वननात् प्रका[p.160]शनाद्वर्णा एव । नेत्याह । **तैश्च मरुद्भिरिति** ॥

120 **नानाकारगकारादिभागयोगीवेति** । कथमिति चेत्तदाह । **ताल्वादिस्थानकरणेति** । वायूनां यो विशिष्टैः स्थानकरणैः संयोगः स एवोपाधिस्तथाविधोपप्लुतरूपप्रदर्शकः ॥

Testimonia

122–123 यथा … वदनस्येति ✻ अथ मुखादिषु खङ्गादिधर्मारोपवद् व्यञ्जकधर्म एव शब्देऽपि आरोप्यते । (NBhū, 408,7–8) ◆ ध्वनयस्तु तुल्यस्थानकरणलब्धजन्मतया परस्परविसदृशतत्तत्पदवाक्यव्यञ्जकानेकविधध्वनिसादृश्येन अन्योन्यविसदृशतत्तत्पदवाक्यसादृश्यानि आपादयन्तः सादृश्योपधानभेदाद् एकमप्यनवयवमपि नानावर्णात्मेवावयवीव चावभासयन्ति, मुखमिव मणिकृपाणदर्पणादयो नियतस्थानमनुपप्लवम् एकमनेकमिवानेकविधस्थानमिव वर्णपरिमाणसंस्थानभेदोपप्लवमिव दर्शयन्ति ॥ (TB, 63,3–6)

M K P C S O Q V Ga Va

119 एष] P C S Q V O Ga ◆ एव M ◆ एव ते K ◆ एव एष Va

119 भिव्यज्यमान-] भिव्यञ्जमान- S V^{ac}

119–120 -संयोगोपाधि-] -संप्रयोगोपाधि- M K

120–121 वशोपप्लवमान- … -दुच्चरित-] वशोपप्लव/// ///दुच्चरित- M

120 -नानाकार-] नाकार- K O ◆ n.a. M

120 -योगीव] -योगी च Q ◆ n.a. M

120–121 चञ्चलत्वा-] च चलत्वा- K ◆ n.a. M

121 उच्चरित-] P M K C ◆ उच्चारित- S Q V O Ga Va

121 ते] P M C S ◆ के K ◆ ते तं Q O Ga Va ◆ तं V^{ac} ◆ सो तं V^{pc}

121 काल्पनिका भागा] P M K C S ◆ काल्पनिका भावा Q V^{ac} O ◆ काल्पनिकाकारम् V^{pc}-Ga Va

121 भासन्ते] अवभासयन्ते V^{pc}Ga Va

121–122 चोपाधिवशाद्] चोपाधिवशाः सत्यमपि K

122–123 रूपमवभासमानम् … शब्दो] रूपमवभा/// ///ब्दो M

श्यामदीर्घादिरूपं वदनस्येति । नादात्मकोऽपि हि शब्दो वीणावेणुमृदङ्गपटहादिव्यञ्जकभेदेन नानात्वमुपगच्छन् दृश्यते । तस्मान्न पारमार्थिका एव ते वर्णा न च स्फोटस्य व्यञ्जका इति क्व व्यस्तसमस्तविकल्पाः प्रभवेयुः । उपाधिभेदेन प्रतिभासमाना असत्याकाराश्च तेऽर्थप्रत्ययान्वयव्यतिरेकानुविधायिनो दृश्यन्ते ॥

तेन यदुच्यते शब्दकल्पनायां कल्पनाद्वैगुण्यमिति तत्रैकगुणापि कल्पना नास्ति का कथा द्वैगुण्यस्य इति ॥

तस्मात् स्फोटात्मकादेव शब्दादर्थप्रत्ययः । वर्णानुविधायित्वं तु तस्यान्यथासिद्धमिति सिद्धम् ॥

Granthibhaṅga

123 नादात्मकोऽपीति । नादात्मकः अवाचकः ॥

M K P C S O Q V Ga Va

123 -रूपं] रूपे C ◆ n.a. M
123 वदनस्येति] P K ◆ वदनस्य C S Q V O Ga Va ◆ n.a. M
123 पि हि] K P^{pc} ◆ हि C S Q V O Ga Va ◆ n.a. M
125 एव ते] एते M^{pc}K
125–126 वर्णा … -प्रत्ययान्वय] व/// ///यान्वय M
125 स्फोटस्य] स्फोट- K ◆ n.a. M
125 व्यस्तसमस्त-] P K ◆ समस्तव्यस्त- C S Q V O Ga Va ◆ n.a. M
126 -भेदेन] -भेद- K ◆ n.a. M
126 -श्च तेऽर्थ-] P C S V O Q Va Ga ◆ श्चार्थ- K ◆ n.a. M
126 -प्रत्ययान्वय-] P C Q V O Ga Va ◆ -प्रत्यया अन्वय- S ◆ -व्यत्ययान्वय- K ◆ ///यान्वय- M
128 -द्वैगुण्यम्] -वैगुण्यम् K
128–131 तत्रैकगुणापि … तस्यान्यथासिद्धम्] तत्रै/// ///थासिद्धम् M
129 का कथा] कथं C ◆ n.a. M
129 द्वैगुण्यस्य] वैगुण्यस्य O ◆ n.a. M
131 -सिद्धमिति सिद्धम्] -सिद्धम् M K

8.2.2 [स्फोटप्रत्यक्षगोचरत्वम्]

NM^{Va}, 152

अपि च ' तार्किकाणामनुमानप्रियत्वात् तत्परितोषायेदमनुमानमभ्यधायि ' न परमार्थतः। परमार्थतस्तु श्रौत्रे प्रत्यये प्रतिभासमानः प्रत्यक्ष एव स्फोटः॥ आह ' किमिदमपूर्वं तस्करचरितं वर्तते ' वर्णाः प्रत्यक्षमुपलभ्यमाना अपि दुर्भगा न प्रत्यक्षाः ' स्फोटः पुनरनवभासमानोऽपि सुभगः प्रत्यक्ष इति॥ उच्यते ' न ब्रूमो वर्णा न प्रत्यक्षा इति। ते पुनरसन्तोऽपि उपा-

Testimonia

136–141 ते पुनरसन्तो ... बाधकाभावात् ∗ अवर्णकुलशब्दोऽपि स्थानसाम्याद्वनादिवत्। समुदायार्थवाचीति न जातिवचनो भवेत्॥ (ŚV^{Ra}, sphoṭa 49) ◆ अवर्णकुलशब्दोऽपि दीर्घाद्युपाधिभेदेन भिन्नत्वाद्वनादिशब्दवदेकस्यानावच्छिन्नस्य समुदायमाह, न जातिमिति दर्शयति। अवर्णेति।

Notes from editions

135 दुर्भगाः ∗ दौर्भाग्यवन्तः। सुभागः। सौभाग्यवान्॥ (NM^{Va})

M K P C S O Q V Ga Va

132 तत्-] M K V^{pc} Ga Va ◆ om. P C S Q O V^{ac}
132–142 तत्परि- ... एकार्थ-] तत्परि/// /// एकार्थ- M
133 परमार्थतः] परमार्थितः V ◆ n.a. M
133 परमार्थतस्तु] परमार्थस्तु S Va ◆ n.a. M
133 श्रौत्रे] श्रोत्रे K Q ◆ n.a. M
133 प्रतिभासमानः] प्रतिभासमान K ◆ परिभासमानः O ◆ n.a. M
134 -पूर्वं] -पूरन् K ◆ n.a. M
134 तस्करचरितं] तस्कराचरितं V^{pc} Ga Va ◆ n.a. M
134 प्रत्यक्षमुपलभ्यमाना] वर्णाप्रत्य⁻⁻पलभ्यमाना K ◆ n.a. M
135 दुर्भगा] दुर्भग वा K^{ac} ◆ दुर्भगः वा K^{pc} ◆ n.a. M
135 न प्रत्यक्षाः] om. Q^{ac} ◆ न प्रत्यक्षः V O ◆ प्रत्यक्षाः C ◆ n.a. M
135 -नवभासमानो] -नवभानवभासमानो P^{pc} ◆ -वभासमानो V O ◆ n.a. M
135 इति] इत्यत्र S ◆ n.a. M
136 न²] om. O ◆ n.a. M

133 श्रौत्रे ∗ For the reading *śrautre pratyaye* cf. 96 above.

134 प्रत्यक्षमुपलभ्यमाना ∗ In K the sentence reads *kim idam apūran taskaracaritaṃ varttate varṇāḥ varṇāpratya⁻⁻palabhyamānā api durbhagaḥ vā na pratyakṣāḥ*. Although its sense is unclear to me, I still kept the variants in the critical apparatus, because here M is not available here and thus K is the only witness of β.

धिवशाद्वदनदैर्घ्यादिवद् अवभासन्ते । शब्दस्त्वेको निरवयवः प्रतीयते । तथा च पदमिति वाक्यमिति एकाकारा प्रतीतिरस्ति । न च भिन्ना वर्णास्तस्यामालम्बनीभवन्ति । न हि सामान्यप्रत्ययो व्यक्त्यालम्बनोऽवयविप्रत्ययो वावयवालम्बनः । न च सेनावनादिबुद्धिवद् अयथार्था पदवाक्यबुद्धिः ' बाधकाभावात् ॥

8.2.2.1 [शब्दैकत्वानौपाधिकत्वम्]

एकार्थप्रत्यायकत्वोपाधिकृतेयमेकाकारा बुद्धिरिति चेत् ' एकार्थप्रतीति- NM^{Shu}, 341

Testimonia

(ŚVT^{Ra}, sphoṭa 49) ◆ यथा गौरित्येकमिदं पदमित्येकपदावभासिनी धीरस्ति लौकिकपरीक्षकाणाम् । न चेयमनालम्बना, नापि वर्णालम्बना, तेषां नानात्वात् । न च सेनावनवदौपाधिकी … । (TB, 70,5–7)

140–141 सेना … बुद्धिः ⁕ एकत्वोपचारो वा वनादिवत् । (SphS, 23, 95,3)

142 एकार्थ- … बुद्धिरिति ⁕ गौरित्येकमतित्वं तु नैवास्माभिर्निवार्यते । तद्ग्राह्यैकार्थताभ्यां च शब्दे स्यादेकतामतिः ॥ (ŚV^{Ra}, sphoṭa 120) ◆ यदपि केवलं प्रतीयमानस्यैव गकारादेरेकार्थसंश्लेषकारितमेकाकारं विज्ञानमुपजायते, तदपि वर्णत्रयात्मकैकगोपदालम्बनम् । एकपदत्वं चैकार्थकत्वेनैकबुद्धिग्राह्यत्वेन चेत्याह । गौरित्येकमतित्वं त्विति ॥ (ŚVT^{Ra}, sphoṭa 120) ◆ ज्ञेये तु तद्ग्राह्यतयैकार्थकारितया वैकत्वभ्रमः । (SphS, 23, 95,2) ◆ एकबुद्धिग्राह्यतयैकार्थकारितया च शब्देष्वेकतां ब्रुवन् । (SphS, 25, 96,7)

Notes from editions

139 आलम्बनीभवन्ति ⁕ पूर्वोक्तप्रत्येकसमुदायविकल्पदुष्टत्वात् ॥Va

M K P C S O Q V Ga Va

137 प्रतीयते] प्रतीयेत S ◆ n.a. M

138 एकाकारा] एकाकार- V Ga ◆ n.a. M

138 च] om. K ◆ n.a. M

139 -स्तस्यामालम्बनी] -स्तस्यालम्बनी O ◆ n.a. M

139–140 व्यक्त्यालम्बनोऽवयविप्रत्ययो] om. O ◆ n.a. M

139–140 व्यक्त्यालम्बनो] P^{pc}K Ga Va ◆ व्यक्त्यालम्बने P^{ac} ◆ व्यक्त्यालम्बनतो C S Q ◆ व्यक्तालम्बनेतो V^{ac} ◆ व्यक्त्यालम्बनेता V^{pc} ◆ n.a. M O

140 वावयवालम्बनः] वावयवालम्बनतः S ◆ n.a. M

142 प्रत्यायकत्वोपाधि-] M K P^{ac} C ◆ प्रत्यायवत्वोपाधि- P^{pc}O ◆ प्रत्यायकोपाधि- S ◆ प्रत्यवयवतोपाधि- V ◆ प्रत्ययत्वोपाधि Q ◆ प्रत्ययवत्वोपाधि Ga Va

142 -कारा] -कार- M K

रिदानीं कुतस्त्या । पदवाक्यप्रतीतिपूर्विका हि पदार्थवाक्यार्थप्रतीतिः ' पदार्थवाक्यार्थप्रतीत्याख्यकार्यैक्याच्च पदवाक्यबुद्धिरेकाकारेति दुरुत्तरमितरेतराश्रयत्वम् । औपाधिकत्वं च सामान्यावयविबुद्धेरपि सुवचम् ॥

बाधसन्देहरहितप्रतीतिदार्ढ्यात्तत्र तत्परिहार इति चेत् ' तदितरत्रापि समानम् । तस्मात् पदबुद्धेः पदस्फोटो वाक्यबुद्धेश्च वाक्यस्फोटो विषय इति प्रत्यक्ष एव स्फोटः । तत्र पदस्फोटात् पदार्थप्रतिपत्तिर्वाक्यस्फोटाच्च वाक्यार्थप्रतिपत्तिः ॥

8.2.3 [वाक्यस्फोटः]

8.2.3.1 [वाक्यनिरवयवत्वम्]

NM^Va, 153 आह ' यदि निरवयवः स्फोटात्मा शब्दो भवति वाक्यमपि शब्द एव '

Granthibhaṅga

145 **औपाधिकत्वं च सामान्यावयविबुद्धेरपीति** । अत्र यद्येकार्थप्रतीतिजनकत्वादेकत्वमुच्यते 'तद्'दाहदोहाद्येकार्थ[158r]कारितोपाधिनिबन्धनः सामान्यप्रत्ययोऽपीत्यतिप्रसङ्गः ॥ ◆◆◆ तद्] तदा Sha

Testimonia

144–145 पदार्थ- … इतरेतराश्रयत्वम् ⁎ तदर्थबोधाद्यदि च व्यक्तमन्योन्यसंश्रयः ॥ … पदरूपावधिविशेषमुपकल्पयन् दुरुत्तरमितरेतराश्रयमाविशति । (SphS, 26cd, 96,14–16)

145 औपाधिकत्वं … सुवचम् ⁎ यदि तावद्वर्णग्रहणसापेक्षत्वात् काल्पनिकः पदप्रत्ययः इति, जात्यादिप्रत्यया अपि कल्पनीयाः स्युरिति जात्यादीनां परमार्थसत्त्वं हीयेत । (SphS, 35, 105,13–106,1)

Notes from editions

150 वाक्यमपि शब्द एव ⁎ वाक्यस्फोटः, पदस्फोटः, वर्णफोटः इत्यनुक्रमश्चेत् वर्णपक्षेऽपि इदं

M K P C S O Q V Ga Va

145 -श्रयत्वम्] -श्रयम् P ◆ -श्रयत्वात् O
145 औपाधिकत्वं] औपाधिकं O
145 च] om. C
146 तत्परिहार] PK ◆ परिहार CSQVOGaVa ◆ n.a. M
147 -बुद्धेश्च] -बुद्धेः P
148 एव] एष V ◆ n.a. M
148 पद-] om. K ◆ n.a. M
148 -प्रतिपत्ति-] -प्रतीति- S ◆ n.a. M
148 -स्फोटाच्च] -स्फोटाद् K ◆ n.a. M
150 स्फोटात्मा] यदि स्फोटात्मा CS

तस्य पदात्मकास्त्ववयवा मा भूवन्। तस्य चेत् पदात्मानोऽवयवा भवन्ति ' पदस्यापि तर्हि वर्णात्मानोऽवयवा भवन्तु ॥

उच्यते ' किंचिदुच्छ्वसितमिव मे हृदयम्। मन्ये भविष्यत्यायुष्मतो विवेकालोकः। बोध्यमानो भोत्स्यसे किंचित्। ध्वन्युपाधिभेदप्रवृत्तवर्णभेदावभासविप्रलब्धबुद्धिं भवद्विधं बोधयितुं पदस्फोटएष निरवयवोऽस्माभिर्दर्शितः। परमार्थतस्तु पदस्फोटो वाक्यावयवभूतो नास्त्येव। निरवयवमेव वाक्यं निरवयवस्यैव वाक्यार्थस्य बोधकम्। यथा पदस्यावयवा न सन्ति तथा वाक्यस्यावयवाः पदानि इति। तथा चाहुः ' वाक्ये पदानामसत्त्वात् त-

Testimonia

154–155 ध्वन्युपाधि … ऽस्माभिर्दर्शितः ∗ यदेतत् पदपदार्थज्ञानं विभ्रमरूपमन्तराले वाक्यवाक्यार्थप्रतिपत्तेरेवोपायभूतं बोद्धव्यम्। तस्मान्निरंशत्वेऽपि वाक्यवाक्यार्थयोः प्रक्रम एव प्रथमसमय एव रूपं तयोर्नावधार्यत इति ॥ (VP[Iyer], vṛtti ad 2.410)

157–158 यथा … न पदानीति ∗ पदे न वर्णा विद्यन्ते वर्णेष्ववयवा न च। वाक्यात् पदानामत्यन्तं प्रविभागो न कश्चन ॥ (VP[Rau], 1.74)

Notes from editions

समानमेव। अतश्च पूर्वोक्तकल्पनाद्वयानतिपातः ॥ (NM[Va])

158 पदानि इति ∗ “न सन्ति” इत्याकर्षः ॥ (NM[Va])

M K P C S O Q V Ga Va

151 पदात्मानो] पदात्मनो Q^{ac} V Ga ◆ पदा/// M

152 वर्णात्मानो] वर्णात्मनो K O ◆ n.a. M

153 -मिव] P K Q Va ◆ -मेव C S V O Ga ◆ n.a. M

154 भोत्स्यसे] P M K Ga Va ◆ भोत्स्यते S ◆ वोत्स्यसे C Q V^{ac}

154 किंचित्] किञ्चित्तु M K

154–155 उपाधि- … निरवयवो] उपा/// ///वो M

155 -विप्रलब्ध-] विपुलं O ◆ n.a. M

155 एष] एव S Q ◆ n.a. M

155–156 निरवयवो … वाक्यं] om. S

156 परमार्थतस्तु] परमार्थितस्तु V ◆ परमार्थस्तु K ◆ n.a. S

156–158 वाक्यं … वाक्ये] वाक्यं/// ///क्ये M

158 पदानि इति] न पदानीति S ◆ n.a. M

158 -मसत्त्वात्] -मसत्त्वात् असत्त्वं V^{pc}Ga

158–159 वाक्ये पदानामसत्त्वात् तदर्थे च पदार्थानां निरवयवौ वाक्यवाक्यार्थाविति ∗ Source unknown. The first sixteen syllables could form the first hemistich of an *anuṣṭubh*.

दर्थे च पदार्थानां निरवयवौ वाक्यवाक्यार्थाविति । अवयवकल्पनायां हि यथा वाक्यस्यावयवाः पदानि पदानामवयवा वर्णा एवं वर्णानामप्यवयवैर्भवितव्यम् । तदवयवानामप्यवयवान्तरैरिति आनन्त्यात् का व्यवस्था स्यात् । वर्णान् प्राप्य तु यद्यवयवकल्पनातो विरन्तव्यं तद्वाक्य एव विरम्यताम् । एकघनाकारा हि वाक्यार्थबुद्धिस्तथाविधादेव वाक्यादुत्पत्तुमर्हति । वृद्धव्यवहाराद्धि शब्दार्थे व्युत्पद्यन्ते व्यवहर्तारः । तत्रास्य पदस्य प्रयोग एव
NM^{Va}, 154 न केवलस्य दृश्यते ' व्यवहारानङ्गत्वात् । वाक्यं तु प्रयोगार्हमिति तत्रैव व्युत्पत्तिस्तत एवार्थसम्प्रत्ययः । अवयवप्रतिभासस्तु भ्रममात्रम् ॥

8.2.3.2 [वाक्यार्थनिरवयवत्वम्]

अर्थोऽपि वाक्यस्यैक एव नरसिंहाकारः । जात्यन्तरं हि नरसिंहो नाम ।

Testimonia

159–161 अवयवकल्पनायां … भवितव्यम् ✳ पदानि वाक्ये तान्येव वर्णास्ते च पदे यदि । वर्णेषु वर्णभागानां भेदः स्यात् परमाणुवत् ॥ (VP^{Rau}, 2.28)
167–168 अर्थोऽपि … सिंहार्थः ✳ गवये नरसिंहे चाप्येकज्ञानावृते यथा । भागं जात्यन्तरस्यैव सदृशं प्रतिपद्यते ॥ (VP^{Rau}, 2.90) ◆ सतामवयवानां हि स्याद्वा सदृशता न वा । सादृश्यं नरसिंहादौ युक्तं जात्यन्तरे सति ॥ ($\text{ŚV}^{\text{Dvā}}$, vākya 124)

Notes from editions

165 व्यवहारानङ्गत्वात् ✳ न हि पदेन व्यवहरन्ति, अपि तु वाक्येन ॥ (NM^{Va})
166 अवयव- ✳ अवयवः पदादिरूपः ॥ (NM^{Va})

M K P C S O Q V Ga Va

159 च] PMKCS ◆ om. QVOGaVa
159–161 अवयव- … अवयवान्तरै-] अव/// ///-यवान्तरै- M
160 वर्णा एवं] om. C ◆ n.a. M
161 का] क्व MK ◆ का वा C
162–164 वर्णान् … वृद्ध-] वर्णान्/// ///-द्ध- M
162 विरन्तव्यं] विरम्यते K ◆ n.a. M
163 एकघनाकारा] K ◆ एका घनाकारा P ◆ एकघटनाकारा CSQVOGaVa ◆ n.a. M
164–166 प्रयोग … प्रतिभासस्तु] प्र/// ///-सस्तु M
165 न केवलस्य] केवलस्य न K ◆ n.a. M
167 अर्थो] अर्थ O
167 पि] पि च MK
167–169 नाम … नाग-] नाम/// ///-ग- M

न तत्र नरार्थो नापि सिंहार्थः। एवं पदार्थेभ्योऽन्य एव वाक्यार्थः ' पानकादिवत्। यथा हि पानकं शर्करानागकेसरमरिचादिभ्योऽर्थान्तरमेव ' यथा च सिन्दूरहरिताललाक्षादिभ्योऽर्थान्तरमेव चित्रम् ' यथा वा षड्जर्षभगान्धारधैवतादिभ्योऽर्थान्तरमेव ग्रामरागः ' तथा पदेभ्यो वाक्यं पदार्थेभ्यो वाक्यार्थः॥

8.2.3.3 [वाक्यांशानामर्थानुगमत्वम्]

कथं तर्हि तदंशावगम इति चेत् ' कल्पनामात्रं तत् ' नासौ परमार्थः॥

Granthibhaṅga

171 अर्थान्तरमेव ग्रामराग इति। ग्रामरागो यत्रांशतया षड्जादयः स्वराः स्थिताः॥

Testimonia

170 यथा … चित्रम् ⁕ चित्रस्यैकस्य रूपस्य यथा भेदनिदर्शनैः। नीलादिभिः समाख्यानं क्रियते भिन्नलक्षणैः॥ (VP[Rau], 2.8) ◆ चित्ररूपावभासिनी च प्रख्या अवयवगतनीलादिरूपभेदेऽपि, नार्थान्तरगोचरतां जहाति। न ह्यर्थान्तरसमवायिनीलानीलादिमात्रं चित्रम्, अवयविनो नीरूपतया अचाक्षुषत्वप्रसङ्गात्। (SphS, 24, 95,19–96,1):

Notes from editions

173 तदंशावगमः ⁕ तदंशतया प्रतीतिः॥ (NM[Va])

M K P C S O Q V Ga Va

168 न तत्र] PK ◆ तत्र न CSQVOGaVa ◆ n.a. M

168 एवं] एवञ्च K ◆ n.a. M

169 हि] PK ◆ om. CSQVOGaVa ◆ n.a. M

169 पानकं] पानकः Q^{pc}Va ◆ n.a. M

169 शर्करा-] om. Q^{ac} ◆ शंकरा C ◆ n.a. M

169 -केसर-] -केशर- Ga

169 मरिचादिभ्यो] मरिचादिभ्यो भ्य O V^{ac} ◆ मरिच्यादिभ्यो Va

169 र्थान्तरमेव] र्थान्तरं P

170 -मेव²] -मिव VO

170 वा] च MK

171–172 षड्ज- … वाक्यार्थः] षड्ज-/// ///-क्यार्थः M

171–172 पदार्थेभ्यो] परार्थेभ्यो K ◆ n.a. M

173 परमार्थः] परमार्थतः P

168 एवं ⁕ The K reading with *ca* conveys the clause as an afterthought of the previous sentence, while it is instead the main issue: that the thing meant by the sentence is different from the single word-meanings, is spelled in this very sentence, beginning with *evam*.

NM[Shu], 342 तच्छब्दानुगमे तदर्थानुगमदर्शनात् पारमार्थिकत्वं भागानामिति चेत् ' न ' कूपसूपयूपानामनेकाक्षरानुगमेऽप्यर्थानुगमाभावात् । न च केवलानुगममात्रेण तत्कारणभावो वक्तुं शक्यो ' रेणुपटलानुगामितया करितुर-

Granthibhaṅga

176–177 करितुरगादिवदिति । यथा सत्सु करितुरगादिषु गच्छत्सु रेणुपटलस्योद्गमदर्शनात्तत्कारणता कल्प्यते । एवं पिपीलिकापङ्क्तिरपि कदाचिद् रेणुपटलोद्गमपूर्वभाविनी दृश्यत इति तस्या अपि तत्कारणत्वप्रसङ्गः ॥

Testimonia

175 न … अर्थानुगमाभावात् ⁕ कूप सूप यूप इति । यदि हि वर्णव्यत्ययकृतमर्थान्तरगमनं स्याद् भूयिष्ठः कूपार्थः सूपे स्यात् सूपार्थश्च कूपे कूपार्थश्च यूपे युपार्थश्च कूपे सूपर्तश्च यूपे यूपार्थश्च सूपे। (VMBh[Ki], 32,3–6) ◆न कूपसूपयूपानामन्वयोऽर्थस्य दृश्यते । अतोऽर्थान्तरवाचित्वं संघातस्यैव गम्यते ॥ (VP[Rau], 2.169) ◆ यत् कूपयूपसूपादौ समानेऽप्युपबन्धने । नास्त्यर्थानुगमः कश्चित्तत्र शब्दोऽपराध्यति ॥ (ŚV[Dvā], vākya 161)

176–177 रेणु- … -प्रसङ्गात् ⁕ एवं पिपीलिकापङ्क्ते रेणुचक्रान्वये सति । गजाश्वोपजनापायेऽप्यतादर्थ्यमशक्तितः। अस्त्येव च गजाश्वेषु सामान्यं रेणुकारणम् ॥ (ŚV[Dvā], vākya 163cd–164)

Notes from editions

176–177 रेणु- … -प्रसङ्गात् ⁕ करितुरगादौ गच्छति रेणुरुत्तिष्ठति । तत्रैव मार्गे अकस्मात् पिपीलिकापि गच्छति । अत्र पिपीलिकापि रेणूद्गमहेतुः स्यात् ॥ (NM[Va])

M K P C S O Q V Ga Va

174–176 दर्शनात् … केवलानुगम] दर्शनात्/// ///-वलानुगम M

174 -गमदर्शनात्] -गमादर्शनात् V

174 पारमार्थिकत्वं] पारमार्थिकत्वमेव P ◆ n.a. M

175 न] om. P ◆ n.a. M

175 -यूपसूपा-] P K ◆ -सूपयूपा- S Q V O Ga Va ◆ -सूपधूपा- C ◆ n.a. M

175 -मनेकाक्षरानुगमे] P ◆ -मेकाकानुगमे K ◆ -मेकाक्षरानुगमे C S Q V O Ga Va ◆ n.a. M

175 प्यर्थानु-] स‐‐र्थानु- K ◆ n.a. M

176 शक्यो] शक्यते S

176 -गामितया] -गमितय्य V O

177–178 करितुरगादिवत् … वाक्यार्थावगमोपायतया] करितुरगादिवत्/// ///वाक्यार्थोपायतया M

176–177 -तुरगादिवत्] M K Q Ga Va ◆ -तुरङ्गादिवत् P C S O ◆ -तुंगादिवत् V

गादिवत् पिपीलिकापङ्क्तेरपि दृश्यमानायास्तत्कारणत्वप्रसङ्गात् । तस्मात् प्रकृतिप्रत्ययांशवद् असत्यपदार्थपरिकल्पनं वाक्यार्थावगमोपायतयाश्रीयते । न त्वर्थस्तदीयस्तत्राश्वकर्णादिवद् उपलभ्यते ॥

8.2.3.4 [असत्यस्य सत्योपयता]

असत्यमपि हि सत्योपायतां प्रतिपद्यमानं दृश्यते । अलीका हि दं-

Granthibhaṅga

179 **अश्वकर्णादिवदिति** । अश्वकर्णाख्या ओषधिः । न तत्राश्वार्थः कश्चिन्नापि कर्णार्थः इति ॥

Testimonia

177–179 तस्मात् … उपलभ्यते * तस्मादनर्थकैरेव विना जातिगुणान्वयात् । प्रकृतिप्रत्ययाद्यन्तपदभागविवर्जितैः ॥ वाक्यैरेव विशीष्टोऽर्थः स्वतन्त्रैः प्रतिपाद्यते । भागशः कथितोपायैरश्वकर्णाजकर्णवत् ॥ (ŚV^{Dvā}, vākya 180–181)

179 न … उपलभ्यते * यथाश्वकर्ण इत्युक्ते विनैवाश्वेन गम्यते । कश्चिदेव विशिष्टोऽर्थः सर्वेषु प्रत्ययस्तथा ॥ (VP^{Rau}, 2.36)

180 असत्यम् … दृश्यते * सत्यं वस्तु तदाकारैरसत्यैरवधार्यते । असत्योपाधिभिः शब्दैः सत्यमेवाभिधीयते ॥ (VP^{Rau}, 3.2 dravya 2) ◆ शशशृङ्गाद्यपोद्धृत्य वाक्यार्थो न हि दृश्यते ॥ असत्यैर्गम्यमानेऽर्थे सत्यता नेत्युदाहृतम् । स्वरूपेणासतो दृष्टं नोपायत्वं हि कस्यचित् ॥ (ŚV^{Dvā}, vākya 339–340ab) ◆ अनवयवमेव वाक्यमनाद्यविद्योपदर्शितालीकवर्णपदविभागमस्या निमित्तमिति केचित् । (TB, 61,5)

M K P C S O Q V Ga Va

177 पिपीलिकापङ्क्तेरपि] पिपीलिकादिपङ्क्तेरपि P ◆ n.a. M

178 असत्य-] PCSQ ◆ असत्य-त्य- K ◆ तदसत्य- O ◆ असत्- V Ga Va ◆ n.a. M

178 वाक्यार्थावगमोपायतया-] वाक्यार्थोपयतया- M ◆ वाक्यावगमोपायतया- O

178 -श्रीयते] श्रूयते P

180 असत्यमपि] असत्यपि O

180–181 अपि हि … चासत्यान्येव] अपि हि/// ///-त्यान्येव M

180 हि] PMK ◆ om. CSQVO Ga Va

180 -पद्यमानं] -पाद्यमानं S ◆ n.a. M

180 अलीका हि] अलीकादि- V^{ac} O ◆ n.a. M

180 अलीका हि * The example can also be understood as a compound, *alīkāhidaṃśādayaḥ*, “false (*alīka*) snake (*āhi*) bites, etc. (*daṃśādayaḥ*)”.

शादयः सत्यमरणकारणं भवन्ति । लिप्यक्षराणि चासत्यान्येव सत्यार्थ-
NM^{Va}, 155 प्रतिपत्तिमादधति ॥

स्वरूपसत्यानि तानीति चेत् ' न ' रेखारूपतया तेषामप्रतिपादकत्वात् । गकारोऽयमित्येवं गृह्यमाणा रेखा अर्थप्रत्ययहेतवः । ता येन रूपेण सत्यास्तेन नार्थप्रतिपादिकाः । येन चार्थप्रतिपादिकाः तेन न सत्या इति ॥

8.2.3.5 [प्रकृतिप्रत्ययविभागापरमार्थिकत्वम्]

ननु ' प्रकृतिप्रत्ययाद्यंशा अपि परमार्थसन्त एव ' तथा प्रतिभासाद् ' अर्थप्रत्ययहेतुत्वाच्च ॥

Notes from editions

183 स्वरूपसत्यानि तानीति चेत् ⁎ अलिदंशभ्रमः खलु सत्य एव । रेखा अपि सत्या एव ॥ (NM^{Va})

184 येन ⁎ रेखात्वेन । येन च वर्णत्वेन ॥ अलिदंशभ्रमेऽपि, भ्रमत्वेन न तस्य मरणहेतुत्वम् । अपि तु प्रमात्त्व[sic]भ्रान्त्यैव ॥ (NM^{Va})

M K P C S O Q V Ga Va

181 -कारणं] -कारणे C ◆ -कार्थकारणं K ◆ n.a. M

181 चासत्यान्येव] च सत्यान्येव V^{ac} O ◆ ¯¯सत्यान्येव K ◆ ///त्यान्येव M

182 -प्रतिपत्ति-] -प्रतीति- M K

183–184 तेषाम् … अर्थप्रत्यय-] तेषाम-/// ///त्यय- M

183 तेषामप्रति-] P M K ◆ तेषां प्रति- C S Q V^{ac} ◆ तेषां प्रतिपत्ति- O ◆ तेषामर्थाप्रति- V^{pc} Ga Va

184 -मित्येवं] -मिति हि P ◆ -मिति V^{ac} ◆ n.a. M

185–188 -प्रतिपादिकाः … अन्वाख्यानभेदेन] प्रति-/// ///अन्वाख्यानभेदेन M

185 -स्तेन नार्थ-] -स्तेनानर्थ- C

185 -प्रतिपादिकाः] P K V^{pc} Q^{ac} Ga ◆ प्रतिपादकाः C S Q^{pc} V^{ac} O Va ◆ n.a. M

185 -प्रतिपादिकाः] P V^{pc} Ga ◆ -प्रतिपादकाः K C S Q V^{ac} O Va ◆ n.a. M

185 इति] om. S ◆ n.a. M

186 -सन्त] om. K ◆ n.a. M

186 प्रतिभासाद्] प्रतिभास V ◆ n.a. M

186 अर्थ-] तदर्थ- V Ga ◆ n.a. M

नैतदेवम् ' अन्वाख्यानभेदेन तेषां स्वरूपेणेयत्तानिश्चयानुपपत्तेः । भवतीत्यत्र भूशब्दः प्रकृतिः क्वचिदन्वाख्यायते क्वचिद्भवशब्दः । प्रत्ययादेशागमगुणवृद्धिवर्णलोपाद्यन्वाख्यानविसंवादात् कः प्रकृतिप्रत्ययविभागः । कल्पनामात्रं त्वेतद् इयं प्रकृतिरेष प्रत्यय इति । एवं पदानामपि वाक्यात् कल्पनयैवापोद्धारः । तदुक्तम् '

Granthibhaṅga

189 **प्रत्ययादेशेति** । प्रत्ययविसंवादः । क्वचिल्लकारः प्रत्ययः, अन्यत्र 'त्यादय' इत्येवमन्यत्रापि ॥ ◆◆◆ त्यादय] त्वा(त्या?)दय Sha

191–192 **'वाक्यात्' कल्पनयैवेति** । कल्पनया असतामप्यनपोद्धारे वाक्यार्थस्य प्रतिपादयितुमशक्यत्वाद् । असतामपि तेषां कल्पनयोद्धृतानां रेखागवयादीनामिव सत्यार्थप्रतिपादकत्वम् ॥ ◆◆◆ वाक्यात्] वाक्यार्थ- Sha *v.l.*

Testimonia

188 अन्वाख्यानभेदेन ... निश्चयानुपपत्तेः ✳ अन्वाख्यानानि भिद्यन्ते शब्दव्युत्पत्तिकर्मसु । बहूनां संभवेऽर्थानां निमित्तं किंचिद् इष्यते ॥ (VP^Rau^, 2.170)

190–192 कल्पनामात्रं ... कल्पनयैवापोद्धारः ✳ यथा पदे विभज्यन्ते प्रकृतिप्रत्ययादयः । अपोद्धारस्तथा वाक्ये पदानामुपपद्यते ॥ (VP^Rau^, 2.10)

Notes from editions

189 -द्भव- ✳ भव इव आचरति भवति इति क्विप् ॥ (NM^Va^)

M K P C S O Q V Ga Va

188 स्वरूपेणेयत्ता-] स्वरूपेयत्ता- M K

188–197 निश्चयानुपपत्तेः ... अत्र हि] निश्चयानुप-/// ///अत्र हि M

189 -द्भव-] -द्भाव- Q V O ◆ n.a. M

190 लोपाद्यन्वा-] P K V*pc* O*pc* Ga Va ◆ लोपादन्वा- C S Q V*ac* O*ac* ◆ n.a. M

190 -ख्यान-] -ख्याने K ◆ n.a. M

190 कः] क्व K ◆ n.a. M

191 त्वेतद्] एतद् S ◆ n.a. M

191 पदानाम्] P K ◆ पदार्थानाम् C S Q V O Ga Va ◆ n.a. M

191–192 वाक्यात् कल्पनयैवापोद्धारः] K GBh ◆ वाक्यात् कल्पनयोद्धारः P ◆ वाक्यार्थपरिकल्पनयैवापोद्धारः C S Q V O Va Ga ◆ n.a. M

अपोद्धृत्यैव वाक्येभ्यः प्रकृतिप्रत्ययादिवद् ॥ इति ॥

अपि च ' पारमार्थिकत्वे पदानां नियतमविसंवादिरूपं प्रतीयेत । विसंवदति NM^{Va}, 156 तु नानानामाख्यातसाधारणवर्णसन्निवेशदर्शनात् । न नियतमेषां रूपम् । अतः काल्पनिकमेव तत् ' न वास्तवम् । न च निश्चेतुमपि तत् पार्यते । काले-

Granthibhaṅga

193 **अपोद्धृत्यैव वाक्येभ्य इति** अस्य पूर्वमर्धम् । पदं कैश्चिद्द्विधा भिन्नं चतुर्धा पञ्चधापि वा इति ॥

Testimonia

193 अपोद्धृत्यैव ... -प्रत्ययादिवद् ✱ द्विधा कैश्चित् पदं भिन्नं चतुर्धा पञ्चधापि वा । अपोद्धृत्यैव वाक्येभ्यः प्रकृतिप्रत्ययादिवत् ॥ (VP^{Rau}, 3.1 jāti 1)

Notes from editions

193 अपोद्धृत्यैव ... -प्रत्ययादिवद् ✱ वाक्यपदीये तृतीयकाण्डे श्लो॰ १ । वाक्येभ्योऽपोद्धृत्य कल्पनाबुद्ध्या पदं पृथङ् निष्कृष्य कैश्चित्पदं नामाख्यातभेदेन द्विधा भिन्नं कैश्चित्तु नामाख्यातोपसर्गनिपातभेदेन चतुर्धा कैश्चित् नामाख्यातोपसर्गनिपातकर्मप्रवचनीयभेदेन पञ्चधा स्वीकृतम् ततश्चाखण्डवाक्यव्युत्पत्तिरित्यर्थः । (NM^{Shu})

195 न नियतं तेषां रूपम् ✱ भवति इति तिङन्तमपि, भवच्छब्दः सप्तम्यन्तमपि ॥ (NM^{Va})

M K P C S O Q V Ga Va

193 अपोद्धृत्यैव ...] M K GBh ◆ पदं कैश्चिद्द्विधा भिन्नं चतुर्धा पञ्चधापि वा । अपोद्धृत्यैव ... P S V^{pc} Va Ga ◆ पंच कैश्चिद्द्विधा भिन्नं चतुर्धा पञ्चधापि वा । अपोद्धृत्यैव ... C Q V^{ac} O

193 -प्रत्ययादिवद्] -प्रत्ययावद् K ◆ n.a. M

194 प्रतीयेत] प्रतीयते O ◆ प्रतीदते C ◆ n.a. M

194 विसंवदति] P K Q V^{ac} ◆ विसंवदन्ति C S ◆ विसंवदि V^{pc} O ◆ विसंवादि Ga Va ◆ n.a. M

195 नाना-] P K C S ◆ तन O ◆ तेन Q ◆ नन V^{ac} ◆ तत् V^{pc} ◆ तत् Ga Va ◆ n.a. M

195 न] om. P ◆ n.a. M

195 नियतमेषां] P K ◆ नियतं तेषां C S Q V O Ga Va ◆ n.a. M

---

193 अपोद्धृत्यैव ✱ Although in M this portion is lost, judging from the size of the missing part of the leaf and the count of the missing *akṣara*-s one can assume that the first hemistich of the verse was not present in M, nor was it present in the NM text commented upon by Cakradhara, as clear from his gloss.

194 विसंवदति ✱ The syntax of this sentence in the early manuscript tradition is indeed peculiar, so one can understand the reasons behind the conjectures *visaṃvadati tu tat* found in the *editio princeps*, *visaṃvadanti* in S and C, etc.

नदन्तिनागा इत्यत्र हि कीदृशः पदविभागः ' अर्थद्वयोपपत्तेः ' उभयत्र च वर्णतुल्यत्वात् । किं कालेन कृष्णेन दन्तिना अगास्त्वं गत इत्येवमेतानि पदानि व्यवस्थाप्यन्ताम् ' अथ काले समये नदन्ति शब्दायन्ते नागाः करिण इति । तस्मादनियमात् न पदतदर्थविभागः पारमार्थिकः ॥

अथ ' प्रथमप्रतिपन्नवाक्यार्थानुसारेण पदतदर्थविभागो व्यवस्थाप्यते । तर्हि किं तेन तदानीं व्यवस्थापितेन ' वाक्यार्थस्य पूर्वमेव प्रतिपन्नत्वात् ॥

Granthibhaṅga

201 **अथ प्रथमप्रतिपन्नेति** । प्रकरणादिवशेन कालेनदन्तिनागा इत्यस्मादुच्चारिताद् ˙विशिष्टार्थे˙ प्रतिपत्तिर्भवत्येव, भो[158v]जनादिप्रस्तावे सैन्धवमानयेति प्रतिपत्तिवत् ॥

◆◆◆ विशिष्टार्थे] विशिष्टार्थ- Sha

M K P C S O Q V Ga Va

197 हि] om. Va

198 कृष्णेन] कृष्णे S

198–200 दन्तिना … तस्मादनियमान्] दन्तिना/// ///दनियमान् M

198 दन्तिना] P K ◆ दन्तिना हस्तिना C S Q V O Ga Va ◆ n.a. M

198 -स्त्वं] -स्तं C ◆ n.a. M

198 गत] om. V^{pc}Ga ◆ n.a. M

199 समये] समयेन V^{ac} ◆ n.a. M

199 नागाः] रागाः O ◆ n.a. M

200 इति] om. S ◆ n.a. M

200 तस्मादनियमात्] तस्मान्नियमान् S Q O^{ac} V^{ac}

201 प्रथम-] P^{ac} GBh C S Q V O Ga Va ◆ om. M K P^{ac}

202–203 तदानीं … -शब्दयोः] तदा-/// ///-ब्दयोः M

202 पूर्वम्] P K ◆ प्रथमम् C S^{pc}Q V O Ga Va ◆ प्रथमे S^{ac} ◆ n.a. M

198 दन्तिना ∗ I take the *hastinā* addition in C, etc., as the *lectio facilior*, probably caused by an urge for symmetry. Moreover, it would be problematic to explain its independent loss in P and K.

201 प्रथम- ∗ In P, *prathama* is an interlinear integration, apparently by the original scribe. It is also corroborated by the GBh and is thus accepted here as the archetypical reading.

किं च दध्यत्र मध्वत्रेति दधिमधुशब्दयोरिकारोकारान्तयोरदर्शनेऽपि तदर्थसम्प्रत्ययो दृश्यते ॥ NM^{Shu}, 343

तस्मादपि न पारमार्थिकः पदवर्णविभागः । निरस्तावयवमेव वाक्यं तथाविधस्यैव वाक्यार्थस्य वाचकमिति सिद्धम् ॥

8.2.4 [शब्दाद्वैतवादः]

ननु ' यथा पदेषु वर्णा न सन्ति ' वाक्येषु पदानि न सन्ति ' तथा महावाक्येष्ववान्तरवाक्यान्यपि न स्युः । ततः किम् । महावाक्यान्यपि प्रकरणापेक्षया

Testimonia

203 किं च दध्यत्र ∗ प्रकृतिविकृत्योश्च ॥ (MSū, 1.1.10) ◆ अपि च दध्यत्रेत्यत्र इकारः प्रकृतिः यकारो विकृतिरित्य् उपदिशन्ति (ŚBh, 1.1.10)

M K P C S O Q V Ga Va

203 किं च दध्यत्र] किमन्यत्र O ◆ n.a. M

203 मध्वत्रेति] P K C V O Q Va Ga ◆ अत्रेत्यत्र S ◆ n.a. M

203 -शब्दयो-] M K ◆ -पदयो- P C S V O Q Va Ga

203 -रिकारोकारान्तयो-] P K M C S ◆ -रिकारोकारयो- Q V O Ga Va

203 -रदर्शने] P K M^{pc} V^{pc} O^{pc} Ga Va ◆ -र्दर्शने M^{ac} C S Q V^{ac} O^{ac}

205 तस्मादपि] तस्मान् O

205 निरस्तावयवमेव] P M ◆ निरस्तावयव एवं S ◆ निरस्तावयवैव K C ◆ निरस्तावयवम् Q V O Ga Va

206–207 तथाविधस्यैव … पदानि न] त-/// ///न पदानि M

205–206 तथाविधस्यैव] P C S V O Q Va Ga ◆ तथाविधस्य K ◆ n.a. M

207 ननु] ननु च O ◆ n.a. M

207 पदेषु] पदे S ◆ n.a. M

207 वाक्येषु] वाक्येषु च P

207 पदानि न] न पदानि M K

207–208 -वाक्येष्ववान्तर-] -वाक्येश्वपि अवान्तर- P^{ac} ◆ -वाक्ये वान्तर- K

न तात्त्विकानि स्युः। पुनस्ततः किम्। प्रकरणान्यपि शास्त्रापेक्षया न स्युः। ततोऽपि किम्। एकमेवेदं शब्दतत्त्वमविभागमद्वयमापतति॥ उच्यते ' यदि तत्त्वं पृच्छसि बुद्ध्यसे वा तदेवमेवैतत्। शब्दब्रह्मैवेदमद्वयम-

Testimonia

209 प्रकरणान्यपि शास्त्रापेक्षया न स्युः ⁕ शास्त्र एव न वाक्येऽस्ति विभागः परमार्थतः॥ ($\mathrm{VP}^{\mathrm{Rau}}$, 3.8 kriyā 46cd)

211–212 शब्द … विवर्तते ⁕ अनादिनिधनं ब्रह्म शब्दतत्त्वं यदक्षरम्। विवर्ततेऽर्थभावेन प्रक्रिया जगतो यतः॥ ($\mathrm{VP}^{\mathrm{Rau}}$, 1.1)

Notes from editions

209 प्रकरणान्यपि शास्त्रापेक्षया न स्युः ⁕ प्रकरणं निर्दिष्टविषयकम्। शास्त्रं तु समग्रम्॥ ($\mathrm{NM}^{\mathrm{Va}}$)

M K P C S O Q V Ga Va

209 तात्त्विकानि] om. S

209 पुनस्ततः] P C S ◆ ततः M K Q V O Ga Va

209–210 प्रकरणान्यपि … अद्वयमापतति] प्रकरणान्यपि/// ///-द्वयमापतति M

210 एकमेवेदं] एवमेवेदं Q ◆ n.a. M

210 शब्द-] P K ◆ शास्त्र- C S Q V O Ga Va ◆ n.a. M

211 वा] om. Q

211 तदेव-] तदा एव- Va ◆ om. V^{ac} Ga

211 -मेवैतत्] P M K ◆ -मेवैतत् साधो C S Q O Va ◆ तत् साधो V^{ac} ◆ साधो V^{pc}Ga

211 शब्द] शास्त्रे O

211 अद्वयम्] om. M K

NM^Va, 157 नाद्यविद्यावासनोपप्लवमानभेदमर्थभावेन विवर्तते। न तु वाचकाद्भिक्तं वाच्यमपि नाम किञ्चिदस्ति। तस्मात् काल्पनिक एव वाच्यवाचकविभागोऽयम्' अविद्यैव विद्योपाय इति आश्रीयते ॥

Granthibhaṅga

212 **अनाद्यविद्यावासनेति**। अविद्यावशाद्धि वर्णपदावान्तरवाक्यमहावाक्यप्रविभाग इत्यनेन चैतदुक्तं भवति। एकमेवेदं त्रयीरूपं शब्दब्रह्म परब्रह्मप्राप्त्युपायः। तस्य यदिदं विभागेन चातुराश्रम्यप्रतिपादनं तदसत्यम्। मातृमोदकन्यायेन हि तत्तद्वस्तूद्देशेन समीहावतां प्राणिनां बाह्योपायनिषेधेन पश्वर्थिनामिव चित्रादि दर्शयद् बाह्यक्षोभनिवर्तनेन शनैः शनैः शान्ततां दर्शयत् परं क्षेमं दर्शयतीति। तदुक्तम् ॥ [p.161] त्रयीरूपेण तज्ज्योतिः प्रथमं परिवर्तते। पृथक् तीर्थप्रवादेषु 'दृष्ट'भेदनिबन्धनम् ॥ शान्तं विद्यात्मकं ब्रह्म तदुहैतदविद्यया। तया ग्रस्तमिवाजस्रं या निर्वक्तुं न शक्यते ॥ इत्यादि ॥ ◆◆◆ दृष्ट-] दृष्टि- Sha

212 **अर्थभावेन विवर्तत इति**। तथा चाह ॥ शब्दस्य परिणामोऽयमित्याम्नायविदो विदुः। छन्दोभ्य एव प्रथममेतद्विश्वं 'व्यवर्तत' ॥* तस्मादाकृतिगोत्रस्थाद्व्यक्तिग्रामा विकारिणः। मारुतादिव जायन्ते वृष्टिमन्तो बलाहका** इत्यादि ॥ ◆◆◆ *VP^Iyer, 1.120 ◆ **वाक्यप॰ स्वो॰ वृत्तौ (१०१) उद्धृता। आकृतिः सामान्यम्। गोत्रं सादृश्यम्। वाक्यप॰ वृषभटीका [Sha] ◆ व्यवर्तत] प्रवर्तते (VP^Rau, 1.124)

214 **अविद्यैव विद्योपाय इति**। अनेन द्वारेण प्राङ्नीत्या विद्याधिगमस्य सम्भवात्। तदुक्तम् ॥ अतत्त्वे व[159r]र्त्मनि स्थित्वा ततस्तत्त्वं प्रकाशत इति ॥

Testimonia

214 अविद्यैव विद्योपाय ⁕ असत्ये वर्त्मनि स्थित्वा ततः सत्यं समीहते ॥ (VP^Rau, 2.238cd)

Notes from editions

212 विवर्तते ⁕ विविधं प्रतीयते। विविधं परिणमत इति वा। वाक्यपदीये विवर्तपरिणामशब्दौ पर्यायतया [sic, probably meant to be पर्यायतया] प्रयुक्तौ ॥ (NM^Va)

214 विद्योपायः ⁕ ज्ञानसाधनम्। असत्यात्सत्यसिद्धेरिदं मूलम् ॥ (NM^Va)

M K P C S O Q V Ga Va

212 अर्थभावेन] अर्थभेदे S

212–213 न तु … -वाचकविभागोऽयम्] न/// ///-कविभागोऽयम् M

213 तस्मात्] om. P ◆ n.a. M

214 आश्रीयते] आश्रीते O

वाग्रूपता तु तत्त्वं सर्वत्र प्रत्यये ' तदनपायात् । यथोक्तम् '
वाग्रूपता चेदुत्क्रामेदवबोधस्य शाश्वती ।
न प्रकाशः प्रकाशेत सा हि प्रत्यवमर्शिनी ॥

Granthibhaṅga

215 **सर्वत्र प्रत्यये तदनपायादिति** । यथा रुचककुण्डलादीनामपायोपजनेऽपि सुवर्णरूपताया अनपायात्तस्या एव तात्त्विकत्वम्, एवं यत् प्रतीयते तत् सर्वं वाग्रूपतानति-'क्रमेणेति' ॥ ◆◆◆ क्रमेणेति] क्रमणेति J

216 **वाग्रूपता चेदिति** । यावत् पदार्थः घटोऽयमिति न प्रत्यवमृष्टस्तावत् प्रकाशितो न भवति । वाग्रूपताव्यतिरेकेण चान्यस्य प्रत्यवमर्शकत्वं नास्ति । अत उक्तम् । **सा हि प्रत्यवमर्शिनी** इति ॥

217 **न प्रकाशः प्रकाशेत** । प्रकाशोऽप्यप्रकाशः स्यात् ' व्यापारस्य प्रत्यवमर्शस्याकरणात् । प्रकाशरूपतामेवासौ न लभेतेत्यर्थः ॥

Testimonia

215 वाग्रूपता ... तदनपायात् ✻ न सोऽस्ति प्रत्ययो लोके यः शब्दानुगमादृते । अनुविद्धमिव ज्ञानं सर्वं शब्देन भासते ॥ (VP^{Rau}, 1.131)

216–217 वाग्रूपता ... -अवमर्शीनी ✻ वाग्रूपता चेदुत्क्रामेदवबोधस्य शाश्वती । न प्रकाशः प्रकाशेत सा हि प्रतयवमर्शिनी ॥ (VP^{Rau}, 1.132)

Notes from editions

215 सर्वत्र प्रत्यये ✻ प्रत्यये प्रतीतौ । "न सोऽस्ति प्रत्ययो लोके यश्शब्दानुगमादृते" इति हरिः ॥ (Va)

216–217 वाग्रूपता ... -अवमर्शीनी ✻ वाक्यपदीये प्रथमकाण्डे श्लो० १२५ । अवबोधस्य ज्ञानस्य नित्या वाग्रूपता यदि उत्क्रमेत् अपगच्छेत् तदा प्रकाशः न प्रकाशेत सा वाग्रूपता हि यतः प्रत्यवमार्शिनि सविकल्पकरूपा । (NM^{Shu})

217 न प्रकाशः प्रकाशेत ✻ ज्ञानं जातमपि "घटोऽयं" इत्यादिप्रत्यवमर्शः यावन्न जातः, तावत् अर्थप्रकाशात्मकमपि तत् न तथा ज्ञायेत । व्यवहारानुगुण्यापादनमेव ज्ञानकृत्यम् ॥ (NM^{Va})

M K P C S O Q V Ga Va

215 तु] P M K ◆ om. C S Q V O Ga Va

215 सर्वत्र] सर्व- M K

216–218 अवबोधस्य ... वाक्] अवबो-/// ///क् M

216 शाश्वती] P K S ◆ शास्वती C Q V O Ga Va ◆ n.a. M

217 प्रत्यवमर्शिनी] P K ◆ प्रत्यवमर्शिनी इति C S Q V O Ga Va ◆ n.a. M

8.2.4.1 [वाचः त्रैविध्येनावभासनम्]

सा चेयं वाक् त्रैविध्येन व्यवस्थितावभासते ' वैखरी मध्यमा पश्यन्तीति । तत्रेयं स्थानकरणप्रयत्नक्रमव्यज्यमानगकारादिवर्णसमुदायात्मिका वाक् सा वैखरीत्युच्यते । पूर्विखर इति देहेन्द्रियसङ्घात उच्यते । तत्र भवा वैखरी । तदुक्तम् '

Granthibhaṅga

218 **सा चेयं वाक् त्रैविध्येन व्यवस्थितेति** । तत्त्रैविध्यप्रतिपादनं स-र्वाव[p.162]स्थस्य शब्दस्यार्थाविनिर्भागज्ञापनाय ॥

220 **पूर्विखर इति** । पूःशब्देन विखरशब्देन च देहेन्द्रियसङ्घात उच्यत इति प्रसिद्धेन पूःशब्देन साम्यं दर्शयति ॥

Testimonia

218 सा … पश्यन्तीति ∗ वैखर्या मध्यमायाश्च पश्यन्त्याश्चैतदद्भुतम् । अनेकतीर्थभेदायास्त्रय्या वाचः परं पदम् ॥ (VP^Rau, 1.159)

Notes from editions

218 वैखरी … इति ∗ परासंज्ञकस्तु शब्दः अनिर्वचनीय इत्याद्यभिप्रायेणात्र नोक्तः ॥ (NM^Va)

M K P C S O Q V Ga Va

218 व्यवस्थितावभासते] P M K ◆ व्यवस्थितैवावभासते C S Q V O Ga Va
219 तत्रेयं] तत्र येयं P
219 -करण-] -कारण V
219 -समुदायात्मिका] -समुदाया M K
219 वाक् सा] P C S Q ◆ वाचः स्वा V^{ac} ◆ या वाक् सा V^{pc} Ga Va ◆ om. M K
220–222 विखर … -परिग्रहा] विख-/// ///-रि⁻⁻M
220 पूर्विखर] P GBh ◆ विखर M K C S V O Q Va Ga
220 देहेन्द्रिय-] देहींद्रिय- V ◆ n.a. M
220 -सङ्घात] -संघात इति P ◆ n.a. M
220 भवा] भावा V ◆ n.a. M
220–221 वैखरी । तदुक्तम्] वैखरीत्युक्तम् O ◆ n.a. M

220 पूर्विखर ∗ The term *pur*, "fortified town", (changed into *pūr* after *sandhi* in *pūrvikhara*), is attested in both P and the GBh. The word *vikhara* may evoke something physical or concrete, as with *khara*, "hard" or "solid".

220 तत्र भवा ∗ Jayanta may be referring to the application of the *taddhita* suffix in the sense of *tatra bhavaḥ* (Pā, 4.3.53). Incidentally, in Tarkavacaspati, 1962–1969, s.v. the etymology of *vaikharī* is explained differently, as *viśeṣeṇa khaṃ rāti.*

स्थानेषु विधृते वायौ कृतवर्णपरिग्रहा ।
वैखरी वाक् प्रयोक्तॄणां प्राणवृत्तिनिबन्धना ॥ इति ॥

या पुनरन्तःसङ्कल्प्यमाना क्रमवती श्रोत्रग्राह्यवर्णरूपाभिव्यक्तिरहिता वाक् सा मध्यमा इत्युच्यते । तदुक्तम् ' NM^Va, 158

केवलं बुद्ध्युपादाना क्रमरूपानुपातिनी ।

Granthibhaṅga

222–223 'स्थानेषु विधृत इति' । स्थानेषु ताल्वादिषु विधृते प्रतिहते वायौ सति तस्मान्निमित्तात् कृत आत्मलाभाय वर्णानामक्षराणां परिग्रह उपादानं यया । यतः प्राणाख्यस्य वायोर्वृत्तिर्व्यापारो निबन्धनं कारणमस्याः । [159v] प्रयोक्तॄणां उच्चारयितृणां सम्बन्धिनी ॥ ◆◆◆ स्थानेषु विधृत इति] om. J^{ac}

224 या पुनः केवलं 'बुद्ध्युपादाना' बुद्धावेव प्रतिभासते न वैखरीवद् बहिः श्रोत्रेणापि सा मध्यमा ॥ ◆◆◆ बुद्ध्युपादाना] बुद्ध्यापादाना J

226 क्रमरूपानुपातिनी । वैखर्यास्तत्कार्यत्वात्तदवस्थाभाविनः क्रमस्यानुकारानुवर्तिनी । यादृशी मूर्तिरालेखयितव्या 'तथा विविधैव' बुद्धिस्था निरूप्यते । एवं च स्थूलोऽपि शब्दः 'प्रथम'बुद्धौ निवेश्यः सक्रमश्चासौ । बुद्धिनिविष्टत्वमेव 'च' मध्यमत्वम् । एवं च वैखरीधर्मस्य 'क्रमस्यातत्'सन्निवेशलक्षणस्य च पश्यन्तीधर्मस्यानुगमादुभयोर्वाग्धर्मयोर्मध्ये भावान् मध्यमात्वम् । 'प्राणस्य' प्राणाख्यस्य वायोर्व्यापारं हि स्वरूपनिष्पत्तयेऽतिक्रम्यावधीर्य प्रवर्तते सा । ◆◆◆ तथा विविधैव] तथाविधैव Sha ◆ प्रथम-] प्रथमं Sha ◆ च] om. Sha ◆ क्रमस्यातत्-] क्रमस्यात्म- Sha ◆ प्राणस्य] [प्राणवृत्तिमिति] प्राणस्य Sha

Testimonia

222–223 स्थानेषु … -निबन्धना ∗ स्थानेषु विवृते वायौ कृतवर्णपरिग्रहा । वैखरी वाक् प्रयोक्तॄणां प्राणवृत्तिनिबन्धना ॥ (VP^Rau, 1.165)

226–227 केवलं … प्रवर्तते ∗ केवलं बुद्ध्युपादानक्रमरूपानुपातिनी । प्राणवृत्तिमतिक्रम्य मध्यमा वाक् प्रवर्तते ॥ (VP^Rau, 1.166)

Notes from editions

222–231 स्थानेषु … वागनपायिनीति ∗ भारतवचनत्वेनैते श्लोकाः वाक्यपदीयटीकायां पुञ्जराजकृतायां प्रथमकाण्डे १४४ श्लोके लिखिताः । (NM^Shu)

M K P C S O Q V Ga Va

222 विधृते] K GBh ◆ विवृते P C S V O Q Va Ga ◆ n.a. M

224 अन्तः-] अन्तःकरण S

224 -सङ्कल्प्यमाना] P M ◆ -संकल्प्यमान- K C S V O Q Va Ga

224–227 -रूपाभिव्यक्तिरहिता … इति] रूपाभिव्य-/// ///इति M

224–225 सा मध्यमा इत्युच्यते] P K Q ◆ सा मध्यमोच्यते V Ga Va ◆ मध्यमा सोच्यते C S O ◆ n.a. M

प्राणवृत्तिमतिक्रम्य मध्यमा वाक् प्रवर्तते ॥ इति ॥

या तु ग्राह्यभेदक्रमादिरहिता स्वप्रकाशसंविद्रूपा वाक् सा पश्यन्ती इत्युच्यते । तदुक्तम् '

अविभागात्तु पश्यन्ती सर्वतः संहृतक्रमा ।
स्वरूपज्योतिरेवान्तः सूक्ष्मा वागनपायिनी ॥ इति ॥

8.2.5 [स्फोटपक्षोपसंहारः]

$\mathrm{NM}^{\mathrm{Shu}}$, 344 तदलमतिप्रसक्तानुप्रसक्त्या । द्राघीयसी चर्चेयं प्रकृतान्तरायकारिणीति न

Granthibhaṅga

230–231 **अविभागा तु पश्यन्ती** । **अविभागा** अविद्यमानभेदा ' विवक्षाया अभावात् । **सर्वतः** स्वात्मनो विषयाच्च संहृतः तिरोधापितः **क्रमो** यया ' तदवस्थयोर्वाच्यवाचकयोरुभयोरपि क्रमस्याप्रतिभासनात् । स्वात्मैव **ज्योतिः** प्रकाशोऽस्या ' न पुनर्वैखरीवत् परसंवेद्यापि । **सूक्ष्मा** ज्ञेयेनार्थेनासंभिन्नाकारा 'ज्ञान'प्रतिलीनाकारा वा । अत एवोद्भूतेन ज्ञानात्मना रूपेण पश्यति शब्दतत्त्वम् ' न [160r] विवक्षयोपादत्त इति । व्यापाराश्रयया सञ्ज्ञया ज्ञानानुस्यूता शब्दावस्था मध्यमावस्थायाः कारणमुक्ता । **अनपायिनी** च सा ' विषयापगमेऽपि चिदवस्थाया अविचलनादिति ॥ ◆◆◆ ज्ञान] ज्ञानं J

232 [p.163] अथ तस्यां तथाविधायामवस्थायां शब्दरूपानुगमे किं प्रमाणम् इति तदाह । **अलमतिप्रसक्तेति** ॥

Testimonia

230–231 अविभागात्तु … अनपायिनी ⁕ अविभागा तु पश्यन्ती सर्वतः संहृतक्रमा । स्वरूपज्योतिरेवान्तः सूक्ष्मा वागनपायिनी ॥ (VP^{Rau}, 1.167)

M K P C S O Q V Ga Va

228 -क्रमादि-] -कथादि- M K
228–237 -रहिता … विद्यायां हि] -र-/// ///विद्यायां हि M
228 स्वप्रकाश-] स्वप्रकाशा K ◆ n.a. M
228 वाक् सा] om. K ◆ n.a. M
230 अविभागात्तु] अविभाग⁻⁻ K ◆ अविभागा तु Q GBh ◆ n.a. M
230 संहृत-] स⁻त S ◆ संवृत K ◆ n.a. M
231 सूक्ष्मा] सूक्ष्म- P ◆ n.a. M
232 -मति-] -मिति V ◆ n.a. M
232 -] -प्रसंगेन Q ◆ n.a. M
232 -कारिणीति] -कारिणी K ◆ n.a. M

प्रतन्यते । इह त्वेतावतैव नः प्रयोजनम् ' वर्णपदपूर्वको वाक्यार्थप्रत्ययो न भवतीति । वाक्येन लोके व्यवहारात् तस्य चावयवव्यवस्थानुपपत्ते-र्निर्भागमेव तद्वाचकं निर्भागश्च तस्य वाच्योऽर्थ इति । अवान्तरवाक्यमपि प्रयोगयोग्यं व्यवहारकारणमिति तन्न निह्नूयते । अविद्यावस्थेयं वर्तते । तत्रेयं व्यवहारवर्तनी यथादृश्यमानैवास्तु । विद्यायां सर्वमेवेदमसारमिति । पदेन तु वर्णेन वा व्यवहाराभावात् तस्य केवलस्याप्रयोगात् तत्स्वरूपमस्यामपि दशायां न वास्तवमिष्यत इति ॥

Granthibhaṅga

234 **तस्य ˙चावयव˙व्यवस्थानुपपत्तेरिति** । यथा प्रतिपादितं कालेनदन्तिनागा इ-त्यत्र ॥ ◆◆◆ चावयव] चावयवि Sha *v.l.*

Notes from editions

237 विद्यायां सर्वमेवेदमसारमिति ✻ शून्यविवर्तवादः, विज्ञानविवर्तवादः, शब्दविवर्तवादः, ब्र-ह्मविवर्तवादश्चेति चत्वारो विवर्तवादाः प्रायः शब्दभेदमात्रे पर्यवस्यन्ति । निरूपणप्रक्रिया तु समाना ॥ (NM[Va])

237–238 पदेन तु वर्णेन वा ✻ वाक्यमेव कल्पितं चेत् किमु वक्तव्यं प्रत्येकपदानां वर्णानां वा !(Va)

M K P C S O Q V Ga Va

233 नः] PK ◆ पुनः CSQVO Ga Va ◆ n.a. M

233 -प्रत्ययो] PK ◆ -व्यवहारो V^{pc}Ga Va ◆ om. CSQV^{ac}O ◆ n.a. M

234 चावयव-] KGBh ◆ चावयवावयव P ◆ चावयवावयवि- CSQVO Ga Va ◆ n.a. M

235 -र्निर्भागमेव] -र्निर्विभागमेव O ◆ n.a. M

235 निर्भाग-] विभाग- O

236 प्रयोगयोग्यं] प्रयोग्यं S

236 कारणमिति] करणमिति C

237 -वर्तनी] -प्रवर्तनी P ◆ -वर्तिनी O ◆ n.a. M

237 -दृश्यमानैवास्तु] PK$V^{pc}$$O^{pc}$Ga Va ◆ -दृश्यमानैवावस्तु CSQV^{ac} O^{ac} ◆ n.a. M

237 विद्यायां] विद्यायां हि MK

237 -मेवेदमसारमिति] -मेवैतदसारमिति P ◆ -मेवेदं समानमिति O

238 व्यवहाराभावात्] व्यवहारभावात् MV^{ac}

238 केवलस्याप्रयोगात्] केवलस्यप्रयोगात् O

239–241 वास्तवमिष्यत … जनयति] वास्तवमिष्य-/// ///-यति M

NM[Va], 159

तस्मादेकः क्रमविरहितः कल्पितासत्यभागो
वाक्यस्फोटो जनयति मतिं तादृशि स्वाभिधेये ।
वर्णास्त्वेते प्रकृतिलघवः कल्पनैकप्रतिष्ठा-
स्तस्मिन्नर्थे विदधति धियं नेत्यलं तत्कथाभिः ॥

Granthibhaṅga

242 **प्रकृतिलघवः** स्वभावत एव लघवोऽसारा अस्थिराः। परं यदि सङ्कलनाद्यात्मिकायां कल्पनाबुद्धावारूढानां तेषां स्थितिर्न स्वरूपेण क्षणिकत्वादिति ॥

M K P C S O Q V Ga Va

240 -देकः] -देक- Va ◆ n.a. M
240 -विरहितः] -विरहिताः C ◆ n.a. M
240 कल्पितासत्यभागो] कल्पितासद्विभागो V^{pc} Ga Va ◆ कल्पितासविभागो O ◆ n.a. M
241 मतिं] मतिस् M K
241 तादृशि] तादृश्य O ◆ तादृशीं Ga Va
242 प्रतिष्ठास्] प्रविष्टाः O
243 धियं] धिय O

9 [वर्णवादः]

अत्राभिधीयते ' किमयमनुमानमहिम्ना स्फोटाभ्युपगमः प्रत्यक्षप्रतीतिबलवत्तया वा ॥

9.1 [स्फोटकल्पनानुपपत्तिर्वर्णपक्षोपपत्तिश्च]

न तावदनुमानतः स्फोटस्वरूपमुपपादयितुं पार्यते ' परिदृश्यमानविशिष्टानुपूर्वीकवर्णकलापकरणत्वेन अर्थप्रतीतेर्घटमानत्वात् ॥

9.1.1 [क्रमभाविनां सामस्त्यसामर्थ्यम्]

ननु ' व्यस्तसमस्तादिविकल्पैरुत्सादितं वर्णानां वाचकत्वम् ॥

M K P C S O Q V Ga Va

244–246 -मनुमान- … न तावदनु-] -मनु/// ///वदनु- M
244 स्फोटाभ्युपगमः] स्फोटोऽभ्युपगमः Ga ◆ n.a. M
245 वा] om. K^{ac} O ◆ n.a. M
246 -स्वरूप-] -रूप- P
247 -करणत्वेन-] P ◆ -कारणकत्वेन M ◆ -कारणकल्पेन K ◆ -करणेन- C S Q V O Ga Va
248–249 व्यस्तसमस्तादि- … दुर्विकल्पास्ते] व्य/// ///स्ते M
248 -रुत्सादितं] P K C Ga Va ◆ -रुत्पादितं S Q V O ◆ n.a. M

247 -करणत्वेन- ∗ I understand the instrumental of cause as an application of Pā, 2.3.23, [*hetau*] *vibhāṣā guṇe 'striyām*. Thus *karaṇatva*, a *guṇa*, looks better in this causal sense. On Jayanta's usage of *karaṇa* and *kāraṇa*, cf. also Section 9.1.4.1.

नैतद् ' दुर्विकल्पास्ते । व्यस्तानां तावद्वाचकत्वं नेष्यत एव वर्णानाम् । समस्ता एव ते वाचकाः ॥

9.1.1.1 [लौकिको दृष्टान्तः]

यत्तु ' तत्सामस्त्यं नास्ति क्रमभावित्वादिति ' तदसत् ' क्रमभाविनामपि समस्तानां कार्यकारिणामनेकशो दर्शनात् । यथा युगपद्भाविनः समस्तास्त्रयो NM[Va], 160 ग्रावाण एकामुखां धारयन्तो दृश्यन्ते ' तथा क्रमभाविनोऽपि समस्ता ग्रासा एकां तृप्तिमुत्पादयन्तो दृश्यन्ते । एकस्मिन्नपि हि ग्रासे हीयमाने न भ-

Granthibhaṅga

253 उखा स्थाली ॥

Testimonia

252–253 यथा … दृश्यन्ते ⁕ अस्ति खल्वेकाभिधेयधीहेतुभावस्त्रयाणामपि वर्णानामेकस्मरणसमारोहिणां ग्राव्णामिवैकपिठरधारणे, यस्मात् पदमिति व्यपदेशः ॥ (TB, 71.5–6)

Notes from editions

253 ⁕ अधस्ताद्द्वारुणि शिला नासा दारूपरि स्थितमित्यमरः पुट-१३ द्वारोपरितनशिला । इतरपार्श्वत्रयस्थितशिलाभिः सा यते । (Va)

M K P C S O Q V Ga Va

249 एव¹] om. Ga
250 ते] om. M K
251 तत्सामस्त्यं] सामस्त्यं M K
251 -दसत्] -दसत्यम् V^{ac}
252 समस्तानां- … समस्तास्त्रयो] समस्ता/// ///स्तास्त्रयो M
252 यथा] om. O ◆ n.a. M
252 समस्तास्त्रयो] समास्त्रयो V Ga ◆ त्रयो S
253 एकामुखां] एकामुखां तानां O ◆ एकां नासां Va
253 तथा] यथा P
254–255 हि ग्रासे- … -स्तृप्तेः कारणम्] हि ग्रा/// ///कारणम् M
254 ग्रासे] ग्रामे C O

249 दुर्विकल्पास्ते ⁕ Although the Sphoṭavādin's argument begins with a dilemma of either individual or collective phonemes, other alternatives were also proposed, as indicated by the *ādi*; thus the use of the plural, rather than the dual. See Section 8.1.1.

253 एकामुखां ⁕ Interestingly, the variant reading *nāsām* generates in Va a radically different interpretation of the example.

वति तादृशी तृप्तिः । अतः समस्ता एव ते ग्रासास्तृप्तेः कारणम् । न च समस्ता अपि ते ग्रासा युगपत् प्रयोक्तुं शक्याः । तथैकानुवाकग्रहणे संस्थानां क्रमभाविनीनामपि सामस्त्ये सति सामर्थ्यम् ' एकयापि संस्थया विना तदामुखीकरणासम्भवाद् । एवं तावल्लोके सामस्त्यं क्रमभावित्वं च दृष्टम् ॥

Testimonia

256–258 तथैकानुवाक- … -करणासम्भवाद् ✻ यथानुवाकः श्लोको वा सोढत्वमुपगच्छति । आवृत्त्या न तु स ग्रन्थः प्रत्यावृत्ति निरूप्यते ॥ (VP^{Iyer}, 1.84) ◆ अभ्यासानां च लोकेऽपि स्वाध्यायग्रहणादिषु ॥ (ŚV^{Ra}, sphoṭa 74cd) ◆ एकसाधनसंस्थाश्च व्यापारावयवा यदा । स्वरूपतो निरीक्ष्यन्ते यौगपद्यमसत्तदा ॥ किं पुनर्बहवो भिन्ना भिन्नसाधनसंश्रिताः । भवेयुर्यौगपद्येन व्यापाराः क्रमवर्तिनः ॥ (ŚV^{Ra}, sphoṭa 77–78) ◆ लोकेऽपि पदाध्ययनादीनामेकानुवाकग्रहणसाधकत्वम् । (ŚVT^{Ra}, sphoṭa 74)

258 एवं … दृष्टम् ✻ लोकेऽपि पदाध्ययनादीनामेकानुवाकग्रहणसाधकत्वम् ॥ (ŚVT^{Ra}, sphoṭa 74)

Notes from editions

256–257 संस्थानां ✻ संस्था धारणा । प्रकृते तदुपायः ॥ (NM^{Va})

M K P C S O Q V Ga Va

255 तादृशी] तादृशीयन् K ◆ n.a. M
255 ग्रासा-] ग्रामा- C O ◆ n.a. M
256 ग्रासा] ग्रामा C O
256 तथैकानुवाक-] तथैव चार्वाक- C
257–258 सामर्थ्य- … -भावित्वंच] सामर्थ्य/// ///भावित्वंच M
257 एकयापि] P K ◆ एकया C S Q V O Ga Va ◆ n.a. M
257 संस्थया] संस्थयापि K ◆ n.a. M
257 विना] om. Va ◆ n.a. M
258 तदामुखी-] तदासुखी C O ' तदभिमुखी- K ◆ n.a. M
258 तवल्लोके] तावदेव लोके S ◆ तवच्छोके O ◆ n.a. M
258 -भावित्वं च] भाविनां Ga Va

258 तदामुखी- ✻ Both *āmukhīkaraṇa*, "accomplishing", and *abhimukhīkaraṇa*, "propitiating", fit the context, but *āmukhīkṛ-* is the only attested reading in another NM passage in an analogous context (NM^{Va}, I 165,15, see line 347 below). The *anuvāka* example was used by Bhartṛhari (VP^{Rau}, 1.84) in support of the thesis of the fully clear manifestation of the *sphoṭa* only upon hearing the last phoneme of the word or the sentence. In the same context, in the ŚV argumentation, an important role is played by *śakti* (equivalent of *sāmarthya* here), that is a necessary condition, along with the sequential acts, towards a single result.

9.1.1.2 [वैदिको दृष्टान्तः]

वेदेऽपि दर्शपूर्णमासाभ्यामित्यत्रेतरेतरयोगशंसिना द्वन्द्वेन समर्पितसाहित्यानामाग्नेयादियागानां पक्षद्वयप्रयोज्यत्वेन चापरिहार्यक्रमाणामेकाधिका-

Granthibhaṅga

260 **पक्षद्वयप्रयोज्यत्वेनेति**। दर्शे हि त्रयः प्रयुज्यन्ते पूर्णमास्यां च त्रय इति ॥

Testimonia

259–261 वेदे … दृष्टम् ✱ दृष्टश्च पूर्णमासादेः क्रमः संहत्यकारिणः। ($ŚV^{Ra}$, sphoṭa 74ab) ◆ दर्शपूर्णमासाभ्यामित्युपपदसमर्पितसाहित्येतिकर्तव्यताविशिष्टानाम् आग्नेयादीनाम् एकप्रेर्यविशेषणोत्पादकत्वं क्रमेण, करणानामाग्नेयादीनां क्षणिकत्वेन यौगपद्यासम्भवात् ॥ ($ŚVT^{Ra}$, sphoṭa 74)

Notes from editions

260 -द्वय- ✱ पक्षद्वये शुक्लपक्षकृष्णापक्षयोः। दर्शयागे त्रयः पौर्णमास्यां त्रयश्च विहिताः ॥ (NM^{Va})

M K P C S O Q V Ga Va

259 -मित्यत्रेतरेतर-] P ◆ -मितरेतर- M K C S Q O^{pc} ◆ -मितीतरेतर- V Ga Va ◆ -मितिरेतर O^{ac}

259 -योग-] -योगि- S

259 -शंसिना] शंसितानां O

259–260 -साहित्यानाम्] सहितानाम् V O

260 -द्वय-] P K C S Q O ◆ -द्वयो V^{ac} ◆ -द्वये V^{pc}Ga Va ◆ n.a. M

260 -न चापरिहार्य-] -नापरिहार्य- S Q ◆ n.a. M

---

259 दर्शपूर्णमासा- ✱ See Garge, 1952, 267: … "the *Darśapūrṇamāsa* rites are to be repeated on every Moonless and Full-Moon day". The Darśapūrṇamāsa has three components, Āgneya, Upāṃśu and Agnīṣomīya, which need to be performed in a prescribed order (*krama*) (Garge, 1952, 278).

259 द्वन्द्वेन ✱ The copulative compound, *itaretarayogadvandva*, preserves the number of the members grouped in the compound, in this case the two *darśa* and *pūrṇamāsa*, unlike the generic *samahāradvandva*, and thus explicitly points to the need of a sequence.

रसम्पादकत्वं दृष्टम् । तथा ऐन्द्रवायवं गृह्णाति आश्विनं गृह्णाति इति सोमग्रहग्रहणाभ्यासानां समस्तानां क्रमभाविनां चैकप्रधाननिर्वर्तकत्वं दृष्टमिति । अतश्च नायं विरोधः सामस्त्यं च क्रमकारित्वं चेति ॥

एवं क्रमवर्तिनोऽपि वर्णा एकार्थाभिधायिनो भविष्यन्ति ॥ NM[Shu], 345

9.1.1.3 [दृष्टान्तदार्ष्टान्तिकयोर्भेदः]

ननु ' ग्राससंस्थादीनां युक्तं समस्तानां क्रमकारित्वम् ' यतः कार्यमपि तदीयं तृप्त्यादि क्रमेण निर्वर्त्यमानं दृश्यते । वर्णेभ्यस्तु क्रमेण श्रूयमाणेभ्यो न

Granthibhaṅga

261 **तथैन्द्रवायवं गृह्णातीति** । सोमेन यजेतेत्युक्तम् । तत्र कथं यजेतेत्यपेक्षायामैन्द्रवायवं ग्रहं 'आश्विनं ग्रहं गृह्णाति' इत्यादयः सोमग्रहग्रहणाभ्यासा उक्ताः । सोमरसो विशिष्टपात्रस्थः सोमग्रहः । तस्य देवतोद्देशेन यदादानं तद्ग्रहणम् । तेषां ग्रहणानां विशिष्टदेवतोद्देशेन बहूनां यानि सम्पादनानि तान्येव कृतस्य ग्रहणस्य पुनःकरणरूपतयाभ्यासाः । न [160v] ह्यभ्यासं विनासौ सोमरस ऐन्द्रवायवमकृत्वाश्विनः कर्तुं शक्यत इति । ते च क्रमभाविनः । ऐन्द्रवायवो हि तदा भवति यदेन्द्रवायुभ्यां संकल्प्यते । सङ्कल्पश्च न यागं विना भवतीति प्रकृत्यंशो यागः । स च क्रमेण निर्वर्त्यमानोऽपि ज्योतिष्टोमाधिकारलक्षणं प्रधानाधिकारं निर्वर्तयतीति ॥ ◆◆◆ आश्विनं ग्रहं गृह्णाति] om. J^{ac}

Testimonia

261–262 तथा … इति ✻ अभ्यासे चैन्द्रवायवादीनामेकाधिकारनिष्पादकत्वम् । (ŚVT[Ra], sphoṭa 74)

M K P C S O Q V Ga Va

261 ऐन्द्रवायवं] P M K Ga Va ◆ ऐन्द्रवायव्यं C S Q O V^{ac}

261 आश्विनं गृह्णाति] om. Q

261–262 सोमग्रह-] सोम- V Ga Va

262 -निर्वर्तकत्वं] -निर्वर्तकत्वे C ◆ n.a. M

262 दृष्टम्] om. O ◆ n.a. M ◆ इष्टम् Va[क] not found in any ms

263 च[२]] om. O Va ◆ n.a. M

263 -कारित्वं] P K S ◆ -भावित्वं C Q V Ga Va ◆ -भावित्वे O ◆ n.a. M

264 एकार्थाभिधायिनो] P M K ◆ एवार्थाभिधायिनो C S Q V O Ga Va

265 ग्रास-] ग्राम- C O

265 -कारित्वम्] P M K ◆ -भावित्वं C S Q V O Ga Va

266–267 वर्णेभ्य- … दृश्यते] om. V Ga

266 न] om. Q O ◆ n.a. V Ga

यावती तावत्यर्थावगतिमात्रा निर्वर्त्यमाना दृश्यते ॥ NM^Va, 161 यद्येवमाग्नेयादिभ्यस्तर्हि क्रमेण निर्वर्त्यमानं किं कार्यमुपलभ्यते ॥ अवान्तरापूर्वमिति ब्रूमः ' शब्दप्रामाण्यात् । परमापूर्वनिर्वृत्तिस्तु तेषां सामस्त्ये सति सेत्स्यतीति ॥ उच्यते ' अवान्तरापूर्वनिर्वृत्ताविदानीं क्रमभाविनामाग्नेयावयवभूतक्रियाक्ष-

Granthibhaṅga

269 **अवान्तरापूर्वमिति** । भट्टपक्षेऽवान्तरापूर्वं शक्तिरूपम् ' प्रभाकरमते त्ववान्तराग्नेयादिनियोग एव ॥

269 कुतस्तस्यानुपलभ्यमानस्य कल्पनेति चेत्तदाह । **शब्दप्रामाण्यादिति** । आग्नेययागस्य क्रियारूपत्वात् क्षणिकत्वेनान्यप्रधानयागकालेऽनवस्थितत्वेन फलनिर्वृत्तौ सहकार्ययोगात्तत्करणं निष्फलमेव प्रसज्येत । न च निष्फलं प्रमाणभूतशब्द उपदिशतीति तत्कल्पनम् ॥

271–272 **आग्नेयावयवभूतक्रियाक्षणानामिति** । चतुरो 'मुष्टीन्निर्वपतीति' व्रीहीन् अवहन्ति तन्दुलान् पिनष्टीत्यादय आग्नेययागावयवाः क्रियाक्षणाः ॥ ◆◆◆ मुष्टीर्निवपतीति J

Testimonia

271–272 क्रमभाविनामाग्नेयावयवभूतक्रियाक्षणानां ∗ चतुरो मुष्टीन् व्रीहीणां निर्वपति । (*Baudhāyanaśrautasūtra*, e.g., Ch 5, Par. 11, Verse 144.4)

Notes from editions

271 अवान्तरापूर्वनिर्वृत्ता ∗ आग्नेयादिभिरवान्तरापूर्वनिर्वृत्तिर्वक्तव्या चेत्, आग्नेयाङ्गभूतव्रीह्यवहननादिक्रियाभिः प्रथमं किं कार्यं निर्वर्त्यत इति वक्तव्यम् । आहत्यावान्तरापूर्वनिर्वृत्तिश्चेत् प्रकृतेऽपि समानम् ॥ (NM^Va)

M K P C S O Q V Ga Va

267 -त्यर्थावगति-] P C S Q Va ◆ -त्यर्थावति- O ◆ -त्यर्था--- M ◆ -त्यर्थावगम- K ◆ n.a. V Ga

269 परमापूर्व-] परमार्थपूर्व- C

269 -निर्वृत्ति-] निवृत्ति- P S V

271 -निर्वृत्ता-] -निवृत्ता- Ga

271–272 ∗ In GBh^Sha, Shah has emended the plural accusative *muṣṭīḥ* with the masculine counterpart. The word *muṣṭi*, from the suffix *ktic*, is most often found in the masculine gender, as in *muṣṭinā* (Vaidya, 1969–1971, 58.49), but also in the feminine, as in *dṛḍhāṃ muṣṭim* (MBh, 4.5.10). The root *vapu*, too, is attested with both the preverbs *ni* and *nir*. Thus the J reading would be acceptable. The presence of the masculine accusative *caturaḥ*, however, justifies Shah's emendation.

णानां किमवान्तरं कार्यं का वा तस्य निर्वृत्तिरुपलभ्यते। अपि च यथाभिमतं यत् कार्यं यदभिसन्धानेन प्रवृत्तिस्तत् सामस्त्यात् पूर्वं न क्वचिदुपलभ्यते। न ह्यवान्तरापूर्वेण स्वर्गमात्रा काचिदभिनिर्वर्त्यते, शास्त्रार्थस्य तदानीमनिष्पन्नत्वात्। अतः किमवान्तरापूर्वेण कृतेनापि। यत्किंचित् त्ववान्तरापूर्वप्रायं कार्यं वर्णेष्वपि न न दर्शयितुं शक्यते। किं तदिति चेत् स्वरूपग्रहणं संस्कारो वा भविष्यति। तयोः प्रधानकार्यावयवत्वं नास्ति इति चेत्, मा भूदवयवत्वम्, तदुपयोगिता तु विद्यत एव। अवयवावयविव्यवहारस्तु अवान्तरपरमापूर्वयोरपि दुरुपपादः। पदानां तु वाक्यार्थप्रतिपत्तिलक्षणप्रधानकार्यावयवभूतपदार्थज्ञानाख्यकार्यनिर्वर्तकत्वमतिस्पष्टमस्त्येवेति न तेष्वेष

Notes from editions

272 यथाभिमतं ∗ स्वर्गसाधनत्वेन ज्ञात्वा तत्र प्रवर्तते, न तु अवान्तरापूर्वसाधनत्वेन ॥ (NM^Va^)
274 स्वर्गमात्रा ∗ स्वर्गमात्रा स्वर्गलेशः ॥ (NM^Va^)
280–281 तेष्वेष दोषः ∗ एष दोषः अवान्तरापूर्वपरमापूर्वयोर्लेशतोऽपि संबन्धानवगमरूपः ॥ (NM^Va^)

M K P C S O Q V Ga Va

272 अवान्तरं] P C S V O Q Va Ga ◆ अवान्तर- M K
272 का] P M K C S V Q Ga Va ◆ किं O
272–273 अपि … उपलभ्यते] om. V Ga
272 च] om. O ◆ n.a. V Ga
273 यदभि-] P M K ◆ तदभि- C S Q O Va ◆ n.a. V Ga
273 -स्तत् सामस्त्यात्] P M C S Va ◆ -स्तत्सामस्त्य- O ◆ -स्तत्सामर्थ्यात् Q ◆ -स्तत्सामर्थ्या K ◆ n.a. V Ga
275 अनिष्पन्नत्वात्] P C S V O Q Va Ga ◆ असंपन्नत्वाद् M ◆ संपन्नत्वाद् K
275–276 त्ववान्तरापूर्व-] P M^{pc} C S V^{pc} Ga Va ◆ त्ववान्तरापूर्वं K ◆ त्ववान्तरापूर्वा M^{ac} ◆ त्ववान्तरपूर्व- Q O V^{ac}
276 कार्यं] om. M K
276 दर्शयितुं] वर्णयितुं P ◆ ---तुं K
278 विद्यत] भवति O
279 -प्रतिपत्ति-] om. O
280 -निर्वर्तकत्व-] P M K V^{pc} Ga Va ◆ -निर्वर्तक- S Q O V^{ac} ◆ -निवर्तक- C
280 -मस्त्येवेति] -मेव अस्तीति S

NM[Va], 162 दोषः प्रादुःष्यात् ॥

9.1.2 [वर्णसमूहपक्षः]

वर्णानामपि गमनक्रियाक्षणानामिव ग्रामप्राप्तौ ग्रासानामिव तृप्तौ संस्थानामिवामुखीकरणे यद्यपि क्रमोपचीयमानतत्कार्यमात्रासमुन्मेषो नास्ति तथापि तदौपयिकस्वोपलब्धिसंस्कारादिकार्यकरणात् तत्कार्यावयवो न तावत्कृतो भवतीति न समस्तानां क्रमकारित्वमपहीयते। तत्र पूर्वे वर्णा अतीता अप्यु-

Notes from editions

285–286 अप्युपकरिष्यन्ति ✻ घण्टाताडनादौ दश, एकादशेत्यादि संख्यागणनायां अयमंशः स्पष्टः। उपरितनग्रन्थे अयमंशः व्यक्तः ॥ (NM[Va])

M K P C S O Q V Ga Va

281 प्रादुःष्यात्] प्रादुष्यात् M K Va ◆ स्यात् प्रादुष्ष्यात् S
282 ग्रासानाम्] ग्रामाणाम् C O
283 -वामुखी-] -वाभिमुखी- M K
283 क्रमोपचीयमान-] तदोपक्रमोपचीयमान- M K
283 -मात्रासमुन्मेषो] -मात्रसमुन्मेषो M K Va
283 तथापि] तथा C
284 तदौपयिकस्वोपलब्धि-] P ◆ तदौपयिकश्चोपलब्धि- M ◆ तदौपयिकस्योपलब्धि K C S Q V O Ga Va
284 -कार्य-] कार्यस्य V^{pc} Ga Va
284 -करणात्] -कारणात् K C O
284 -कार्यावयवो] -कार्यावयवी V Ga
284 न] P M K C S ◆ om. Q V O Ga Va
285 -मपहीयते] -मपनीयते M ◆ -मपसीयते K ◆ -मुपहीयते O

281 प्रादुःष्यात् ✻ In the South Indian manuscripts of the NM the *visarga* is consistently dropped when followed by a sibilant. This is not an application of *Vārttika* ad Pā, 8.3.36, since the sibilant is not followed by an unvoiced stop, as enjoined by that optional rule. It may be thus considered a regional *sandhi* variant.

283–285 यद्यपि … भवतीति ✻ The interpretation of the tricky passage and the reconstruction of the text hinges on the variants *tadaupayikasvopalabdhi-* vs *tadaupayikasyopalabdhi-*, and *na tāvatkṛtaḥ* vs *tāvatkṛtaḥ*. The received text is arguably the *lectio difficilior*, while in Ga and Va it is smoother, but perhaps trivialised.

पकरिष्यन्ति ' चरमस्तु वर्तमान इतीदृश एवायं काल्पनिकः क्रियाक्षणसमूह इव वर्णसमूहोऽर्थप्रत्यायकः ॥

9.1.3 [सङ्कलनाज्ञानपक्षः]

अथ वा ' क्रमोपलब्धेष्वपि वर्णेषु मानसमनुव्यवसायरूपमखिलवर्णविषयं सङ्कलनाज्ञानं यदुपजायते तद् अर्थप्रत्यायनाङ्गं भविष्यति । दृश्यते च विनश्वरेष्वपि पदार्थान्तरेषु क्रमानुभूतेषु युगपदनुव्यवसायो मानसः शतमाम्राणि भक्षितवान् देवदत्त इति । न चायं प्रत्ययो नास्ति सन्दिग्धो बाध्यते वा । अनभ्युपगम्यमाने चेदृशि समुच्चयज्ञाने तन्निबन्धना भूयांसो व्यवहारा उत्सीदेयुः ॥

Granthibhaṅga

288 **अनुव्यवसायरूपमिति** । 'बाह्येनेन्द्रियेण' व्यवसितस्य निश्चितस्यानु पश्चान् मानसं यन्निश्चयनं सोऽनुव्यवसायः ॥ ◆◆◆ बाह्येनेन्द्रियेण] बाह्येन्द्रियेण Sha

292 **तन्निबन्धना भूयां[161r]सो व्यवहारा इति** । यथा प्रदर्शितम्, शतमाम्राणीत्यादिव्यव/// ///तिः । प्रामाणिकी व्यवस्था ॥

M K P C S O Q V Ga Va

286 चरम-] P M K ◆ चरमवर्ण- C S Q V O Ga Va

286 काल्पनिकः क्रिया-] काल्पनीया- K

288 मानसमनुव्यवसाय-] मानसव्यवसाय- M K

289 सङ्कलना-] संकल्पना- C S V^{ac} O

289–290 विनश्वरेष्वपि] विश्वनरेष्वपि C S O V^{ac}

290 क्रमानुभूतेषु] क्रमभूतेषु M K ◆ क्रमांतर्भूतेषु O

290 -दनुव्यवसायो] -दध्यवसयो P ◆ -दनुव्यवसायमानो S

290 शतमाम्राणि] शतमम्राणि O ◆ शतमम्लानि V

292 तन्निबन्धना … व्यवहारा ✻ From here the text of the GBh is partially lost. Only the left half of fol. 161 is preserved in J, so that only the first half of lines in 161r and 161v is extant. The leaf is broken vertically, where the vertical rulers were drawn to delimit the ornament between the two halves of the layout (see also Section 3.5.1).

9.1.3.1 [सङ्कलनाज्ञाने व्यस्तसमस्तविकल्पानवकाशत्वम्]

स चायं सङ्कलनाप्रत्ययः स्मर्यमाणानुभूयमानप्राक्तनान्त्यवर्णविषयतया सदसद्वर्णगोचरश्चित्ररूप उपेयते । यदि वान्त्यवर्णोऽपि तिरोहिते भवन्नसद्वर्णगोचर एव न चित्राकारः । सोऽर्थप्रतीतिहेतुरेक एव इति निरवकाशा व्यस्तसमस्तविकल्पाः ॥

9.1.3.2 [सङ्कलनाज्ञाने विपरीतक्रमप्रसङ्गानवकाशत्वम्]

NM^{Va}, 163

ननु च ' सङ्कलनाप्रत्ययेऽपि यदि ते वर्णाः क्रमेणावभासन्ते तदसावपि पूर्वोत्पन्नैकैकवर्णबुद्धिनिर्विशेष एव स्याद् इति तदुपारूढा अपि वर्णा नार्थप्रतीतिहेतवो भवेयुः । यदि त्वेकघनस्तबकाकारावभासी स प्रत्ययस्तदा

Testimonia

294–295 स चायं … चित्ररूप उपेयते ∗ यद्वा प्रत्यक्षतः पूर्वं क्रमज्ञातेषु यत् परम् । समस्तवर्णविज्ञानं तदर्थज्ञानकारणम् ॥ तत्र ज्ञाने च वर्णानां यौगपद्यं प्रतीयते । नावश्यं यौगपद्येन प्रत्यक्षत्वेन तद्भवेत् ॥ चित्ररूपां च तां बुद्धिं सदसद्वर्णगोचराम् । केचिदाहुर्यया वर्णो गृह्यतेऽन्त्यः पदे पदे ॥ (ŚV^{Ra}, sphoṭa 109–111) ◆ अपरे तु संस्कारत्रयजन्यां वर्णस्मरणरूपां सङ्कलनात्मिकामिच्छन्तीत्याह (ŚVT^{Ra}, sphoṭa 112)

Notes from editions

295–296 भवन्नसद्वर्णगोचर ∗ स्मर्यमाणानुभूयमानवर्णविषयकत्वकल्पनाक्लेशः अस्मिन् कल्पे नास्ति । आहत्य सर्ववर्णविषयकं एकं मानसिकं ज्ञानमेव भवतु बोधजनकम् ॥ (NM^{Va})

M K P C S O Q V Ga Va

294 स] न M
294 सङ्कलना-] P M K Q Ga Va ◆ -संकल्पना- C S V O
295 पि] om. M K
296 न] om. M^{ac} Va
296–298 चित्राकारः … यदि ते] चित्रा/// ///दि ते M
296 एव] om. K ◆ n.a. M
298 च] P K ◆ om. C S Q V O Ga Va ◆ n.a. M
298 सङ्कलना-] संकल्पना- C V^{ac} O ◆ n.a. M
299 -बुद्धि-] -बुद्धिः K O Va ◆ बुद्धि- M
299 एव स्याद्] स्याद् K ◆ स्यादेव O
300 त्वेक-] त्वेकः Q
300 -घन-] P M K C S ◆ -मना- O V^{ac} ◆ -सुमन- V^{pc} Ga Va ◆ om. Q
300 -स्तबकाकारावभासी] -स्तबकाकारवती Va

तस्मिन् क्रमानवगमाद् विपरीतक्रमा अपि ते वर्णा अर्थप्रतीतिकारिणः स्युः ॥ उच्यते ' विशिष्टानुपूर्वीकवर्णमालानुभवसमनन्तरभावी हि सङ्कलनाप्रत्ययोऽर्थप्रतीतिहेतुः ' न स्तबकाकारपरिच्छेदमात्रम् । विपरीतक्रमाशङ्कनं च तदानीं कुतस्त्यम् । स्तबकावभासे तावत् क्रम एव नास्ति । कस्य वैपरीत्यमवैपरीत्यं वा । यदनन्तरजन्मा तु समुच्चयप्रत्ययः ता विशिष्टक्रमावभासिन्य एव पूर्वभाविन्यो वर्णबुद्धय इति कुतो वैपरीत्यविकल्पः । तस्मात् प्रथमपरिपठननियतानुपूर्व्यास्ते तदनन्तरभाविसमस्तावभासिसङ्कलनाप्रत्ययोपारूढा वर्णा अर्थप्रतीतिकारिण इति न दोषः ॥

NM^{Shu}, 346

Notes from editions

301 अपि ते ∗ तावताऽपि तस्य सर्ववर्णविषकत्वात्[sic] ॥ (NM^{Va})
306 पूर्वभाविन्यो ∗ शब्दबोधात् पूर्वभाविन्यः ॥ (NM^{Va})

M K P C S O Q V Ga Va

301 क्रमानवगमाद्] क्रमानवभासाद् P ◆ क्रमावगमात् M K
302 -पूर्वीक-] -पूर्वी M^{ac}
302 -भावी हि] -भाविनि K
302 सङ्कलना-] संकल्पना- O
303 -प्रतीति-] -प्रतीतेः V Ga Va
303 -परिच्छेद-] -परिच्छेदक- K
303 -क्रमाशङ्कनं] -क्रमाशंकने O
304 कस्य] तस्य K
305 -जन्मा तु] -जन्मायं V^{pc}Ga Va ◆ -जन्मांतर- Q O V^{ac}
305 ता] P M K ◆ तद्- C S Q V^{ac} ◆ यद्- O ◆ ताश्च तद्- V^{pc}Ga ◆ ताश्च Va
305 विशिष्ट-] विशिष्टा M O^{ac}
306 -भाविन्यो] -भागिन्यो O
306–307 प्रथमपरिपठन-] P M K Va ◆ प्रथमपठन- C S Q O V^{ac} ◆ प्रथमावगम- V^{pc}Ga
307 -पूर्व्यास्ते] P Q ◆ -पूर्व्यते C S O V^{ac} ◆ -पूर्वीकाते V^{pc}Ga Va ◆ -पूर्व्याः M K
307 तदनन्तरभावि-] तदन्तरभावि- M
307 -सङ्कलना-] -संकल्पना- C S^{ac} V O
307 -प्रत्ययोपारूढा] -प्रत्ययोपारूढ- O
308 कारिण] -कारिणः स्युः M K Va
308 दोषः] दोषाः C V^{ac}

9.1.4 [पूर्ववर्णसंस्कारसहितान्त्यवर्णपक्षः]

यथा वा पूर्ववर्णजनितसंस्कारसहितोऽन्त्यो वर्ण इति तत्रभवता मीमांसाभाष्यकृता वर्णितं तथा वर्णानामर्थप्रत्यायकत्वमस्तु ॥

9.1.4.1 [संस्कारसामर्थ्यम्]

ननु ' अत्रोक्तं संस्कारस्यार्थप्रतीतिजनकत्वं न दृष्टपूर्वम् ' स्मृतावेव तस्य व्यापार इति ॥

किमियं राजाज्ञा स्मृतिरेव संस्कारेण कर्तव्येति ॥

नेयं राजाज्ञा ' नयाज्ञा त्वेषा । न हि संस्कारो नाम स्वतन्त्रः कोऽपि ध-

Testimonia

309–310 पूर्व … वर्णितं ⁎ पूर्ववर्णजनितसंस्कारसहितोऽन्त्यो वर्णः प्रत्यायक इत्यदोषः (VKG, 38,13)

311–312 ननु … व्यापार इति ⁎ नन्वेकस्मात् वासनापरनाम्नः संस्कारात् कथं कार्यद्वयं भविष्यति ॥ (ŚVT^{Ra}, sphoṭa 102) ◆ एकयैव हि संस्कृत्या कथं कार्यद्वयं भवेत् (ŚVT^{Ra}, vākya 115cd)

313 किम् … कर्तव्येति ⁎ यद्यपि स्मृतिहेतुत्वं संस्कारस्य व्यवस्थितम् । कार्यान्तरेऽपि सामर्थ्यं न तस्य प्रतिषिध्यते ॥ (ŚV^{Ra}, sphoṭa 102)

M K P C S O Q V Ga Va

309 वा] om. V^{pc}Ga

309 न्त्यो] P M K ◆ न्त्य- C S Q V O Ga Va

310 तथा] तथा वा V^{pc}Ga

311 अत्रोक्तं] अत्रोक्त- C ◆ चोक्तं V

311 दृष्टपूर्वम्] दृष्टं S

311 स्मृतावेव] स्मृताविव Q

313 किमियं] किमयं M K

313 स्मृतिरेव] स्मृतेरेव M K

313 कर्तव्येति] कर्त्तव्यतेति M K

314 नयाज्ञा] नायाज्ञा K ◆ याज्ञा M

314–315 धर्मी] धर्मः M K Q ◆ धर्मो V

314 नेयं राजाज्ञा ⁎ The expression *rājājñā* is used, with analogous rhetoric force, in ŚV^{Ra}, abhāva 47b: *na ca rājājñayā sthitam.*

र्मी । किं तु पट्वभ्यासादरप्रत्ययगृहीतेष्वर्थेषु यद् आत्मनः स्मरणे कारणं NM^Va, 164 स संस्कारः । सा च स्मृत्यैव कार्येण कल्प्यमाना शक्तिः । न च शक्तिरूपस्य संस्कारस्य शक्त्यन्तरमर्थप्रतीतिजन्मनि सम्भवति । येनैव कार्येण सा शक्तिः कल्पिता तदपहाय किं कार्यान्तरं कुर्यात् । स्मरणहेतोश्च संस्कारस्य प्रसवकारणमनुभवः । अनुभवहेतोस्त्वस्य नूतनचरितस्य संस्कारस्य जन्मनिमित्तमेव नोत्पश्यामः । तस्मान् नासावर्थप्रतीतिहेतुर्भवति ॥

नैतत् सारम्, वर्णानुभवसंस्कृतमतेः पुंसोऽर्थप्रतीतिदर्शनात् । न हि स्मरणशक्तिः संस्कारः, किं त्वात्मगुणो वासनाख्यः । स च स्मृतिमिवार्थप्रतीतिमपि

Testimonia

316–317 न … शक्त्यन्तरम् ∗ शक्तेः शक्त्यन्तरायोगः (SphS, 7) ◆ न च शक्तौ शक्त्यन्तरयोगोऽवकल्पते, अनवस्थानात् । (ŚVT^Ra, sphoṭa 102)

Notes from editions

319 अनुभवहेतोः ∗ अनुभवः शाब्दबोधात्मकः ॥ (NM^Va)

M K P C S O Q V Ga Va

315 स्मरणे] P M K ◆ स्मरण- C S Q V O Ga Va
316 स] om. K O ◆ सु- C
316 न] om. M^ac
317–319 संस्कारस्य … नूतनचरितस्य] om. K
318 सा शक्तिः कल्पिता] M Va ◆ सा कल्प्यते शक्तिः P C S Q V O Ga ◆ n.a. K
318 तदपहाय] तदापहाय C ◆ n.a. K
319 -कारण-] -करण- S ◆ n.a. K
320 जन्म-] जन्मनि P
320 -र्भवति] -र्भवतीति M K
321 स्मरण-] स्मृति- S
322 संस्कारः] संसारः C

316 सा ∗ Here the feminine *sā* concords with *śakti*, though it logically refers back to the masculine *saṃskāra*, similar to the case discussed in Speijer, 1886, p. 18, fn. 1, *tat satyaṃ sa ātmā*.

321–322 स्मरणशक्तिः संस्कारः ∗ *śakti* is listed as a category in Prābhākaramīmāṃsā (see TR, 20, *dravyaguṇakarmasāmānyasamavāyaśaktisaṃkhyāsādṛśyāny aṣṭau padārthāḥ*), unlike in Vaiśeṣika and in Nyāya.

जनयितुमर्हति । सर्वत्र नो दर्शनं प्रमाणम् । स्मरणजननकौशलमपि तस्य तथादर्शनादवगम्यते । तदिदमनुभवजननमपि ततो दृश्यत एव । वर्णाश्च तदनुभवाश्च व्यतीताः । अन्यच्च शब्दतत्त्वं नानुभूयत इति वक्ष्यामः । अस्ति चार्थप्रतीतिः । नासौ निष्करणिकास्थास्तु । करणव्यतिरेकेण हि सानुद्भवन्ती करणमाक्षिपति । यदस्याः करणं संस्कार इति स्मृतिरिवार्थप्रतीतिरपि तत्कार्यत्वात् तदनुमापिका भवत्येव ॥

Testimonia

323–324 सर्वत्र … अवगम्यते ∗ सर्वत्र नो दर्शनं प्रमाणम् । प्रत्यायक इति हि प्रत्ययं दृष्ट्वा अवगच्छामः । (VKG, 36,15–16)

325 अन्यच्च शब्दतत्त्वं नानुभूयत इति वक्ष्यामः ∗ See Section 9.3 below.

M K P C S O Q V Ga Va

323 -मर्हति] P M K ◆ -मुत्सहति C Q O V^{ac} ◆ -मुत्सह¯ S ◆ -मुत्सहते V^{pc}Ga Va

323 -जनन-] -जन- O

324 -जननम्] -जनम् O^{ac} V^{ac}

324 वर्णाश्च] P V^{pc}C S Q Ga Va ◆ वर्णाः M K ◆ वर्णश्च V^{ac} O

325 अन्यच्च] अन्यश्च O V^{ac}

325 -तत्त्वं] -तत्त्व O

326 निष्करणिकास्थास्तु] P ◆ निष्करणिकास्तु M K ◆ निष्करणिका स्थान- C S Q O V^{ac} ◆ निष्करणिका V^{pc}Ga ◆ निष्करणिका स्यात् Va

326 -व्यतिरेकेण] -व्यतिकरेण S

326 हि] om. M K

327 करणं] कारणं V O

327 संस्कार] M K C ◆ स संस्कार P S Q O V Ga Va

328 -नुमापिका] P M K V^{pc}Ga Va ◆ -नुमानिका C S Q O V^{ac}

326 निष्करणिकास्थास्तु ∗ The received reading is here considered a *lectio difficilior.* The compound *niṣkaraṇikāsthā* is interpreted as a *bahuvrīhi, niṣkaraṇikā āsthā yasyāḥ sā* [*arthapratītiḥ*]. It was apparently trivialised in M and K by expunging the *sthā* part. In part of the *vulgata* the *sthāstu* part has become *sthāna-*, joined in compound to the following clause and deleted by Gangadhara in NM^{Ga}. In NM^{Va} *syāt* is added by conjecture to the NM^{Ga} reading. A similar construction, *śithilitāsthāḥ … ādriyeran sādhavaḥ*, can be seen in NM^{Va}, I 7,8.

यत्तु ' कुतस्तादृशः संस्कार उदेतीति ' जडप्रश्नोऽयम् ' अनुभवहेतुकत्वस्य सुप्रसिद्धत्वात् । तथा चाहुः ' वस्तुधर्मो ह्येष यदनुभवः पटीयान् स्मृतिबीजमाधत्त इति ॥

ननु ' स्मृतिबीजमिति यदुच्यते तत् कथमनुभवबीजं स्यात् ॥

नैष नियमः स्मृतेरेव बीजमिति । अनुभवस्तावत् तथाविधमात्मधर्ममाधत्ते ।
स कार्यभेदेऽपि नोत्पत्तौ कारणान्तरं मृगयते । कार्यभेदश्चास्य तथादर्शनाद- NM^{Va}, 165
वगम्यत इत्युक्तम् ॥

9.1.4.2 [स्मृतिद्वारेण संस्कारसामर्थ्यम्]

अथ वा ' किमनेन निर्बन्धेन । न साक्षादर्थप्रतीतिकारी संस्कारः । स्मृतिद्वारेण
तां करिष्यति । पूर्ववर्णेषु संस्कारात् स्मरणमन्त्यवर्णे श्रोत्रेन्द्रियादनुभव NM^{Shu}, 347
इत्येवं स्मर्यमाणानुभूयमानवर्णकरणकोऽर्थप्रत्ययः स्यात् । को दोषः ॥

Testimonia

330–331 सुप्रसिद्धत्वात् … इति ❋ … सर्वलोकप्रसिद्धं चैतत् । तदुक्तम् । वस्तुधर्मो ह्येष यदनुभवपटीयान् स्मृतिबीजमाधत्ते इति । (ŚVT^{Ra}, sphoṭa 100; PSṬ, 1.5)

Notes from editions

329 तादृशः ❋ तादृशः अनुभवजन्यस्सन् अनुभवहेतुः ॥ (NM^{Va})
334 कार्यभेदे ❋ कार्यविशेषः अनुभवरूपः ॥ (NM^{Va})

M K P C S O Q V Ga Va

329 स्तादृशः] स्तादृश- K ◆ n.a. M
329 उदेतीति] उदेतेति O ◆ उदेति V Ga ◆ n.a. M
329 -हेतुकत्वस्य] P C S ◆ -हेतुकस्य K Q V O Ga Va ◆ n.a. M
330 चाहुः] चाह Ga
330–331 स्मृतिबीजमा-] स्मृतिमा- S
333–334 नियमः स्मृते- … कार्यभेदे] नियमः स्मृ/// ///कार्यभेदे M
333 -स्तावत्] -स्तावदिदानीं K ◆ n.a. M
333 -धत्ते] -दत्ते O ◆ n.a. M
334 कार्यभेदे] P M K ◆ कार्यभेदे भेदो V ◆ कार्यभेदो C S Q O Ga Va
334 -श्चास्य] P M K C S Va ◆ -श्च Q V O Ga
336 निर्बन्धेन । न] M K P^{pc} C S Va ◆ निर्बन्धनेन V O Ga ◆ निर्बन्धेन P^{ac} Q
337 -वर्णे] -वर्ण- M^{pc} K
337 श्रोत्रेन्द्रियादनुभव] -श्रोत्रेन्द्रियानुभव K

ननु ' अनुभवक्रमाहितसंस्कारसामर्थ्यमनुरुध्यमानाः स्मृतयोऽपि क्रमेणोत्पत्तुमर्हन्ति ' न युगपदिति । ततश्च प्राक्तन एव दोषः सामस्त्याभावादिति ॥ नैष दोषः । नानावर्णविषयैः क्रमभाविभिरनुभवैः क्रमोपचीयमानात्मा पुटपाकैरिव कार्तस्वरस्य एक एवात्मनः संस्कारस्तादृगुपाधीयते येन सर्वानेव पूर्वदृष्टान् वर्णानसौ सकृत् स्मरति इति ॥

9.1.4.3 [संस्करात् संस्कारोत्पत्तेरनलौकिकत्वम्]

संस्कारात् संस्कारोत्पत्तिरलौकिकीति चेत् ' नालौकिकी ' स्वाध्यायाध्ययने सिद्धत्वात् । उच्चारणक्रियायाः क्षणिकत्वात्तदाहिते संस्कारान्तरकारिणि संस्कारेऽनिष्यमाणेऽन्त्यमुच्चारणं प्रथमोच्चारणान्न विशिष्येतेति पुरुषायुषेणापि

Notes from editions

341 क्रमोपचीयमानात्मा ∗ प्रथमं एकवर्णविषयकः, ततः वर्णद्वयविषयः एवमुपचीयमानः ॥ (NM[Va])

M K P C S O Q V Ga Va

340 एव] om. M K

341 -वर्ण-] -वर्णक्रम- M K

341 क्रमभाविभिः] om. P^{ac} S

341 क्रमोपचीयमानात्मा] P M K C ◆ क्रमोपचीयात्मा O V^{ac} ◆ क्रमोपचेयात्मा Q V^{pc}Ga - Va ◆ क्रमो---- S

342 -पाकैरिव] -प्रापकैरिव O

342–349 संस्कारस्तादृग् ... वयम्] om. S (three blank lines)

342 -गुपाधीयते] -गुपादीयते Q ◆ n.a. S

342 येन] तेन C ◆ n.a. S

344 चेत् ' नालौकिकी] om. O ◆ n.a. S

344 स्वाध्यायाध्ययने] M K P Ga Va ◆ स्वाध्यायने C Q V O ◆ n.a. S

345 -क्रियायाः] क्रियायां V ◆ n.a. S

346 विशिष्येतेति] विशिष्येते किं V^{ac} ◆ विशिष्येते ततः किं V^{pc} ◆ विशिष्येत । ततः किं Ga ◆ विशिष्येतेति । ततः किं Va ◆ n.a. S

341–342 पुटपाकैरिव कार्तस्वरस्य ∗ Cf. NM[Va], I 273,6–7, NM 2: *yathā vā puṭapākena śodhyamānaṃ śanaiś śanaiḥ / hema niṣpratikāśaṃ tad yāti kalyāṇatāṃ parām.* The example may point to the process of removing impurities from gold by melting it.

नानुवाक एक आमुखीक्रियेत ॥

9.1.4.4 [स्फोटपक्षे कल्पनाद्वैविध्यम्]

ननु ' अयमीदृशः प्रकार एकस्मरणसिद्धये कल्पनीयः ' अर्थप्रतीतिहेतुता वा संस्कारस्य कल्पनीया इति। सर्वथा वयमदृष्टकल्पनातो न मुच्यामहे। तत्र (NM^{Va}, 166) कः संस्कारं प्रति पक्षपातः ' कश्च स्फोटं प्रति विद्वेषः ॥

यदेष कल्प्यते नैष इति। उक्तमत्र तेनैव सुगृहीतनाम्ना भाष्यकारेण शब्दकल्पनायां सा च शब्दकल्पना च इति ॥

ननु ' नास्ति कल्पनाद्वैगुण्यम्। संस्कारो हि यथाप्रसिद्धि स्थित एव। का तत्र कल्पना। न हि वयं स्मरणैककारणत्वं संस्कारधर्ममतिलङ्घितवन्तो भवन्त

Testimonia

349 न मुच्यामहे ⁕ सोऽपि पर्यनुयोगेन नैवानेन विमुच्यते ॥ (ŚV^{Ra}, sphoṭa 91cd)
351–352 शब्दकल्पनायां सा च शब्दकल्पना च ⁕ VKG, 40,11

Notes from editions

351 यदेष ⁕ एषः संस्कारः। एषः स्फोटः ॥ (NM^{Va})
354–355 भवन्त इव ⁕ इदं च संस्कारस्यार्थप्रतीतिहेतुत्वकल्पनपक्षाभिप्रायेण ॥ (NM^{Va})

M K P C S O Q V Ga Va

347 एक] P M^{pc} K C Q ◆ एव M V O Ga Va ◆ n.a. S
347 -क्रियेत] P M K Ga Va ◆ -क्रियते C Q O V^{ac} ◆ n.a. S
349 सर्वथा वयमदृष्ट-] P^{pc} M K Q ◆ सर्वथावयवमदृष्ट- P^{ac} ◆ सर्वथा˘˘˘यमदृष्ट- C ◆ सर्वथेयमदृष्ट- V Ga ◆ सर्वथायमदृष्ट- O ◆ सर्वथा चेयमदृष्ट- Va ◆ n.a. S
349 -कल्पनातो] -कल्पना। अतो Q Va
349 मुच्यामहे] P M K C ◆ पश्यामहे S Q V O Ga Va
350 संस्कारं] संस्कारः M K
350 विद्वेषः] द्वेषो M K
351 यदेष] यदेष संस्कार P^{pc}
351 कल्प्यते] कल्पते M
351 नैष] नैष स्फोटः P^{pc}
353 -प्रसिद्धि-] -प्रसिद्ध O V^{ac}
353 तत्र] तत्- V Q Ga
354 स्मरणैक-] स्मरणेनैक- O

347 आमुखीक्रियेत ⁕ See note on *āmukhī-kṛ-* and *abhimukhī-kṛ-* at line 258 above.
350 प्रति ⁕ See Pā, 1.4.90, *karmapravacanīya* in a distributive sense (*bhāge*).

इव ॥

कथं न लङ्घितवन्तो भवन्तः । सर्ववर्णविषयैकस्मरणकारणता हि भवद्भिरपि कल्पितैव । यैव हि वर्तनी वर्णानामर्थप्रतीतौ सैव स्फोटव्यक्तावपि । तां च कल्पयित्वा शब्दोऽप्यन्यः कल्पित एव । अतश्च संस्कारस्योभयवादिविदितस्य स्मरणकारित्वमुल्लङ्घ्य अर्थप्रत्ययकारित्वं केवलमधिकमस्माभिरभिहितम् । भवद्भिस्तु मूलत एवारभ्य नवं विश्वमुत्थापितम् । अपूर्वस्य शब्दस्य तावदस्तित्वं पुनर्वर्णव्यतिरिक्तत्वं

Notes from editions

356 सर्व- … -कारणता हि ∗ पूर्वपूर्वसंस्कारस्येति शेषः ॥ (NM^{Va})
358–360 अतश्च … -स्माभिरभिहितम् ∗ सिद्धे वस्तुनि अतिरिक्तधर्ममात्रकल्पनमत्र, भवतस्तु धार्मिणोऽपि कल्पनम् । इदं सर्वं संस्कारस्यार्थप्रत्ययहेतुत्वपक्षे । स्मृतिहेतुत्वपक्षे त्वस्यापि नावकाशः ॥ (NM^{Va})
361 अपूर्वस्य ∗ अपूर्वस्य सूक्ष्मस्य स्फोटाख्यस्य ॥ (NM^{Va})

M K P C S O Q V Ga Va

356 लङ्घितवन्तो भवन्तः] लंघितवन्तः M K
356 सर्व-] P M K V^{pc} Ga Va ◆ सर्वथा C S Q O V^{ac}
356 -वर्ण-] -वर्णक- M K
356 -कारणता हि] P M K ◆ -कारिता C S Q V O Ga Va ◆ -कारणिका Va^{च}
356–357 भवद्भिरपि] भवद्भिः M K
358 प्यन्यः] P M K C S ◆ न्यः Q V O Ga Va
358 एव] M K C ◆ एवम् P S Q V O Ga Va
358–359 अतश्च] ततश्च M K ◆ स तच्च C
359 संस्कारस्योभय-] P M K C Va ◆ संस्कारोभय- Q V O Ga ◆ उभय- S
359 -विदितस्य] -विहितस्य V Ga
360 -मधिक-] P M K ◆ om. C S Q V O Ga Va
360 एवारभ्य नवं] एवारभ्याभिनवं M K Va
361 -मुत्थापितम्] -मुत्पादितम् P
361 अपूर्वस्य] अपूर्व- M
361 -व्यतिरिक्तत्वं] -व्यतिरिक्तं S

पुनरनवयवत्वं कल्पितमिति कथं न कल्पनागुरुत्वम् । तदुक्तम् '

सद्भावव्यतिरेकौ च तथावयववर्जनम् । $\mathrm{NM}^{\mathrm{Va}}$, 167
तवाधिकं भवेत्तस्माद्यत्नोऽसावर्थबुद्धिषु ॥ इति ॥

9.1.4.5 [स्फोटव्यञ्जकत्वानुपपत्तिः]

9.1.4.5.1 [वर्णानां स्फोटव्यञ्जकत्वानुपपत्तिः]

यत् पुनरवादि ' प्रथमवर्णबुद्धिवेलायामेव व्यक्तं स्फोटतत्त्वमुत्तरोत्तरवर्णबुद्धिभिरतिशयिततरप्रत्ययविषयतां नीयते रत्नतत्त्ववद् इति ' स एष विषम

Granthibhaṅga

363 सद्भावव्यतिरेकौ चेति । स्फोट/// /// क्रियतेऽसौ वर्णेभ्योऽर्थबुद्धिजन्मन्येव क्रियतां कल्पनाला///

Testimonia

363–364 सद्भाव- … ऽसावर्थबुद्धिषु ⁂ सद्भावव्यतिरेकौ च तथावयववर्जनम् । तवाधिकं भवेद्यस्माद्यत्नोऽसावर्थबुद्धिषु ॥ ($\mathrm{ŚV}^{\mathrm{Ra}}$, sphoṭa 94)

Notes from editions

363–364 सद्भाव- … ऽसावर्थबुद्धिषु ⁂ श्लोकवार्तिके स्फोटवादे श्लो॰ ९४ । तव स्फोटवादिनः स्फोटसद्भावः तस्य च वर्णेभ्यो व्यतिरेकः सावयवे पदे गम्यमाने तद्विपरीतं निरवयवत्वं च कल्पनीयम् तस्मादवश्याश्रयणीयः संस्कारादिकल्पनांशः अर्थबुद्धावेवाश्रयणीयो न स्फोटाभिव्यक्तावित्यर्थः । ($\mathrm{NM}^{\mathrm{Shu}}$)

M K P C S O Q V Ga Va

362 -रनवयवत्वं] P ◆ -रवयं K ◆ -रवयवत्व CS ◆ -रवयव- QOV^{ac} ◆ ----- M ◆ -रवयवरहित्यं V^{pc}Ga Va
362 कल्पितमिति] कल्पनमिति Q
362 कथं न] कथमनव- P
364 तवाधिकं] न बाधिकं O
364–366 बुद्धिषु इति … -तिशयिततर-] बुद्धिषु इति/// ///तिशयिततर- M
365 -वर्ण-¹] om. K ◆ n.a. M
365 -मेव] -मिव Ga ◆ n.a. M
365 व्यक्तं] व्यक्त- O ◆ n.a. M
365 -वर्ण-²] PKCS ◆ om. QVOGaVa ◆ n.a. M
366 -प्रत्ययविषयतां] -प्रत्ययतां QVOGa
366 एष] एव O

365–366 प्रथमवर्णबुद्धिवेलायामेव … रत्नतत्त्ववद् इति ⁂ See Section 8.2.1.4.3.

उपन्यासः। रत्नस्य हि सावयवत्वात् प्रथमप्रत्ययाविषयीकृतसूक्ष्मतरावयवविशेषग्राहिणामुत्तरोत्तरप्रत्ययानाम् अस्ति तत्रावकाशः। स्फोटस्तु वर्णस्वरूपवदनंश इति तत्स्वरूपसर्वस्वमाद्येनैव वर्णेन व्यक्तम्। (NM[Shu], 348) किमिदानीमन्ये वर्णाः करिष्यन्ति। एकदेशव्यक्तिस्तु निरवयवस्य वर्णस्येव न सम्भवति। यथोक्तम् '

अल्पीयसापि यत्नेन शब्दमुच्चरितं मतिः।
यदि वा नैव गृह्णाति वर्णं वा सकलं स्फुटम्॥ इति॥

Testimonia

372–373 अल्पीयसापि … स्फुटम् ∗ ŚV[Ra], sphoṭa 10

Notes from editions

370 निरवयवस्य ∗ वाक्यस्येत्यध्याहारः॥ (NM[Va])

372–373 अल्पीयसापि … स्फुटम् ∗ श्लोकवार्तिके स्फोटवादे श्लो॰ १०। अल्पीयसापि यत्नेन उच्चरितं शब्दं यदि मतिः सकलं वर्णं न गृह्णाति तदा वर्णानामवयवसिद्धिः स्यात् साकल्यवैकल्यग्रहणे हि अवयवसिद्धिः नैवमस्तीति भावः। (NM[Shu])

372 अल्पीयसापि ∗ अल्पीयसा एकवर्णोच्चारणानुकूलप्रयत्नेनोच्चारितः यदा एको वर्ण [sic] तदैव समग्रमपि वाक्यं मतिः गृह्णीयात्, अथ वा कदापि वा न गृह्णीयात्, वाक्यस्फोटस्य निरवयवत्वात्॥ (NM[Va])

M K P C S O Q V Ga Va

367 उपन्यासः] उपमन्यासः M[pc]K

368 -प्रत्ययानाम्] -विषयाणाम् O

368 वर्ण-] वर्णं C

369–370 किमिदानीमन्ये वर्णाः] किमित्येकवर्णा C

371 यथोक्तम्] om. K

372 -मुच्चरितं] P M K ◆ -मुच्चारितं C S Q V O Ga Va

योऽपि द्वितीयो दृष्टान्त उदाहारि ' यथानुवाकः श्लोको वा प्रथमसंस्थया गृहीतोऽपि संस्थान्तराभ्यासैः स्फुटतरपरिच्छेदो भवति ' तथा स्फोटोऽपि प्रथमवर्णव्यक्तो वर्णान्तरैरतिशयिताभिव्यक्तिर्भविष्यति इति ' सोऽपि न सदृशो दृष्टान्तः ' श्लोकानुवाकयोरनंशत्वानुपपत्तेः । केचिदवयवा वर्णात्मानः पदात्मानो वा प्रथमायां बुद्धावपरिस्फुरन्तः संस्थाभ्यासलब्धातिशयायां तस्यां NM^{Va}, 168

Granthibhaṅga

374 'यथानुवाकः श्लोको वेति' । आवृत्त्या न तु स ग्रन्थः प्रत्यावृत्ति निरूप्यत इति ॥ आवृत्त्या [p. 164] 'आ///' ///ति प्रत्यावृत्तिनिरूपणमस्ति ॥ ◆◆◆ यथानुवाकः श्लोको वेति] the *pratīka* is lost in J and absent in Sha Gra ◆ आ-] अ- Sha

Testimonia

374 यथानुवाक- … श्लोको वा ✱ यथानुवाकः श्लोको वा सोढत्वमुपगच्छते । आवृत्त्या न तु स ग्रन्थः प्रत्यावृत्ति निरूप्यते ॥ VP^{Iyer}, 1.84 ◆ यथानुवाकग्रहणे संस्थाभ्यासनकल्पितः । स्थिरः करोति संस्कारः पाठस्मृत्यादिपाटवम् NM^{Va}, I 273,3–4, NM 2

M K P C S O Q V Ga Va

374 उदाहारि] उदहारि P O

374 वा] पि वा S

374 प्रथम-] प्रथमा P

374 -संस्थया] -संस्थाया V^{ac}

375 संस्थान्तराभ्यासैः] P M K Q Va ◆ संस्थानान्तराभ्यासैः C S O^{pc} V Ga ◆ स्थानांतराभ्यासैः O^{ac}

375 स्फुटतर-] स्फुटतरं Va

375 -परिच्छेदो] P M ◆ -परिच्छेद्यो K ◆ -परिच्छिन्नो C S Q V O Ga ◆ परिच्छिन्नो Va

376 -वर्णव्यक्तो] -वर्णव्यक्तौ O ◆ -वर्णव्यतिरिक्तो S^{ac} ◆ om. Va

376 -ताभिव्यक्ति-] -तव्यक्ति- K

377–378 वर्णात्मानः पदात्मानो] पदात्मानो वर्णात्मानो M K

377 वर्णात्मानः] वर्णात्मनः V^{ac}

378 पदात्मानो] पदात्मनो V O

378 बुद्धावपरि-] बुद्धौ परि- M K ◆ बुद्धावपि परि- C

प्रकटीभवन्ति। स्फोटस्त्वेको वर्ण इव निरंश इति कस्तत्र बुद्धेरतिशययोगः। तस्मादयमपि न सङ्गतो दृष्टान्तः ॥

9.1.4.5.2 [ध्वनीनां स्फोटव्यञ्जकत्वानुपपत्तिः]

येऽपि मन्वते ' ध्वनिव्यङ्ग्यत्वात् स्फोटस्य न तत्र वर्णविकल्पावसर इति ' तेऽपि न सम्यग्दर्शिनः ' पराणुद्य वर्णप्रतीतिं ध्वनिभ्यः शब्दप्रतीतेरनुत्पादात् ' अतिद्रुतोच्चिचारयिषया अनुपलक्ष्यमाणवर्णविभागाच्च शब्दादर्थप्रत्ययाभावात् ॥

अथ ' ध्वनयः शब्दव्यक्तिमादधानाः स्थानकरणानुरोधेनासत्यमेव वर्णभेद-

Notes from editions

382 पराणुद्य ∗ पराणुद्य परित्यज्य ॥ (NM[Va])
383 अनुपलक्ष्यमाण- ∗ उच्चरितस्य वाक्यस्य श्रवणे इति अर्थसिद्धम् ॥ (NM[Va])

M K P C S O Q V Ga Va

379 प्रकटी-] om. S
379 -भवन्ति] -भविष्यन्ति O Va
379 -स्त्वेको वर्ण] P M K C S ◆ -स्त्वेकवर्ण Q V O Ga Va
379 इव] एव O
379 इति] om. M K
379 कस्तत्र] P M K ◆ तत्र को C S Q V O Ga Va
381 पि] P M K ◆ पि च C S Q V O Ga Va
381 वर्ण-] वर्णवत् तद्- V^{pc}
382 पराणुद्य] पराणुभ्यः Q O V^{ac} Ga
382 -प्रतीतिं] -प्रतीतेः Q ◆ -प्रतीति- S^{ac} Ga ◆ -प्रतीत- S^{pc}
383 अतिद्रुतोच्चिचारयिषया] अतिद्रुतोश्चारविषय O
383 अनुपलक्ष्यमाण-] P M K ◆ अनुपलभ्यमान- C S Q V O Ga Va
383 -विभागाच्च] -विभागाश्च V O ◆ -विभाषायांश्च C
385 -व्यक्ति-] -शक्ति- Q
385 -करणानु-] -कारणानु- M^{pc}K
385–386 वर्णभेदमुप-] वर्णमुप- O

381 ध्वनिव्यङ्ग्यत्वात् … -विकल्पावसर इति ∗ See Section 8.2.1.4.4.
385–386 ध्वनयः … खङ्गादय इत्युच्यते ∗ See Section 8.2.1.4.4

मुपदर्शयन्ति ' श्यामादिरूपमिव मुखस्य खड्गादय इत्युच्यते ' तदप्यसत् ' असत्यत्वे निमित्ताभावात् । प्रतीयन्ते हि निर्बाधया बुद्ध्या वर्णाः । तदतिरिक्तस्तु शब्दो न प्रतीयते । यश्च न प्रतीयते सोऽस्ति ये च प्रतीयन्ते ते न सन्तीत्युच्यमाने शशो नास्ति विषाणमस्तीति स्यात् । तस्मादयमपि न कल्पनागौरवपरिहारक्षमः पन्थाः । अतः सुष्ठूक्तं ' शब्दकल्पनायां सा च शब्दकल्पना च इति । तस्मात् स्फोटप्रतिपत्तौ यः क्रम आस्थेयः सोऽर्थप्रतिपत्तावास्थीयतामिति किं तेन स्फोटेन ॥

9.1.5 [व्युत्पत्तिपक्षः]

अन्ये तु उपलब्ध्यनन्तरसत्ताकानां वर्णानामर्थप्रत्यायकत्वमाचक्षते । तदिह

Granthibhaṅga

393 उपलब्ध्यनन्तरसत्ता'कानामिति'/// ◆◆◆ -कानामिति] -कानादि Sha

Testimonia

389 शशो … स्यात् ✳ ध्रुवं शशविषाणेन खरशृङ्गस्य तद्भवेत् ॥ (ŚV^{Dvā}, vākya 129cd)
390–391 शब्दकल्पनायां सा च शब्दकल्पना च ✳ VKG, 40,11, see line 352 above.

M K P C S O Q V Ga Va

386 श्यामादि-] श्यामाभि- C
386 तदप्यसत्] तदसत् P^{ac} ◆ om. M K
387 निमित्ताभावात्] निमित्तत्वात् P^{ac} ◆ निमित्तात् P^{pc}
387 निर्बाधया] निर्विवादया P
387–388 तदतिरिक्तस्तु] तदितिरिक्तस्तु M K V^{ac} ◆ तदतिरिक्तास्तु O
388 यश्च न प्रतीयते] om. K
389 -त्युच्यमाने] -त्युपमाने O
389–390 तस्मादयमपि] तदयमपि S
390 कल्पना-] om. O
390 अतः सुष्ठूक्तं] अत उक्तं शोभनं S
392 -प्रतिपत्तावा-] -प्रतिपत्तावेवा- V^{pc}Ga ◆ -प्रतीतावेवा- Va
392 किं] किमिव P
392 तेन] om. M K
392 स्फोटेन] om. P

387 निमित्ताभावात् ✳ The P reading is congruous only if interpreted as *'nimittatvāt* or *'nimittāt*, though no indication of the *avagraha* is present in the manuscript.

NM[Va], 169 नेष्यते ' क्षणिकत्वाद्वर्णानामुपलब्धेरूर्ध्वं सत्तानुपपत्तेः । सर्वथा व्युत्पत्त्यनुसारेण वर्णानामर्थप्रत्यायकत्वम् । तद्यथा पुरा दृष्टं तथाभ्युपगम्यत इति । तदुक्तम् ' यावन्तो यादृशा इति ॥

यत्त्वत्र प्रतीपमुक्तं ' कियन्तः कीदृशा इति ' तत्र प्रतीतयः प्रष्टव्याः न
NM[Shu], 349 तपस्विनो वयमिति यत् किंचिदेतत् ॥

9.1.5.1 [व्युत्पत्तौ विपरीतक्रमप्रसङ्गानवकाशत्वम्]

यत् पुनरभ्यधायि ' क्रमव्यत्यासप्रयुक्ता अपि वर्णाः प्रत्यायका भवेयुः क्रम एव वा स्फोटः स्याद् इति ' तदपि न पेशलम् । क्रमो हि नाम कालभेदः ।

Granthibhaṅga

399–400 ///˚म˚ एव वा ˚स्फोट स्यादिति˚ । शब्दस्य अर्थप्रतीतिहेतो˚र्वर्णाति˚///
◆◆◆ म] स Sha ◆ स्फोट स्यादिति] स्फोटादिति J^{ac} Sha ◆ वर्णाति-] वर्णादि Sha

Testimonia

396 यावन्तो यादृशा ✻ यावन्तो यादृशा ये च यदर्थप्रतिपादने । वर्णाः प्रज्ञातसामर्थ्यास्ते तथैवावबोधकाः ॥ (ŚV[Ra], sphoṭa 69)

Notes from editions

397 प्रतीपमुक्तं ✻ 'यावन्तो यादृशा' इत्यस्य प्रतिकक्ष्यतया ॥ (NM[Va])

M K P C S O Q V Ga Va

394 नेष्यते] ना˘˘क्षते O ◆ नाचक्षते Va[क]
397 तत्र] om. O
397–399 प्रष्टव्याः … क्रम एव] प्रष्टव्या/// ///क्रम एव M
397 न] न तु P ◆ n.a. M
399 -प्रयुक्ता] -युक्ता O ◆ n.a. M
400 स्फोटः] स्फोटगती M
400 काल-] स काल- Q V O Ga

394–395 सर्वथा … तथाभ्युपगम्यत इति ✻ See Section 8.1.6.
394 सर्वथा ✻ I.e., *kṣaṇikatve nityatve vā.*
396 यावन्तो यादृशा ✻ See line 70 above.
397 कियन्तः कीदृशा इति ✻ See line 76 above.
398 यत् किंचिदेतत् ✻ The expression *yat kiṃcid etat* is used by Jayanta also elsewhere with similar rhetorical force, e.g. in NM[Va], II 579,3.
399–400 क्रमव्यत्यास- … स्फोटः स्याद् इति ✻ See Section 8.1.5.

न च काल एव स्फोटो भवितुमर्हति। क्रमोऽपि च न स्वतन्त्रः प्रतिपादकः पदार्थान्तरवृत्तिर्वा ' किं तु वर्णाश्रित एव। तत्र चोक्तम् '

द्वये सत्यपि तेनात्र विज्ञेयोऽर्थस्य वाचकः।
वर्णाः किं नु क्रमोपेताः किं नु वर्णाश्रयः क्रमः॥
क्रमः क्रमवतामङ्गमिति किं युक्तिसाध्यता।
धर्ममात्रमसौ तेषां न वस्त्वन्तरमिष्यते॥

तस्माद्ये यावत्क्रमका यमर्थं प्रत्याययन्तो वर्णा दृष्टास्ते तत्क्रमका तमर्थं

Granthibhaṅga

401–402 [161v] क्रमस्तु केषां क्रम इति। सापेक्षत्वात् सर्वथा परतन्त्र इ--युं///

Testimonia

403–406 द्वये … -मिष्यते ∗ द्वये सत्यपि तेनात्र विज्ञेयो ऽर्थस्य वाचकः। वर्णाः किं नु क्रमोपेताः किं नु वर्णाश्रयः क्रमः॥ क्रमः क्रमवतामङ्गमिति किं युक्तिसाध्यता। धर्ममात्रमसौ तेषां न वस्त्वन्तरमिष्यते॥ (ŚV[Dvā], śabdanityatā 285–286)

Notes from editions

403 द्वये ∗ क्रमविशिष्टा वर्णा वाचकाः? अथ वा वर्णानां क्रमः वाचकः? इति पक्षद्वये क्रमस्य वर्णाश्रितत्वेनाप्रधानत्वात् प्रथमपक्ष एव साधीयान्॥ (NM[Va])

403–406 द्वये … -मिष्यते ∗ श्लोकवार्तिके शब्दनित्यताधिकरणे २८५--२८६। क्रमोपेता वर्णा वर्णक्रमो वा वाचक इति द्वये सत्यपि क्रमोपेता वर्णा एव वाचकः न तु वर्णक्रमः स हि वर्णानां धर्ममात्रं न वस्त्वन्तरं तस्मात्प्रतीयमाना क्रमोपेता वर्णा एव वाचक इति भावः। (NM[Shu])

M K P C S O Q V Ga Va

401 च न] न च O
402 पदार्थान्तर-] पदान्तर- M S
402 वर्णाश्रित एव] वर्णाश्रितो वा S ◆ n.a. M
402 तत्र चोक्तम्] तत्रोक्तं O ◆ n.a. M
404 क्रमः] क्रमाः C
405 क्रमः] क्रमा C
405 क्रमवता-] क्रमकृता- O
406–407 -मिष्यते … तत्क्रमका] -मिष्यते/// ///त्क्रमका M
407 यावत्क्रमका] यत्क्रमका K ◆ n.a. M
407 प्रत्याययन्तो] प्रत्यायन्तो S ◆ n.a. M
407 वर्णा दृष्टास्ते] P K ◆ दृष्टा वर्णास्ते C S Q V O Ga Va ◆ n.a. M
407 तत्क्रमका] P M K ◆ तत्क्रमका वर्णाः C S Q V O Ga Va

प्रत्याययिष्यन्ति इति न स्फोटादर्थावगतिः। तदेवं कार्यानुमानमर्थापत्तिर्वा न स्फोटसिद्धये प्रभवतीति स्थितम् ॥

9.2 [लोकव्यवहारे वर्णपक्षानुपपत्तिरिति प्रतिपक्षः]

NM^{Va}, 170 यदप्यभाणि ' शब्दादर्थं प्रतिपद्यामह इति व्यवहारः स्फोटपक्षसाक्षितामवलम्बत इति ' तदप्यसारम् ' वर्णानां वाचकत्वे यथोक्तनीत्या साधिते तत्पक्षेऽपि तथा व्यवहारोपपत्तेः ॥

ननु ' कथमुपपत्तिः। संस्कारस्तावन् न शब्दशब्देनोच्यते। न हि तथा लोके प्रसिद्धिः। संस्कारे च वाचके व्युत्पत्तिरपि दुरुपपादा। परावगतिपूर्विका हि शब्दात् स्वयमवगतिः। न च परस्थः संस्कारः परस्य प्रतीतिमुपजनयन्

Testimonia

410–411 शब्दादर्थं ... -मवलम्बत ✻ नन्वेवमपि शब्दादर्थं प्रतिपद्यामह इति लौकिकं वचनमनुपपन्नं स्यात् (VKG, 38,14)

Notes from editions

414 संस्कारे च ✻ शब्दानां नष्टत्वात्, तत्संस्काराणामेव वाचकत्वं सिद्धं भवति ॥ (NM^{Va})

M K P C S O Q V Ga Va

408 प्रत्याययिष्यन्ति] प्रत्याययन्ति S
408 -गतिः] -गतिरिति V Ga
408 तदेवं] तदेवं न Ga
409 न] om. V O Ga
409 स्थितम्] P M K ◆ सिद्धम् S Q V O Ga Va ◆ सिद्धे C
410 शब्दादर्थं] शब्दादथ Va
411 -मवलम्बत] P M C S Q O ◆ -मवलंबित K ◆ -मेवालम्बते V Ga ◆ -मालम्बते Va
411 ऽसारम्] ऽसारे C
413 मुपपत्तिः] -मपत्तिः O
413 संस्कारस्तावन्] शब्दस्तावन् O
414 -रपि] -रपि तु M
414 दुरुपपादा] दुरुपपदा C
414 परावगति-] पदावगति- K
414 -पूर्विका] -पूर्वा S
415 स्वयमवगतिः] P M K ◆ स्वावगतिः C S Q O V Ga Va
415 संस्कारः] om. C

410–411 शब्दादर्थं ... -मवलम्बत ✻ See Section 8.2.1.1

ग्रहीतुं शक्यः ' परोक्षत्वात् । वर्णेष्वपि शब्दशब्दो वर्तमानः प्रतिवर्णं वा वर्तेत वर्णसमुदाये वा । प्रतिवर्णं वर्तमाने शब्दशब्दे न शब्दादर्थप्रतिपत्तिः स्याद् ' एकस्य वर्णस्य वाचकत्वायोगात् । समुदाये तु न वर्तितुमर्हति शब्दशब्दः ' जातिशब्दत्वात् । द्विवचनबहुवचनान्तव्यक्तिशब्दप्रयोगे हि न तत्सामानाधिकरण्येन जातिशब्द एकवचनान्तः प्रयुज्यते । न हि भवति देवदत्तयज्ञदत्तौ पुरुष इति धवखदिरपलाशा वृक्ष इति । तथा गकारौकारविसर्जनीयाः शब्द इत्यपि न स्यात् ॥

वनशब्दवत्तर्हि समुदायवाची भविष्यति शब्दशब्दो वनं वृक्षा न जातिशब्दवदिति चेत् ' न ' तत्र समुदायिव्यतिरेकनिर्देशदर्शनाद् ' आम्राणां वनं

M K P C S O Q V Ga Va

417 -समुदाये] -समुदायो O
417 वर्तमाने] P ◆ प्रवर्त्तमाने M K ◆ वर्तमाने च C S Q V O Ga Va
417 शब्दशब्दे] शब्दे Ga
417 न] om. O
417 शब्दादर्थ-] शब्दार्थ- O
418 न] om. V[ac]
418 वर्ति-] प्रवर्त्ति- M K
419 -व्यक्ति-] -व्यक्त- C[ac]
419 -शब्दप्रयोगे] -शब्दाप्रयोगे C ◆ -शब्दे प्रयोगे M
419–420 न तत्सामानाधि-] P C S ◆ न सामानाधि- M K ◆ तत्सामानाधि- Q V Ga ◆ तस्मात् सामानाधि- O Va
420 -करण्येन] -करण्येन न V Ga Va
422 स्यात्] P M K ◆ om. C S Q V O Ga Va
423 वन- … न] वनं वृक्षाः इति वनशब्दवत्तर्हि समुदायवाची भविष्यति शब्दशब्दो, न Va
424 -शब्द-] om. S
424 समुदायि-] P M K ◆ समुदाय- C S Q V O Ga Va
424 -व्यतिरेक-] व्यतिरेके Q[ac]
424 -निर्देशदर्शनाद्] -निर्देशाद् P ◆ -दर्शनाद् S Q[ac]

423–424 वनशब्दवत्तर्हि … न जातिशब्दवदिति * The conjecture in Va is partially justified — especially the *iti* after *vanaṃ vṛkṣāḥ*— since the passage is particularly problematic. Even this *iti*, however, is not supported anywhere in the manuscript tradition, thus the more difficult reading has been received here.

कपित्थानां वनमिति। न चैवमिह व्यतिरेकनिर्देशोऽस्ति ' गकारादीनां शब्द इत्यदर्शनात् ॥

NM[Shu], 350 NM[Va], 171

ब्रूयाद् ' आम्रादयो वनमित्यभेदेनापि वनशब्दः प्रयुज्यते ' तथेहापि गकारादयः शब्द इति प्रयोच्यते । एतदपि नास्ति । वनादौ भेदव्यपदेशवशेन प्रतिव्यक्ति चाप्रयोगेण सिद्धे समुदायशब्दत्वे समुदायसमुदायिनोरभेदोपचारादाम्रादयो वनमिति युज्यते प्रयोक्तुम् । इह तु गकारादीनां शब्द इति न कदाचिदपि व्यतिरेकनिर्देशो दृश्यते ' प्रतिवर्णव्यक्ति च प्रयोगो दृश्यत इति समुदायशब्दत्वमघटमानम् । तत्सर्वथा वर्णवादिनामनुपपन्नोऽयं व्यपदेशः शब्दादर्थं प्रतिपद्यामह इति ॥

M K P C S O Q V Ga Va

425 चैवमिह] चैवं M O
425 व्यतिरेकनिर्देशो] व्यतिरेको S
426 इत्यदर्शनात्] इति दर्शनात् C V^{ac}
427 ब्रूयाद्] P M K ◆ अथ ब्रूयाद् C S Q V O Ga Va
427 प्रयुज्यते] प्रयुज्येत S
428 शब्द इति] शब्दायति O
428 प्रयोच्यते] P M K V^{pc}Ga Va ◆ प्रयोच्यन्ते C S Q ◆ प्रयोज्यते V^{ac} ◆ प्रयुज्यंते O
428 एतदपि] तदपि O^{pc}
429 -वशेन] -वशेन न M
429 प्रतिव्यक्ति] प्रवृत्ति C
429 चाप्रयोगेण] P C ◆ चाप्रयोगे न S Ga ◆ चाप्रयोगे न च M K ◆ चाप्रयोगे V O Va ◆ वाप्रयोगे Q
429 सिद्धे] प्रसिद्धे V^{pc}Ga
430–431 गकारादीनां] गादीनां C
431–432 न … इति] om. O
431 व्यतिरेक-] वृत्तिरेक- C ◆ n.a. O
431–432 प्रतिवर्ण- … दृश्यत] om. V Ga Va ◆ n.a. O
432 -व्यक्ति] P M K S Q ◆ -व्यक्तिं C ◆ n.a. V O Ga Va
432 च] P C S Q ◆ om. M K ◆ n.a. V O Ga Va
433 वर्ण-] वर्णशब्द- V^{pc}Ga Va
433 शब्दादर्थं] शब्दार्थं M^{ac} K C

9.2.1 [लोकव्यवहाराप्राधान्यत्वमिति सिद्धान्तः]

उच्यते ' किमनेनोपपन्नेनानुपपन्नेन वा कृत्यम् । यद्ययमुपपद्येत ततः किम् । अथापि नोपपद्येत ततोऽपि किम् । न हि लोकव्यपदेशनिबन्धना वस्तुस्थितिर्भवति ॥

ननु ' शास्त्रकारा अप्येवं वा व्यवहरन्ति भावमाख्यातेनाचष्टे इति ॥

न शास्त्रकारव्यवहारादपि अप्रामाणिकोऽर्थः शक्यतेऽभ्युपगन्तुम् । कतरच्चेदं प्रमाणं लोकव्यपदेशो नाम । अनुमानं तावत् प्रतिक्षिप्तम् । प्रत्यक्षमपि प्रतिक्षेप्स्यते । न चान्यत् स्फोटसिद्धौ प्रमाणं क्रमते । तदस्थानेऽयं लोकव्य-

Granthibhaṅga

437 **शास्त्रकारा इति** अनेन निरुक्तकारयास्काचार्यान् परामृशति । अ/// ///ति ।

Testimonia

437 भावमाख्यातेनाचष्टे ∗ भावमाख्यातेनाचाष्टे (Sarup, 1967, 1.1, p. 28,1).

Notes from editions

435–436 वस्तुस्थितिर्भवति ∗ किन्तु प्रमाणाधीनेति शेषः ॥ (Va)

437 भावमाख्यातेनाचष्टे ∗ भवत्पक्षे हि संस्कारेणाचष्टे इति स्यात् ॥ (Va)

M K P C S O Q V Ga Va

434 -मुपपद्येत] P M K S ◆ -मुपपद्यते Q V O Ga Va ◆ -मुपपद्येते C

435 नोपपद्येत] P M K C ◆ नोपपद्यते S Q V O Ga Va

435 ऽपि] न K

435 -निबन्धना] -निबन्धनो K

437 वा] P M K C S ◆ om. Q V O Ga Va

438 व्यवहारादपि] व्यवहाराद् O

438 अप्रामाणिको] अप्रमाणको M K

439–440 लोक- … प्रमाणं] om. O

439 -व्यपदेशो] व्यवहारो S^{ac} ◆ n.a. O

439 नाम । अनुमानं] नानुमानं K ◆ n.a. O

440 प्रतिक्षेप्स्यते] प्रत्यक्षेप्स्यति V^{ac} ◆ n.a. O

440 -दस्थाने] -दवस्थाने S O V^{ac}

437 भावमाख्यातेनाचष्टे ∗ Here Varadacharya's interpretation is questionable, because the *Nirukta* quote is not about *saṃskāra*-s but rather about the singular number of *ākhyātena*, used also by experts and not only by common people, as in *śābdāt* above.

439–440 प्रत्यक्षमपि प्रतिक्षेप्स्यते ∗ See Section 9.3 below.

पदेशनिरूपणस्फोटाटोपः ॥

9.2.2 [तत्रान्त्यवर्णपक्षोपपत्तिः]

न चात्यन्तमसङ्गतोऽयं वर्णपक्षे लौकिको व्यपदेशः । पूर्ववर्णजनितसंस्कारसहिते तावदन्त्यवर्णे वाचके सुसङ्गत एवायं व्यपदेशः ' तस्य शब्दत्वादेकत्वाच्च ॥

9.2.3 [तत्र सङ्कलनाज्ञानपक्षोपपत्तिः]

NM^{Va}, 172 सङ्कलनाप्रत्ययोपारूढवर्णवाचकत्वपक्षेऽपि न दोषः । न हि भेदशब्दसहित एष शब्दशब्दः प्रयुज्यते गकारादिभ्यः शब्दादर्थं प्रतिपद्यामह इति । केवलस्तु जातिशब्द एकवचनान्तो बहुष्वपि वर्णेषु न विरुद्धः ॥

9.2.4 [तत्र स्फोटानुपपत्तिः]

किं च ' स्फोटपक्षे सुतरामनुपपन्नोऽयं व्यपदेशः ' शब्दादिति प्रातिपदिकार्थस्याभावात् । न हि वर्णवत् स्फोटे शब्दशब्दं प्रयुञ्जानो दृश्यते व्यवहर्तृजनः ॥

M K P C S O Q V Ga Va

441 -निरूपण-] P M K ◆ -निरूपणेन C S Q V O Ga Va
441 -स्फोटाटोपः] स्फुटाटोपः M K
442 चात्यन्तमसङ्गतो] चात्यंतसंगतो Q O V^{ac}
442 लौकिको व्यपदेशः] लौकिव्यपदेशः M ◆ लौकिकव्यपदेशः K ◆ लौकिकोपदेशः C
443 -वर्णे] वर्ण- K
443 सु-] om. O
443 तस्य] तस्य च S
445 दोषः] दोषा P^{ac}
446 इति] P M K C Va ◆ om. S Q V O Ga
448–449 -पदिकार्थस्या-] -पदिकस्य अर्थस्या- Q V O Ga
449 शब्द-] om. O
449 -शब्दं] P M K Va ◆ -शब्दत्वं C S Q O V^{ac} Ga
449 प्र-] om. C

9.3 [स्फोटाप्रत्यक्षत्वम्]

9.3.1 [श्रोत्रग्राह्यत्वमिति शब्दस्य धर्मः]

अर्थप्रतिपत्तिहेतुत्वं तु शब्दलक्षणमसाधु ' धूमादिभिर्व्यभिचारात् । अथापि प्रक्रमपर्यालोचनया श्रोत्रग्राह्यत्वविशिष्टमर्थप्रतिपत्तिहेतुत्वं शब्दलक्षणमभिधीयते ' तदिदं स्फोटं प्रति न सिद्धम् ' तस्य श्रोत्रप्रत्ययविषयत्वाभावात् । श्रोत्रग्राह्यत्वमेव च तदितरव्यवच्छेदक्षममिति तदेव लक्षणं युक्तम् । किमुभयोपादानेन । श्रोत्रग्राह्यत्वं च वर्णेषु एवास्ति नार्थान्तरस्य इति वर्णा एव शब्दः । तदुक्तम् '

Granthibhaṅga

451 प्रक्रम्याभिधानात् **श्रोत्रग्राह्यत्वविशिष्टमिति** । गौरिति///

M K P C S O Q V Ga Va

450 तु] P C S Q O ◆ om. M K V Ga Va
451 प्रक्रम-] क्रम- C
451 श्रोत्र-] श्रौत्र Va
451 -ग्राह्यत्व-] -ग्राहित्व- O V^{ac}
451 -विशिष्टमर्थ-] -विशिष्ट- Ga
452 न सिद्धम्] निषिद्धं P
452 श्रोत्र-] श्रौत्र- V^{pc}Va ◆ श्रौत्रे V^{ac}
453 -ग्राह्यत्वमेव] -ग्राहित्वमेव O ◆ -ग्राह्यत्वमेतव S
453 च] om. M K
453 लक्षणं] P M K ◆ om. C S Q V O Ga Va
453–454 किमुभयोपादानेन] किमुभयपदोपादानेन M K
454 श्रोत्रग्राह्यत्वं] श्रोत्रग्राहित्वं O
454 एवास्ति] P M K ◆ एव C S Q V O Ga Va
454 वर्णा] वर्ण M K
455 शब्दः] शब्दाः P O
455 तदुक्तम्] om. K

परस्परानपेक्षाश्च श्रोत्रबुद्ध्या स्वरूपतः ।
वर्णा एवावसीयन्ते न पूर्वापरवस्तुनी ॥ इति ॥

9.3.1.1 [सत्तया जात्या वा न व्यभिचारः]

श्रोत्रग्राह्यत्वं शब्दलक्षणं सत्तादावप्यस्ति इति चेत् ' न ' श्रोत्रेणैवेत्यवधारणस्य विवक्षितत्वात् ॥

NMVa, 173 श्रोत्रमनोभ्यां ग्रहणादसिद्धमवधारणमिति चेत् ' न ' समानजातीयव्यवच्छे-
NMShu, 351 दार्थत्वादवधारणस्य चक्षुरादीन्येव तेन व्यवच्छेद्यन्ते ' न मनः ॥

Granthibhaṅga

456 ///परिकल्पिता गकाराद्यारम्भकाः परमाणव उच्यन्ते । परशब्दे/// ///इति

Testimonia

456–457 परस्परानपेक्षाश्च … -वस्तुनी ∗ परस्परानपेक्षाश्च श्रोत्रबुद्ध्या स्वरूपतः । वर्णा एवावगम्यन्ते न पूर्वापरवस्तुनी ॥ (ŚV^Ra^, sphoṭa 9)

Notes from editions

456–457 परस्परानपेक्षाश्च … -वस्तुनी ∗ श्लोकवार्तिके स्फोटवादे श्लो॰ ९ । ``गकारौकारविसर्जनीयाः ते च श्रोत्रग्रहणाऽऽ इति भाष्ये गकारादीनामेव श्रौत्रत्ववचनात् पूर्वं —वर्णकारणीभूता अवयवाः अपरं गत्वमवयवी गोशब्दत्वं समुदायः स्फोटश्च नावगम्यन्ते किन्तु वर्णा एवावगम्यन्ते इत्यर्थः । (NM^Shu^)

457 पूर्वापरवस्तुनी ∗ शब्दहेतुः, तत्कार्याणि वा श्रौत्रबुद्ध्या न विषयीक्रियन्ते ॥ (NM^Va^)

458 सत्तादावप्यस्ति ∗ सत्ता शब्दगतसत्तादिः ॥ (NM^Va^)

460 समानजातीय ∗ समानजातीयत्वं बहिरिन्द्रियत्वेन ॥ (NM^Va^)

M K P C S O Q V Ga Va

456 परस्परानपेक्षाश्च] परस्परानपेक्षत्वाच् C ◆ परस्परानपेक्षश्च Q O V^ac^
456 श्रोत्र-] श्रौत्र- Va
456–458 स्वरूपतः … श्रोत्रग्राह्यत्वं] स्व/// ///त्वं M
459 विवक्षितत्वात्] विवक्षत्वात् V^ac^
460–462 -ग्रहणादसिद्धम् … व्यभिचार इति] ग्रहणा/// ///इति M
460 न] om. K ◆ n.a. M
460–461 -व्यवच्छेदार्थत्वादव-] -व्यवच्छेदकत्वादव- K ◆ -व्यवच्छेदत्वादव- C ◆ n.a. M
461 -धारणस्य] -धारणस्य विवक्षत्वात् V^ac^ ◆ -धारणस्य विवक्षितत्वात् V^pc^Ga ◆ n.a. M
461 तेन] om. K ◆ n.a. M

456 परस्परानपेक्षाश्च ∗ In J, due to the loss of support, no *pratīka* is extant. The correlation of this *Granthibhaṅga* fragment with the present passage of the NM is highly conjectural.

तथापि शब्दत्वेन व्यभिचार इति चेत् ' न ' जातिमत्त्वे सतीति प्रक्रमलभ्यविशेषणापेक्षणात् । स्तनयित्नुनादप्रभृतिभिरपि न व्यभिचारः ' तेषां शब्दत्वाभ्युपगमात् । तदुक्तं भाष्यकृता ' द्विविधश्चायं शब्दो वर्णात्मा ध्वनिमात्रश्च इति ॥

9.3.1.2 [श्रोत्रग्राह्यत्वमिति विशेषनस्यावश्यकत्वम्]

अर्थप्रत्यायकत्वं तु न लक्षणमित्युक्तम् ' अगृहीतसम्बन्धे वर्णात्मन्यपि शब्दे तदभावेनाशब्दत्वप्रसङ्गात् ' कालान्तरे च सम्बन्धबुद्धौ सत्यां तस्यैव

Testimonia

464 द्विविधश्चायं … -मात्रश्च ∗ द्विविधश्चायं शब्दो वर्णात्मको ध्वनिरूपश्च । NBh^{Tha}, 2.2.40

Notes from editions

463–464 शब्दत्वाभ्युपगमात् ∗ मीमांसकैस्तु ध्वनेः वायुधर्मत्वमेव स्वीकृतम् ॥ (Va)

M K P C S O Q V Ga Va

462 शब्दत्वेन] शब्दत्वे O Va ◆ n.a. M
462 सतीति] सन्तीति S
463–466 प्रभृतिभिरपि … अर्थप्रत्यायकत्वं] प्रभृ/// ///त्यायकत्वं M
464 द्विविधश्चायं] द्विविधस्त्वयं K ◆ n.a. M
464 ध्वनिमात्रश्च] ध्वनिश्च S ◆ n.a. M
466 अर्थ-] अथ O ◆ -- K ◆ n.a. M
466 -प्रत्यायकत्वं] -प्रत्यायकत्वे C O
466 न] om. C
466 वर्णात्मन्यपि] P M K C Va ◆ वर्णात्मनि S Q V O Ga
467 तदभावेनाशब्दत्व-] तदभावेन शब्दत्व- Q O ◆ तदभावेनाशब्द- S
467 कालान्तरे च] P M K ◆ कालान्तरेण C S Q V O Ga Va
467 सम्बन्ध-] om. Q
467 सत्यां] सत्यं च Ga Va
467 तस्यैव] तस्येव O ◆ सत्येव V^{ac} ◆ om. V^{pc}Ga

462 शब्दत्वेन ∗ I understand *vyabhicāra* as the *ativyāpti* of the *lakṣaṇa*, and *śabdatva* as the *dharmin* to which the property *śrotragrahyatva* would wrongly apply. Transposing it to an *anumāna*, it can be formulated as follows: *śabdaḥ itarebhyo bhinnaṃ, śrotragrahyatvāt. yan naivaṃ tan naivam. sphoṭādivat.* According to the objector, even though *śabdatva* would be expected to be a *vipakṣa*, it is actually a *pakṣa*, because it also possesses *śrotragrahyatva*.

शब्दत्वमिति न व्यवस्थितमिदं लक्षणम् ॥

यदपि ' शब्दस्वरूपनिरूपणप्रसङ्गे तदभिधेयानां जातिगुणक्रियादीनां शब्दताशङ्कनं तत्परिहरणं च ' तदपि किमाशय इति न विद्मः ' तेषामतिविभक्तरूपग्रहणात् ॥

अतः श्रोत्रग्राह्यस्य शब्दत्वात् स्फोटस्य च श्रोत्रग्राह्यत्वाभावाद् वर्णवादिनामेव शब्दादर्थं प्रतिपद्यामह इत्यनुकूलो लोकव्यपदेशः ' न स्फोटवादिनामिति स्थितम् ॥

9.3.2 [पदवाक्याभिन्नत्वम्]

9.3.2.1 [पदवाक्याभिन्नत्वं न गोत्ववत्सामन्यत्वम्]

कथं पुनः श्रोत्रग्रहणत्वं स्फोटस्य न मृष्यते ' यावता पदं वाक्यमिति श्रो-

Testimonia

469–470 यदपि … च ∗ यत्तर्हि तदिङ्गितम् चेष्टितम् निमिषितम् सः शब्दः । न इति आह, क्रिया नाम सा । यत्तर्हि तत् शुक्लः नीलः कृष्णः कपिलः कपोतः इति सः शब्दः । न इति आह, गुणः नाम सः । यत्तर्हि तत् भिन्नेषु अभिन्नम् छिन्नेषु अच्छिन्नम् सामान्यभूतम् सः शब्दः । न इति आह, आकृतिः नाम सा । VMBh^{Bha}, paspaśā 2

M K P C S O Q V Ga Va

468–469 न व्यवस्थितम् … -प्रसङ्गे] न व्यवस्थित/// ///ङ्गेन M
468 न व्यव-] P M K C S ◆ अव्यव- V Ga Va ◆ व्यव- Q O
468 -स्थितमिदं लक्षणम्] स्थितम् C ◆ n.a. M
469 यदपि] यद्यपि C ◆ n.a. M
469 -निरूपण-] -निरूपणा- K ◆ n.a. M
469 -प्रसङ्गे] P C S Q V O ◆ -प्रसङ्गेन M K Ga Va
470 च] om. P
470 तदपि] तदलं M K
470 किमाशयम्] किमाशय C
472 श्रोत्रग्राह्यस्य- … च] om. M K
472 -ग्राह्यस्य] -ग्राहस्य C ◆ n.a. M K
473 लोक-] P M K C Va ◆ शब्द- S ◆ रूप- Q O V^{ac} ◆ om. V^{pc}Ga
473 -व्यपदेशः] -व्यपदेशे V^{ac}

469–470 यदपि … तत्परिहरणंच ∗ See line 96

त्रकरणकमेकाकारं ज्ञानं प्रत्यात्मवेदनीयमस्ति । न च तस्य वर्णा आलम्बनीभवेयुरित्युक्तम् । न युक्तमुक्तम् । इह हि शाबलेयादौ प्रतिपिण्डं गौरिति बुद्धिरुपजायमाना सकलपिण्डसाधारणं रूपं विषयीकरोतीति गोत्वसामान्यं तदिष्यते । एवं यदि प्रतिवर्णं पदं पदमिति वाक्यं वाक्यमिति मतिरुपजायेत जातिवत्तर्हि पदं वाक्यं च सर्ववर्णवृत्ति किमपि रूपमुपगच्छेम । न त्वेवमस्ति मतिः ॥ NM^{Va}, 174

Testimonia

477–481 इह … मतिः ✻ अनारब्धे च गोशब्दे गोशब्दत्वं कथं भवेत् । वर्णसामान्यवच्चापि न तत्कल्पनमर्हति ॥ (ŚV^{Ra}, sphoṭa 66); परस्परविभक्तस्वरूपतया हि शाबलेयबाहुलेयादिपिण्डाः प्रत्यक्षमुपलभ्यन्ते । स्थिते च व्यक्तिभेदे सर्वत्र गौरिति तदभेदप्रत्ययस्यानन्यविषयत्वादिष्यत एव गोत्वजातिः । इह पुनः – गकारव्यक्तयो भिन्नाः शाबलेयादिपिण्डवत् । (NM^{Va}, I 521,6–8, NM 3)

Notes from editions

479 प्रतिवर्णं ✻ न हि प्रत्येकं वर्णेषु पदत्वस्य वाक्यत्वस्य वा प्रतिसन्धानं कस्यापि भवति ॥ (NM^{Va})

M K P C S O Q V Ga Va

476 -कारं] -कारं च P
476 ज्ञानं] om. O
476 -वेदनीयमस्ति] om. S
476 च तस्य] P M K C S ◆ चास्य Q V O Ga Va
478 -साधारणं] -साधारण- M K
479 -वर्णं] -वर्ण- K
479 पदं] प्रतिपदं M K
479 वाक्यं] om. C
480 -रुपजायेत] M K V^{pc}Ga Va ◆ -रुपजायेते V^{ac} ◆ -रुपजायते P S Q O ◆ -रुपजायते त C
480 -वर्ण-] om. S
480 -वृत्ति किमपि] -वृत्तिकमपि M ◆ -वृ///मपि K
480–481 रूपमुपगच्छेम] P M C ◆ रूपगच्छेम K ◆ रूपमभ्युपगच्छेम S Q V O Ga ◆ रूपमवगच्छेम Va
481 न त्वेव-] नन्वेव- C O
481 मतिः] P M K ◆ प्रतीतिः S Q V O Ga Va ◆ प्रतीति C

9.3.2.2 [पदवाक्याभिन्नत्वं न पटवदवयवित्वम्]

यथा च तन्त्वाद्यवयवघटितपटादिकार्यविषयम् आद्यनयनसन्निपातसमय एव भेदोपग्रहरहितमवयविज्ञानमुदेति तथा क्रमसमुच्चरदेकैकवर्णस्वरूपोपग्रहनिरपेक्षम् यदि पदमिति वाक्यमिति ज्ञानं भवेत् तत् पटादिकमवयविनमिव पदं वाक्यमेकरूपमनुमन्येमहि । न त्वेवमस्ति । न हि तन्तुभिरिव पटो वर्णैः पदमारभ्यते ॥

Testimonia

482–485 यथा … अस्ति ∗ यथाभिनवं पटं दृष्ट्वा … तन्तुव्यतिषङ्गजनितोऽयं तन्तुव्यतिशङ्गविनाशात् तन्तुविनाशात् विनाश्यतीत्यवगच्छति । न एवं शब्दस्य किञ्चित् कारणमवगम्यते यद्विनाशाद्विनङ्क्ष्यति । (ŚBh, 1.1.21) ◆ पृथङ् न चोपलभ्यन्ते वर्णस्यावयवाः क्वचित् । न च वर्णेष्वनुस्यूता दृश्यन्ते तन्तुवत् पटे ॥ (ŚV[Ra], sphoṭa 11) ◆ अपि च, सावयवस्य हि पटादेस्तन्त्वादयोऽनारब्धकार्याश्च प्रतीयन्ते । न तु तथा वर्णावयवानामुपलब्धिरित्याह । पृथङ् नेति । तन्तुवदिति वैधर्म्यनिदर्शनम् ॥ (ŚVT[Ra], sphoṭa 11) ◆ सावयवे हि वस्तुनि द्विधा अवयवा दृश्यन्ते, आरब्धकार्याश्चानारब्धकार्याश्चेति । इह पुनरारब्धकार्या अनारब्धकार्या वा पटे तन्त्वादय इव वर्णे न क्वचिदवयवा उपलभ्यन्ते । (NM[Va], I 524,10–525.2, NM 3)

486 पटो ∗ यथा कटं चिकीर्षन्तो विरणानि ŚBh, 1.1.16

M K P C S O Q V Ga Va

482 तन्त्वाद्यवयव-] तत्त्वावयव- O
482 -घटित-] P M K ◆ -परिघटित- C S Q O V^{ac} ◆ -परिघट्टित- V^{pc}Ga Va
483 भेदोपग्रह-] P M K S ◆ भेदो पि ग्रह- C ◆ भेदग्रह- Q V O Ga Va
483–484 -रहितम् … -स्वरूपोपग्रह-] om. S
483 -समुच्चरदेकैक-] -समुच्चाराद् एकैक- Q O V^{ac} ◆ n.a. S
484 -निरपेक्षम्] -निरपेक्षे O
484 तत्] om. C
484 पटादिक-] पटादि- M^{ac} ◆ घटादिक- P ◆ पदादिक- Va
485 वाक्यमेक-] P M K ◆ वाक्यमेकैक- C S Q V O Ga Va
486 पटो] पटो वीरणैरिव कटः M K Va

486 पटो ∗ The additional example found in M and K, and received in Va, may derive from the *Śābarabhāṣya.*

यत्तु ' गौर्भूर्नौरिति झगिति एव ज्ञानमभेदग्राहि दृश्यते ' तदेकाच्त्वादुपाधेः । भिन्नाजुपश्लेषे तु देवदत्त इत्यादौ नानाक्षरग्रहणमेव विलम्बितमनुभूयते । न चैवं पटादिबुद्धिषु तदवयवाः कदाचिद्विच्छेदेनावभासन्ते । तस्मान् नावयवीव न जातिरिव पदं वाक्यमभिन्नमवभासते ॥

9.3.2.3 [स्फोटशब्दत्वसामान्ययोर्भेदः]

ननु ' यासौ शब्दः शब्द इति बुद्धिः सैवेयं स्फोटबुद्धिः ॥

Testimonia

487–488 यत् … अनुभूयते ✻ शैघ्र्यादल्पान्तरत्वाच्च गोशब्दे सा भवेदपि । देवदत्तादिशब्देषु स्फुटो भेदः प्रतीयते ॥ ($ŚV^{Ra}$, sphoṭa 121)

489–490 तस्मान् … वाक्यमभिन्नमवभासते ✻ तत्रापि प्रतिवर्णं हि पदस्फोटो न गम्यते । न चावयवशो व्यक्तिस्तदभावान् न चात्र धीः । प्रत्येकं चाप्यशक्तानां समुदायेऽप्यशक्तया । तत्र यः परिहारस्ते स नोऽत्रापि भविष्यति ॥ ($ŚV^{Ra}$, sphoṭa 92–93)

491 ननु … बुद्धिः ✻ ननु च सर्वशब्देषु शब्दः शब्द इत्येका बुद्धिरस्ति । (Bṛh, 119.3)

M K P C S O Q V Ga Va

487 गौर्भूर्नौरिति] C ◆ गौर्भूर्गौरिति P ◆ गौर्द्यौर्नौरिति M K ◆ गौर्गौरिति S Q V O Ga Va

487 झगिति] P C S ◆ झटिति M K ◆ om. Q V O Ga Va

487 एव] P C S O ◆ एवं M Q V Ga Va ◆ ए- K

487 तदेकाच्त्वादुपाधेः] P C S ◆ तदेकाज्त्वादुपाधेः Q ◆ तदेकस्त्वादुपाधेः O V^{ac} ◆ तदेकाजुपाधेः M K V^{pc} Ga Va

489 चैवं] चैव C

489 पटादिबुद्धिषु] पटादिषु M K

490 न] om. V O Ga Va

490 -रिव] -रिव वा V^{pc} Ga Va

491 ननु] ननु च Q V Ga Va

491 शब्दः शब्द] P M K S ◆ शब्दशब्द C ◆ शब्दशब्दा Q V O ◆ शब्दशब्दाद् Ga Va

491 इति] P M K C S ◆ om. Q V O Ga Va

487 तदेकाच्त्वादुपाधेः ✻ "Due to the contingency of having a single vowel (*ac*)". The application of *sandhi* rules such as *co kuḥ* (Pā, 8.2.30), i.e., in this case, the change of *c* into *k*, is prohibited in some grammars in the context of Pāṇinian *pratyahāra*-s (see HNAV, 2.107).

किमिदानीं यदेव शब्दत्वं सामान्यं स एव स्फोटः ॥ मैवम् ' स्फोट एवासौ । न शब्दत्वसामान्यं तत् । सामान्यं हि तदुच्यते यत्रैकव्यक्तिदर्शने व्यक्त्यन्तरानुसन्धानं शाबलेयग्रहणे बाहुलेयस्येव । इह तु न गकारग्रहणे वकारानुसन्धानमिति नेदं सामान्यम् । एकरूपस्त्वयं प्रतिभासः शब्दतत्त्वविषय एव । शब्दतत्त्वं च स्फोट इति ॥

NM^{Va}, 175

Testimonia

493 सामान्यं हि तदुच्यते ⁎ अपर आह । तिष्ठतु तावत् दूरत एव गत्वाद्यपरसामान्यं महासामान्यमपि शब्दत्वं वर्णेषु नोपपद्यते ॥ व्यक्त्यन्तरानुसन्धानं यत्रैकव्यक्तिदर्शने । तत्रैकरूपसामान्यमिष्यते तत्कृतं च तत् ॥ गकारश्रुतिवेलायां न वकारावमर्शनम् । बाहुलेयपरामर्शः शाबलेयग्रहे यथा ॥ शब्दः शब्दोऽयमित्येवं प्रतीतिस्त्वप्रयोजिका । एषा हि श्रोत्रगम्यत्वं उपाधिमनुरुध्यते ॥ (NM^{Va}, I 550,12–551.2, NM 3)

494–495 इह तु … वकारानुसन्धानमिति ⁎ न च गकारादिष्वेकवर्णग्रहे सति वर्णान्तरावमर्शो भवति पाचकादिवत् । (Bṛh, 120.4–5)

Notes from editions

492 शब्दत्वं सामान्यं ⁎ शब्दः इति शब्दः शब्दसामान्यमाचष्टे, तदेव किल शब्दत्वम् ॥ (NM^{Va})

M K P C S O Q V Ga Va

492 शब्दत्वं] शब्दत्व- M K Va
493 शब्दत्व-] शब्दस्य- M^{ac} ◆ शब्दत्वं V Ga Va
494 व्यक्त्यन्तरा-] व्यक्ततरा- K ◆ व्यक्तंतरा- V O
494–495 बाहुलेयस्येव … व-] om. C
495 -ग्रहणे] -ग्रहणे न Va ◆ n.a. M C
495 व-] Q O V^{ac} Va ◆ ब- P ◆ च- K ◆ ⁻ S ◆ अ- V^{pc} Ga ◆ n.a. M C
495 नेदं] न S
495 सामान्यम्] सामान्यमिति M K
495 प्रतिभासः] शब्दप्रतिभासः P ◆ प्रतिभासतः V^{ac}
496 इति] एव P

495 व- ⁎ Here I am adopting the vulgata reading, because neither of the singular readings of P and K is fully convincing.

उच्यते ' आं ज्ञातम् । अमुनैव हि भयेन कैश्चित् स्फोटशङ्किभिः शब्दत्वसामान्यमपह्नुतम् । अस्थान एव तु अयं तेषां सन्त्रासः । न हि शब्दत्वं स्फोटः । प्रतिवर्णं हि शब्दः शब्द इति बुद्धिरस्ति । न च वर्णा स्फोटः । तदिदं शब्दसामान्यमेव शब्दबुद्धेरालम्बनम् ' न स्फोटः । सामान्यसिद्धौ तु व्यक्त्यन्तरानुसन्धानमकारणमिति प्रागेव निर्णीतमेतत् । तस्मान्न शब्दबु- NM^{Shu}, 352

Granthibhaṅga

497 कैश्चित् स्फोटशङ्किभिरिति प्राभाकरैः ' भाट्टा हि गत्वादि/// ///धानाभावात् ॥

Testimonia

497–498 अमुनैव … सामान्यमपह्नुतम् ∗ किं पुनः कारणं श्रोत्रग्राह्यतैवात्र गृह्यते । न पुनर्गोत्ववच्छब्दत्वमाश्रीयते । (Bṛh, 119.7–120.1)

501 प्रागेव … एतत् ∗ समानबुद्धिग्राह्येऽपि सामन्येऽवस्थिते क्वचित् । भवत्यन्यानुसन्धानं क्वचिद्वा न भवत्यपि ॥ (NM^{Va}, I 551,7–8, NM 3)

Notes from editions

497 कैश्चित् ∗ प्राभाकरैः ॥ (NM^{Va})

M K P C S O Q V Ga Va

497 आं] PCSQ ◆ आ MKVOGaVa
497 भयेन] उभयेन O
497 स्फोट-] स्फोटा- Q
497 -शङ्किभिः] MKVa GBh ◆ -शङ्कितैः PSQVOGa ◆ om. C
497–498 शब्दत्व-] PMKVa ◆ शब्दतत्त्व- CSQVOGa
498 तु] om. K ◆ n.a. M
498 तेषां] PK ◆ om. CSQVOGaVa ◆ n.a. M
499 हि शब्दः] om. S
499 च] हि MK
499 वर्णा] PMKCSQ ◆ वर्णः V^{pc}Ga ◆ वर्ण- OV^{ac}Va
499 स्फोटः] स्फोटाः C
500 तदिदं … स्फोटः] om. C
500 शब्द-] PSQOV^{ac} ◆ शब्दत्व- MKV^{pc}GaVa ◆ n.a. C
500 -रालम्बनम्] -रवलम्बनं S ◆ n.a. C
500 न] न च O ◆ n.a. C
501 व्यक्त्यन्तरा-] व्यक्त्यान्तरा- S
501 निर्णीतमेतत्] निर्णीतमिदं Q ◆ निर्णीतम् VGaVa

497 उच्यते ∗ The *ucyate* is here marking the introduction of the *siddhānta*, following the punctuation of P and K. The editions, however, have it as the end of the *pūrvapakṣa*.

द्वावपि स्फोटोऽवभासते पदवाक्यबुद्धाविवेति । अतश्च सत्यमाह ' यदियमेककार्यकारित्वनिबन्धना वनपृतनादिबुद्धिसमानयोगक्षेमैव पदवाक्यबुद्धिरिति । न च जात्यादिबुद्धिष्वसमाश्वासः ' वैलक्षण्यस्य दर्शितत्वात् ॥

9.3.2.4 [वाच्यबुद्धिवाचकबुद्ध्योर्नेतरेतराश्रयत्वम्]

NM^{Va}, 176

यदपि ' एककार्यकारित्वनिबन्धनायामभेदबुद्धावितरेतराश्रयपरिचोदनम् एकार्थप्रतीतिपूर्विका पदवाक्यबुद्धिः पदवाक्यबुद्धिपूर्विका चैकार्थप्रतीतिरिति ' तदपि न सम्यक् । स्मर्यमाणानुभूयमानवर्णजनितैवेयमर्थप्रतीतिरित्यवोचाम ' नाभिन्नपदपरिच्छेदपूर्विकेति कुत इतरेतराश्रयत्वम् ॥

9.3.2.5 [वाचकभिन्नत्ववाच्यभिन्नत्वयोः सङ्गतिः]

ब्रूयात् ' पदवाक्ययोरेकत्वमन्तरेण कथं पदार्थवाक्यार्थप्रतीतिरेकरूपा भवेदिति ' सोऽयमतीव मुग्धालापः । प्रतीतिभेदाभेदौ हि विषयभेदाभेदावनु-

Notes from editions

508 नाभिन्न- ✱ अभिन्नं—अखण्डम् ॥ (NM^{Va})

M K P C S O Q V Ga Va

502 -विवेति । अतश्च] P M K ◆ -वित्येतच्च S Q V Ga ◆ -वित्येतावच्च C ◆ -विवेत्येकश्च Va ◆ -विद्येतश्च O

502–503 यदियमेक] यदिदमेक K

503 -क्षेमैव] -क्षमैव P

504 च] om. C

504 जात्यादिबुद्धि-] P M K C Va ◆ जात्यादि- S Q V O Ga

504 वैलक्षण्यस्य] वैलक्षिण्यस्य K ◆ वैलक्षण्य- S O^{ac}

504 दर्शितत्वात्] -दर्शनात् S

506 -प्रतीति- … चैकार्थ-] om. C

507 -जनितैवेयमर्थ-] P M K Va ◆ -जनितेयमर्थ- C S Q V O Ga

508 नाभिन्न-] न चाभिन्न- S

508 -च्छेदपूर्विकेति] -च्छेदपूर्वकेति Ga ◆ om. K

508 इतरेतराश्रयत्वम्] इतरेतराश्रयम् P

509 पदार्थ-] P M K C S ◆ पद- Q V O Ga Va

510 हि] om. S

510 -भेदाभेदावनु-] -भेदाभेदमनु- M K

505 एककार्य- … -परिचोदनम् ✱ See line 145 above.

रुध्येते ' नोपायभेदाभेदौ । भिन्नैरपि लोचनालोकान्तःकरणप्रभृतिभिरुपायैः अभिन्नार्थग्राहिणी बुद्धिरुपजन्यत एव । तदिह पदार्थबुद्धेरेकत्वात् पदार्थ एको भवतु योऽस्या विषयः ' न त्वेकं पदं यत्कारणमिति । वाक्यार्थबुद्धेरप्येकत्वादेको वाक्यार्थो भवतु ' न तु एकं वाक्यम् । वर्गीकरणकारणं तु क्रमभाविनां बहूनां वर्णानामेतद्भवति यदेकार्थप्रतिपादकत्वम् ' न त्वभेदमेव पदवाक्ययोर्गमयतीति । विप्रलब्धा एव च वैयाकरणाः पदवाक्ययोरप्यभेदं मन्यन्ते किल शब्दादनन्यभूत एव शब्दार्थ इति । स पुनरेषां व्यामोह एव '

Notes from editions

512 उपजन्यत एव ✱ एवं एकेनैव चक्षुषा घटोऽपि गृह्यते, पटोऽपि गृह्यते ॥ (NM^{Va})
513 त्वेकं ✱ एकत्वं अखण्डत्वम् ॥ (NM^{Va})
517 शब्दादनन्यभूत ✱ शब्दार्थयोरविनाभावात् ॥ (NM^{Va})

M K P C S O Q V Ga Va

511 -भेदाभेदौ] -भेदाभेदः K ◆ -भेदाभेदं M
511 लोचना-] om. K
511 -करण-] -करणे Q^{ac} ◆ -करणेण Q^{pc}
512 एव] एवेति P
513 एको] एकार्थो O
513 स्या] स्य O
513 पदं] om. O
513 यत्कारणमिति] यत्करणमिति S ◆ तत्कारणमिति M
513 वाक्यार्थ-] करण- S^{ac}
514–515 भवतु … क्रमभाविनां] भव/// ///नां M
514 न तु] ननु C O ◆ n.a. M
514 -कारणं] -कारकं Ga ◆ n.a. M
514 तु] P K C ◆ om. S Q V O Ga Va ◆ n.a. M
515 त्वभेदमेव] तु भेदमेव O
516 एव च] om. M K
516 -रप्यभेदं] -रन्यभेदं V^{ac}
517 मन्यन्ते … स पुनरेषां] मन्य/// ///नरेषां M
517 शब्दार्थ] स शब्दार्थ K ◆ n.a. M
517 -रेषां] -रेष M K
517 एव] om. Ga

तद्भेदस्य दृढप्रमाणसिद्धत्वात् । शब्दाध्यासस्तु प्रतीतिविरुद्धत्वेन नेष्यत इत्यलं तत्कथया ॥

तस्मात् प्रत्यक्षगम्योऽपि न भवति स्फोट इति स्थितम् ॥

9.4 [वाक्यार्थावयवित्वम्]

NM[Va], 177

ननु ' अभिन्नत्वाद्वाक्यार्थबुद्धेर्विषयभेदाभेदानुवर्त्तित्वाच्च बुद्धिभेदाभेदयोरभिन्नो वाक्यार्थः स्यात् ॥

बाढम् ' अभिन्नो न त्वनवयवः ' पटादेरभिन्नस्यापि सावयवत्वात् ॥

यत्तु निरवयवत्वमुच्यते तदतीव संवित्परामर्शकौशलशून्यव्याहृतम् '

अंशाः सन्ति न सन्तीति चिन्तात्यन्तमसङ्गता ।

Granthibhaṅga

518 **शब्दाध्यासस्त्विति** । शब्दाकाराध्यारोपेणार्थस्य///

525 ///˙अंशाः सं˙[162r]**ति न सन्तीति** । निरंशश्चेत् प्रमाणेनोप˙लभ्यते˙ तथाविधोपलम्भादेवांशाभाव˙सिद्धिः˙ । किमंशाभावप्रतिपादनचिन्तया ' प्रत्यक्षं चांशानामुपलम्भादिति ॥

◆◆◆ अंशाः सं-] This part is lost in the broken support, but can be inferred from the extant, following text. ◆ ˙-लभ्यते] -लभ्येत Sha˙ ◆ ˙-सिद्धिः] -सिद्धेः Sha˙

M K P C S O Q V Ga Va

518 तद्भेदस्य] तद्वेदस्य P^{ac}

520 -गम्यो] -गम्ये K ◆ n.a. M

520 भवति] P M K C ◆ om. S Q V O Ga Va

520–521 इति स्थितम् … बुद्धिभेदा-] इति स्थितम् /// ///भेदा- M

520 स्थितम्] P M K ◆ सिद्धम् C S Q V O Ga Va

521 ननु] न तु C O ◆ n.a. M

521 -वर्त्तित्वाच्च] P K C S ◆ -वृत्तित्वाच्च Q V O Ga Va ◆ n.a. M

521 बुद्धि-] बुद्ध्य- Ga

523 अभिन्नो] अनवयवो S

523 त्वनवयवः] त्ववयव- C ◆ त्ववयवः K^{ac} O

523–525 पटादे- … -मसङ्गता] पटा/// ///मसङ्गता M

523 पटा-] पदा- K ◆ घटा- O Va

524 यत्तु] सत्तु K ◆ n.a. M

524 -शून्य-] -शून्यं O ◆ n.a. M

525 न] P C S V O Q Va Ga ◆ om. K ◆ n.a. M

निरंशस्त्वस्ति नास्तीति युक्तं चिन्तयितुं सताम् ॥

पदतदर्थभेदस्य प्रतिवाक्यं विस्पष्टमवभासमानत्वाद् ' अनुपगृह्यमाणावयवविभागयोश्च वाक्यवाक्यार्थयोरनवभासमानत्वात् ॥

अस्त्यवयवप्रतीतिः ' सा तु भ्रान्ता इति चेत् ' न ' बाधकाभावात् । भ्रान्तेश्च बीजं किमपि वक्तव्यम् ॥

सादृश्यमिति चेत् ' कस्य केनेति न विद्मः । यदि हि क्वचिन् मुख्या अवयवाः प्रसिद्धा भवेयुस्तत्सादृश्यादितरत्र तदभावेऽपि भ्रम इति गम्येत । न त्वे-

Granthibhaṅga

531 सादृश्यमिति चेदिति । यादृशा एव स्थानकरणादिसामान्याद् देवदत्त गामभ्याज इत्यादौ वाक्येऽभिव्यञ्जका ध्वनयः ' तादृशा एव गामानय इत्यत्रापि वाक्य इति । ध्वनिसादृश्याद्यथा तत्र गोशब्दोऽस्त्येवमत्राप्यस्तीति भ्रमः ॥

Notes from editions

526 सताम् ⁕ सावयवत्वं प्रत्यक्षसिद्धम् । निरंशत्वं तु युक्तिसिद्धम् । तत्र तु विप्रतिपत्तिः स्यात् । अतः निरंशत्वं कथमित्येव विचारणीयम् ॥ (NM^{Va})

M K P C S O Q V Ga Va

526–528 सताम् … -मानत्वात्] सताम्/// ///मानत्वात् M
527 पदं] C ◆ n.a. M
527 विस्पष्ट-] विसृष्ट- C ◆ n.a. M
527 -मवभासमानत्वाद्] PK ◆ -मनवभासमानत्वात् C ◆ -माभासमानत्वाद् SQVO Ga Va ◆ n.a. M
527 अनुप-] अनु- KO ◆ n.a. M
527–528 -वयवविभागयोश्च] -वयविभागयोश्च K ◆ n.a. M
528 वाक्यवाक्यार्थयो-] पदवाक्ययो- Q ◆ n.a. M
528 -रनवभास-] -रवभास- O
529 अस्त्यवयव-] अथास्त्यवयव- MK ◆ अस्तु अवयव- Va
529 सा तु भ्रान्ता] om. S^{ac}
529 बाधकाभावात्] वाधकभावाद् OV^{ac}
530 बीजं किमपि] किमपि बीजं MK
531 कस्य केनेति] केन कस्येति O
531 हि] om. MK
532 -स्तत्-] PKQVa ◆ -स्तस्मात् CSVOGa ◆ n.a. M
532 गम्येत] PMVa ◆ गम्यते CSQVGa ◆ ग--- K ◆ अवगम्यते O

527 पद- … -मवभासमानत्वाद् ⁕ This and the next ablative give reasons in support of the statement made in the preceding stanza.

वमस्ति ' सर्ववाक्यानामभागत्वात् । नरसिंहे हि नरावयवाः सिंहावयवाश्च
NM^{Shu}, 353 पृथक्पृथगनुभूताः प्रत्यभिज्ञायन्ते । तद्वदिहाप्यभ्युपगम्यमाने नूनं क्वचिद् वा-
NM^{Va}, 178 क्ये सत्यत्वमवयवानामेषितव्यम् । चित्रेऽपि सिन्दूरहरितालादिरूपम् पानके
त्वगेलादिरसः ग्रामरागेऽपि षड्जर्षभगान्धारादिस्वरजातं पृथगवगतमिति न

Notes from editions

533 अभागत्वात् ✱ त्वन्मत इति शेषः ॥ (NM^{Va})
536 त्वगेलादि- ✱ त्वक् परिकरसुगन्धद्रव्यम् ॥ (NM^{Va})

M K P C S O Q V Ga Va

533 सर्व-] P M K Va ◆ पूर्व- C S Q V O Ga
533 -वाक्यानाम्] -वाक्यानामपि V^{pc}Ga Va
533 हि] P M K C ◆ पि S Q V O Ga Va
533 नरावयवाः] वरावयवाः C
534 पृथक्पृथगनुभूताः] *conj.* ◆ पृथक्पृथगनुभूताश्च P ◆ पृथगनुभूताः M K ◆ पृथक्पृथगवयवाः C S Q O V^{pc} ◆ पृथक् पृथक् V^{pc}Ga Va
534 तद्वद् … क्वचिद्] त/// ///चिद् M
534 -दिहाप्यभ्युप-] K O Va ◆ -दिहाभ्युप- P C S Q V Ga ◆ n.a. M
534–535 वाक्ये] P M K V^{pc}Ga Va ◆ वाक्ये हि C S Q V^{ac} ◆ वाह्ये हि O
535 सत्यत्व-] P M K C Va ◆ असत्त्व- S Q O V^{ac} ◆ सत्त्व- V^{pc}Ga
535 सिन्दूरहरितालादि-] P M K C ◆ हरितालसिन्दूरादि- S Q V O Ga Va
535 -रूपम्] om. P^{ac}
536 त्वगेलादि-] P M K V^{pc}Ga Va ◆ त्वगैलादि- C S Q V^{ac} ◆ त्वगैरिकादि- O
536 पि] om. M K
536 -र्षभगान्धारादि-] -र्षभादि- M K ◆ -र्षभगान्धार- P
536 पृथगव-] पृथगेव V^{ac}
536–538 -गतमिति … चित्राद्बुद्धयस्तर्हि] -गतमिति/// ///बुद्धयस्तर्हि M

533–534 नरसिंहे हि नरावयवाः सिंहावयवाश्च पृथक्पृथगनुभूताः प्रत्यभिज्ञायन्ते ✱ See Section 8.2.3.2 above.

534 पृथक्पृथगनुभूताः ✱ The reading of the vulgata is not satisfactory, because without the word *anubhūta*, which is found in P, M and K, the gist of the argument is lost: in order to explain the error by similarity one must have experienced before (as indicated by the past participle) the reality of the parts that are recognized. Stemmatically, both the repetition of *pṛthak* and the absence of *ca* are supported; thus the syncretic conjecture.

535–536 चित्रेऽपि सिन्दूरहरितालादिरूपम् पानके त्वगेलादिरसः ग्रामरागेऽपि षड्जर्षभगान्धारादिस्वरजातं ✱ See Section 8.2.3.2 above.

ते निर्भागदृष्टान्ताः ॥

चित्रादिबुद्धयस्तर्हि दृष्टान्ता इति चेत् ' बाढम् ' वाक्यार्थबुद्धिरपि निर्भागा इष्यत एवास्माभिः ' बुद्धीनां निराकारत्वेन सर्वासामनवयवत्वात् । अर्थौ दृष्टान्तदार्ष्टान्तिकयोः सावयव एव । तस्मान्न निर्भागौ वाक्यवाक्यार्थाविति युक्तम् ॥

9.4.1 [वाक्यव्यवहारे पदवर्णोपयोगित्वम्]

यदप्यभ्यधायि ' वृद्धव्यवहारतः सम्बन्धबुद्धिर्वाक्यवाक्यार्थयोरेव न पदतदर्थयोः ' पदेन व्यवहाराभावाद् इति ' तदप्यसाधु । वाक्यादपि व्युत्पत्तिर्भवन्ती पदार्थपर्यन्ता भवति इत्येवं हि पदतदर्थसंस्कृ-

Granthibhaṅga

544 पदार्थपर्यन्ता भवति आवापोद्वापकल्पनया ॥

Notes from editions

544 भवति ∗ वाक्यार्थस्याखण्डस्य खण्डितत्वादिति हेतुः ॥ (NM^{Va})

M K P C S O Q V Ga Va

537 -दृष्टान्ताः] -दृष्टांतः Q ◆ n.a. M

538 दृष्टान्ता] दृष्टान्त S Q V

538 वाक्यार्थ-] वाक्य- M K

539 बुद्धीनां] बुद्धीनां हि S

539 निराकारत्वेन] P C S Q ◆ निराकरणत्वेन O ◆ निरकत्वेन V^{ac} ◆ निरंशत्वेन M K Va ◆ निरंशकत्वेन V^{pc}Ga

539 -मनवयवत्वात्] -मभ्युपगतत्वात् M K

540 निर्भागौ] निरवयवौ M K

542 -भ्यधायि] -भिधायि C V O

542 -व्यवहारतः] -व्यवहार्थः V^{ac} ◆ -व्यवहारेण V^{pc}Ga

542 -र्वाक्य-] वाक्यार्थ- V ◆ om. Ga

543 पदेन] पदे K

543–544 व्यवहाराभावाद् ... पदार्थपर्यन्ता] व्यवहाराभा/// ///दार्थपर्यन्ता M

543 व्यवहाराभावाद्] व्यवहारभावाद् V^{ac}

544 इत्येवं] एवं Va

542–543 वृद्धव्यवहारतः ... व्यवहाराभावादिति ∗ See line 164ff.

तमतेरभिनवकविविरचितादपि वाक्यादर्थप्रतीतिरुपपत्स्यते । तदावापोद्वापरचनावैचित्र्येण वाक्यानामानन्त्याद् अशक्या प्रतिवाक्यं व्युत्पत्तिः । सापि नापेक्षिष्यते । इतरथा हि सावश्यमपेक्ष्यते ॥

यत्तु ' केवलं पदं न प्रयुज्यते तेन तदसत्यमिति ' तदप्यसत् ' महावाक्यस्थानेऽवान्तरवाक्यं न प्रयुज्यत इति तदप्यसत्यं स्यात् ॥

स्वार्थे तत् प्रयुज्यत इति चेत् ' पदमपि स्वार्थे क्वचित् प्रयुज्यत एव । यत्र

Granthibhaṅga

548–549 रक्तः पटो भवति इति **महावाक्यं** रक्ताख्येन गुणेन पटस्य सम्बन्धप्रतिपादनार्थम् । **अवान्तरवाक्यं** तु पटो भवति इति । स्वार्थश्चास्य पटसत्तासम्बन्धलक्षण इति ॥

550–551 **यत्र पदान्तराणामर्थ इति** । यथा संव्रियतामपाव्रियतामित्यस्यार्थेऽर्थप्रकरणादिलभ्ये द्वारमिति केवलं प्रयुज्यत इति ॥

Notes from editions

546 व्युत्पत्तिः ⁕ वाक्यार्थस्य पदार्थातिरिक्तत्वे, अखण्डत्वे च वाक्यशक्तिग्रहः अशक्य एव ॥ (NM^{Va})

M K P C S O Q V Ga Va

545 -कविविरचितादपि] P M C ◆ -विचिरचितादपि K ◆ -विरचितादपि Q V O Ga Va ◆ -रचितादपि S

545 वाक्यादर्थ-] P M K ◆ वाक्याद् वाक्यार्थ- C S Q V O Ga Va

546 -रचना-] M K C ◆ -वचना- P ◆ -रचन- S ◆ -रचनाक्रम- Q ◆ -रचक्र- O V^{ac} ◆ -परतन्त्र- V^{pc}Ga ◆ -चक्र- Va

547 हि] ◆ om. M K

547 सावश्य-] सादृश्य- S

547 -मपेक्ष्यते] P C S Q O V^{ac} ◆ -मपेक्ष्येत M K V^{pc}Ga Va

548 तेन] इति V O Ga Va

548 तदसत्यमिति] om. O

549–550 वान्तरवाक्यं … तत् प्रयुज्यत] वान्तरवा/// ///युज्यत M

549 -प्यसत्यं] -प्यसत्ये C ◆ n.a. M

550 स्वार्थे क्वचित्] क्वचित् स्वार्थे Q

545 अभिनवकविविरचितादपि ⁕ The reading *abhinavaviracitād* with the omission of *kavi* in the vulgata is apparently smoother, and *kavi* could in principle have been caused by a gloss that crept into the text. Yet, due to stemmatic reasons, I rather assume that it was the archetypical reading, later trivialised by the tradition.

548 केवलं पदं … तदसत्यमिति ⁕ See line 164.

पदान्तराणामर्थोऽर्थप्रकरणादिना लभ्यते तत्र यावदप्राप्तं पदमेव केवलमुच्चारयन्ति । ग्रन्थग्रहणाद्यवसरेषु च स्वरूपावधारणमपि फलवद्वर्णानाम् ॥ NM^{Va}, 179

9.4.2 [वाक्यकार्यार्थं पदानामावश्यकत्वम्]

मा वा फलवत्त्वं पदवर्णानां भूत् । तथापि रथावयवानामिव रथकार्येष्वपर्याप्तशक्तीनामपि स्वरूपसत्त्वमनिवार्यम् ॥

कार्यान्तराय रथावयवाः प्रभवन्तीति चेत् ' पदवर्णा अपि कार्यान्तरे प्रभ-

Granthibhaṅga

555 **कार्यान्तराय रथावयवा इति** । कार्यान्तरं रथादन्यत् काष्ठमात्रसाध्यं दर्शनं वा ॥

555 **वर्णा अपि कार्यान्तर इति** । यथाकारादयो विष्णवादिवाचकाः ॥

Testimonia

553–555 मा … प्रभवन्तीति ⁕ न च यत्रैकशोऽशक्तिस्तत्र सर्वेष्वशक्तता । रथाद्यङ्गानि दृश्यन्ते शाल्यादिवहनादिषु ॥ शक्तिस्तत्रास्ति काचिद्धि वहने सा समर्थ्यते । सङ्घातेन तु वर्णानां प्रत्येकं काचिदिष्यते ॥ न ह्यर्थावयवः कश्चित् प्रत्येकं तैः प्रतीयते । समस्तस्याथवा कश्चिद् बोधलेशोऽत्र जायते ॥ रथस्यापि तु यत् कार्यं शाल्यादिवहनं न तत् । प्रत्येकं दृश्यते किञ्चिन् मनागपि यथेहितम् ॥ (ŚV^{Ra}, sphoṭa 86–89)

Notes from editions

554 स्वरूपसत्त्वम् ⁕ प्रत्येकमिति शेषः ॥ (NM^{Va})

M K P C S O Q V Ga Va

551 पदान्तराणामर्थो] पदानामर्थो V Ga
551 यावदप्राप्तं] यावत् प्राप्तं O
551 पदमेव] तावत् पदमेव Va
552–553 -ग्रहणाद्यवसरेषु … मा वा] ग्रह/// /// वा M
552 -ग्रहणाद्यवसरेषु] P K C S ◆ -ग्रहणावसरेषु Q V O Ga Va ◆ n.a. M
552 च] om. K ◆ n.a. M
552–553 फलवद् … तथापि] om. C
553 रथा-] यथा- P
554 -कार्येष्वपर्याप्त-] -कार्येष्वप्यपर्याप्त- P
554 -सत्त्वमनिवार्यम्] -सत्त्वपरिवार्यं O
555 कार्यान्तराय] M K GBh ◆ कार्यान्तराय रथादु P C S V O Ga Va ◆ कार्यान्तराय रथे Q
555 रथावयवाः] द्रव्यावयवाः Q
555 कार्यान्तरे] वाक्यार्थांतरे Q ◆ कार्यांतरेण O ◆ n.a. M
555–556 प्रभविष्यन्ति] प्रभविष्यन्तीति K ◆ n.a. M

विष्यन्ति । रथकार्यैकदेशमात्रां कामपि रथावयवाः कुर्वन्तीति यदि उच्यते पदान्यपि वाक्यकार्यैकदेशं कमपि कुर्वन्त्येव ' वर्णा अपि केचिदर्थवन्तो भवन्त्येव इति । तस्मान्नासन्तः पदवर्णाः ॥

9.4.3 [अवयवान्तरत्वप्रसङ्गे उपलब्ध्यनुपलब्धिविरुद्धत्वम्]

यत् पुनरवादि ' वाक्यस्येव पदानि पदानामिव वर्णा वर्णानामप्यवयवान्तराणि स्युरिति ' तदिदमपूर्वं पाण्डित्यम् । न हि घटः सावयव इति परमाणुभिरपि सावयवैर्भवितव्यम् ' परमाणवो वा निरवयवा इति घटे-

Granthibhaṅga

557 **वर्णा अपि केचिदिति** । पदे ये वर्णाः प्रकृतिप्रत्ययादयः स्वा[162v]र्थेन चार्थवन्तस्ते ॥

M K P C S O Q V Ga Va

556–557 रथावयवाः … अपि] om. C
556 रथावयवाः] रथाः S ◆ n.a. C
556 यदि] P M K Va ◆ यद् S Q V O Ga ◆ n.a. C
556 उच्यते] उच्येत M K ◆ n.a. C
557–559 वर्णा अपि … वाक्यस्येव पदानि] वर्णा अपि/// ///नि M
558 इति] om. Va ◆ n.a. M
559–560 -मप्यवयवान्तराणि] -मवयवान्तरणानि न M^{ac} ◆ -मप्यवयवान्तरणानि न M^{pc}-K ◆ -मपि चावयवान्तराणि S
560 -मपूर्वं] -मपूर्व- S Q V
560 हि] om. M
560 घटः सावयव] P M K C ◆ घटाः सावयवा S V Q O Ga Va
561–562 परमाणवो … -र्भवितव्यम्] P M K C Va ◆ om. S Q V O Ga
561–562 परमाणवो … -नुपलब्धी हि] परमाणवो/// ///ब्धी हि M
561 वा] P C Va ◆ om. K ◆ n.a. M S Q V O Ga
561–562 घटेनापि तथा] P K ◆ घटो नापि तथा C ◆ घटैरपि निरवयवैः Va ◆ n.a. M S Q V O Ga

559–560 वाक्यस्येव पदानि … वयवान्तराणि स्युरिति ✻ See line 161.
561–562 परमाणवो … -र्भवितव्यम् ✻ The whole clause is missing in the vulgata but it is present in Va, where it could only have been inherited it from M. Presently, however, the part of the leaf of M that may have contained this line is lost due to damage, so it is possible that M was in a much better condition when it was consulted by Va.

नापि तथा भवितव्यम् । उपलब्ध्यनुपलब्धी हि वस्तूनां व्यवस्थापिके । यद्यथोपलभ्यते तत्तथा भवति । यद्यथा नोपलभ्यते तत्तथा न भवति । वाक्यपदयोश्च भागा उपलभ्यन्ते न वर्णानाम् । सूक्तं ह्येतत् '

अल्पीयसापि यत्नेन शब्दमुच्चरितं मतिः ।
यदि वा नैव गृह्णाति वर्णं वा सकलं स्फुटम् ॥ इति ॥

तस्माद् बालिशचोद्यमिदम् ' वर्णस्याप्यवयवा भवन्तु वाक्यपदयोरपि वा मा भूवन्निति ॥

Testimonia

565–566 अल्पीयसापि … स्फुटम् ∗ अल्पीयसापि यत्नेन शब्दमुच्चरितं मतिः । यदि वा नैव गृह्णाति वर्णं वा सकलं स्फुटम् ॥ (ŚV^{Ra}, sphoṭa 10) ◆ तत्र पूर्वं गकारावयवनिराकरणप्रतिज्ञां तावत् साधयितुमाह । अल्पीयसापीति । सावयवस्य हि पटादेः सकलप्रतिपत्त्यप्रतिपत्तिव्यतिरेकेणापि विकलप्रतीतिर्दृष्टा । गकारस्य तु नैव ग्रहणम्, सकलस्य वा ग्रहणम् न तु पटवद् विकलस्येत्यर्थः ॥ (ŚVT^{Ra}, sphoṭa 10)

Notes from editions

565–566 अल्पीयसापि … स्फुटम् ∗ श्लोकवार्तिके स्फोटवादे श्लो॰ १० । यदि वर्णाः सावयवाः स्युस्तदा कस्यचिदवयवस्य कदाचिद्ग्रहणं स्यात्कदाचिन्न स्याच्चैवमस्ति अतो निरवयवास्ते इति भावः । (NM^{Shu})

M K P C S O Q V Ga Va

562 व्यवस्थापिके] व्यवस्थापके V^{ac} ◆ व्यवस्थापिते K S
563 तत्तथा न भवति] न तत् तथा M K
563–564 वाक्यपदयोश्च] पदवाक्ययोश्च M K
564–565 वर्णानाम् … मतिः यदि] वर्णाना/// ///दि M
564 सूक्तं ह्येतत्] P ◆ उक्तं ह्येतत् K ◆ तथा हि उक्तमेतत् C S Q V Ga Va ◆ तथा युक्तमेतत् O ◆ n.a. M
565 अल्पीयसापि] अल्पीयसा S ◆ n.a. M
565 शब्द-] वर्ण- Q ◆ n.a. M
565 -मुच्चरितं] P K C ◆ -मुच्चारितं S Q V O Ga Va ◆ n.a. M
566 वा] om. M^{ac} C
567 बालिशचोद्यमिदम्] देलिशब्दोचितमिदम् O ◆ बेलिशचोदितमिदम् V^{ac} ◆ बालिशचोदितमिदम् Q V^{pc} Ga Va
567 वाक्यपदयोरपि] पदवाक्ययोरपि Ga Va
567 वा] om. S
568 भूवन्निति] भूदिति K

564 सूक्तं ह्येतत् ∗ The following verse is also quoted at line 372 above.

9.4.4 [अवयवानुगामित्वात् वाक्यवाक्यार्थयोरवयवित्वम्]

$\mathrm{NM}^{\mathrm{Shu}}$, 354

इतश्च सावयवौ वाक्यवाक्यार्थौ ' पदोपजनापायाभ्यां तदर्थोपजनापायदर्शनात् । अनयैव युक्त्या पदभागा अपि प्रकृतिप्रत्ययादयस्तात्त्विका इत्यवगन्तव्याः । न कल्पनामात्रप्रतिष्ठाः । वृत्तं वृत्तेण इत्यत्र प्रकृत्यर्थानुगमे प्रत्ययार्थो भिद्यते । वृत्तं घटमिति प्रत्ययार्थानुगमे प्रकृत्यर्थो भिद्यते । तत्र योऽर्थो यं शब्दमनुगच्छति स तस्यार्थ इत्यवसीयते । तत् कथमसत्या भागाः ॥

Notes from editions

569 पदोपजनापायाभ्यां ✻ पदोपजननापायौ—पदेन साकमन्वयव्यतिरेकौ ॥ ($\mathrm{NM}^{\mathrm{Va}}$)

M K P C S O Q V Ga Va

569 इतश्च] P M K Va ◆ अतश्च S V O Ga ◆ आतश्च C Q
569 सावयवौ वाक्यवाक्यार्थौ] सावयवो वाक्यवाक्यार्थो O
569 -जनापायाभ्यां] P M K C ◆ -जननापायाभ्यां S Q V O Ga Va
569–570 -जनापायदर्शनात्] P M C ◆ -जननापायदर्शनात् S Q V O Ga Va ◆ जनापाद्- K
570–571 इत्यवगन्तव्याः] इत्यवगंतव्यः O ◆ इत्यवगन्तव्यं V Ga
571 न] om. Q O V^{ac}
571 कल्पना-] -कलना S O V^{ac}
572 -मिति] -मित्यत्र S ◆ n.a. M
572 प्रत्ययार्थानुगमे] प्रत्यर्थानुगमे K ◆ प्रत्ययानुगमे O ◆ ///नुगमे M
573 कथमसत्या] किमसत्या P

यत् पुनः ' कूपसूपयूपादौ सत्यपि वर्णानुगमेऽर्थानुगमो न दृश्यते तेन चाकारणमर्थप्रतीतेः वर्णानुगम इत्युक्तं ' तदयुक्तम् ' यतो नान्वयव्यतिरेकाभ्यामनुत्पन्ना प्रतीतिरुत्पाद्यते ' येन कूपादौ तदुत्पादनमाशङ्क्यते । सिद्धायां तु प्रतिपत्तौ वाचकभागेयत्तानियमपरिच्छेदेऽनयोः व्यापारः । न चैकत्र वर्णा-

Granthibhaṅga

575 **यत् पुनः कूपसूपेति** । आह च । यत् कूपसूपयूपेषु समानेऽप्युपबन्धने । नास्त्यर्थानुगमः 'कश्चिन्न शब्दोऽत्रापराध्यति' ॥ 'अन्वयव्यतिरेकाभ्यां नापूर्वार्थो'ऽवधार्यते । सङ्कीर्णेऽवगते ह्यर्थे ताभ्यां शक्तिर्नियम्यत इति ॥ ◆◆◆ कश्चिन्न शब्दोऽत्रापराध्यति] conj. ◆ कश्चिन्न शब्दोऽत्र पराध्यति J ◆ क[श्चित् तन्न शब्दो ऽपराध्यति] Sha ◆ अन्वयव्यतिरेकाभ्यां नापूर्वार्थो] conj. ◆ अन्वयव्यतिरेकाभ्यां न पूर्वार्थो J ◆ नान्वयव्यतिरेकाभ्यामपूर्वार्थो Sha

Testimonia

575 कूप … उत्पाद्यते ✻ यत् कूपयूपसूपादौ समानेऽप्युपबन्धने । नास्त्यर्थानुगमः कश्चित्तन्न शब्दोऽपराध्यति ॥ नान्वयव्यतिरेकाभ्यामपूर्वार्थावधारणम् । संसृष्टेऽवगतेऽर्थे हि ताभ्यां शक्तिर्नियम्यते ॥ (ŚV^{Dvā}, vākya 161–162)

Notes from editions

576–577 नान्वयव्यतिरेकाभ्याम् ✻ अन्वयव्यतिरेकौ हि ज्ञापकौ । न तु कारकौ । अन्वयव्यतिरेकाभ्यां नोत्पद्यत इत्यन्वयः ॥ (NM^{Va})

M K P C S O Q V Ga Va

575 न] तु C ◆ n.a. M
575 तेन] न KO ◆ इति न Q ◆ n.a. M
576 चाकारण-] कारण- Q ◆ n.a. M
576 -प्रतीतेः] -प्रतीते CO
577 -मनुत्पन्ना] -मुत्पन्ना V^{ac} SO
577 -रुत्पाद्यते] -रुत्साद्यते C
577 -शङ्क्यते] PMKCS ◆ -शङ्क्येत QVOGaVa
577 सिद्धायां] प्रसिद्धायां MKVa
578 प्रतिपत्तौ] प्रतीतौ Ga
578 भागेयत्ता … चैकत्र] भा/// ///चैकत्र M
578 -भागेयत्ता-] PKSV^{pc}GaVa ◆ -भागेयंता CQOV^{ac} ◆ n.a. M
578 -नियम-] -नियमा C ◆ n.a. M
578 नयोः] तयोः KQ^{pc} ◆ n.a. M
578–579 वर्णानुगमाद्] PMKCSVa ◆ वर्णानुगमे VGa ◆ वर्णानुगम- Q^{pc}O ◆ वर्णानुगमो Q^{ac}

575–576 कूपसूपयूपादौ … वर्णानुगम इत्युक्तम् ✻ See line 175.

नुगमाद् अर्थानुगमो दृष्ट इत्यन्यत्रादृश्यमानोऽपि हठादापादयितुं युक्तः ॥

9.4.5 [वर्णप्रत्यायकत्वे नान्यथासिद्धत्वम्]

रेणुपटलानुगतपिपीलिकापङ्क्तिद्वारकव्यभिचारोद्भावनमपि न पेशलम् ' पांसुपटलविकलपिपीलिकापङ्क्तिदर्शनेन तस्यास्तत्प्रति कारणत्वाभावनिश्चयात् । करिकरभतुरगप्रभृतीनां तु प्रत्येकं व्यभिचारेऽपि दृढप्राणिरूपसामान्यानपायात् तत्कारणमेव धूलिपटलमवगम्यते ॥

9.4.6 [अश्वकर्णादिपदे नावयवार्थपरित्यागः]

NM^{Va}, 181 यदपि ' अश्वकर्णादाववयवार्थलोपादन्यत्राप्येवमिति कथितं ' तदपि न

Notes from editions

581–582 -निश्चयात् ∗ अन्यथा करितुरगादीनामपि तद्धेतुत्वं न स्यादित्यर्थः ॥ (NM^{Va})

M K P C S O Q V Ga Va

579 अर्थानुगमो] P M K C Va ◆ अर्थागमो S ◆ पदार्थानुगमो Q ◆ पदार्थागमो O V^{ac} ◆ अनुगमो V^{pc} Ga

580–581 -द्वारक- … -पङ्क्ति-] om. S

581 -स्तत्प्रति] P M K C ◆ -स्तत्प्रतीति- S Q O V Ga Va

581 -कारणत्वाभाव-] P M K ◆ -कारत्वाभाव- C ◆ -कारित्वाभाव- S Q V Ga Va ◆ -कारिताभाव- O

582 दृढ-] P M K ◆ बहु- S Q V O Ga Va ◆ महा- C

582 -रूप-] om. M K

583 तत्-] तत्तत्- V Ga

583 -कारणमेव] -कार्यमेव M K

584 यदपि … कथितं] यद/// ///तं M

584 यदपि] यद्यापि C

584 -लोपा-] -लोका- K ◆ n.a. M

584 मिति] -मति- V^{ac} ◆ n.a. M

584 तदपि न] यच्चति C ◆ तथापि न O

580–581 रेणुपटलानुगत- … -दर्शनेन ∗ See line 176.

584 अश्वकर्णादाववयवार्थ- … कथितं ∗ See line 179.

चतुरश्रम् । अश्वकर्णशब्दो हि क्वचिदर्थप्रकरणवशान् न्यग्भवदवयवशक्तितया तिरस्कृतावयवार्थो वस्त्वन्तरव्यक्तौ न सर्वात्मनावयवार्थाभावः । व्यस्तत्वेन सामस्त्येन वा पुनः प्रयोगान्तरे तदर्थसम्प्रत्ययदर्शनाद् ' अश्वमारोह कर्णे कुरु कुण्डलमिति व्यस्तयोः प्रयोगः ' तुरगश्रोत्रे तु प्रतिपिपादयिषितेऽश्वकर्ण इति समस्तप्रयोगोऽपि तदर्थापरित्यागी दृश्यत इति ' न सर्वात्मना निरर्थका भागाः ॥

9.4.7 [अन्वाख्यानविसंवादेऽपि न पदासत्यत्वम्]

यत् पुनः ' अन्वाख्यानविसंवादात् प्रकृतिप्रत्ययविभागनियमो नावकल्पत

Notes from editions

585 अश्वकर्णशब्दो … -वशान् ✱ ओषधिविशेषेऽपि अश्वकर्णसादृश्यादेव तत्प्रयोग इति न सर्वथाऽर्थशून्यत्वम् ॥ (NM^{Va})

M K P C S O Q V Ga Va

585 -शब्दो] -शब्दे C
585 -शक्तितया] -शक्तित्रया C
586 -वयवार्थो] M K ◆ -वयवार्थ- P C S Q O V Ga Va
586 -वयवार्था-] -वयवार्थ- O ◆ -ववार्थ- Q V^{ac} ◆ -वयवा- K
586–588 भावः ' व्यस्तत्वेन … कर्णे कुरु] भावः व्य/// ///क्तने कुरु M
587 सामस्त्येन] समस्तत्वेन K ◆ n.a. M
587 पुनः] om. C ◆ n.a. M
587 प्रयोगान्तरे] प्रयो जनने C ◆ n.a. M
588 कुरु] om. Ga Va
588 तु] om. M K
588–591 प्रतिपिपादयिषिते … -विभागनियमो] प्रतिपिपादयिषिते /// ///नियमो M
588 प्रतिपिपादयिषिते] P M S V^{pc} Ga Va ◆ प्रतिविवादयिषिते K ◆ प्रतिपिपादयिष्यते C ◆ प्रतिपादयिषिते Q ◆ प्रतिपादयिष्यते O V^{ac}

586 -वयवार्थो ✱ The received reading is not supported by the stemma. The compound, -*vayavārthavastvantara*-, however, does not quite make sense ; hence the deviation from the general policy adopted in this edition.
591 अन्वाख्यान- … नावकल्पत ✱ See line 188.

इति ' एतदपि न युक्तम् ' आप्ततरोक्तीनां प्रामाण्यात् । त्रिमुनिव्याकरणमिति पाणिनिमतमेव हि प्रकृतिप्रत्ययविभागमवितथं प्रत्येष्यामः । कियत्यपि चांशे प्रायेण सर्वेषामन्वाख्यातॄणामविवादः । विकरणादिविसंवादमात्रं तु अकिञ्चित्करम् । अतः पारमार्थिकत्वात् प्रकृतिप्रत्ययांशयोर्न कल्पनामात्रेण पृथक्करणम् ॥

9.4.8 [स्वराद्युपायैर्वर्णसाम्ये पदविभागसम्भवत्वम्]

यदप्यवर्णि ' वर्णसाम्यात् पदविभागज्ञानं दुर्घटं कालेनदन्तिनागा इति '- तदप्यसारम् ' स्वरस्मरणादीनां पदभेदावगमोपायानां सम्भवात् । सराम

Granthibhaṅga

598–599 [p.165]सराम इति । आख्यातपक्षे प्रत्ययस्वरेणान्तोदात्तः । पदद्वयपक्षे स इति 'प्रातिपदिक'स्वरेणोदात्त राम इति च कर्षात्वतोर्घञोऽन्त उदात्त* इत्यन्तोदात्तः । सह रामया वर्तत इति तु बहुव्रीहौ पूर्वपदप्रकृतिस्वरेणाद्युदात्तः ॥ ◆◆◆ *Pā 6.1.159

Notes from editions

598–599 सराम इति ✻ सृ गतौ इति धातोः उत्तमपुरुषबहुवचने आख्यातस्यान्तोदात्तत्वम् । बहुव्रीहित्वे आद्युदात्तत्वम् । अन्यत्र उदात्तत्वम् ॥ (NM^{Va})

M K P C S O Q V Ga Va

592 इति ' एतदपि] इति तदपि O

592 युक्तम्] साधु Q

592 -मुनि-] -गुणि- V

593 -मतमेव] -मत एव M K

593–594 प्रकृति- … -मविवादः] प्र/// ///मविवादः M

593 -विभागमवितथं] -विभागवितथं O ◆ -भागमपि तथा K ◆ n.a. M

593 प्रत्येष्यामः] प्रत्येच्यामः K ◆ n.a. M

594 विकरणादि-] विकरादि- K

594–595 अकिञ्चित्करम् । अतः] अकिञ्चित्करमतं M

597–598 यदप्यवर्णि … -स्मरणादीनां] य/// ///णादीनां M

597 -साम्यात्] -सामान्याद् V Ga Va ◆ n.a. M

597 पदविभाग-] पादविभाग- K ◆ अपि भाग- V Ga ◆ n.a. M

597 -ज्ञानं] om. V^{ac} ◆ n.a. M

597–598 वर्णसाम्यात् … -नागा इति ✻ See line 197.

598–599 सराम इति ✻ The expression *sarāmaḥ* may be read as the finite verb *sarāmaḥ*,

इति आख्यातस्यान्यत् स्वरादिरूपं नाम्नोऽन्यत्। नामत्वेऽपि स इति राम इति द्वे चेत् पदे तयोरन्यद्रूपम्। सह रामया वर्तत इत्यैकपद्येऽप्यन्यद्रूपम्। अभियोगविशेषवतां च सर्वं सुगममिति नाशक्यः पदविभागपरिच्छेदः॥ NM^{Va}, 182

9.4.9 [ईषद्विकृतावपि पदार्थसम्प्रत्ययः]

यदपि ' दध्यत्र मध्वत्र इति तथाविधपदरूपादर्शनेऽपि तदर्थसम्प्रत्यय इ-

Testimonia

602–603 यदपि दध्यत्र ... सोऽपि न दोषः ∗ इकारसादृश्यं च यकारस्योपलभ्यते तेनापि तयोः प्रकृतिविकारभावो लक्ष्यते (ŚBh, 1.1.10)

M K P C S O Q V Ga Va

599 नाम्नो] नाम्ना M^{ac}

599 न्यत्] न्य K

600–601 द्वे चेत् पदे ... -विशेषवतां] द्वे चै/// ///विशेषवतां M

600 द्वे चेत् पदे] P ◆ द्वे चैत्पदे K ◆ द्वे चै/// M ◆ च द्वे पदे S Q V O Ga Va ◆ द्योतते C

600 रामया] P K S Q ◆ जामया C ◆ तामया O V^{ac} ◆ रामेण V^{pc} Ga Va ◆ n.a. M

600 इत्यैकपद्ये] P K S ◆ इत्येकपदे C Q V O Ga Va ◆ n.a. M

600 प्यन्यद्रूपम्] रूपमिति Va ◆ n.a. M

601 च] om. Ga Va

601 सर्वं] सर्व- C

601 सुगममिति] P M K ◆ सुभगमिति C S Q V O Ga Va

601 नाशक्यः] नाशक्यं M K C

602 यदपि] यदत्र S ◆ यद्यपि C

602 -पद-] om. M K

602 -रूपादर्शने] -रूपदर्शने Q O ◆ कूपदर्शने V^{ac} ◆ -परस्पर्शने C

602 तदर्थ-] अतदर्थ- P

603 इत्युक्तम् ... तत्प्रत्यभिज्ञानाद्] इ/// ///नाद् M

"we go", or as the *bahuvrīhi* compound *sarāmaḥ*, "he is with Ramā", as suggested in the *Granthibhaṅga*, or even as *sa rāmaḥ*, "he is Rāma", with the *visarga* of *saḥ* dropped according to Pā, 6.1.132, *etattadoḥ sulopo 'kor anañsamāse hali*.

602–603 दध्यत्र ... -सम्प्रत्यय इत्युक्तं ∗ See line 203.

त्युक्तं ' सोऽपि न दोषः । यतस्त एवैते पदे ईषद्विकृते तत्प्रत्यभिज्ञानाद् अर्थप्रत्यभिज्ञानाच्च इति केचित् ' अथ वा इगन्तदधिमधुपदवद् यणन्तयोरपि विषयान्तरे साधुत्वात् । तथैव तद्विदां व्युत्पत्तेर्यणन्तेऽपि पदेऽर्थप्रतिपादके भविष्यत इति । अलमेवंप्रायैः कदाशाव्याहृतैः ॥

9.4.10 [असत्यपदानां न सत्योपायत्वम्]

NM[Shu], 355 अपि च ' पदानामसत्यत्वे किमर्थ एष तद्व्युत्पत्तावियान् प्रयत्नो वृद्धैराधीयते । असत्यमपि सत्योपायतां प्रतिपद्यत इति चेत् ' न ' अदृष्टत्वात् ।

Testimonia

604–606 अथ वा … भविष्यतः ✻ वर्णान्तरमविकारः (MSū, 1.1.16) ◆ न च दध्यत्रेति अत्र प्रकृतिविकारभावः शब्दान्तरमिकाराद्यकारः । न हि यकारं प्रयुञ्जाना इकारमुपाददते … न च सादृश्यमात्रं दृष्ट्वा प्रकृतिर्विकृतिर्वोच्यते । न हि दधिपिटकं दृष्ट्वा कुन्दपिटकं च प्रकृतिविकारभावेऽवगम्यते (ŚBh, 1.1.16)

M K P C S O Q V Ga Va

603 दोषः] दोषाय K ◆ n.a. M
603 एवैते] एव ते P ◆ एते S ◆ n.a. M
603 ईषद्विकृते] ईषद्विवृते P ◆ णषद्विकृते C ◆ n.a. M
603–604 अर्थप्रत्यभिज्ञानाच्च] P M[pc] ◆ अर्थप्रत्यभिज्ञाच्च M[ac] ◆ च K C S Q V O Ga Va
605 तथैव] P M K Ga Va ◆ तथैव च C S Q V O
605 तद्विदां] P M K S ◆ तद्विधा C Q ◆ तद्विधां V O ◆ तद्विधाद् Ga Va
605 व्युत्पत्तेर्यणन्ते] व्युत्पत्तुर्यणान्ते Ga ◆ व्युत्पत्तेर्बणन्ते K ◆ व्युत्पत्तेर्यणान्ते M
605–606 पदे … -व्याहृतैः] पदे/// ///हृतैः M
606 भविष्यत] भविष्यतः C V ◆ n.a. M
606 -व्याहृतैः] -व्याकृतैः C Q V ◆ -व्याहतैः O
607 एष तद्व्युत्पत्ता-] Ga Va ◆ एष व्युत्पत्ता- M K ◆ एतद्व्युत्पत्ता- P S ◆ एव तद्व्युत्पत्ता- C Q V O ◆
608 -धीयते] -स्थीयते M K
608–609 चेत् … येऽत्रोदाहृतास्ते] चेद्/// ///येऽत्रोदाहृतास्ते M
608 चेत् ' न ' अदृष्टत्वात्] P K Q Va ◆ चेददृष्टत्वाद् C S V Ga ◆ वेददृष्टत्वाद् O ◆ चे/// M

ग्रलीका हि दंशादयः सत्यमूर्च्छाहेतवो येऽत्रोदाहृतास्ते तथा न भवन्ति ' विषवद् विषाशङ्काया ग्रपि तत्कार्यहेतुत्वात् । शङ्का हि नाम बुद्धिः । बुद्धिश्च न न कारणम् । न चासती बुद्धिः ॥

9.4.11 [लिप्यत्तराणां सत्यत्वम्]

यदपि ' लिप्यत्तराणामसत्यानां सत्यार्थप्रतिपादकत्वमुच्यते ' तदप्यनभि-

Granthibhaṅga

610 शङ्काया ग्रपि तत्कार्यहेतुत्वादिति । शङ्काविषेणापि मरणं दृश्यते यतः ॥

Testimonia

612 लिप्यत्तरा- … -प्रतिपादकत्वमुच्यते ∗ ये ऽपि रेखादयो दृष्टा वर्णानां प्रतिपादकाः । न ते स्वेनापि रूपेण परमार्थत्ववर्जिताः ॥ वर्णात्मना न सत्याश् चेत् सर्वभावेष्व् ग्रयं विधिः । पदार्थान्तररूपेण न सत्यं किञ् चिद् इष्यते ॥ parencite[nirālambana 160–161]SV :1978

M K P C S O Q V Ga Va

609 हि] om. O ◆ n.a. M
609 -मूर्च्छा-] -मूर्छादि- P ◆ n.a. M
609 येऽत्रोदाहृतास्ते] P V Ga Va ◆ यत्रोदाहृतास्ते M K C S Q O
610 विषवद्] P M K ◆ om. C S Q V O Ga Va
610 विषाशङ्काया] ◆ विषाशङ्कया P ◆ विषशङ्काया M K
611 न न] न तु C ◆ न O
611 कारणम्] करणं M
612–613 लिप्यत्तराणाम- … रेखास्तावत्] लिप्यत्तरा/// ///रेखास्तावत् M

609 ग्रलीका … येऽत्रोदाहृतास्ते ∗ Or, as a compound, *alīkāhidaṃśādayaḥ*, "false (*alīka*) snake (*āhi*) bites, etc. (*daṃśādayaḥ*"). See line 180.

611 न न ∗ I understand *na na* as a double negation, as in line 276 above, as well as, e.g., in NM[Va], I 628,18 and II 73,3.

612 लिप्यत्तरा- … -प्रतिपादकत्वमुच्यते ∗ See line 181.

NM[Va], 183 ज्ञभाषितम् । रेखास्तावत् स्वरूपतः सत्यास्ताश्च खण्डिकोपाध्यायोपदेशसंस्कृतमतेर्वर्णानुमापिका भवन्ति । तथा सम्बन्धग्रहणाद् रेखानुमितेभ्यश्च वर्णेभ्योऽर्थप्रतिपत्तिरिति नासत्यः सत्योपायः । अयं गकार इति तु सामानाधिकरण्यभ्रमः ' लिङ्गलिङ्गिनोरभेदोपचारात् । यथा प्रस्थमिताः सक्तवः प्रस्थशब्देनोच्यन्ते तथा रेखातो गकारानुमानाद् रेखैव गकार इत्युच्यते । एवमनिष्यमाणे लिप्यनभिज्ञस्यापि ततोऽर्थप्रतिपत्तिः स्याद् ' रेखाणामस-

Notes from editions

613 खण्डिको- * खण्डिका—वेदभागः, अनुवाकवत् ॥ (NM[Va])

615 अयं गकार इति तु * रेखायामिति शेषः ॥ (NM[Va])

M K P C S O Q V Ga Va

613 -ज्ञ-] -ज्ञा- V^{ac} ◆ n.a. M

613 सत्या-] सत्य- Ga

613 खण्डिको-] पण्डितो- M K

613 -पाध्यायोपदेश-] -पदेश- S^{ac}

613–614 -संस्कृत-] -संस्कृते C

614 -मतेर्वर्णानु-] मते वर्णानु- C ◆ -मते वर्णानु- O

614 -मापिका] -मानिका K

614–616 -ग्रहणाद् … सामानाधिकरण्य-] ग्रहणाद्/// ///सामानाधिकरण्यं M

614 -मितेभ्यश्च] -मितेश्च K S ◆ n.a. M

615 नासत्यः सत्योपायः] नासत्याः सत्योपायाः V^{pc}Ga Va ◆ n.a. M

615 अयं गकार इति तु] अयं तु गकार इति P ◆ n.a. M

616 -करण्य-] -करण्यं M K

616 प्रस्थमिताः] प्रस्थापिता C

617–619 -शब्देनोच्यन्ते … विद्यमानत्वात्] शब्देनोच्य/// ///विद्यमानत्वात् M

617 रेखातो] P K ◆ रेखातोऽपि C S Q V O Ga Va ◆ n.a. M

618 एवमनिष्यमाणे] एवमन्विष्यमाणे O ◆ n.a. M

613 खण्डिकोपाध्यायोपदेश * A mention of a *khaṇḍikopadhyāya* can be found in VMBh[Ki], 1.1.1, värtt. 13, p. 41, *yaḥ udātte kartavye anudāttaṃ karoti khaṇḍikopādhyāyas tasmai capeṭāṃ dadāti …*

615 अयं गकार इति तु * See line 184.

त्यवर्णात्मनां विद्यमानत्वात् । न चैवमस्ति । तस्माद् वर्णानुमानपुरःसरैव रेखाभ्योऽर्थावगतिः । अभ्यस्तत्वाद् विषयस्य सूक्ष्मत्वाच्च कालस्य क्रमो न लक्ष्यते । न त्वन्यथा ततोऽवगतिः ॥

तस्मात् पारमार्थिकत्वात् पदतदर्थानां न निरवयवौ वाक्यवाक्यार्थाविति स्थितम् ॥

यत् पुनः ' वाक्यभागपदवर्णापह्नववर्त्मना शब्दब्रह्मैवाद्वयमुपदर्शयितुमुपक्रम्यते ' तत्र पुरस्तात् सविस्तरं समाधिमभिधास्यामः ॥

Granthibhaṅga

620 **अभ्यस्तत्वाद्विषयस्येति** । अविनाभावस्मृत्यभावेऽपि रेखावगमसमनन्तरं वर्णावगतेः ॥

M K P C S O Q V Ga Va

619 -वर्णात्मनां] -वर्णानां Va ◆ n.a. M
619–622 चैवमस्ति … पदतदर्थानां] चैव/// ///पदतदर्थानां M
619 वर्णानुमान-] वर्णावर्णानुमान- C O V^{ac} ◆ n.a. M
620 अभ्यस्तत्वाद्] अभ्यस्तत्वात्तु P ◆ n.a. M
622 पदतदर्थानां] पदमतदर्थानान् K ◆ पदपदार्थानां O
623 स्थितम्] om. S
624–626 -वर्त्मना … -त्रैविध्यं] वर्त्म/// ///त्रैविध्यन् M
624 -ब्रह्मैवाद्वय-] -ब्रह्मैव- O
624 -मुपदर्शयितुमुप-] -मुद्दर्शयितुमुप- P
625 -क्रम्यते] -क्रमते O ◆ n.a. M
625 पुरस्तात्] परस्तात् P ◆ पुरस्थात् C ◆ n.a. M

624–625 वाक्यभाग- … -क्रम्यते ✱ See line 211.
625 समाधिमभिधास्यामः ✱ The discussion on *śabdādvaita* takes place in NM[Va], II 478,18–487,5, NM 9.

9.4.12 [वाचस्त्रैविध्ये प्रामाण्याभावः]

यत्पुनरवादि ' वाचस्त्रैविध्यं तदपि नानुमन्यन्ते ।
एकैव वैखरी वाग् वागिति लोके प्रसिद्धा हि ॥
अन्तःसंजल्पो वर्ण्यते मध्यमा वाक्
सोऽयं बुद्ध्यात्मा नैष वाचः प्रभेदः ।
बुद्धिर्वाच्यं वा वाचकं वोल्लिखन्ती

Granthibhaṅga

630 'बुद्धिर्वाच्यं' वेति । घटमहं प्रतिपादयामीति वाच्यमुल्लिखन्ती, घटशब्दमुच्चारयामीति तु वाचकमुल्लिखन्ती ॥ ◆◆◆ बुद्धिर्वाच्यं] बुद्धिर्वाच्यं [वाचकं] Sha

Notes from editions

630 वोल्लिखन्ती ✻ उल्लिखन्ती बुद्धिरित्यन्वयः ॥ (NM[Va])

M K P C S O Q V Ga Va

626 -विध्यं] -विद्यं O V[ac]
627 एकैव] एकैक M[ac]
627 लोके] P M K ◆ om. C S Q V O Ga Va
628 -संजल्पो] -सजल्पो V ◆ -संकल्पो Ga
629 सोऽयं] सेयं V Ga Va ◆ से O
629–631 बुद्ध्यात्मा … जह्राति] om. O
629–631 वाचः … बोधभावं] वाच/// ///भावं M
629 वाचः] वाचां K ◆ n.a. O
630 -र्वाच्यं] -र्वाक्यं C ◆ n.a. M O
630 वा] P GBh ◆ om. K C Q V Ga Va ◆ n.a. M O
630 वोल्लिखन्ती] P S ◆ वोल्लिखंते V ◆ चोल्लिखन्ती K Q Ga Va ◆ चेल्लिखंती C ◆ n.a. M O

626–627 यत् … प्रसिद्धा हि ॥ ✻ This is in *āryā* meter of the *pathyā* variety (Varakale, 1927, 2.3, p. 28), with the expected absence of *jagaṇa* (i.e., *madhyaguru*, a group of four morae with a heavy syllable in the middle) in uneven positions, as well as a light syllable (*pra*) as the sixth group in the second hemistich (see Varakale, 1927, 2.1–2). The metric form of this passage, unnoticed in previous editions of the NM, was brought to my attention by Kei Kataoka.
626 वाचस्त्रैविध्यं ✻ See line 218.
630 वा ✻ The *vā*, which is needed *metri causa*, is attested to only in GBh and P.
630 वोल्लिखन्ती ✻ *vollikhantī* is attested to, indirectly, also by the GBh, because the first *vā* implies the second one.

रूपं नात्मीयं बोधभावं जहाति ॥
पश्यन्तीति तु निर्विकल्पकमतेर्नामान्तरं कल्पितं $\mathrm{NM}^{\mathrm{Va}}$, 184
विज्ञानस्य हि न प्रकाशवपुषो वाग्रूपता शाश्वती ।
जातेऽस्मिन् विषयावभासिनि ततः स्याद्वावमर्शो गिरो
न स्याद्वापि न जातु वाग्विरहितो बोधो जडत्वं स्पृशेत् ॥

9.5 [स्फोटनिराकरणोपसंहारः]

तदास्तामियं शब्दब्रह्मचर्चा । प्रकृतमनुसरामः ˈ

Granthibhaṅga

633 ˚स्व˚प्रकाशवपुषो वाग्रूपता शाश्वती नैव काचित् सम्भवतीत्यर्थः । तदेवाह । जातेऽस्मिन्निति ॥ ◆◆◆ स्व-] न Sha

Notes from editions

634 जाते ✳ विषयप्रकाशके ज्ञाने जाते, तत्र शब्दस्य परामर्शः स्यात् न वा न तत्र निर्बन्धः । परन्तु शब्दाविषयकत्वमात्रात् विषयाविषयकत्वं न भवेत् । शब्दाननुविद्धा प्रतीतिः स्यादेव ॥ ($\mathrm{NM}^{\mathrm{Va}}$)

635 जडत्वं ✳ जडत्वं–घटादिवन्निर्विषयत्वम् ॥ ($\mathrm{NM}^{\mathrm{Va}}$)

M K P C S O Q V Ga Va

632 निर्विकल्पक-] निर्विकल्पिक- Q
632 -मतेर्नामान्तरं] -मेतन्नामान्तरं V O ◆ -मतन्नामान्तरं C
633 हि] om. S
633 वाग्रूपता] वाग्रूपतो C
633 शाश्वती] P M C V O ◆ शास्वती K Q Ga Va ◆ शास्वता S
634 जाते] ज्ञाते V^{ac}
634–635 स्याद्वावमर्शो … जडत्वं] स्याद्वा/// ///जडत्वं M
634 गिरो] गिरान् K ◆ n.a. M
636 तदास्तामियं] तदास्तादियं O
636 शब्द-] om. Ga
636 -ब्रह्म-] om. C
636 -चर्चा] -चर्चाः K

इति विततया वर्णा एते धिया विषयीकृता 637
दधति पदतां वाक्यत्वं वा त एव च वाचकाः । 638
न पुनरपरः शब्दः श्रोत्रे विभात्यवबोधने 639
न च विधिहतो वाच्ये बुद्धिं विधातुमसौ क्षमः ॥ 640

Granthibhaṅga

637 **इति विततयेति** । क्रमोपलब्धवर्णविषयया सङ्कलनारूपविततया ॥
640 **न च विधिहत इति** । विधि[163r]ना दैवेन हतः । यथा सकलसदुपलम्भकप्रमाणाविषयस्तद्वद्य इत्यर्थः । बहुना वा क्लेशेन तस्य निराकरणादाक्रोशः ॥

Notes from editions

637 विततया ∗ विततया—एवं विस्तरेण प्रतिपादितया रीत्या वर्णाः धिया विषयीकृताः पदतां, वाक्यतां वा दधति । न त्वतिरिक्तं पदं वाक्यं वा । कृतामिति पाठे तत् पदतामित्यादेर्विशेषणम् ॥ (NM^Va^)
640 विधिहतो ∗ विधिहतः—दुर्भगः । असौ—स्फोटः ॥ (NM^Va^)

M K P C S O Q V Ga Va

637 -कृता] कृतां Ga
638 पदतां] पदतां त्वं C ◆ पदत्वं O V^{ac}
638–639 वाक्यत्वं वा … -बोधने] वाक्यत्वं वा/// ///धने M
639 पुनरपरः] PKS ◆ चापरो C ◆ खलु च परो Q ◆ चापरे O V^{ac} ◆ च तदपरः V^{pc}Ga Va ◆ n.a. M
639 शब्दः] PK ◆ वर्णः CSQ ◆ वर्णाः O V^{ac} ◆ स्फोटः V^{pc}Ga Va ◆ n.a. M
639 श्रोत्रे] KCQOVa ◆ श्रौत्रे PSVGa ◆ n.a. M
639 बोधने] वोधे C V^{ac}
640 विधिहतो] विधिहते K

10 Foliation

p.127) 1 151v7 K 88v11 P 233r5 C 239v10 S 158r3 O 189r12 V 367 Ga 143 Va
p.128) 7 कश्चि[189v]दस्ति V
p.129) 11 प्रतिजानाते ॥[144]ननु Va
p.129) 14 वर्णात्म[233v]नः C
p.129) 15 अतो[152r]न प्रमाणम् K
p.129) 16 चाप्तप्रणी[240r]तत्वम् S
p.132) 26 सत्ता[145]मात्रेण Va
p.132) 28 नित्यः[158v]शब्द O
p.133) 33 प्रती[368]तावेव Ga
p.133) 34 एकव[190r]क्तृ- V
p.133) 35 -पु[234r]रुष- C
p.134) 41 वाचकाः ॥[146]वर्णविषया Va
p.134) 43 -जनि[240v]त- S
p.135) 47 अन्त्यवर्ण///[152v]अन्तरं K
p.137) 57 प्रत्यायि[234v]ष्यन्तीति C
p.137) 58 तथा[147]विध- Va
p.137) 61 ///[90r]येण P
p.137) 61 व्या[159r]पाराभावात् O
p.137) 63 -प्रयुक्ता[190v]अपि V
p.138) 64 चि[3r2]न्तनीयः M
p.138) 65 किमप्य[369]धिकं Ga
p.139) 72 वर्तते[241r]परावगति S
p.139) 73 कमर्थं[148]प्रतिपादयन्तो Va
p.140) 80 सर्वथा[235r]र्थप्रतीति- C
p.141) 82 [250r]क्षपणादक्ष- Q
p.141) 85 -र्थौ विभक्त्य[153r]र्थश्च द्वयम् K
p.142) 88 इति[90v]व्यवहारस्स्यात् P
p.142) 89 ऽर्थ[149]प्रतिपादके Va
p.143) 94 -प्रतिपत्ति[191r]स्स शब्दः V
p.145) 97 -प्रतिपत्तिः स[370]शब्दः Ga
p.145) 99 भव[159v]न्तु भवन्ती O
p.145) 100 कार्यता[241v]मुपयायात् S
p.146) 102 त्वन्यथासिद्धम्[150]का पुन- Va
p.146) 103 -प्रतीतेरुप[235v]प्लवते C
p.146) 103 -प्रतीतेरुपप्लव[250v]ते वर्णा- Q
p.146) 103 ///[3v2]प्रतिपत्तिमादधाति M
p.149) 118 प्रयोच्यन्त इति ॥[151]अपरे Va
p.149) 118 स्फोटस्य[91r]व्यञ्जकाः P
p.150) 121 -प्रध्वं[153v]सिनः के K
p.151) 123 दर्शयन्ति[191v]नादात्मको V
p.151) 125 न पा[251r]रमार्थिका Q
p.151) 126 तेऽर्थप्रत्य[236r]यान्वय- C
p.151) 128 यदु[242r]च्यते S
p.151) 130 -प्रत्ययो[371]वर्णानु- Ga
p.152) 133 स्फोटः ॥[152]आह Va
p.152) 134 -चरितं व[160r]र्तते O
p.153) 141 ----द्[4r]¯कार्थप्रत्यायकत्वो- M
p.154) 144 -वाक्यार्थ[91v]प्रतीत्याख्य- P
p.154) 145 औपाधि[251v]कत्वं च Q
p.154) 150 प्रतिपत्तिः ॥[153]आह Va
p.154) 150 निर[236v]वयवः C
p.155) 153 -च्छ्वसितमेव[192r]मे हृदयम् V
p.155) 154 भोत्स्य[154r]से किञ्चित्तु K
p.155) 157 बोधकम्[242v]यथा S
p.156) 162 -कल्प[372]नातो Ga
p.156) 164 ///य व्यवहाराद्[4v]धि शब्दार्थे M
p.156) 164 पदस्य [252r]प्रयोग Q
p.156) 165 वाक्यं तु[154]प्रयोगार्हम् Va
p.157) 169 -केसरमरिचा[92r]दिभ्यो P
p.157) 170 -मरिच्यादिभ्योऽर्थान्तर[160v]मेव O
p.157) 170 -लाक्षादिभ्योऽर्थान्तरमे[237r]व

चित्रम्C

p.160) 181 सत्य[192v]मरण- V

p.160) 182

-प्रतिपत्तिमादधति ॥[155]स्वरूपसत्यानि Va

p.160) 184 येन[252v]रूपेण Q

p.160) 185 चार्थ[154v]प्रतिपादका- K

p.160) 186 प्रतिभा[243r]सादर्थ- S

p.162) 193 तदुक्तम् ।[373]पदं Ga

p.162) 193 चतुर्धा[237v]पञ्चधापि C

p.162) 193 ///द्[5r]इति अपि च M

p.162) 195 -वर्णस[92v]न्निवेशदर्शनात् P

p.162) 195 नियत[156]तेषां Va

p.163) 201 प्रथम[161r]प्रतिपन्न- O

p.164) 203 मध्वत्रे[253r]ति दधि- Q

p.164) 208 -वाक्यान्यपि[193r]प्रकरणापेक्षया V

p.166) 212 -भेदम[243v]र्थभेदे S

p.166) 212 -भेदमर्थ[238r]भावेन C

p.166) 212 -भावेन[157]विवर्तते Va

p.168) 221 तदुक्तम् ।[374]स्थनेषु Ga

p.169) 222 कृतव[155r]र्णपरिग्रहा K

p.169) 225 तदुक्तम्[158]केवलं Va

p.169) 226 बुद्ध्युपादाना[93r]क्रमरूपानुपातिनी
P

p.169) 226 क्रमरूपानुपाति[253v]नी प्राण- Q

p.171) 235 ///[5v]स्य वाच्योऽर्थ M

p.171) 237 विद्या[238v]यां C

p.171) 238 वर्णानां वा[161v] व्यवहाराभावात् O

p.172) 240 इति ॥[159]तस्माद् Va

p.172) 241 -विभागो[193v]वाक्यस्फोटो V

p.173) 246 बलवत्तया वा[244r]न तावदनु- S

p.174) 249 व्यस्तानां ता[254r]वद्वाचकत्वं Q

p.174) 251 यत्तु[375]तत्सामस्त्यं Ga

p.174) 253 दृश्यन्ते ॥[160]तथा Va

p.175) 256 ग्रासा यु[93v]गपत् P

p.176) 260 आग्नेया[239r]दियागानां C

p.176) 260 आग्नेयादिया[155v]गानां K

p.177) 264 ///[6r]--आ एकार्थाभिधायिनो M

p.178) 268 दृश्यते[161]यद्येवम् Va

p.178) 268 कार्य[254v]मुपलभ्यते Q

p.178) 271 अवान्तरापू[194r]र्वनिर्वृत्ता- V

p.179) 272 किमवा[162r]न्तरं O

p.179) 274 अवान्तरापूर्वेण[244v]स्वर्ग- S

p.179) 278 -व्यवहार[94r]स्त्ववान्तर- P

p.179) 280 -भूतप[239v]दार्थ- C

p.180) 281 प्रादुष्यात् ॥[162]वर्णानामपि Va

p.180) 284 -कार्यस्य[376]करणात् Ga

p.181) 286 इतीदृ[255r]श एवायं Q

p.181) 291 सन्दिग्धो[156r]बाध्यते K

p.182) 298 विकल्पाः ॥[163]ननु Va

p.182) 298 ///[6v]-दि ते वर्णाः M

p.182) 299 निर्विशेष एव स्या[194v]दिति
तदुपारूढा V

p.182) 300 त्वेकघ[245r]नस्तबक- S

p.183) 301 प्रत्ययस्त[240r]दा तस्मिन् C

p.183) 301 अपि ते[94v]वर्णा P

p.183) 303 संकल[162v]नाप्रत्ययो O

p.183) 304 नास्ति[255v]कस्य Q

p.185) 315 स्मरण[164]कारणं Va

p.185) 317 -मर्थप्र[377]तीतिजन्मनि Ga

p.185) 320 -प्रतीतिहे[240v]तुर्भवति C

p.186) 323 जनयितु[256r]मुत्सहति Q

p.186) 324 अवगम्य[95r]ते तदिदमनु- P

p.186) 325 इति वक्ष्यामः ।[245v]अस्ति S

p.186) 326 निष्करणि[195r]का करण- V

p.186) 328 तत्कार्यत्वात्[156v]तदनुमापिका K

p.187) 330 ///[7r]-----त् तथा M

p.187) 333 अनुभव[163r]स्तावत् O

p.187) 334 आधत्ते ।[165]स कार्यभेदो Va

p.188) 341 सामस्त्याभावादिति[241r]नैष C

p.188) 342 संकार[256v]स्तादृगुपाधीयते Q

p.189) 348 एकस्म[95v]रणासिद्धये P

p.189) 349 -कल्पनातो[378]न पश्यामहे Ga

p.189) 349 अतो न[166]पश्यामहे Va

p.190) 356 कारिता[195v]भवद्भिरपि V

p.190) 361 तावद[246r]स्तित्वं S

p.191) 362 व्यतिरिक्तत्वं[157r]पुनरवयं K

p.191) 362 ///[7v]कल्पितम् M

p.191) 362 कल्प[257r]नागुरुत्वम् Q

p.191) 363 तदुक्तम् ।[167]सद्भाव- Va

p.191) 363 सद्भाव[241v]व्यतिरेकौ C

p.191) 366 स ए[163v]व विषम O

p.192) 373 स्फुट[96r]म् इति P

p.193) 378 -लब्धा[168]तिशयायां Va

p.194) 379 बुद्धे[379]रतिशययोगः Ga

p.194) 382 परागुभ्यो[257v]वर्ण- Q

p.194) 385 अथ[242r]ध्वनयः C

p.195) 386 रूपमिव[196r]मुखस्य V

p.196) 394 सत्तानुपपत्तेः ।[169]सर्वथा Va

p.196) 396 -गम्यत इति[246v]यावन्तो S
p.196) 396 यादृशाः[8r]इति यत्त्वत्र M
p.196) 397 किय[157v]न्तः कीदृशाः K
p.196) 397 तत्र[96v]प्रतीतयः P
p.196) 399 ग्रभ्यधा[164r]यि क्रम- O
p.197) 402 पदा[258r]र्थान्तर- Q
p.198) 408 वर्णास्त[242v]मर्थं C
p.198) 410 सिद्धम् ॥[170]यदप्यभाणि Va
p.198) 411 तद[380]प्यसारं Ga
p.199) 417 वर्तमाने च[196v]शब्दशब्दे V
p.199) 423 समुदायवाची[97r]भविष्यति P
p.199) 423 शब्दशब्दो[258v]वनं वृक्षा Q
p.200) 428 वनादौ[171]भेदव्यपदेश- Va
p.200) 430 समुदायसमु[243r]दायिनोरभेदो- C
p.200) 430 समुदायि⁻⁻[8v]⁻भे⁻पचारादाप्रा- M
p.200) 430 प्रयोक्तु[247r]मिह तु S
p.200) 432 तत्[164v]सर्वथा O
p.200) 433 वा[158r]दिनाम् K
p.202) 445 एकत्वाच्च ॥[172]सङ्कलना Va
p.202) 445 वाचक[259r]त्वपक्षे Q
p.202) 445 दोशा । न[381]हि भेद- Ga
p.202) 448 स्फो[97v]टपक्षे P
p.202) 448 -मनुपपन्नो[197r]यं व्यपदेशः V
p.203) 451 -विशिष्टमर्थ[243v]प्रतिपत्ति- C
p.204) 460 विवक्षितत्वात् ॥[173]श्रोत्रमनो- Va
p.205) 462 व्यभिचार इ[9r]ति चेत् न M
p.205) 463 व्यभिचारः ते[247v]षां शब्द- S
p.205) 466 लक्ष[259v]णमित्युक्तम् Q
p.205) 467 शब्दे तद[165r]भावेन- O
p.206) 469 जाति[158v]गुणक्रिया- K
p.206) 471 -ग्रह[98r]णाद् ग्रतः P
p.207) 476 श्रोत्र[244r]करणकम् C
p.207) 476 वर्णा[174]ग्रालम्बनी- Va
p.207) 477 शाब[382]लेयादौ Ga
p.207) 478 पिण्डसा[197v]धारणं V
p.208) 485 ग्रनुमन्येम[260r]हि न त्वेवमस्ति Q
p.210) 493 स्फोटः[175]मैवम् Va
p.210) 494 -दर्शने व्य[98v]क्त्यन्तरा- P
p.210) 495 ///का[9v]रानुसन्धानमिति M
p.210) 495 -सन्धान[248r]मिति S
p.211) 499 -वर्णं हि[244v]शब्दः C
p.211) 500 स्फोटः[165v]तदिदं O
p.212) 503 -समान[159r]योगक्षेमैव K
p.212) 504 वैलक्षण्यस्य[260v]दर्शितत्वात् Q
p.212) 506 चैकार्थ[176]प्रतीतिरिति Va
p.212) 509 रूपा[383]भवेदिति Ga
p.213) 515 क्रमभा[99r]विनां P
p.214) 521 इतिसिद्धम् ॥[177]ननु Va
p.214) 521 विषय[245r]भेदाभेदानु- C
p.214) 523 ग्रभिन्नस्या[261r]पि सावयव- Q
p.214) 523 -स्यापि सा[248v]यवत्वात् S
p.214) 525 ///म[10r]संगता M
p.215) 529 वाधकभावा[166r]द् भ्रान्तेश्च O
p.216) 534 गम्य[198v]माने V
p.216) 535 एषितव्यम् ॥[178]चित्रे Va
p.216) 535 सिन्दूरहरिता[159v]लादि K
p.217) 539 -कारत्वेन[99v]सर्वासामनवयव- P
p.217) 542 एव[384]न पद- Ga
p.217) 544 वाक्या[245v]दपि C
p.217) 544 वाक्यादपि[261v]व्युत्पत्ति- Q
p.219) 551 पदा[179]न्तराणामर्थो Va
p.219) 552 -रूपावधारण[249r]मपि S
p.220) 556 कार्यैकदेश[10v]मात्रां M
p.220) 560 तदि[166v]दमपूर्वं O
p.221) 563 यथोपलभ्य[262r]ते तत्तथा Q
p.221) 563 न भवति[199r]वाक्यपदयोश्च V
p.221) 564 -लभ्यन्ते न[100r]वर्णानाम् P
p.221) 566 स्फुटमि[246r]ति तस्मा- C
p.222) 569 भुवन्निति ॥[180]इतश्च Va
p.222) 571 इत्यव[160r]गन्तव्याः K
p.223) 575 पुनः[385]कूपसूप- Ga
p.224) 583 तत्त[262v]त्कारणम् Q
p.224) 584 ग्रवगम्यते ॥[181]यदपि Va
p.225) 585 ग्रश्वक[249v]र्णशब्दो S
p.225) 587 -र्थसम्प्र[246v]त्ययदर्शनाद् C
p.225) 588 ⁻र्ण[11r]कुरु कुण्डलमिति M
p.225) 589 दृश्यत[100v]इति न P
p.226) 592 प्रामा[167r]ण्या O
p.226) 593 पाणि[199v]निमतमेव V
p.227) 599 नाम्नोऽन्यत् ।[182]नामत्वे Va
p.227) 602 -परिच्छेदः[263r]यदपि Q
p.228) 603 इत्युक्तं[160v]सोऽपि K
p.228) 607 ग्रपि च[386]पदानाम् Ga
p.229) 609 दंशादयः[247r]सत्य- C
p.230) 613 खण्डकोपा[183]ध्यायोपदेश- Va
p.230) 615 वर्णेभ्यो[250r]र्थप्रति- S
p.230) 615 ग्रयं तु गका[101r]र इति P
p.231) 619 -वर्णात्मनां[11v]विद्यमानत्वात् M

p.231) 620 -स्तत्वात्तु वि[263v]यस्य Q
p.231) 621 न त्व[200r]न्यथा ततो V
p.231) 625 -क्रम्यते[167v]तत्र O
p.233) 632 जहाति ॥[184]पश्यन्तीति Va
p.233) 633 प्रकाश[247v]वपुषो C

Part III

Appendix

11 Tables of errors

11.1 Conjunctive readings of the γ family

- *grahaṇatvāt*] *grahaṇāt* (II 149,4) γ
- *pi hi*] *hi* (II 150,6) P ^{ac} γ
- *pratipatti*] *pratīti* (II 149,9) γ
- *te vikalpāḥ*] *vikalpāḥ* (II 150,10) γ
- *vadanasyeti*] *vadanasya* (II 151,6) γ
- *vyastasamasta*] *samastavyasta* (II 151,8) γ
- *vyaktyālambano* (II 152,6)] *vyaktyālambanato* γ
- *tatparihāra*] *parihāra* (II 152,15) γ
- *ekaghanākārā*] *ekaghaṭanākārā* (II 153,15) γ
- *na tatra*] *tatra na* (II 154,3) γ
- *yūpasūpānām*] *sūpayūpānām* (II 154,10) γ
- *api hi*] *api* (II 154,15) γ
- *apratipādakatvāt*] *pratipādakatvāt* (II 155,1–2) γ
- *padānām*] *padārthānām* (II 155,9) γ
- *vākyāt kalpanayoddhāraḥ*] *kalpanayaivāpoddhāraḥ* (II 155,10) γ
- *eṣāṃ*] *teṣāṃ* (II 156,1) γ
- *pūrvam*] *prathamam* (II 156,8) γ
- *śabda*] *śāstra* (II 156,16) γ
- *vāgrūpatā tu*] *vāgrūpatā* (II 157,3) γ
- *vyavasthitāvabhāsate*] *vyavasthitaivāvabhāsate* (II 157,7) γ
- *naḥ*] *punaḥ* (II 158,9) γ
- *vākyārthapratyayo*] *vyavahāro* / *om.* (II 158,9) γ
- *kāritvaṃ*] *bhāvitvaṃ* (II 160,15) γ
- *yad*] *tad* (II 161,6) γ
- *nanu ca*] *nanu* (II 163,1) γ
- *ntyo*] *ntya* (II 163,13) γ
- *smaraṇe*] *smaraṇa* (II 163,13) γ
- *arhati*] *utsahati* (II 164,9) γ
- *bhede*] *bhedo* (II 165,1) γ
- *svādhyāyādhyayane*] *svādhyāyayane* (II 165,12) γ
- *mucyāmahe*] *paśyāmahe* (II 166,1) γ
- *karaṇatā hi*] *kāritā* (II 166,7) γ
- *kevalam adhikam*] *kevalam* (II 166,11) γ
- *uccaritaṃ*] *uccāritaṃ* (II 167,10) γ
- *paricchedo*] *paricchinno* (II 167,13) γ
- *kas tatra*] *tatra ko* (II 168,2) γ
- *anupalakṣyamāṇa*] *anupalabhyamāna* (II 168,5) γ
- *varṇā dṛṣṭāḥ*] *dṛṣṭā varṇās* (II 169,14) γ
- *sthitam*] *siddham* (II 169,16) γ

- *svayam avagatiḥ*] *svāvagatiḥ* (II 170,6) γ
- *na syāt*] *na* (II 170,14) γ
- *samudāyi*] *samudāya* (II 170,16) γ
- *nirūpaṇa*] *nirūpaṇena* (II 171,13) γ
- *pratipadyāmaha iti*] *pratipadyāmahe* (II 172,3) γ
- *śabdam*] *śabdatvam* (II 172,5) γ
- *lakṣaṇaṃ yuktaṃ*] *yuktaṃ* (II 172,10) γ
- *evāsti*] *eva* (II 172,11) γ
- *kālāntare ca*] *kālāntareṇa* (II 173,9) γ
- *matiḥ*] *pratītiḥ* (II 174,5) γ
- *ghaṭita*] *parighaṭita* (II 174,6) γ
- *eka*] *ekaika* (II 174,9) γ
- *śabdatva* (II 175,6–7)] *śabdatattva* γ
- *teṣāṃ santrāsaḥ*] *santrāsaḥ* (II 175,7) γ
- *jātyādibuddhiṣu*] *jātyādiṣu* (II 175,14) γ
- *janitaiveyaṃ* (II 176,1–2), *jānitaṃ yaṃ*] *janiteyaṃ* γ
- *sthitam*] *siddham* (II 176,15) γ
- *sarva* (II 177,12)] *pūrva* γ
- *artha*] *vākyārtha* (II 178,10) γ
- *yady*] *yad* (II 179,6) γ
- *itaś*] *ataś* (II 180,1) γ
- *dṛḍha*] C *mahā, bahu* (II 180,15) γ
- *sugamam*] *subhagam* (II 182,2) γ
- *tathaiva* (II 182,8)] *tathaiva ca* γ
- *viṣavad viṣāśaṅkayā*] *viṣāśaṅkayā* (II 182,14) γ
- *loke prasiddhā*] *prasiddhā* (II 183,14) γ
- *śabda, varṇaḥ, varṇāḥ*] *sphoṭaḥ* (II 184,8) γ
- *bhāvānāṃ*] *varṇānāṃ* (II 185,6) γ
- *ādhīyate*] *āśrīyate* (II 186,10) γ
- *yathāha*] *om.* (II 186,15) γ
- *yogyatva*] *yogyatā* (II 187,9) γ
- *pratipattis tato*] *pratipattir ato* (II 187,13) γ
- *samudāyātmakaṃ*] *samūhātmakaṃ* (II 188,5) γ
- *bhūyāpi*] *bhūya* (II 188,9) γ
- *vyavayitoccāriteṣv* [...] *upapādayiṣyate*] *om.* (II 189,5) γ
- *viratavirata*] *virata* (II 189,19) γ
- *pradhāna*] *pradhāne* (II 190,7) γ
- *vākyārthānavagame*] *vākyārthāvagame* (II 191,11) γ
- *prāktanena ca*] *prāktanena* (II 192,8) γ
- *ekaṃ*] *eka* (II 192,10) γ
- *pūrvapada*] *pada* (II 192,17) γ
- *saṃskārasyaikatvāt*] *saṃskārasyaivaikatvāt* (II 192,17) γ
- *avacchedakatvaṃ*] *avacchedakatve* (II 196,1) γ
- *sthāpanaṃ*] *sthānaṃ* (II 196,13) γ
- *kṛtottara*] *kṛtottarottara* (II 196,15) C S Q V[pc] O
- *turagam iti* (II 198,3)] *turagaṃ* γ
- *pūrva*] *sarva* (II 200,6) γ
- *adhigacchantīti*] *adhigamayantīti* (II 202,7) γ
- *abhihitānām anvaya*] *abhihitānvaya* (II 202,13) γ
- *padārthakasya*] *padārthasya* (II 202,14) γ
- *padam anyānurakta* (II 204,2)] *padasāmānyānurakta* γ
- *avagamayati* (II 205,10)] *avagamayatīti* γ
- *kārakāni* (II 206,4)] *kāraṇāni* γ
- *pratyabhijñānāt* (II 206,4)] *pratijñānāt* γ
- *ca*] *om.* (II 207,11) γ
- *upapatsyate* (II 208,13)] *utpatsyate* γ
- *upāyābhāvāt* (II 209,4)] *ubhayābhāvāt* γ
- *kin tu vyutpatti*] *vyutpattiś* (II 212,11) γ
- *tu*] *om.* (II 213,2) γ

- *anvitānanvita* (II 214,3–4)] *ananvita* γ
- *kriye ete* (II 215,1)] *ete kriye* γ
- *viśeṣe*] *viśeṣo* (II 215,16) γ
- *iyam iyaṃ*] *iyaṃ* (II 216,16) γ
- *pratyayau hi*] *pratyayau* (II 217,15) γ
- *niyogasyādhātu*] *niyogasya dhātu* (II 217,16) γ
- *iti vadan*] *iti* (II 219,18) γ
- *tadupa-*] *upa-* (II 220,7) γ
- *anyathāpi tat*] *anyathā tat* (II 220,8) γ
- *vedārtha*] *vedārthasya* (II 220,18) γ
- *jīvatsv api*] *jīvatsu* (II 220,19) γ
- *kim*] *kim anena* (II 221,12) γ
- *kaścit*] *kaiścit* (II 222,18) γ
- *pratipadyeta*] *pratipatsyate* (II 223,5) γ
- *prasiddheś* (II 223,12)] *siddheś* γ
- *sopānāntarita*] *sopānāntara* (II 224,19) γ
- *gāvyādi*] *gavyādi* (II 225,1) γ
- *gāvyādiṣu* (II 225,16)] *gavyādiṣu* γ
- *tṛṣṇā-* (II 226,11)] *tṛṣā-* γ
- *kāraṇaka* (II 226,14)] *karaṇaka* γ
- *vidhiṃ*] *vidhiṃ vā* (II 226,18) γ
- *vācaspater api*] *vācaspater* (II 227,4) γ
- *apaśabda*] *apaśabde* (II 228,16) γ
- *vidhiyate iti*] *abhidhiyate iti* (II 229,2) γ
- *sambhāvyeta*] *sambhāvyate* (II 230,4) γ
- *pramāṇāpekṣayā vā*] *pramāṇāpekṣayā* (II 230,8) γ
- *eṣā*] *aśeṣā* (II 230,12) γ
- *tvadabhimata*] *abhimata* (II 230,15) γ
- *gāvyādy* (II 230,16)] *gavyādy* γ
- *gāvyādy* (II 231,6)] *gavyādy* γ
- *kaṃ*] *kiṃ* (II 233,4) γ
- *adhīyānam* (II 233,4)] *adhīyamānam* γ
- *saṃskāram* (II 235,9)] *vidhis saṃskāram* γ
- *prayogopāyasya* (II 235,12)] *prayogopāya* C Q V O, *prayogopa* S
- *tadvārake* (II 235,14)] *tatkārake* γ
- *vidhīyeta*] *vidhīyate* (II 237,12) γ
- *ama roge*] *amo roge* (II 238,17) γ
- *sarva*] *sakala* (II 243,13) γ
- *vyāpāraṃ* (II 244,3)] *vyāpāraḥ* γ
- *prasakti*] *prasakta* (II 244,5) γ
- *samarthānāṃ* (II 244,8)] *samāsārthānāṃ* γ
- *tatkuto* (II 244,10)] *kuto* γ
- *itaravākya* (II 245,2)] *itara* γ
- *-śodhana*] *-codana* (II 245,13) γ
- *cāmaraṇānto*] *ca maraṇānto* (II 246,10) γ
- *vyāhṛtaṃ*] *vyākṛtaṃ* (II 246,19) γ
- *dṛśyante*] om. (II 248,11) γ
- *gāvyādayo*] *gavyādayo* (II 248,16) γ
- *gāvyādi* (II 249,7)] *gavyādi* γ
- *avalambantām*] *ālambantām* (II 249,10) γ
- *dhṛtam*] *avadhṛtam* (II 254,6) γ

11.2 Conjunctive readings of the β family

- *sphoṭa*] *sa sphoṭa* (II 148,7) β
- *rtho* (II 148,12)] *rtho vibhaktyarthaś ca* β
- *om. iti*] *iti* (II 148,13) β
- *idaṃ tv anyathāsiddham*] *om.* (II 148,14) β
- *api* (II 149,9)] *om.* β
- *sphoṭa* (II 150,10)] *sphoṭasya* β
- *carame* (II 150,14)] *carama* β
- *saṃyogopādhi* (II 151,3)]

saṃprayogopādhi β
- *eva te* (II 151,8)] *ete* β
- *iti siddham* (II 151,14–15)] *om.* β
- *ekākārā* (II 152,9)] *ekākāra* β
- *pada* (II 152,17)] *om.* β
- *ca* (II 152,17)] *om.* β
- *varṇātmāno* (II 153,3)] *varṇātmano* β
- *kiṃcit* (II 153,5)] *kiñcit tu* β
- *kā* (II 153,13), *kā vā*] *kva* β
- *pi* (II 154,2)] *pi ca* β
- *yathā* (II 154,4)] *yathā hi* β
- *vā* (II 154,6)] *ca* β
- *pratipattim* (II 154,16)] *pratītim* β
- *svarūpeṇeyattā* (II 155,6)] *svarūpeyattā* β
- *padayor* (II 156,10)] *śabdayor* β
- *advayam* (II 156,19)] *om.* β
- *sarvatra* (II 157,3)] *sarva* β
- *samudāyātmika* (II 157,8–9)] *samudāyā* β
- *vāk sā* (II 157,9)] *om.* β
- *kramādi* (II 158,3)] *kathādi sā* β
- *vidyāyāṃ* (II 158,13)] *vidyāyāṃ hi* β
- *matiṃ* (II 159,2)] *matis* β
- *te vācakāḥ* (II 159,11)] *vācakāḥ* β
- *tat sāmastyaṃ* (II 159,12)] *sāmastyaṃ* β
- *ekāṃ* (II 160,1)] *ekā* β
- *aniṣpannatvād* (II 161,8)] *asaṃpannatvād* M, *saṃpannatvād* K
- *kāryaṃ* (II 161,9)] *om.* β
- *ivāmukhī* (II 162,2)] *ivābhimukhī* β
- *kramo* (II 162,2)] *tadopakramo* β
- *mātrāsamunmeṣo*] *mātrasamunmeṣo* (II 162,2) β
- *mānasam anuvyavasāya* (II 162,7)] *mānasa vyavasāya* β
- *kramānubhūteṣu* (II 162,9)] *kramabhūteṣu* β
- *pi* (II 162,14)] *om.* β
- *kramānavagamād* (II 163,4), *kramānavabhāsād*] *kramāvagamād* β
- *te* (II 163,10)] *om.* β
- *syuḥ* (II 163,12)] *om.* β
- *iyaṃ* (II 163,16)] *ayaṃ* β
- *smṛtir* (II 163,16)] *smṛter* β
- *kartavyeti* (II 163,16)] *karttavyateti* β
- *bhavati* (II 164,6)] *bhavatīti* β
- *ca* (II 164,11)] *om.* β
- *hi* (II 164,13)] *om.* β
- *anurudhyāmānāḥ* (II 165,7)] *anurudhyamānā* β
- *eva* (II 165,6)] *om.* β
- *varṇa* (II 165,9)] *varṇakrama* β
- *saṃskāraṃ* (II 166,1)] *saṃskāraḥ* β
- *vidveṣaḥ* (II 166,1)] *dveṣaḥ* β
- *varṇa* (II 166,7)] *varṇaka* β
- *api* (II 166,8)] *om.* β
- *navaṃ* (II 166,11)] *abhinavaṃ* β
- *upanyāsaḥ* (II 167,5)] *upamanyāsaḥ* M^{pc}K
- *varṇātmānaḥ padātmāno* (II 167,16)] *padātmāno varṇātmāno* β
- *apari* (II 166,16)] *pari* β
- *iti* (II 168,1)] *om.* β
- *tad apy asat* (II 168,8)] *om.* β
- *tena* (II 168,15)] *om.* β
- *vartamāna* (II 170,9)] *pravarttamāna* β
- *vartitum* (II 170,10)] *pravarttitum* β
- *sphoṭāṭopaḥ* (II 171,13)] *sputāṭopaḥ* β
- *laukiko* (II 171,14)] *laukika* β
- *ca* (II 172,10)] *om.* β
- *ubhayopādānena* (II 172,11)] *ubhayapadopādānena* β
- *varṇā* (II 172,11)] *varṇa* β
- *prasaṅge* (II 173,11)] *prasaṅgena* β
- *api* (II 173,12)] *alaṃ* β

- *śrotra* [...] ca (II 173,14)] *om.* β
- *padaṃ* (II 174,3)] *pratipadaṃ* β
- *om. viraṇair iva kaṭaḥ*] *viraṇair iva kaṭaḥ* (II 174,9–10) β
- *paṭādibuddhiṣu* (II 174,13)] *paṭādiṣu* β
- *śabdatvaṃ*] *śabdatva* (II 174,16) β
- *sāmānyam* (II 175,3)] *sāmānyam iti* β
- *śaṅkitaiḥ*] *śaṅkibhiḥ* (II 175,6) β
- *ca* (II 175,7)] *hi* β
- *bhedābhedāv* (II 176,5–6)] *bhedābhedam* β
- *eva ca* (II 176,12)] *om.* β
- *eṣāṃ* (II 176,13)] *eṣa* β
- *asty* (II 177,9)] *athāsty* β
- *bījaṃ kim api* (II 177,10)] *kim api bījam* β
- *yadi hi, yad iha, yadyaha* (II 177,11)] yadi β
- *pi* (II 178,1)] *om.* β
- *ṛṣabhagāndhārādi* (II 178,2)] *ṛṣabhādi* β
- *vākyārtha* (II 178,3)] *vākya* β
- *anavayavatvāt* (II 178,4)] *abhyupagatatvāt* β
- *nirbhāgau* (II 178,6)] *niravayavau* β
- *hi* (II 178,12)] *om.* β
- *rathād* (II 179,4)] *om.* β
- *ucyate* (II 179,6)] *ucyeta* β
- *avayavāntarāṇi* (II 179,10)] *avayavāntaraṇāni na* β
- *tat tathā na bhavati* (II 179,16)] *na tat tathā* β
- *vākyapadayoś* (II 179,16)] *padavākyayoś* β
- *rūpa* (II 180,16)] *om.* β
- *kāraṇam* (II 180,16)] *kāryam* β
- *artha* (II 181,3)] *artho* β
- *tu* (II 181,6)] *om.* β
- *matam* (II 181,10)] *mata* β
- *pada* (II 182,4)] *om.* β
- *ādhīyate* (II 182,11)] *āsthīyate* β
- *khaṇḍiko* (II 182,17)] *paṇḍito* β
- *samānādhikaraṇya* (II 183,3)] *samānādhikaraṇyaṃ* β
- *ādadhānā* (II 185,10)] *dadhānā* β
- *uccāritānām*] *uccaritānām* (II 186,5) β
- *pi* (II 186,7)] *om.* β
- *tu* (II 186,11)] *ca* β
- *padārthapratītiṃ* (II 187,3)] *padārthabuddhiṃ* β
- *kāryā* (II 187,4)] *kāryo* β
- *nāvakalpeta* (II 187,9)] *nāvakalperan* β
- *om. iti*] *iti* (II 188,2) β
- *kālpanika* (II 188,3)] *kālpanikaṃ* β
- *vākyārtha* (II 188,6)] *vākyārthe* β
- *naitad yuktaṃ* (II 188,6)] *om.* β
- *ādhāsyanti* (II 188,10)] *ādhāsyantīti* β
- *paratra* (II 188,11)] *om.* β
- *kāryadvayaṃ padāni*] *padāni kāryadvayaṃ* (II 188,15) β
- *bhinnatvāt* (II 189,2)] *vibhinnatvāt* β
- *cānantara* (II 189,5)] *cānantaram eva* β
- *atyantaṃ* (II 189,11)] *atyanta* β
- *gamakavāco* (II 189,13)] *gamakabhāvavāco* β
- *ca* (II 189,15)] *om.* β
- *hi* (II 189,17–18)] *om.* β
- *na budhyante*] *nāvabudhyante* (II 190,4) β
- *ca* (II 190,9)] *tu* β
- *vadad* (II 190,12)] *vadan* β
- *śābdatve* (II 190,15)] *śābdatve tu* β
- *mūlatvāt*] *tanmūlatvāt* (II 190,16) β
- *śvetam* (II 191,14)] *śvetim* β
- *evaṃ śveto* (II 191,15), eva ca śveto P] *evañ cec chveto* β
- *adīdṛśan* (II 192,6)] *adīdiśan* β
- *ca saṃskāreṇa* (II 192,7)]

saṃskāreṇa ca β
- *saṃskāreṇa* (II 192,8)] *saṃskāreṇa ca* β
- *pada* (II 192,15)] *padasya* β
- *pīvara* (II 192,15)] *pivara* β
- *padārtha* (II 193,12)] *padārthapada* β
- *carama* (II 193,15)] *antya* β
- *jñānasya hi* (II 194,1)] *jñānāhita* β
- *vināśa* (II 194,2)] *avināśa* β
- *pada* (II 194,10)] *om.* β
- *rūpeṇa* (II 194,13)] *krameṇa* β
- *jñānena* (II 195,1)] *jñānena ca* β
- *ca* (II 195,6)] *om.* β
- *bāhye* (II 195,19)] *bāhya* β
- gocaracārīṇi] *gocarāṇi* (II 195,21) β
- *padajñānasahāyāt* (II 196,9)] *dvitīyapadajñānasahāyāt* β
- *ca* (II 196,12)] *om.* β
- *om. hi*] *hi* (II 197,2) β
- *vinaśyad* (II 197,3)] *om.* β
- *avasthaṃ* (II 197,4)] *om.* β
- *brūyāt* (II 197,5)] *brūyāḥ* β
- *bhūtayā* (II 197,5)] *bhūtayā ca* β
- *buddhimātreṇa* (II 197,5–6)] *om.* β
- *sahasaiva* (II 197,13)] *om.* β
- *krameṇa* (II 197,15)] *om.* β
- (II 198,2)*paryālocana*] *paryālocanā* β
- *tasmiṃś* (II 198,10)] *tataṣ* β
- *prathamaṃ* (II 198,13)] *tatprathamaṃ* β
- *prayuktam* (II 198,13)] *vṛttam* β
- *padaṃ* (II 198,13)] *om.* β
- *api* (II 199,14)] *om.* β
- *ca* (II 199,15)] *om.* β
- *sahitena* (II 200,3)] *sāhityena* β
- *padārtha* (II 200,5)] *om.* β
- *apramāṇam*] *apramāṇatvam* (II 200,9) β
- *pratyayāsambhavād*] *pratipattyasambhavād* (II 200,12) β
- *smṛtir* (II 200,16)] *smṛtir apy* β
- *smaraṇenānu* (II 201,3)] *saṃsmaraṇenānu* β
- *śakyo* (II 201,6)] *śakyate* β
- *vā*] *om.* (II 201,17) β
- *te*] *tu* (II 202,1) β
- *tathābhihitās* (II 202,6)] *yathābhihitās* β
- *'rtham avagamayati vyutpattim antareṇa*] *vyutpattinirapekṣo 'rtham avagamayati* (II 202,8–9) β
- *tadanvitā*] *tadānvitā* (II 202,11) β
- *vākyārthasaṃpratyayo* (II 202,14)] *vākyārthasya pratyayo* β
- *pravibhāgāś*] *vibhāgāś* (II 202,15) β
- *tu* (II 202,18)] *ca* β
- *tu* (II 203,3)] *om.* β
- *rūpād upāyāt* (II 203,4)] *rūpānapāyāt* β
- *upeyaṃ* (II 203,4)] *upeyāṃ* β
- *bandhana* (II 203,7)] *om.* β
- *avadhāraṇaṃ* (II 203,9)] *avadhāraṇañ ca* β
- *padārthayor* (II 203,9)] *tadarthayor* β
- *sā* (II 203,12)] *sa* β
- *vyutpattyāvakalpate* (II 203,14)] *vyutpattāv avakalpate* β
- *anenaiva* (II 204,3)] *anena* β
- *tu gośabdasya na* (II 204,8)] *na gośabdasya* β
- *kṛtopadarśanāt* (II 204,13)] *bhūtopadarśanāt* β
- *yenākāṅkṣito* (II 205,1)] *yena kāṅkṣito* β
- *ca* (II 205,10)] *om.* β
- *sati* (II 206,7)] *om.* β
- *evaṃ* (II 206,9)] *ittham* β
- *om. tat*] *tat* (II 206,18) β
- *na* (II 207,5)] *na na* β
- *pariniścayāc* (II 207,17)] *paraniṣṭhayā* β

- *upagacchāmahe* (II 207,18)] *upagacchāma* β
- *dvāpodvāpa* (II 208,6)] *dvāpābhyām* β
- *racanā* (II 208,6)] *aracanā* β
- *bhavantī* (II 209,10)] *om.* β
- *saṃsṛṣṭa* (II 210,14)] *saṃsṛṣṭas* β
- *hy*] *tv* (II 211,2) β
- *katham*] *kaṣṭam* (II 211,4) β
- *pravāda*] *pralāpa* (II 211,18) β
- *om. syāt*] *syāt* (II 211,18) β
- *śuddhatvam* (II 212,5)] *śuddhatvād* β
- *padasyārtho* (II 212,17)] *śabdasyārtho* β
- *asyārtha*] *tasyārtha* (II 213,1) β
- *kiyati* [...] *śaktiḥ* (II 213,4)] *om.* β
- *kiyantaṃ* [...] *muñcati* (II 213,5–6)] *om.* β
- *tadaṅguly* (II 214,6)] *aṅguly* β
- *om. ca* (II 214,11)] *ca* β
- *ceti* (II 214,16)] *iti* β
- *eva nānvīyamānābhidhānaṃ* (II 215,4)] *om.* β
- *abhidhānam*] *abhidhānakriyā so'yam* (II 215,4–5) β
- *anye* (II 215,13)] *anye tu* β
- *jñāpakatvāt* (II 215,14)] *jñāpakatvāt tu* β
- *kā tarhīyaṃ* (II 215,15)] *tarhi keyaṃ* β
- *asaṃsṛṣṭaṃ ca kāryaṃ* (II 217,13)] *asaṃsṛṣṭa kāryaṃ* β
- *yujyate, dṛśyate*] *vidyate* (II 218,7) β
- *abhigantavyaḥ* (II 219,17)] *adhigantavyaḥ* β
- *vadhāryate*] *vadhāryeta* (II 220,19) β
- *atīndriye rthe niyatā* (II 221,5)] *tadatīndriye rthe niyatāt* β
- *purassarā* (II 222,8)] *purassara* β
- *tad* (II 222,9)] *om.* β
- *bodhakatvād* (II 222,9)] *bodhakatva* β
- *apratipādakatva* (II 222,9)] *om.* β
- *lakṣaṇam aprāmāṇyam apojjhato* (II 222,9)] *lakṣaṇaprāmāṇyākṣepe* β
- *pari* (II 222,13)] *om.* β
- *kṛtabuddhir api* (II 222,13)] *om.* β
- *vedam*] *cedam* (II 223,17) β
- *eva* (II 223,18)] *eva tāvac* β
- *niṣedhabodho* (II 224,2)] *niṣedhāvabodho* β
- *pratyakṣādi* (II 224,3)] *om.* β
- *pramitiṣu* (II 224,5)] *om.* β
- *api* (II 224,7)] *om.* β
- *sādhutve*] *sādhvasādhutve* (II 224,12) β
- *tadvidhau / siddhe cāsādhutve tanniṣedhe*] *tadvidhiniṣedhe* (II 224,12) β
- *itaretarāśrayam*] *itaretarāśrayatvam* (II 224,13) β
- *tāvaty* (II 225,2)] *om.* β
- *hema* (II 225,3)] *hima* β
- *sambandhaḥ sa* (II 225,4)] *sambandhaḥ śabdaḥ sa* β
- *sādhavaḥ* (II 225,11)] *sādhavaś ca* β
- *etac* (II 225,15)] *tac* β
- *asādhutvaṃ* (II 225,17)] *cāsādhutvaṃ* β
- *sādvasādhu* (II 225,18)] *om.* β
- *atisūkṣmayāpi* (II 226,1)] *atisūkṣmayā* β
- *ca* (II 226,9)] *om.* β
- *aprāpteḥ* (II 226,9)] *prāpteḥ* β
- *niyamaṃ*] *niṣedhaṃ* (II 226,18) β
- *śabdānupadarśya*] *śabdāt pradarśya* (II 227,1) β
- *grahaṇa* (II 227,2)] *grahaṇena* β
- *parameṣṭhino pi* (II 227,3)] *parameṣṭhino* β
- *śabdānupadarśya*] *iti* (II 227,14) β
- *hi* (II 227,16)] *ca* β
- *nivṛtti* (II 228,8)] *nirvṛtti* β

- *pracuraḥ* (II 228,12)] *pracura* β
- *parokṣasyādṛṣṭasya* (II 229,4–5)] *parokṣasya* β
- *sārvatrikī* (II 229,13)] *sārvatrika* β
- *apy* (II 230,1)] *om.* β
- *sikṣādīnām* (II 230,1)] *sīkṣādīnām* β
- *plavane* (II 230,3)] *plavanaṃ* β
- *yad* (II 230,9)] *yo* β
- *prayoga* (II 231,3)] *vyavahāra* β
- *anyatamaḥ kila vyākaraṇasya* (II 231,15–16)] *anyatamaṃ kila* β
- *evāvagamyate* (II 231,18)] *avagamyate* β
- *vargād* (II 232,12)] *vargāder* β
- *vidher* (II 232,13)] *nidher* β
- *prayojanāntaram* (II 232,15)] *prayojanāraṃbham* β
- *śabdopadeśa*] *śabdetaropadeśa* (II 232,15) β
- *satas* (II 232,16)] *om.* β
- *vahatsv* (II 233,11)] *om.* β
- *bhaviṣyati* (II 233,13)] *bhavati* β
- *suvyāhṛtam*] *sādhuvyāhṛtam* (II 233,17) β
- *iti* (II 234,2)] *om.* β
- *ca* (II 234,8)] *om.* β
- *varṇayos* (II 234,15)] *varṇa* β
- *rūḍha*] *śākhi* (II 235,4) β
- *iti* (II 235,4)] *om.* β
- *vā* (II 235,13)] *om.* β
- *pi* (II 236,4)] *om.* β
- *janikartuḥ* (II 236,6)] *janir* β
- *pi dambher* (II 236,8)] *pīdam* β
- *vacanasaṃjñā* (II 236,10)] *vācanasya* β
- *codyam* (II 236,14)] *coditam* β
- *iti cātra* (II 236,14)] *iti ca* β
- *ktvā* (II 236,15)] *tvā* β
- *vyākaraṇasya* (II 236,16), *vyākaraṇam asya* Q] *vyākaraṇam* β
- *skhalantīti* (II 236,16)] *skhalanti* β
- *tubhyaṃ* (II 237,3)] *tubhya* β
- *iti* (II 237,14)] *om.* β
- *hi* (II 237,15)] *om.* β
- *api* (II 238,1)] *iha* β
- *ca* (II 238,3)] *om.* β
- *bhavati* (II 238,15)] *bhavatīti* β
- *yata* [...] *asti ca* (II 238,19–239.1)] *om.* β
- *pāṭha* (II 239,1)] *om.* β
- *cānarthakaḥ* (II 239,4)] *anarthakaḥ* β
- *vacanatvasya* (II 239,7)] *vacanatva* β
- *dvitīyasya*] *dvitīya* (II 239,7) β
- *ca* (II 239,11)] *om.* β
- *niyama* (II 239,12)] *om.* β
- *kṛśam api na* (II 240,3)] *na kṛśam api* β
- *ādye* (II 240,10)] *ādya* β
- *kriyāyāḥ*] *kriyayā* (II 240,10) M ^{pc}K
- *adhikaraṇasaṃjñā* (II 241,9)] *adhikaraṇatvaṃ* β
- *apsu pacatīti syāt* (II 241,11)] *om.* β
- *sthito* (II 241,11)] *om.* β
- *ekaikakārakādhāratve*] *ekaikādhāratve* (II 241,14) β
- *tal* (II 241,14)] *om.* β
- *avyāpārarūpatvād* (II 242,1)] *avyāparatvād* β
- *kriyārthitayā* (II 242,4)] *kriyārthatayā* β
- *ity* (II 242,6)] *om.* β
- *kriyayā cāptum iṣṭatamam* (II 242,8)] *kriyayāptum iṣṭam* β
- *tat* (II 242,12)] *om.* β
- *kārakatvam* (II 242,14)] *kārakam* β
- *upeya*] *upeyā* (II 242,16) M ^{ac}K
- *kriyāyāḥ upāyaḥ*] *kriyā tadupāyaṃ* (II 242,16) β
- *taṇḍulān* (II 243,1)] *taṇḍulādīn* β
- *om. kriyāsampadyam*] *kriyāsampadyam* (II 243,4) β

- *tarhi* (II 243,11)] *sa tarhi* β
- *uccārito* (II 244,2)] *uccarito* β
- *om. kṛt*] *kṛt* (II 244,7) β
- *tad atrāpi* (II 244,8)] *tatrāpi* β
- *iti* (II 244,11)] *om.* β
- *sāmarthye* (II 244,13)] *om.* β
- *iti* (II 244,15)] *om.* β
- *tathā* (II 244,16)] *om.* β
- *ca prātipadika* (II 244,16)] *om.* β
- *pratiṣedha* (II 245,4)] *niṣedha* β
- *vāvacanānarthakya* (II 245,7)] *vacanānarthakya* β
- *prasaṃgena* (II 245,9)] *atiprasaṃgena* β
- *anuharatīti phalina* (II 245,16)] *anuvahatīti phalā* β
- *barhiṇau*] *barhiṇaṃ* (II 245,17) β
- *vṛtti*] *vṛttis* (II 246,15) β
- *sūtraṃ* (II 246,15)] *sūtras* β
- *tathaiva* (II 247,13)] *tathā* β
- *ekāntena* (II 248,1)] *ekānto* β
- *apabhraṣṭā* (II 248,11)] *bhraṣṭā* β
- *te cen na* (II 248,15)] *na cet* β
- *adhyavasātuṃ* (II 248,17)] *addhyavasthātuṃ* β
- *āhatya* (II 249,2)] *abhihatya* β
- *vācī* (II 249,7)] *vādī* β
- *eva* (II 249,9)] *om.* β
- *om. ca*] *ca* (II 249,14) β
- *so* (II 249,15)] *om.* β
- *pādā māṣā* (II 250,3)] *māṣāḥ pādā* β
- *āśrayaḥ*] *āśrayāḥ* (II 250,13) β
- *acchinno*] *avicchinno* (II 250,15) β
- *kalpate* (II 251,16)] *kalpyate* β
- *ativyā* (II 252,1)] *avyā* β
- *yadi* (II 253,4)] *om.* β
- *panasa* (II 253,12)] *panase* β
- *nara*] *tara* (II 254,1) β
- *pati, bhūpati* (II 254,1)] *nṛpati* β
- *śūdra*] *śudratā* (II 254,1) β
- *śravaṇottara* (II 254,3)] *grahaṇāntara* β
- *śāsana* (II 254,4)] *śāsanam* β
- *phalasaṃyogam* (II 254,8)] *phalopayogam* β
- *pramāṇatvaṃ* (II 254,9)] *pramāṇatāṃ* β
- *siddhau* (II 254,11)] *prasiddhau* β
- *niṣedhayos*] *pratiṣedhayos* (II 254,11) β
- *viṣayārthatvā*] *viṣayatvā* (II 254,13) β
- *satyam uktaṃ*] *satyaṃ* (II 254,13) β
- *ādiṣṭa* (II 255,1)] *ādiśiṣṭa* β
- *vaidikam* [...] *vidhi* (II 255,1–2)] *om.* β
- *śakyam* (II 255,2)] *yuktam* β
- *gambhīra* (II 255,5)] *om.* β
- *ha vā* (II 255,11)] *bhavā* β
- *yad apaśabdaḥ* (II 255,12)] *yo paśabdaḥ* β
- *upayogīni* (II 255,12)] *upayogīny eva* β
- *apabhāṣitaṃ* (II 255,14)] *api bhāṣitaṃ* β
- *iva*] *vad* (II 255,15) β
- *śabdasvarūpaṃ*] *svarūpaṃ* (II 256,5) β
- *ucyate iti*] *ucyateti* (II 256,7) β
- *sādhubhir* (II 256,13)] *sādhur* β
- *śabda* (II 256,16)] *prayoga* β
- *phalatva* (II 257,3)] *phala* β
- *vāda* (II 257,4)] *om.* β
- *vedaś ... niṣprayojanaḥ* (II 257,10)] *vedāś ... niṣprayojanāḥ* β
- *vedaveda*] *vedavat* (II 258,2) β
- *paramārthatas* (II 258,3)] *paramārthas* β
- *brūmo* (II 258,12)] *bruve* β
- *avagatya*] *avagamya* (II 258,18) β
- *praṇītavān*] *om.* (II 258,18) β
- *om. paṇḍita*] *paṇḍita* (II 259,9) β
- *asūtram* (II 259,13)] *asaṃbaddham* β
- *paramaṃ*] *prathamaṃ* (II 260,6) β
- *vā* (II 261,6)] *vai* β
- *śruta* (II 262,2)] *śruti* β

11.3 Singular readings in K

- *dṛśyante* (II 207,9) M] *dṛśyate* K
- *paraniṣṭhayā* (II 207,17) M] *pariniṣṭhayā* K
- *tv* (II 208,5) M] *vā* K
- *navadhāraṇāt* (II 213,9) M] *navadhārakāraṇāt* K
- *cokto bhihitānvaye* (II 215,18) M] *cekto bhihitānvayo* K
- *doṣa* (II 216,6) M] *deśa* K
- *niṣkṛṣṭa* (II 216,18) M] *nikṛṣṭa* K
- *parāpekṣīṇi* (II 217,18) M] *parāpekṣaṇī* K
- *vyākaraṇena* (II 222,11) M] *vyākaraṇe* K
- *analaṃ na* (II 226,7) M] *analaṃ* K
- *prayojana* (II 226,14) M] *prayojanaṃ* K
- *apaśabdānām* (II 228,11) M] *apaśaktānām* K
- *śruyamāṇayor* (II 229,11) M] *śrayamāṇayor* K
- *pramāṇabhāva* (II 229,11) M] *pramāṇābhāva* K
- *na* (II 230,7) M] *om. na* K
- *vāg* (II 230,12) M] *vā* K
- *mūlamanvādi* (II 232,1) M] *mūlatayādi* K
- *ākāṃkṣati* (II 232,15) M] *āṃkāṃkṣati* K
- *prayogapravāhād* (II 233,7) M] *prayogād* K
- *bhavati* [...] *prayojanam* (II 233,9–10) M] *om. bhavati* [...] *prayojanam* K
- *kathyate* (II 234,3) M] *kalpyate* K
- *mahatī* (II 235,10) M] *mahatīti* K
- *kaścid vyākaraṇena* (II 235,13–14) M] *kañcid vyākaraṇe* K
- *vyākaraṇam* (II 235,15) M] *vyākaraṇe* K
- *aviravika* (II 236,12) M] *aviravi* K
- *anantaran* (II 237,3) M] *antaran* K
- *janme janme* (II 237,3) M] *janme* K
- *bhavatīti* (II 238,6) M] *bhavati* K
- *nagara* (II 238,7) M] *naga* K
- *kambalada* (II 238,7) M] *kaṃ ida* K
- *kecana* (II 238,12) M] *kenacana* K
- *tv evaṃ* (II 238,14) M] *tvam evam* K
- *kṛte* (II 238,14) M] *pi tu te* K
- *lṛṭ* (II 239,11) M] *om. lṛṭ* K
- *luṅ* (II 239,11) M] *lud* K
- *kriyopalabhyate* (II 240,4) M] *kriyayopalabhyate* K
- *karmmaśabdaḥ* (II 240,9) M] *karmmaḥ* K
- *copādhyāyasya* (II 240,11) M] *coddhyāyasya* K
- *dvayor apy* (II 241,14) M] *dvayo py* K
- *atiśāyanaḥ* (II 242,3–4) M] *itiśāyanaḥ* K
- *na* (II 242,7) M] *na hi* K
- *anivāryam* (II 242,7) M] *anirvāryam* K
- *na vācakaḥ* (II 243,2–3) M] *nu vācakaḥ* K
- *vyavasthāpanād* (II 245,7) M] *vasthāpanād* K
- *sthūlodara* (II 246,2) M] *sthūloda* K
- *asti* (II 248,3) M] *om. asti* K
- *prabhavā* (II 248,9) M] *prabhāvā* K
- *sarva* (II 248,9) M] *sarvā* K
- *bhavantīti* (II 255,13) M] *bhavanti* K
- *kṛśānupāna* (II 255,15) M] *kṛśānupā* K
- *śaṃkopaplavamāna* (II 256,15) M] *śaṃkopaplavatmāna* K
- *bhavatu ko* (II 257,3) M] *bhavato* K

- *manvānas* (II 257,15) M] *mayānas* K
- *teṣāṃ* (II 258,11) M] *keṣāṃ* K
- *hitam* (II 259,7) M] *hita* K
- *saṃskāra* (II 260,12) M] *saṃskāraṇa* K
- *malakalile* (II 261,6) M] *malakalikhe* K

11.4 Singular readings in M in relation to K

- *hi* (II 179,10)] K; *om.* M
- *pūrvapadāvacchedenottarottara* (II 196,11)] K; *pūrvapadāvacchedo nottarottara* M
- *padoparāga* (II 197,1)] K; *paroparoga* M
- *pratipatteḥ* (II 200,9)] K; *pratīteḥ* M
- *aparaṃ na saṃsarggapratīter* (II 209,18)] K; *aparaṃ saṃsarggaprīter* M
- *labhavet* (II 212,1)] K; *bhavet* M
- *āvāpodvāpa* (II 212,17)] K; *āpodvāpa* M
- *tadvanmātraṃ* (II 213,7)] K; *tanmātraṃ* M
- *sarvārtham* (II 213,15)] K; *sarvārthakam* M
- *syātām* (II 215,3)] K; *syatām* M
- *eva nābhidhīyamānānvayaḥ* (II 215,5)] K; *evābhidhīyamānānvayaḥ* M
- *om. jāti* (II 215,9)] K; *jāti* M
- *ca* (II 217,11)] K; *om.* M
- *adyatve* (II 220,16)] K; *anyatve* M
- *vyavahārānusāreṇa* (II 222,15)] K; *vyavahānusāreṇa* M
- *hy ācaṣṭe* (II 223,7) Ω, *vyācaṣṭe*] K; *ācaṣṭe* M
- *anārabhyāt* adhītau, *anārabhyādhītau* (II 223,16)] K; *anārabhyātītau* M
- *śabdatvādi* (II 224,6)] K; *śabdatvāti* M
- *pāmarādiḥ lokaḥ* (II 225,1) Ω, *pāmarādiḥ*] K; *pāramādiḥ lokama* M
- *pi* (II 225,6)] K; *hi* M
- *kāraṇatvaṃ* (II 225,14)] K; *karaṇatvaṃ* M
- *teṣāṃ* (II 227,6)] K; *te teṣāṃ* M
- *phalaś* (II 228,17)] K; *palaś* M
- *anārabhyādhītayoḥ* (II 229,11)] K; *anārabhyādhītayo* M
- *vedasyeti* (II 229,12)] K; *vedasyaiti* M
- *sa dūram* (II 230,3) Ω, *tu sudūram*] K; *sudūram* M
- *vyavahāriṇo* (II 230,16)] K; *vyahāriṇo* M
- *pratiyoga* (II 231,4)] K; *prayoga* M
- *vaidya* (II 231,7)] K; *vaidyaka* M
- *niyama* (II 232,4)] K; *nimayama* M
- *daṇḍa* (II 232,5)] K; *daṇḍā* M
- *sāddhyatām* iti, *sādhyatām* (II 232,9)] K; *sāddhyatām itaḥ* M
- *kalpāt* Ω, *bālyāt* (II 233,11)] K; *kalpā* M
- *saṃbhavati* (II 234,7)] K; *sa saṃbhavati* M
- *prayojanāntarāṇi* (II 233,18)] K; *prayojanād antarāṇi* M
- *abhimukhī* Va (II 235,9), *āmukhī* KΩ] *ābhimukhī* M
- *tṛ* (II 236,5)] K; *tri* M
- *tathaiva* (II 236,9)] K; *tathaiva ca* M
- *vārttikakāro* (II 236,8)] K; *vārttikāro* M
- *vyāpāyād* (II 236,9)] K; *vyapāyād* M
- *upayogo* (II 237,8)] K; *upāyogo* M

- *cāha* (II 237,13)] K; *ca* M
- *saṃjñayā* (II 238,13)] K; *saṃjñā* M
- *prātipadikam* (II 238,17)] K; *prātipadipadikaṃ* M
- *rūpāt* (II 239,2)] K; *svarūpāt* M
- *tiṅbhiḥ* (II 239,13)] K; *tiṅaḥ* M
- *ucyatāṃ* (II 239,13)] K; *ucyantāṃ* M
- *svarūpataś* (II 239,18)] K; *rūpātaś* M
- *kārakasandarbha* (II 241,2)] K; *sandarbha* M
- *kartur* (II 241,12)] K; *takarttur* M
- *tasya* (II 242,14)] K; *satya* M
- *kriyāsādhāraṇatvāt*] K; *kriyāsādhanatvāt* (II 242,14) M
- *sāddhyaikasya* (II 242,14) Ω, *om.*] K; *sāddhyaika* M
- *pāribhāṣikaḥ* (II 242,15)] K; *pāribhāṣitakaḥ* M
- *sambandhanibandhanaḥ* (II 242,15)] K; *sabandhanibanaḥ* M
- *acetanākarttṛtva* (II 243,11) Ω, *acetanānām akarttṛtva*] K; *acetanakarttṛtva* M
- *samāsā* (II 244,7)] K; *samānā* M
- *gosanu* (II 244,13)] K; *goratha* M
- *na hi* (II 244,14) Va, *na*] K; *na ca* M
- *prātipadikam* (II 244,16)] K; *prātidikam* M
- *saṃjñā* (II 244,17)] K; *saṃjña* M
- *samānaś* Va *samāna* (II 245,5)] K; *samānasya* M
- *pradātavyaṃ* (II 246,16)] K; *pradātavya* M
- *uttamam* (II 246,16)] K; *uttam* M
- *samāna* (II 247,18)] K; *samana* M
- *prāptau* (II 250,8)] K; *prāpto* M
- *śaraṇāvagamā* (II 250,10)] K; *śaraṇāgamā* M
- *samaya* (II 251,7)] K; *om.* M
- *karaṇake* (II 253,4) Ω *karaṇakenaiva*] K; *karaṇe* M
- *vyākaraṇādhyayayana* (II 253,5)] K; *vyākaraṇādhyayana* M
- *śrotrendriya* (II 253,7)] K; *śrotriya* M
- *prāmāṇya* (II 253,10)] K; *prāṇya* M
- *prāmāṇyam* (II 253,10)] K; *prāṇyam* M
- *vyākaraṇa* (II 253,15)] K; *vyākaṇa* M
- *ativarttate* (II 253,16)] K; *ativarttete* M
- *asādhubhir* (II 255,14)] K; *adhātubhir* M
- *deśādyaśakyatvam* (II 256,3)] K; *deśāśakyatvam* M
- *pradarśita* (II 259,4)] K; *pradirśita* M
- *pavitraṃ* (II 260,6)] K; *om.* M

11.5 Singular readings of P

- *te cārthapratipādakāḥ* (II 148,13)] *te pratipādakāḥ* P
- *paṭādikaṃ* (II 174,8)] *ghaṭādikam* P
- *pratibhāsaḥ* (II 175,4)] *śabdapratibhāsaś* P
- *kṣemaiva* (II 175,14)] *kṣamaiva* P
- *eva* (II 176,7)] *eveti* P
- *kāryeṣv* (II 179,3)] *kāryeṣv apy* P
- *katham* (II 180,6)] *kim* P
- *tad* (II 182,4)] *atad* P
- *vikṛte* (II 182,5)] *vivṛte* P
- *mūrchā* (II 182,13)] *mūrchādi* P
- *ayaṃ* (II 183,3)] *ayaṃ tu* P
- *abhyastatvāt* (II 183,8)] *abhyastatvāt tu* P
- *upadarśayitum* (II 183,11)] *uddarśayitum* P

- *purastāt* (II 183,12)] *parastāt* P
- *varṇeṣu* (II 185,1)] *varṇeṣu ca* P
- *vākyārthāvagatiḥ* (II 185,3)] *vākyārthāvasayaḥ* P
- *vākyeṣu* (II 185,16)] *vākye* P
- *padārthebhyas* (II 186,11)] *tadarthebhyas* P
- *vākyam* (II 189,15)] vākyaṃ, *yathoktam* P
- *padānāṃ* (II 190,8)] *padārthānāṃ* P
- *siddher* (II 191,1)] *siddhe* P
- *kṛto* (II 192,11)] *kṛta* P
- *pratināyakasya* (II 193,14)] *pratirodhakasya* P
- *eva* (II 196,17)] *eva ca* P
- *janana* (II 197,2)] *jānana* P
- *vinaśyad* (II 197,3)] *na vinaśyad* P
- *etad* (II 197,6)] *etad apy* P
- *paraḥ* (II 197,11)] *paramaḥ* P
- *pratyayo* (II 198,1)] *pratyayo pi* P
- *paṭutaras* (II 200,4)] *paṭutamas* P
- *padānāṃ vākyatvāyogād* (II 202,3)] *padārthānāṃ vākyārthatvāyogād* P
- *gamyate* (II 202,15)] *dṛśyate* P
- *apekṣyate* (II 203,7)] *apekṣate* P
- *vyavahāreṣu* (II 203,11)] *vyavahāre* P
- *apekṣyate* (II 203,12)] *apekṣyante* P
- nāto'paraḥ (II 205,2)] *nāparaḥ* P
- *saha vyāpārāt* (II 207,13)] *savyāpārāt* P
- *paryantāpi* (II 208,7)] *paryantā* P
- *artho* (II 209,8)] *ato* P
- *pi* (II 211,2)] *hi* P
- *ananvitābhidhānād* (II 211,18)] *ananvitābhidhānatvād* P
- *gotva* (II 213,6)] *go* P
- *aṅgulyāgra* (II 214,1)] *aṅgulyagrādi* P
- *pūrvam anvaya* (II 215,3)] *pūrvapakṣatva* P
- *kadācid* (II 216,6)] *kācid* P
- *pratyāyayanti* (II 216,16)] *pratyāyanti* P
- *hi* (II 218,11)] *tu* P
- *iti* (II 219,17)] *om.* P
- *śakyate* (II 220,8)] *śakyato* P
- *kalpanāsambhavāt* (II 220,8)] *kalpanā kriyeta* P
- *vyutpattāv* (II 223,5)] *pratipattāv* P
- *cintyam* (II 223,6)] *cintyate* P
- *cintyatām* (II 223,18)] *cintyam* P
- *ca* (II 224,20)] *om.* P
- *loke* (II 224,20)] *lokeṣu* P
- *anadhigata* (II 225,1)] *anavadhigata* P
- *vidhitsatāṃ* (II 226,18)] *vidhitsatā* P
- *karaṇa* (II 227,12)] *kāra* P
- *ca* (II 228,17)] *cāpi* P
- *madhyama* (II 231,4)] *madhyame* P
- *prayojanatā* (II 232,5)] *prayojanāt* P
- *na* (II 232,5)] *na tu* P
- *prāyaśo* (II 232,6)] *prāyo* P
- *śāstra* (II 232,8)] *śāstre* P
- *śaraṇatā* (II 233,2)] *kāraṇatā* P
- *pṛṣati ityādi* (II 235,16)] *pṛṣatyādi* P
- *tasya* (II 235,19)] *tasyāpi* P
- *vidyate* (II 237,8)] *dṛśyata* P
- *tāvad* (II 237,12)] *bhaved* P
- *nirūpyate* (II 238,10)] *vicaryate* P
- *lakṣaṇaṃ na* (II 238,10)] *lakṣaṇena* P
- *abhipreyante* (II 240,11)] *abhiprīyanta* P
- *prasajyeta* (II 241,9)] *prasajyate* P
- *rātrāv aśnāti* (II 241,17)] *rātrau cāśnāti* P
- *tathā* (II 244,13)] *tathā ca* P
- *pratyayayor* (II 245,6)] *prātipadikayor* P

- *tu* (II 246,2)] *ca* P
- *bhayān* (II 246,2)] *bhiyā* P
- *vasaraḥ* (II 248,3)] *vatāraḥ* P
- *prayoga* (II 252,7)] *prayoge* P
- *eva cāsādhutva* (II 253,2)] *evāsādhutva* P

11.6 Conjunctive readings of the δ family

- *uccarita*] *uccārita* (II 151,4) δ
- *api*] *om. api* (II 173,9) δ
- *na bhavati*] *na* (II 176,15) δ
- *hi*] *pi* (II 177,13) δ
- *sindūraharitālādi*] *haritālasindūrādi* (II 178,1) δ
- *ghaṭas sāvayava*] *ghaṭās sāvayavāḥ* (II 179,10) δ
- *paramāṇavo* ... bhavitavyaṃ] *om.* (II 179,11) δ
- *uccaritaṃ*] *uccāritaṃ* (II 179,18) δ
- *janāpāyābhyāṃ*] *jananāpāyābhyāṃ* (II 180,1) δ
- *evāsau*] *eva* (II 186,14) δ
- *arhati*] *arhatīti* (II 187,4) δ
- *abhidhātrī ca*] *abhidhātrī* (II 190,8) δ
- *abhidhāne*] *abhidhāna* (abhidhāya Va *II* 190,13) δ
- *vākyārtha*] *vākya* (II 191,7) δ
- *om. tataḥ*] *tataḥ* (II 192,13) δ
- *ekaṃ*] *eka* (II 192,17) δ
- *iva*] *eva* (II 192,18) δ
- *tathāpi* (II 193,11)] *tathā* δ
- *anupalabhyamānena satāpi*] *anupalabhyamānenāpi satā* (II 194,3) δ
- *varṇāvagama*] *varṇānugama* (II 194,13) δ
- *varṇa*] *om.* (II 195,3) δ
- *viśiṣṭaṃ*] *viśiṣṭa* (II 195,10) δ
- *svābhidhānāva-*] *svābhinnāva-* (II 195,11) δ
- *padārtha*] *pada* (II 196,17) δ
- *ādya* (II 197,16)] *antya* δ
- *vastunī dve*] *dve vastunī* (II 198,9) δ
- *saṃskāraḥ* ... 30 akṣ ... punaḥ] *saṃskāra punaḥ* (II 200,3) δ
- *smaraṇād*] *smaryamāṇād* (II 201,7) δ
- *smaraṇā-* (II 201,8)] *smaryamāṇā-* δ
- *hi* (II 202,8)] *om.* δ
- *iti kutaḥ*] *iti* (II 202,13) δ
- *śābda*] *śabda* (II 203,13) δ
- *ekaikasya*] *ekasyaiva* (II 206,3) δ
- *yathā*] *yathā hi* (II 206,3) δ
- *sarvāṇy eva* (II 206,4)] *om.* δ
- *vinaika-*] *vinaivaika-* (II 206,10) δ
- *kārya* (II 206,11)] *kāritva* δ
- *tu*] *om.* (II 207,2) δ
- *om. śuddhānāṃ*] *śuddhānāṃ* (II 207,5) δ
- *vidāpi*] *vidā* (II 208,2) δ
- *atrāpi* (II 211,8)] *anyāpi* δ
- *tu* (II 212,1)] *om.* δ
- *aviruddhaṃ* (II 212,2)] *na viruddhaṃ* δ
- *jñapti*] *jñāna* (II 212,6) δ
- *padārtha* (II 212,12)] *padāntara* δ
- *anyair*] *anyonyam* (II 213,5) δ
- *doṣāṇām anapāyāt* (II 213,12)] *doṣānapāyāt* δ
- *vaditum*] *veditum* (II 214,4) δ
- *tattvaṃ* (II 219,1)] *tattvair* δ
- *vayam api*] *vayasi* (II 220,16) δ
- *avadhūya* (II 222,11)] *anavadhūya* δ
- *aṅgatva* (II 223,12)] *aṅga* δ
- *samarpaka-*] *saṃparka-* (II 223,12) δ
- *gāvyā-* (II 225,13)] *gavyā-* δ
- *tad ucyatāṃ*] *dṛśyatāṃ* (II 227,7)

δ

- *jñātaṃ*] *jātaṃ* (II 234,1) δ
- *kāraṇasya* (II 235,13)] *karaṇasya* δ
- *abhihito*] *abhihite* (II 239,6) δ
- *gāvyā-* (II 247,19)] *gavyā-* δ

11.7 Conjunctive readings of C with β and P

- *ādadhāti* (II 150,2)] *ādadhati* βC
- *kalpānikābhāva* (II 151,4)] *kālpanikābhāga* βC
- *sa saṃskāra* (II 164,14)] *saṃskāra* βC
- *śabdād artham* (II 171,5)] *śabdārtham* M^{ac}KC
- *nāśakyaḥ* (II 182,3)] *nāśakyaṃ* βC
- *etat* (II 186,1)] *tat* βC
- *hi* (II 187,14)] *om.* βC
- *pada* (II 193,7)] *om.* βC
- *ekārtho* (II 206,2)] *evam ekārtho* βC
- *eṣāṃ* (II 207,7)] *eṣān na* βC
- *anupādeya* (II 222,1)] *anupāya* M*n.a.*KC
- *śrautra* (II 224,7)] *śrotra* β, *śrotraḥ* C
- *jīvino* (II 227,3)] *jīvino pi* β, *jīvine pi* C
- *kārakaṃ kārakaṃ* (II 240,16)] *kārakaṃ* βC
- *ā* (II 247,15)] *om.* βC
- *upagamyate*] *upakramyate* (II 251,15) βC
- *apanīyate* (II 252,5)] *apanīyeta* βC
- *roma* (II 252,16)] *gadgadaroma* βC
- *eva* (II 187,10)] *eva ca* PC
- *viramya* (II 194,6) (*om.* O)] *viramyaviramya* PC
- *svārtha* (II 195,5)] *svārthe* PC
- *bhavaty* (II 195,17)] *tadbhavaty* PC
- *eva* (II 196,3)] *eva ca* PC
- *saṃskareṇeva* (II 197,9)] *saṃskareṇaiva* PC
- *na* (II 198,8)] *om.* P^{ac}C
- *yathaiva* (II 200,12)] *tathaiva* PC
- *ca* (II 203,13)] *om.* PC
- *sannihitārthoparakto* (II 213,1)] *sannihito rthoparakto* P^{ac}C^{ac}
- *doṣo nvitābhidhāne* (II 215,17)] *doṣānvitābhidhāne* P^{ac}C
- *paṭhitau* (II 223,15)] *paripaṭhitau* PC
- *uccārita* (II 234,8)] *uccarita* PC
- *kapratyayo* (II 238,6)] *kaḥ pratyayo* PC
- *eva* (II 238,12)] *evaṃ* PC
- *nirvartyatvāt* (II 243,8)] *nivartyatvāt* PC
- *mārgāntaram* (II 249,10)] *sargāntaram* P^{ac}C
- *mādṛśa* (II 251,7)] *sādṛśa* P^{ac}C
- *gamyāpi* (II 254,2)] *gamyādi* P^{ac}C^{ac}

11.8 Conjunctive readings of P and S

- *śabdābhidheyatām* (II 249,17)] *śabdāntarābhidheyatām* PSβ
- *svair*] *svais svair* (II 250,17) PSβ
- *tu* (II 250,3)] *om.* PS
- *hetutām* (II 251,9)] *hetutvām* PS
- *valādīnām* (II 252,6)] *valānām* PS

- *vādaḥ* (II 252,10)] *vāda* $P^{ac}S$
- *pramāṇaṃ* (II 252,11)] *tāvat pramāṇaṃ* PS
- *pūrvīka* (II 252,17)] *pūrvaika* PS
- *pada* (II 252,17)] *śabda* PS
- *vaiyākaraṇopadeśa* (II 253,6)] *vyākaraṇopadeśa* PS
- *kāle* (II 253,13)] *kāle ca* PS
- *kṛtakakapaṭārya* (II 254,1)] *kṛtakapaṭārya* PS
- *liṅgam* (II 254,4)] *liṅgam apy* PS
- *vit* (II 255,4)] vat$P^{ac}S$
- *upalabhyate* (II 255,7)] *upalabhyata iti* PS
- *saprayojano* (II 257,12)] *saprayojane* PS
- *prapaṃcaṃ*] *prapaṃca* (II 257,14) PS
- *anāditvād* (II 258,2)] *anāditvād vā* PS
- *vā* (II 258,2)] *om.* PS
- *saṃskārādi* (II 258,9)] *saṃskāra* PS
- *eva* (II 258,10)] *evātra* PS
- *ke* (II 258,11)] *ke ca* PS
- *nipuṇadarśita* (II 259,8)] *nipuṇapradarśibhir darśita* PS
- *dūṣaṇāny* (II 259,11)] *dūṣaṇādy* PS
- *kartuṃ* (II 260,2)] *kartu* $P^{ac}S$
- *matam adhigata* (II 260,3)] *matam adhigatam adhigata* PS
- *ca* (II 260,8)] *hi* PS
- *ihāpy uktam* (II 260,10)] *om.* PS
- *svasmṛtau paṭhitau* (II 261,1)] *smṛtau paṭhitaḥ* PS
- *vācaṃ* (II 261,3)] *vedaṃ* PS
- *sulabha* (II 261,9)] *subhaga* PS

11.9 Conjunctive readings of the ε family

- *atra*] *eva* QOV^{ac} (II 149,10)
- *yasyānavayavaḥ*] *yasyāvayavaḥ* QOV^{ac} (II 150,5)
- *om. ca*] *ca* ε (II 151,1)
- *tadarthe ca*] *tadarthe* ε (II 153,10)
- *bhava*] *bhāva* ε (II 155,8)
- *ikārokārantayor*] *ikārokārayor* ε (II 156,10)
- *nirastāvayavam eva*] *nirastāvayavaṃ* ε (II 156,12)
- *na tāvat*] *tāvat* ε (II 162,4)
- *janmā tu*] *janmāntara* QOV^{ac} (II 163,8)
- *cāsya*] *ca* ε (II 165,1)
- *śabdo py*] *śabdo* ε (II 166,9)
- *varṇabuddhibhir*] *buddhibhir* ε (II 167,4)
- *pratyayaviṣayatām*] *pratyayatām* ε (II 167,4)
- *tv eko*] *tv eka* ε (II 168,1)
- *parāṇudya*] *parānubhyaḥ* QOV^{ac} (II 168,4)
- *kāla*] *sa kāla* ε (II 169,7)
- *gakāraukāra*] *gakārokāra* ε (II 170,13)
- *evam eva*] *evam* ε (II 171,9)
- *prātipadikārthasya*] *prātipadikasyārthasya* ε (II 172,4–5)
- *ca tasya*] *cāsya* ε (II 173,18)
- *bhedopagraha*] *bhedagraha* ε (II 174,6)
- *padārtha*] *pada* ε (II 176,4)
- *varttitvāc*] *vṛttitvāc* ε (II 177,1)
- *grahaṇādyavasareṣu*] *grahaṇāvasereṣu* ε (II 179,2)
- *āśaṅkyate*] *āśaṅkyeta* ε (II 180,10)
- *gamakatvaṃ*] *gamakatve* QOV^{ac} (II 187,6–7)
- *abhidhātryā*] *abhidhāvyāpāra* QO, V*n.a.*(II 190,12)
- *api vā*] *api* ε (II 194,8)

- *atha*] *athā* QOV^{ac} (II 194,10)
- *karaṇaṃ*] *kāraṇaṃ* QOV^{ac} (II 195,18)
- *karaṇaṃ*] *kāraṇaṃ* ε (II 195,17)
- *viśeṣya*] *viśeṣa* ε (II 198,8)
- *viṣayā*] *viṣaya* ε (II 200,6)
- *bhāvināṃ*] *bhāvinā* ε (II 201,17)
- *svārthābhidhāyitvena*] *svārthābhidheyatvena* ε (II 208,12)
- *śabdākhya*] *śabdākhyaṃ* ε (II 209,9)
- *eva hi*] *eva* ε (II 209,16)
- *vācitā*] *vācyatā* ε (II 210,14)
- *saṃsargaviṣaya*] *viṣayasaṃsarga* ε (II 212,3)
- *tu*] *om.* ε (II 212,13)
- *eva*] *api* QOV^{ac} (II 212,17)
- *saṃhatya*] *saṃhata* QOV^{ac} (II 213,2)
- *padasyāprayogāt*] *padasya prayogāt* QOV^{ac} (II 213,8)
- *vābhihitānvayaḥ*] *vābhir ivānvayaḥ* QOV^{ac} (II 214,14)
- *prakṛtyā*] *prakṛti* QOV^{ac} (II 217,15)
- *veda*] *vede* Q^{ac}OV (II 219,18)
- *uta*] *hata* QO, *ta* V^{ac} (II 221,14)
- *gāvyādibhir*] *gavyādibhir* ε (II 221,17)
- *kevalaiḥ*] *kaivalaiḥ* QOV^{ac} (II 222,18)
- *parijñāto pi*] *parijñāto* ε (II 223,2)
- *karaṇa*] *om.* ε (II 223,10)
- *gāvyādayo*] *gavyādayo* ε (II 224,16)
- *ubhaye pi*] *ubhaye* ε (II 227,2)
- *sarasvatyā api*] *sarasvatyā* ε (II 227,5)
- *apramādokta*] *apramādottha* QV, *aprasādottha* O (II 228,9)
- *gāvyādīnām*] *gavyādīnām* ε (II 252,9)

11.10 Conjunctive readings of Q and V

- *bhavatsu*] *om.* QV^{ac} (II 149,14)
- *padātmāno*] *padātmano* Q^{ac}V^{ac} (II 153,2)
- *tatra kalpanā*] *tatkalpanā* QV (II 166,5)
- *nanu*] *nanu ca* QV (II 174,15)
- *na tv*] *nanu* QV (II 176,8)
- *chābdatva*] *chabdatva* QV^{ac} (II 209,14)
- *vyatiṣaktārtha*] *vyatiṣiktārtha* QV^{ac} (II 209,15)
- *surā*] *purā* QV (II 233,18)
- *yasya*] *api* QV (II 234,1)
- *anārabhyādhīto*] *ārabhyādhīto* QV (II 234,5)
- *iti*] *om.* QV (II 235,19)
- *vyavāyāt*] *vyapāryāt* QV (II 236,9)
- *jñātaras santi me*] *jñātaram aṃtime* QV (II 237,2)
- *rāghavasya ceti*] *rāghavasya iti* QV (II 237,3)
- *parityāgād*] *tyāgād* QV (II 238,17)
- *tatra*] *om.* QV (II 239,1)
- *bhūyad*] *bhūyād* QV^{ac} (II 239,2)
- *arhati*] *arhatīti* QV (II 239,5)
- *yogi*] *yogo* QV^{ac} (II 240,3)
- *sa sampradānam*] *tatsampradānam* QV (II 240,9)
- *kāṣṭhaika*] *koṣṭaika* QV^{ac} (II 241,5)
- *yad*] *om.* QV^{ac} (II 243,7)
- *prayojako*] *prayojaka* QV (II 244,3)
- *ekārthānvayitvam*] QV^{ac} *ekārthānvayatvam* QV^{ac} (II 244,9)
- *iti*] *om.* QV^{ac}, ΩV^{pc} *iti* (II 244,14)
- *viparyaya*] *viparyayā* QV (II 245,18)
- *ca*] *om.* QV(II 246,1)

- *iti*] *om.* QV (II 246,1)
- *kṛt*] *om.* QV (II 246,4)
- *yathoditaṃ*] *yathocita* Q^{pc}V (II 247,9)
- *jagat*] *om.* QV (II 247,15)
- *śabdā*] *śabdānāṃ* QV (II 248,15)
- *iti*] *om.* QV (II 249,3)
- *patati*] *patitaḥ* QV (II 249,4)
- *siddhaṃ*] *om.* QV (II 249,7)
- *iti anekaśabdavācyas*] *om.* QV^{ac} (II 249,16)
- *api*] *api tu* QV (II 249,17)
- *kiṃ*] *om.* QV (II 250,3)
- *gāvyādayo*] *gavyādayo* QV (II 250,9)
- *iti yuktam*] *ity uktam* QV (II 250,9)
- *śaraṇāvagamā na tān*] *śaraṇāvagamānan* QV^{ac} (II 250,10)
- *gāvyādibhyo*] *gavyādibhyo* QV(II 250,12)
- *gāvyādayaḥ*] *gavyādayaḥ* QV (II 250,14)
- *nanu*] *om.* QV (II 251,5)
- *gāvyādiṣu*] *gavyādiṣu* QV (II 251,8)
- *trāsa*] *om.* QV (II 252,1)
- *pari*] *parī* QV (II 252,10)
- *liṅgam*] *liṅgaṃ tv* QV^{ac} (II 252,13)
- *pratyakṣatām*] *pratyayatām* QV^{ac} (II 253,16)
- *ācārataś*] *ācarataś* Q^{ac}V (II 253,17)
- *veṣa*] *veśa* QV (II 254,1)
- *rūpaṃ*] *svarūpaṃ* QV (II 254,6)
- *duṣyati*] *dadhyati* QV (II 254,9)
- *nanu*] *om.* QV (II 254,11)
- *vidhaṃ*] *vidha* QV (II 255,2)
- *vegā*] *vegāḥ* QV (II 255,6)
- *vānavakāśam*] *anavakāśam* QV (II 255,15)
- *suśakatvāt*] *suśakyatvāt* QV (II 256,6)
- *paryanuyojyatā*] *paryanuyojanā* QV (II 258,2)
- *praṇītavān*] *kṛtavān* QV (II 258,17)
- *carakaḥ*] *carakaṃ* QV (II 258,18)
- *pratikṣiptāni*] *pratikṣeptavyāni* Q, *pratikṣiptavyāni* V^{ac} (II 259,12)
- *āha ca*] *āha* QV (II 260,5)
- *ābhiyoga*] *prayoga* QV (II 260,16)
- *yadi hi*] *yadiha* QV (II 261,14)
- *lakṣaṇasāmyam*] *lakṣaṇam* QV^{ac} (II 262,4)

11.11 Conjunctive readings of O and V

- *anuyogena naivānena*] *anuyogenaivānena* V^{ac}O (II 150,6)
- *pratyakṣāḥ*] *pratyakṣaḥ* VO (II 152,2)
- *anavabhāsamāno*] *avabhāsamāno* VO (II 152,2)
- *nya eva*] nya˘˘eva V^{ac}O (II 154,4)
- *maricādibhyo*] *maricādibhyo bhya* V^{ac}O (II 154,5)
- *eva*] *iva* VO (II 154,6)
- *paṭalānugāmitaya*] *paṭalānugāmitayya* VO (II 154,11–12)
- *alīkāhi*] *alīkādi* V^{ac}O (II 154,15)
- *cāsatyāny*] *casatyāny* V^{ac}O (II 154,16)
- *ādadhati*] *ādadhāti* VO (II 154,17)
- *sahityānām*] *sahitānām* VO (II 160,9)
- *varṇāḥ*] *varṇaś* V^{ac}O (II 164,11)
- *anyac ca*] *anyaś ca* V^{ac}O (II 164,11)
- *karaṇaṃ*] *kāraṇaṃ* VO (II 164,11)
- *na*] *om.* VO (II 169,16)
- *grāhyatva*] *grāhitva* V^{ac}O (II 172,8)

- *nāvayaviva na*] *nāvayaviva* VO (II 174,13–14)
- *niraṃśas*] *niraṃśās* V^{ac}O (II 177,6)
- *tena*] *iti* VO (II 178,13)
- *pipīlikā*] *pippīlikā* VO (II 180,13)
- *travidhyaṃ*] *traividyaṃ* V^{ac}O (II 183,13)
- *padatāṃ*] *padatvaṃ* V^{ac}O (II 184,7)
- *sāṃkarya*] *saṃkarya* V^{ac}O (II 194,10)
- *saṃskāreṇa*] *saṃskāreṇa ca* VO (II 195,6)
- *durupapādaḥ*] *durapavādaḥ* V^{ac}O (II 198,6)
- *viśeṣye*] *viśeṣe* VO (II 198,9)
- *anupapannā*] *anupapanna* V^{ac}O (II 198,11)
- *śaktā*] *śaktās* V^{ac}O (II 199,4)
- *draṣṭum*] *dṛṣṭaṃ* VO (II 199,4)
- *smṛtī*] *smṛte* V^{ac}O (II 200,7)
- *yadi*] *yadi vākyasya vākyārthe padasya padārthe iti yadi* VO (II 202,9–11).
- *taṭa*] *tada* V^{ac}O (II 205,15)
- *tathāpi na na*] *tathāpi na* V^{ac}O (II 208,8)
- *panthāḥ*] *paṃthā* VO (II 209,14)
- *āvāpodvāpa*] *avāpodvāpa* V^{ac}O (II 212,17)
- *ākāṃkṣita*] *ākāṃkṣitā* V^{ac}O (II 213,1)
- *nupalambhāt*] *nupalambāt* V^{ac}O (II 215,6)
- *saṃsargāvagati*] *saṃsargān nāvagati* V^{ac}O (II 217,13)
- *vyutpattyabhāva*] *vyutpattyābhāva* V^{ac}O (II 219,17)
- *hastaḥ*] *hasta* VO (II 220,1)
- *sādhvasādhu*] *sādhusādhu* VO (II 222,3)
- *kalañja*] *kalañjasya* VO (II 224,1)
- *vāśitādiṣu*] *vāśatādiṣu* V^{ac}O (II 225,10)
- *prayojanavattām*] *prayojanavatām* VO (II 231,8)
- *tat*] *uta* VO (II 231,9)
- *utprekṣanta*] *utprekṣyaṃta* VO (II 246,7)
- *gṛhīto*] *grahīto* VO (II 246,12)
- *kakṣyā*] *kakṣā* VO (II 248,9)
- *vācakasyaiko*] *vācakasyai* V^{ac}O (II 250,5)

11.12 Conjunctive readings of S, Q and V

- *dṛṣṭāntā*] *dṛṣṭānta* VSQ (II 178,3)
- *apūrvaṃ*] *apūrva* VSQ (II 179,10)
- *iti*] *om.* VSQ (II 232,6)
- *pravādād*] *pravāhād* VSQ (II 233,7)
- *nāgama*] *na cāgama* VSQ (II 233,10)
- *hi*] *om.* VSQ (II 233,15)
- *vyaktikatvam*] *vyaktitvam* VSQ (II 234,11)
- *vādināṃ*] *vidāṃ* VSQ (II 234,14)
- *anālaṃbanaḥ*] *anālaṃbamānaḥ* V^{ac}SQ (II 234,15)
- *tv āha*] *cāha* VSQ (II 235,18)
- *tathā*] *om.* VSQ (II 236,6)
- *śabda*] *śabdasya* VSQ (II 236,9)
- *ādi*] *om.* VSQ (II 238,1)
- *na*] *om.* VSQ (II 239,5)
- *utpadyerān*] VSQ *utpadyerān / samastapakṣe ityādipatitam* (II 239,9)
- *nirūpaṇam*] *rūpam* V, *rūpaṇam* SQ (II 239,12)
- *nirṇetum*] *nirṇītum* VSQ (II 239,19)
- *īpsitatamaṃ*] *īpsitam* VSQ (II

242,5)
- *kriyopayogitvam*] *kriyayopayogitvam* VSQ (II 242,12)
- *cet tābhyāṃ tarhi*] *cet tarhi* VSQ (II 244,10)
- *pratiṣedhaphalaṃ*] *pratiṣedhāya* VSQ (II 245,2)
- *darśī tatra*] *darśaty atra* V, *darśīty atra* SQ (II 246,3)
- *buddhitaro*] *buddhir* VSQ (II 246,4)
- *cāha*] *ca* VSQ (II 246,8)
- *upapādyate*] *upapadyate* VSQ (II 247,5)
- *gāvyādīnāṃ*] *gavyādīnāṃ* VSQ (II 247,17)
- *prayoga*] *om.* VSQ (II 248,6)
- *sambhāvanābhaṅgura*] *sambhāvanāṅkura* VSQ (II 248,16)
- *tad*] *om.* VSQ (II 248,19)
- *viśeṣe tarhi*] *tarhi viśeṣe* VSQ (II 249,5)

11.13 Readings of P, M and K found in V

- *anugater* CSQV^{ac}O] *avagater* PMKV^{pc}GaVa (II 150,12)
- *votsya, botsu* CQV^{ac}O] *bhotsya* PMKSV^{pc}GaVa (II 153,5)
- *lopādanva* CSV^{ac}O^{ac}AQ] *lopādyanva* PMKV^{pc}O^{pc}GaVa (II 155,8)
- *tasmān niyamān* CSQV^{ac}O^{ac}] *tasmād aniyamān* PMKV^{pc}O^{pc}GaVa (II 156,6)
- *darśane* M^{ac}CSQV^{ac}O^{ac}] *adarśane* PM^{pc}KV^{pc}O^{pc}GaVa (II 156,10)
- *om. vyavahāro* CSV^{ac}O^{ac}AQ] *vākyārthapratyayo* PMK, *vyavahāro* V^{pc}O^{pc}GaVa (II 158,9)
- *naivāvastu* CSV^{ac}O^{ac}AQ] *naivāstu* PMKV^{pc}O^{pc}GaVa (II 158,13)
- *nirvartakam* CSQV^{ac}O] *nirvartakatvam* PMKV^{pc}GaVa (II 161,15)
- *anumānikā* CSQV^{pc}O] anumāpikā, PMKV^{ac}GaVa (II 164,15)
- *sarvathā* CSQOV^{ac}] *sarva* PMK V^{pc}GaVa (II 166,7)
- *visarjanīyaḥ* CSQVOM^{ac}V^{ac}] *visarjanīyāḥ* PM^{pc}K^{pc}V^{pc}GaVa (II 170,14)
- *śabdaḥ* CSQVOV^{ac} *om.*] *śabdaḥ* PMKV^{pc}GaVa (II 170,14)
- *tvagai* CSQVO] *tvage*, PMKV^{pc}GaVa (II 178,1)
- *padārthaḥ* CSQVO] *padārthārthaḥ* PMKV^{pc}GaVa (II 188,2)
- *na gacchati* CSQVOV^{ac}] *gacchati* PMKV^{pc}GaVa (II 191,14)
- *viśeṣaṇa* SQVOV^{ac}] *viśeṣya* PMKCV^{pc}GaVa (II 198,10)
- *vyautpattika* CSQVOV^{ac}] *autpattika* PMKV^{pc}GaVa (II 203,10)
- *ca* CSQVOV^{ac}] *om.* PMKV^{pc}GaVa (II 219,3)
- *śaktivat* CSQOV^{ac}GaVa] *śabdavat* PMKV^{pc} (II 228,9)
- *tathā* CSQOV^{ac}] *tatra* PM*n.a.*KV^{pc}GaVa (II 229,2)
- *ca* CSQOV^{ac}] *om.* PMKV^{pc}GaVa (II 229,3)
- *ṇamul* CSQOV^{ac}] *ṇamulam* PMKV^{pc}GaVa (II 236,15)
- *na* CSQOV^{ac}] *om.* PMKV^{pc}GaVa (II 241,14)
- *yaḥ* CSQOV^{pc}] *yaḥ kartā* PMKV^{ac}GaVa (II 243,10)
- *prātipādikānām* CSQOV^{ac}] *prakṛtikānām* PMKV^{pc}GaVa (II 245,8)
- *gavyāder* CSQOV^{ac}] *gāvyāder* PMKV^{pc}GaVa (II 247,2)

11.14 Lists of polygenetic readings

PCO:

- *ity* (II 233,18)] *ityādy* PCO
- *bahiṣkṛta* (II 245,18)] *bahiṣkṛtaṃ* PCO

PO:

- *śabdaḥ* (II 172,12)] *śabdāḥ* PO
- *na* naḥ (II 187,7)] *na* PO

OCK:

- *anavayavaḥ* (II 177,2)] *avayavaḥ* K^{ac}CO

OCSV:

- *saṅkalanā* (II 163,11)] *saṅkalpanā* CS^{ac}VO

CVO:

- *duravagama*] *duradhigama* CVO (II 148,1)
- *idam*] *idaṃ tv* CVO (II 148,14)
- *nanu na* (II 149,3)] nanuCVO
- *niravayavam eva* (II 153,7)] *niravayava eva* CV^{ac}O
- *abhyadhāyi* (II 178,7)] *abhidhāyi* CVO
- *varṇānumāna* (II 183,7)] *varṇāvarṇānumāna* CV^{ac}O
- *sāmarthyā* (II 185,5)] *sāmarthya* CV^{ac}O
- *kārya eva* (II 207,7)] *kārye eva* CVO
- *pāṇiḥ* (II 220,1)] *pāṇinir* CVO
- *jāś* (II 228,7)] *jā* CVO
- *prayojanavattāṃ* (II 230,7)] *prayojanavatāṃ* CVO
- *ānuṣaṃgikatvāc* (II 233,19)] *anuṣaṃgikatvāc* CVO
- *niṣṭham iti kāṣṭhaiḥ* (II 241,5)] *niṣṭam iti kāṣṭaiḥ* CVO
- *śrautre* (II 252,16)] *śrotre* CVO
- *antyajanapada* (II 257,11)] *antyapada* CV^{ac}O

SV:

- *vyajyate* (II 150,5)] *vyajyato* VS
- *bhyvyajyamānas* (II 151,2)] *bhivyañjamānas* VS
- *bhūya* (II 190,2)] *bhūta* VS
- *śāntiḥ* (II 199,8)] *śantiḥ* S^{ac}V^{ac}
- *māṃsam* (II 221,9)] *māsam* VS
- *prabhṛti* (II 233,11)] *prabhṛtiṣu* VS
- *abrāhmaṇādi* (II 236,10)] *brahmaṇādi* VS
- *pṛṣṭvā* (II 237,10)] *ṣṭvā* V^{ac}S
- *kambalada* (II 238,7)] *kambala* VS
- *tiṅaḥ*] *tiṅaś ca* VS (II 239,9)
- *varṇyamānam*] *varṇamānam* VS (II 245,2)
- *śiṣyo* (II 247,12)] *śiṣṭo* VS
- *vācaka* (II 248,8)] *vācakā* VS
- *doṣarahito-* (II 252,16)] *doṣārahito-* V^{ac}S

SQ:

- *eṣa* (II 153,6)] *eva* QS
- *-tvenacāpariharya-*] *-tvenāpariharya-* QS (II 160,9)
- *nirdeśadarśanād* (II 170,17)] *darśanād* Q^{ac}S
- *vyutpattes* (II 240,17)] *utpatteḥ* QS

PSVO:

- *prathamaṃ* (II 192,6)] *prathama* PS^{pc}VO

SVO:

- *uccaritāt*] *uccāritāt* SVO (II 148,6)
- *asthāne* (II 171,13)] *avasthāne* SV^{pc}O
- *anutpannā* (II 180,9)] *utpannā*

SV^{ac}O
- *bhāgeyattā* (II 180,10)] *bhāgeyaṃtā* SV^{ac}O
- *vāna* (II 199,12)] *vana* SV^{ac}O
- *asaṃsṛṣṭā* (II 201,16)] *asaṃspṛṣṭā* SVO
- *apekṣyamānāyāṃ*] *apekṣamānāyāṃ* SVO (II 203,15)
- *śakatakāryaṃ* (II 207,12)] *śakataṃ* SV^{ac}O
- *nava* (II 208,13)] *na* SV^{ac}O
- *tena* (II 225,11)] *te* SV^{ac}O

OS:
- *savayavatvāt* (II 167,5)] *savayatvāt* S^{ac}O^{ac}
- *ādhāsyati* (II 188,4)] SO^{ac}
- *tu* (II 211,17)] *om.* SO
- *vyarthau* (II 226,3)] *vyaktau* SO
- *na* [...] *śaktivat* (II 228,10)] *om.* SO
- *niyogagarbho* (II 232,18)] *niyogarbho* SO
- *phalā* (II 233,15)] *phala* SO
- *anyathaivaṃ* (II 236,14)] *anyathaiva* SO
- *saukaryāc* (II 252,9)] *saukāryāc* SO

OQC:
- *kaṃcid* (II 219,16)] *kiṃcid* CQ^{ac}O

11.15 Readings introduced by Gangadhara

- *sphoṭābhyupagamaḥ* (II 159,5)] sphoṭo'bhyupagamaḥ Ga
- *eva* (II 159,11)] *om.* Ga
- *eva* (II 167,3)] *iva* Ga
- tasyaiva, tasyeva, *ca tasyaiva* (II 173,10)] *ca* Ga
- *eva* (II 176,13)] *om.* Ga
- *vākyapadayor* (II 179,20)] *padavākyayor* Ga
- *pratipattau* (II 180,10)] *pratītau* Ga
- *vyutpatter* (II 182,8)] *vyutpattur* Ga
- *saṃjalpo* (II 183,15)] Ga saṃkalpo, V sajalpo,
- *śabda* (II 184,5)] *om. śabda* Ga
- *jānāty evāsau* (II 184,5)] *jānātīvāsau* Ga
- *pratipattis tato*] Ga Va *pratipattau* (II 187,13),
- *om. ca* (II 190,16)] *ca* Ga
- *sāmānyena* (II 197,4)] *sāmānye* Ga
- *pada* (II 203,9)] *om.* Ga
- ananvite'rthe (II 209,3)] *ananvitārthe* Ga
- *anvayo na* (II 211,17)] 'nanvayo Ga
- *na* (II 214,6)] *om.* Ga
- *tata eva* ca, *tata eva* (II 220,16)] *tataś ca* Ga
- *siddhir* (II 224,13)] *siddher* Ga
- *ca* (II 225,16)] *om.* Ga
- *pi* (II 226,13)] *om.* Ga
- *loke* (II 228,11)] *loka* Ga
- *niyamo* (II 228,15)] *vidhiniyamo* Ga
- *eva* (II 233,10)] *om.* Ga
- *gaṇapaṭhitatvād* (II 236,10)] *gaṇāpaṭhitatvād* Ga
- *anantyāc* (II 237,13)] *syāc* Ga
- *divyaṃ* (II 237,13)] *divya* Ga
- *asaṃbhavāt* (II 237,15)] *sambhavo* Ga
- *iti* (II 245,6)] *api* Ga
- *svarūpa* (II 247,10)] *rūpa* Ga
- *śabda* (II 249,1)] *śabdam* Ga
- *kriyate* (II 250,3)] *om.* Ga

- *iha ca* (II 250,6)] *ca iha* Ga
- *anadhigata* (II 250,15)] S *adhigata* Ga
- *gaṇātmaka* (II 252,17)] *guṇātmaka* Ga
- *hi* (II 253,9)] *om.* Ga
- *abhāvārthatvena* (II 254,12)] *bhāvārthatvena* Ga
- *ācāmanādi* (II 255,1)] *ācāmana* Ga

11.16 Readings introduced by Varadacharya

- *om. eva*] *eva* (II 149,4) Va
- *om. bhāvāt*] *bhāvāt* (II 149,5) Va
- *ukhāṃ*] Va *nāsāṃ* (II 159,14) (but A *reads* nānāṃ, O *reads* tānāṃ),
- *eva na citrākāraḥ* (but *the* M *reading is* uncertain)] *eva citrākāraḥ* (II 162,15) Va
- *stabakākārāvabhāsī*] *stabakākāravatī* (II 163,3) Va
- *niṣkaraṇikāsthāna, niṣkaraṇikāsthāstu, niṣkaraṇikāstu*] *niṣkaraṇikā syāt* (II 164,12) Va
- *sarvathā* vayam, sarvathāyam, *sarvatheyam*] *sarvathā ceyam* (II 165,17) Va
- *sphuṭatara*] *sphuṭataram* (II 167,13) Va
- *prathamavarṇavyakto*] *prathama* (II 167,14) Va
- *pratipattāv*] *pratītāv* (II 168,14) Va
- *om. vanaṃ vṛkṣaḥ iti*] *vanaṃ vṛkṣaḥ iti* (II 170,15) Va
- *vanaṃ vṛkṣā na*] *na* (II 170,16) Va
- *śrotra*] *śrautra* (II 172,8) Va
- *śrotra*] *śrautra* (II 172,9) Va
- *śrotra*] *śrautra* (II 172,13) Va
- *vyavacchidyante*] *vyavacchedyante* (II 173,2) Va
- *abhyupagacchema, upagacchema*] *avagacchema* (II 174,5) Va
- *paṭādikam, ghaṭādikam*] *padādikam* (II 174,8) Va
- *om. na*] *na* (II 175,3) Va
- *etaś, ataś*] *ekaś* (II 175,13) Va
- *asty athāsty*] *astv* (II 177,9) Va
- *bhavatīti*] *bhavati* (II 178,9) Va
- *racanā, vacanā, racakra, paratantra*] *cakra* (II 178,11) Va
- *om. tāvat*] *tāvat* (II 179,1) Va
- *eveti*] *eva* (II 179,7) Va
- *ghaṭenāpi tathā*] *ghaṭair api* (II 179,12) Va
- *om. niravayavair*] *niravayavair* (II 179,12) Va
- *rūpam*] *rūpam iti* (II 182,2) Va
- *spṛeśet*] *smṛśet* (II 184,4) Va
- *vākyārthe*] *vākyārthe* 'pi (II 185,4) Va
- *vākyārtha*] *vā vākyārtha* (II 186,2) Va
- *sannidhiyogyatva*] *yogyatāsannidhi* (II 187,9) Va
- *om. tātparya*] *tātparya* (II 187,10) Va
- *prasiddho*] *prasiddhiḥ* (II 188,2) Va
- *abhidhāne, abhidhāna*] *abhidhāya* (II 188,2) Va
- *eveti*] *eva* (II 190,14) Va
- *pādārthyan* nāma, *pādārthānām*] *pārārthyaṃ nāma* (II 191,2–3) Va
- *na dṛśyate sa* kiṃ, *dṛśyate kiṃ*] *dṛśyate na* (II 191,13) Va
- *saṃpratyayaḥ*] *pratyayaḥ* (II 192,2) Va
- *kalpanayā*] *kalpanāyā* (II 192,4) Va
- *iva*] *eva* (II 193,7) Va
- *tajjñānānantaraṃ*] *tadajñānānantaraṃ* (II 196,12) Va

- *kāryakāraṇa*] *viśeṣe pramāṇa* (II 197,7) Va
- *saṃskāra*] *saṃkāra* (II 197,8) Va
- *utpadyate, upapadyate, upapatsyate*] *utpatsyate* (II 197,17) Va
- *aśvam*] *turagam* (II 198,5) Va
- *adṛṣṭaṃ*] *adṛṣṭā* (II 199,3) Va
- *kramāt*] *trayāt* (II 200,7) Va
- *grahaṇāt*] *grahāt* (II 200,10) Va
- *pathā*] *vṛthā* (II 201,12) Va
- *om. tu*] *tu* (II 202,5) Va
- *om. aśvanayana ... iti vākyād*] *aśvanayana ... iti vākyād* (II 203,6–7) Va
- *kevalasya*] *kevala* (II 205,11) Va
- *prāpta*] *prāpya* (II 205,12) Va
- *abhidadhati*] *abhidadhanti* (II 206,1) Va
- *evam* ekārtho, *ekārtho*] *evārtho* (II 206,2) Va
- *atha*] *artha* (II 206,18) Va
- *anvitārtha*] *anvitārthaṃ* (II 207,13) Va
- *kṛṣṇānvitasyāpi tadarthasya*] *kṛṣṇānvitasya* (II 208,4) Va
- *duravagamatvāt*] *duravagamāt* (II 208,4) Va
- *vākyānyevāvāpo*] *vākyānyāvāpo* (II 208,6) Va
- *kiṃ padāntara*] *padāntara* (II 209,1) Va
- *kurvanti kārakāṇīty*] *kārakāṇi kurvanti ity* (II 209,2) Va
- *ananvitatve*] *anabhihitatve* (II 211,2) Va
- *śābde*] *śabde* (II 211,12) Va
- *kriyā*] *kriyādi* (II 211,14) Va
- *nānumanyante*] *nānumanyate* (II 212,8) Va
- *om. sā*] *sā* (II 212,11) Va
- *yāvantam*] *yāvat tam* (II 213,5) Va
- *yogyaiś ca sannihitaiś ca*] *sannihitaiś ca* (II 213,5) Va
- *saṃvedanaṃ*] *saṃvedana* (II 215,5) Va
- *tarhy ayam ābhidhāniko*] *tarhy ābhidhānikī* (II 216,5) Va
- *guṇa, guṇaguṇa*] *guṇaguṇi* (II 216,8) Va
- *avagata*] *anugata* (II 216,18) Va
- *vadhiḥ*] *vidhiḥ* (II 217,6) Va
- *nirapekṣa*] *nirapekṣe* (II 218,5) Va
- *mataye*] *mitaye* (II 218,15) Va
- *rasārdre, rasāndre, rasadbhir*] *tu sāndre* (II 219,2) Va
- *hṛdayam*] *hṛdaya* (II 219,2) Va
- *so'py aham iva ... anyam* upāsīta so'py] so'py (II 219,8) Va
- *padārtha*] *tadartha* (II 220,7) Va
- *pūrvoktena*] *pūrvoktina* (II 220,13) Va
- *pratipadyāmahe*] *pratipādyāmahe* (II 220,17) Va
- *vedaś cārthaś ca*] *vedārthaś ca* (II 221,6) Va
- *kiṃ tu*] *tāni* (II 221,7) Va
- *kuṭumbinam ātmānaṃ*] *kuṭumbinamānaṃ* (II 221,10) Va
- *vyacakṣaṇo pi*] *vyacakṣaṇo* (II 223,7) Va
- *kḷptādhikārau kalpyādhikārau*] *kḷptādhikārī kalpyādhikārī* (II 223,16) Va
- *pramāṇātītatvāt*] *pramāṇātītavāt* (II 224,3) Va
- *tān* anumātum, *anumātum*] *tāvad anumātum* (II 225,5) Va
- *tac*] *etac* (II 225,7) Va
- *vidheyāṃś*] *praviṣedhyāṃś* (II 226,18) Va
- *kṛtaśabda*] *kṛtāpaśabda* (II 228,5) Va
- *prāpte*] *prāptau* (II 229,2) Va
- *śabdāpaśabdaprayogasya*] *suśabdāpaśabdayor* (II 229,3) Va
- *sārvatrikī*] *sārvatriko* (II 229,13) Va

- *adhyetavyam*] *adhyeyam* (II 230,1) Va
- *anitaretara*] *itaretara* (II 230,1) Va
- *om. nāpabhāṣitavai*] *nāpabhāṣitavai* (II 230,9) Va
- *om. jñātaḥ su*] *jñātaḥ su* (II 230,10) Va
- *om. sa*] *sa* (II 231,2) Va
- *tasya prayojanatayā*] *tasyāprayojanatayā* (II 231,4) Va
- *om. idam*] *idam* (II 232,14) Va
- *om. yuktā*] *muktā* (II 233,2) Va
- *manaso vā buddher vā*] *buddher vā* (II 235,13) Va
- *tatra tatra śiṣṭāḥ*] *tatra tatra* (II 236,4) Va
- *iti cātra*] *iti cātra ca* (II 236,14) Va
- *kathamitthaṃsu siddhāprayogaś ced iti*] *katham* (II 236,14) Va
- *mety uktveti*] *me ity* (II 237,1) Va
- *ityādayaś ca*] *ityādayo* (II 238,7) Va
- *om. ca*] *ca* (II 239,1) Va
- *asādhutvaṃ*] *adhātutvaṃ* (II 239,4) Va
- *om. kriyāsu kārakāṇi*] *kriyāsu kārakāṇi* (II 240,11) Va
- *kāraka ... nupapatteḥ*] *om. kāraka ... nupapatteḥ* (II 240,16) Va
- *labhata*] *labhyata* (II 241,3) Va
- *tamabarthaṃ*] *tam arthaṃ* (II 241,3) Va
- *om. hi*] *hi* (II 241,4) Va
- *om. ca*] *ca* (II 244,6) Va
- *viśeṣavidhitvena*] *vidhiśeṣatvena* (II 245,1) Va
- *om. sarvaṃ*] *sarvaṃ* (II 245,15) Va
- *kapardī, kaḍanī*] *kaṭandī* (II 246,15) Va
- *mukho vedaḥ*] *mukhe vedāḥ* (II 246,20) Va
- *om. taṃ*] *taṃ* (II 247,10) Va
- *kuśāgrīya*] *kuśāgra* (II 248,7) Va
- *anekārthatvaṃ ca*] *anekārthatvaṃ* (II 250,4) Va
- *yathaiva mlecchānāṃ*] *yathaiva* (II 250,16) Va
- *kva vā*] *vā* (II 251,5) Va
- *āvagatārtha*] *āvagamārtha* (II 254,3) Va
- *śāstrāṇi*] *śāstraṃ ca* (II 258,8) Va
- *om. varṇa*] *varṇa* (II 259,10) Va
- *graha*] *grahaṇa* (II 259,14) Va
- *paramaṃ*] *paramā* (II 260,7) Va
- *bhaṭṭajayanta*] *jayantabhaṭṭa* (II 262,13) Va

11.17 Conjunctive readings of Ga and Va

- *kālpanikābhāgā*] *kālpanikāram* V[pc], *kalpānikākāram* GaVa (II 151,4)
- *bhavitvaṃ ca*] *bhāvināṃ* GaVa (II 160,7)
- *śabdaśabda*] *śabdaśabdād* GaVa (II 174,15)
- *sāmyāt*] *sāmānyāt* GaVa (II 181,14)
- *viśeṣavatāṃ ca*] *viśeṣavatāṃ* GaVa (II 182,2)
- *eva*] *eṣa* GaVa (II 182,10)
- *asti yataḥ*] *asti* GaVa (II 185,14)
- *pade*] *padeṣu* GaVa (II 185,15)
- *pratipattis tato*] *pratipattau* GaVa (II 187,13)
- *paṭutaraḥ*] *paṭutara* GaVa (II 192,14)
- *ācakṣuḥ, ācakhyuḥ*] *ācacakṣuḥ* GaVa (II 194,17)
- *avacchedakatve, avacchedakatvaṃ*] *avacchedakatva* GaVa (II 196,1)
- *karma ca karaṇaṃ* ca, *karma*

karaṇaṃ ca] *karma karaṇaṃ* GaVa (II 196,3)
- *vedaṃ*] *cedaṃ* GaVa (II 201,8)
- *padasya tu*] *padasya* GaVa (II 202,11)
- *kadambaka*] *kadamba* GaVa (II 203,2)
- *na*] *yathāhuḥ na* GaVa (II 204,7)
- *śābda*] *śabda* GaVa (II 212,3)
- *procchvasadbhiḥ*] *prollasadbhiḥ* GaVa (II 218,18)
- *yā caiṣā*] *ya caiṣā* GaVa (II 219,4)
- *vedasya*] *cet tasya* GaVa (II 220,4)
- *vyavahāra*] *vyavahāraṃ* GaVa (II 223,2)
- *anṛṣau*] *asmādṛśe* GaVa (II 223,7)
- *samarpakatvam, samparkitvaṃ*] *samparkatvaṃ* GaVa (II 223,12)
- *ciram abhyasta*] *cirābhyasta* GaVa (II 225,6)
- *avācakasya ca*] *avācakasya* GaVa (II 228,3)
- *itaretarāśrayaṃ*] *itaretarāśrayatvaṃ* GaVa (II 231,1)
- *bhūyad iti*] *bhūyac* GaVa (II 239,2)
- *pāte*] *yāne* GaVa (II 240,7)
- *tad*] *tadarthaṃ kartur* GaVa (II 242,5)
- *kāraka*] *kārakatva* GaVa (II 242,14)
- *so'pi anyena so'pi anyena*] *so'pi tadanyena so'pi tadanyena* GaVa (II 247,14)
- *varṇāśramāṇā*] *varṇāśramāṇām* GaVa (II 254,1)
- *api vā*] *api* GaVa (II 256,10)
- *tena*] *etena* GaVa (II 257,6)
- *visaṃsthulatvam*] *visaṃṣṭhulatvam* GaVa (II 259,6)
- *sāmagrya*] *sāmargya* GaVa (II 260,8)
- *mata*] *mataṃ* GaVa (II 262,2)

12 Internal divisions of interesting manuscripts

12.1 Internal divisions of M

NM 6 [*ki* (3r) – *khaḥ* (32v3)] *-ntanīyaḥ avyatireke ta eva te varṇā iti kathan na bodhakā* (II 147,7) ... *sidhyanti +++++++++++++ ++++++++++ya mañjaryāṃ ṣaṣṭham āhnikam*

NM 7 [*khaḥ* (32v3) – *ghu* (53v5)] *evaṃ pramāṇapadārthe parīkṣite sati ... duḥkhaṃ saṃtyajya niśreyasamakhilabhayātītam āptuṃ yateta / bhaṭṭajayantasya kṛtau nyāyamañjaryāṃ saptamam āhnikaṃ samāptam / śivam iti*

NM 8 [*ghu* (53v5) – *ṅḹ* (74r6)] *ātmānantaraṃ vibhāgasūtre śarīranirdeśāt ... gatabhayam apavartaṃ śāśvataṃ so 'bhyupaiti / nyāyamañjaryām aṣṭamam āhnikam*

NM 9 [*ṅḹ* (74r6) – *co* (93r7) (*co*)] *evaṃ śarīrādau duḥkhaparyante ... kṣipram ālambanīyaḥ / iti nyāyamañjaryān navamam āhnikam*

NM 10 [*co* (93r7) – *che* (107v3)] *saṃśayādeḥ padārthagaṇasya ... iti hi vyāharad vṛttikāraḥ / iti bhaṭṭajayantakṛtau nyāyamañjaryān daśamam āhnikam*

NM 11 [*che* (107v4) – *je* (123v5)] *++ yavānantaraṃ prathamasūtre tarkasyoddeśād ... vācyaḥ parair abhihitasya tathā samādhiḥ / nyāyamañjaryām ekādaśam āhnikam*

NM 12 [*je* (123v5) – *jhau* (142v6)] *chalānantaraṃ jāter uddeśāt ... prapannajanasaṃkalpakalpavṛkṣāya śambhave / iti bhaṭṭajayantakṛtau nyāyamañjaryān dvādaśam āhnikam / nyāyamañjarī samāptā / hariḥ namaś śivāya /*

12.2 Internal divisions of K

NM 1 [1r–26r10] *hariḥ oṃ mahāgaṇapataye namaḥ namaś śāsvatikānandajñānaiśvaryamayātmane ... jaḍamatitvam uktaṃ bhavet* [ornament] *iti bhaṭṭajayantaviracitāyān nyāyamañjaryyāṃ prathamam āhnikaṃ* [ornament]

NM 2 [26r10–62r10] *evaṃ pramāṇānāṃ sāmānya- ... parigrāhyan tasmāt pravaramunigītaṃ sumatibhiḥ* [ornament] *iti bhaṭṭajayantaviracitāyān nyāyamañjaryyān dvitīyam āhnikaṃ* [ornament]

NM 3: **[62r10–95r4** *upamānānantaraṃ śabdasya vibhāgasūtre ... kaviravikalaśaktir yyukta evendumauliḥ* [ornament] *iti bhaṭṭajayantakṛtau nyāyamañjaryyān tṛtīyam āhnikaṃ* [ornament] *namaś śivāya*

NM 4 [95r4–122v3] *evaṃ kṛtakatve varṇānāṃ sādhite* ... *yadi na dhīḥ parikhidyate vaḥ* [ornament] *iti bhaṭṭajaya +++ nyāyamañjaryyāñ caturtham āhnikaṃ* [ornament]
NM 5 [122v3–151v8] *atha yad uktaṃ vāstavasya* ... *tac chabdasya nirastam ity akaluṣaṃ prāmāṇyam asya sthitaṃ* [ornament] *iti bhaṭṭajayantakṛtau nyāyamañjaryāṃ pañcamam āhnikaṃ* [ornament]
NM 6 [151v7–178v9] *nanu nādyāpi śabdasya* ... *siddhyanti sarve puruṣārthasārthā* [ornament] *iti + ṭṭajayantakṛtau nyāyamañjaryāyāṃ ṣaṣṭham āhnikaṃ* [ornament]
NM 7 [179v9–187v10] *evaṃ pramāṇapadārthe parīkṣite* ... *kiṃ sa evāyaṃ stambha ity ekaṃ jñāna +* (NM^{Va}, II 308,10)

12.3 Internal divisions of P

12.3.1 The NM portion

NM 1 [i.3r–46v16] *+++ lāviharaṇodyataiḥ* (NM^{Va}, I 3,9)[1] ... *nanu nādyāpi ca+++m avatiṣṭhate / sambhavaitihye* (NM^{Va}, I 167,9)
NM 2 [i.48r1–100v20] *+++ yam ādadhānasya* (NM^{Va}, I 172,7)[2] ... *parigrāhyaṃ tasmāt pravaramunigītaṃ sumatibhiḥ // ity āc + ryaśitikaṇṭhasvāmilikhitabhaṭṭajayantakṛtau nyāyamaṃjaryāṃ dvitīyam āhnika +++* [The last *akṣara*-s are continued on 101r. The first lines of 101r, however, are wiped off and illegible]
NM 3 [i.101r4–149r10] *+++ śāt tasya +++ ty ucyamāne paryāyamātroccāraṇād* (NM^{Va}, I 396,1) ... *kaviravi + laśaktir yukta evendumauliḥ // iti kāśmīrikācāryā (rju) nasvāmiputraśītikaṇṭhāsvāmilikhitāyāṃ bhaṭṭajayantasya kṛtau nyāyamaṃjaryāṃ tṛtīyam āhnikam // oṃ namaḥ śrīmahāgaṇapataye // oṃ namaś śrīśāradāyai kaśmīrade++++ //*
NM 4 [ii.2r1–46r12] *(+++)// tathā ca mīmāṃsakaiḥ pratihetur iha gīyate* (NM^{Va}, I 574,10) ... *tac chrūyatāṃ yadi na dhīḥ parikhidyate vaḥ // ity ācāryaśitikaṇṭhasvāmilihitāyāṃ nyāyamaṃjaryāṃ bhaṭṭajayantaviracitāyāṃ caturtham āhnikam // oṃ namo mahāgaṇapataye //*
NM 5 [ii.46r15–88v11] *prapannāya vipannānāṃ duḥkhitānāṃ sukhātmane /* ... *tacchabdasya nirastam ity akaluśaṃ prāmāṇyam asya sthitam // ity ācāryaśītikaṇṭhasvāmilikhitāyāṃ bhaṭṭajayanta +++ au +yama (ṃja) ryāṃ paṃcamam āhnikam // oṃ namaś śrīśāradāyai +++*
NM 6 [ii.88v11– 129r4 (NM^{Va}, II 262,12)] *oṃ nanu nādyāpi śabdasya* ... *sidhyanti sarve puruṣārthasārthāḥ // ity ācāryaśitikaṇṭhasvāmilikhitāyāṃ bhaṭṭajayantasya kṛtau nyāyamaṃjaryāṃ ṣaṣṭham āhnikam // oṃ namaś śrīmahāgaṇapataye bhīmasvāmine //*

[1]Fol. i.1 is missing, fol. i.2 is not properly digitized (only parts of i.2v are visible).
[2]Fol. i.47 is not available in the images; foll. i.89 and i.90 were possibly stuck together, and for this reason i.89v and i.90r could not be photographed.

NM 7 [ii.129r4–153v18] *evaṃ pramāṇapadārthe parīkṣite ... duḥkha + santyajya niśśreyasam akhilabhayā +++ yateta // ity ācāryārjunasvāmiputraśitikaṇṭhasvāmili +++ bhaṭṭajayantakṛtau nyāyamaṃjaryāṃ saptamam āhnikam // oṃ nama ++++ ṇapataye bhīmasvāmine //*

NM 8 [ii.153v18–175v7] *ātmānantaraṃ vibhāgasūtre śarīra +++ ... gatabhayam apavargaṃ śāśvataṃ so bhyupeti // ity ācāryārjunasvāmiputraśitikaṇṭhasvāmilikhitāyāṃ bhaṭṭajayantasya kṛtau nyāyamaṃjaryāṃ aṣṭamam āhnikam // śrīmahāgaṇeśāya bhīmasvāmine // oṃ namaś śrīśāradāyai //*

NM 9 [ii.175v8–204v12] *evaṃ śarīrādau duḥkhaparyante heye prameye nirṇīte ... panthāḥ kṣemāya mokṣādhigamasamucitaḥ kṣipram ālambanīyaḥ // prameyapadārthaḥ // ity ācāryārjunasvāmiputraśitikaṇṭhasvāmilikhitāyāṃ bhaṭṭajayantasya kṛtau nyāyamaṃjaryāṃ navamam āhnikam // oṃ namaś śrī śāradāyai // oṃ namo mahāgaṇapataye //*

NM 10 [ii.204v18– 224r (NM^{Va}, II 583,4)] *saṃśayādeḥ padārthagaṇasya pramāṇaprameyapadasaṃgṛhītasyāpi nyāyapravṛttiprayojanatayā pṛthagvyutpādanīyatvasya prāg eva samarthitatvāt ... prāyaiś śakyo na pakṣaḥ kṣapayitum iti hi vyāharadvṛttikāraḥ // avayavapadārthaḥ // ity ācāryārjunasvāmiputraśitikaṇṭhasvāmilikhitāyāṃ bhaṭṭajayantasya kṛtau nyāyamaṃjaryāṃ daśamam āhnikam // avayavapadārthasiṃhaḥ pranirastasamastadūṣaṇahariṇa (ga) ṇaḥ vādī .. nighātārthaṃ śitikaṇṭhasvāminā mayā hṛdi nihitaḥ // oṃ namo mahāgaṇapataye // oṃ namaś śrī śāradāyai kaśmīradeśavāsinyai //*

NM 11 [ii.224r18–245r4] *avayavānantaraṃ prathamasūtre tarkasyoddeśād uddeśānukrameṇa tasya lakṣaṇam āha ... vācyaḥ parair abhihitasya tathā samādhiḥ // ity ācāryārjunasvāmiputraśitikaṇṭhasvāmilikhitāyāṃ bhaṭṭajayantasya kṛtau nyāyamaṃjaryām ekādaśam āhnikam // śrīmahāgaṇeśāya namaḥ //*

NM 12 [ii.245r5– 271r3] *chalānantaraṃ jāter uddeśāt tasyāḥ sāmānyalakṣaṇaṃ tāvad āha ... prapannajanasaṅkalpakalpavṛkṣāya sambhave // ity ācāryārjunasvāmiputraśitikaṇṭhasvāmilikhitāyāṃ bhaṭṭajayantasya kṛtau nyāyamaṃjaryām dvādaśam āhnikam // samāptā ce* [19] *yaṃ nyāyamaṃjarī // śiṣyān adhyāpayituṃ śitikaṇṭhasvāminā guruṇā* [408a1] *gautamamatatattvavidā tvaritaṃ śrīnyāyamañjarī likhitā // oṃ namaś śrī* [2] *śāradāyai // oṃ namo mahāgaṇapataye // iti śubham astu lekha* [3] *kapāṭhakayoḥ // śāke 1394 āśva śu ti 10 //*

12.3.2 The unidentified Vaiśeṣika work

[Incipit] [281r3] *ihātmany arthaviśeṣāliṃgite tattvajñānam ābhyāsikaṃ niśśreyasanibandhanatayā prāpaṃcitam vaiseṣikaśāstreṣu // tac cābhyāsikaṃ tattvajñānaṃ śarīrādivivekenānumānād ātmano 'dhigame saty upapadyate*

[Explicit] [286r17] *iti +++ṃ saṃkīrṇās saṃpradarśitāḥ // saṃkīrṇa ekatra niyatā (aneka* +i)+++ *vimuktaye vyadhita (yaṃ)* +++

12.3.3 The fragment of the Raghuvaṃśa

There are seven unnumbered folios, bound at the end of the codex containing a portion of the RaV, *sarga* 14–15. The text contains emendations and/or glosses, and it is punctuated with half *daṇḍa*-s below the line, as in the NM parts, in addition to the single and double *daṇḍa*-s at the end of hemistiches. The verses are numbered. Between verses the gloss *yugalakam* (two stanzas as a syntactic unity) is also observed.

- One recto folio with RaV, 15.11–16. Incipit: *tasyamārga* [...].
- One folio with lost foliation, but with the abbreviation *ra ghu*, followed by *paṇca* on the bottom left margin, containing RaV, 15.17–21.
- One recto folio with RaV, 14.65, followed by *sāhaṃ tapaḥ sūryaniviṣṭadṛṣṭir ūrdhvaṃ*, ending abruptly with just four lines of text.
- One verso folio containing RaV, 14.69–71, with visible *ghu* abbreviation, followed by *catu*, and visible original foliation 45.
- One recto folio containing RaV, 14.72–75
- One verso folio containing RaV, 14.76–79 with *ghu* abbreviation, followed by *catu*, and original foliation 46.
- One blank recto folio.
- One blank verso folio.
- One recto folio with RaV, 15.41cd–45ab.
- One verso folio with the abbreviation *ra ghu*, followed by *paṇca*, with original foliation 54 on the bottom left margin, containing RaV, 15.45cd–49.
- One recto folio with RaV, 15.22–26, partly faded and illegible.
- One verso folio with the abbreviation *ra ghu*, followed by *paṇca*, with original foliation 50, containing RaV, 15.27–30.
- One recto folio with RaV, 15.31–35.
- A fragment of a verso folio, containing RaV, 15.36–38.

12.4 Internal divisions of C

NM 1 [1v–42v10] *oṃ śrīgaṇeśāya namaḥ oṃ namaḥ śivāya gurave // oṃ namaḥ śāśvatikānaṃdajñānaiśvaryamayātmane ... jaḍamatitvam uktaṃ bhavet // iti prathamam āhnikam //*

NM 2 [42v10–98v6] *evaṃ pramāṇānāṃ sāmānyalakṣaṇe ... parigrāhyaṃ tasmāt pravaramunigītaṃ sumatibhiḥ // iti dvitīyam āhnikam //*

NM 3 [98v6–149r1] *upamānānāṃtaraṃ śabdasya vibhāgasūtre nirdeśāt ... kavir aviralaśaktir yukta eveṃdumauliḥ // iti tṛtīyam āhnikam //*

NM 4 [149r1–189r4] *evaṃ kṛtakatve varṇānāṃ sādhite sati ... tac chrūyatāṃ yadi na dhīḥ parikhidyate vaḥ // iti caturtham āhnikam //*

NM 5 [189r4–233r5] *oṃ prasannāya vipannānāṃ duḥkhitānāṃ sukhātmane ... ity akaluṣaṃ prāmāṇyam asya sthitam iti nyāyamaṃjaryāṃ paṃcamam āhnikam //*

NM 6 [233r5–274v6] *nanu nādyāpi śabdasya niraṇāyi pramāṇatā ... sidhyaṃti sarve puruṣārthasārthāḥ iti bhaṭṭajayaṃtasya kṛtau nyāyamaṃjaryāṃ ṣaṣṭam āhnikam //*

NM 7 [274v6–302v7] *oṃ pramāṇa evaṃ pramāṇapadārthe parīkṣite sati ... niḥśreyasamakhilatayātītam āptuṃ yateta // jayaṃtabhaṭṭakṛtau nyāyamaṃjaryāṃ saptamam āhnikam //*

NM 8 [302v7–325r9] *ātmānaṃtaraṃ vibhāgasūtre śarīranirdeśāt ... gatabhayam apavargaṃ śāśvataṃ so bhyupaiti // bhaṭṭajayaṃtakṛtau nyāyamaṃjaryām aṣṭamam āhnikaṃ //*

NM 9 [325r9–354v3] *evaṃ śarīrādau duḥkhaparyaṃte ... bhaṭṭajayaṃtakṛtau nyāyamaṃjaryāṃ navamam āhnikaṃ //*

NM 10 [354v2–375v1] *saṃśayāde paramātmāṇas tu pramāṇaprameyapadasaṃgṛhītasyāpi ... iti hi vyāharad vṛttikāraḥ avayavapadārthaḥ // bhaṭṭajayaṃtakṛtau nyāyamaṃjaryāṃ daśamam āhnikaṃ samāptam //*

12.5 Internal divisions of S

NM 5 [210r1–239v10] [The beginning of NM 5 is missing] *kalpitaṃ tu tat vaktum aśakyaṃ kalpanayaiva* (NM^{Va}, II 20,12) ... *ity akaluṣaṃ prāmāṇyam asya sthitam // iti nyāyamañjaryāṃ pañcamam āhnikam //*

NM 6 [239v10–272r15] *oṃ namo gurave sarasvatīrūpāya // nanu nādyāpi śabdasya ... sidhyanti sarve puruṣārthasārthāḥ // ⟦ity ācāryaśitikaṇṭhasvāmilikhitāyāṃ⟧ bhaṭṭajayantasya kṛtau nyāyamañjaryāṃ ṣaṣṭam āhnikam //*

NM 7 [272v15–294r13] *oṃ namaḥ śrīmahāgaṇapataye bhīmasvāmine // evaṃ pramāṇapadārthe parokṣite sati ... niḥśreyasam akhilabhayātītam āptuṃ yateta // ⟦ity ācāryārjunasvāmiputra⟧ iti bhaṭṭajayantakṛtau nyāyamañjaryāṃ saptamam āhnikam*

NM 8 [295r1–309v15] *oṃ namo mahāgaṇapataye bhīmasvāmine // ātmānantaraṃ vibhāgasūtre śarīranirdeśāt ... iti coditaṃ parihṛtaṃ tad bhāṣyakāreṇa* [stops abruptly here (NM^{Va}, II 405,14), with about one fourth of the *āhnika* missing]

12.6 Recomposition of Q

The two manuscripts DC 10663 and AA 5329 were originally a single document, as explained in Section 3.4.7.

DC 10663

NM 1 [1v–41v] *oṃ svasty astu // śrī gaṇeśāya namaḥ // namaḥ śāsvatikānāṃda ... samakṣam amunātmano jaḍamatitvam uktaṃ bhavet // 7 // iti śrījayaṃtabhaṭṭakṛtau śrīnyāyamaṃjaryāṃ prathamam āhnikaṃ //*

NM 2 [43r–97v] *oṃ svasty astu // śrī gaṇeśāya namaḥ // evaṃ pramāṇānāṃ ... parigrāhyaṃ tasmāt pravaramunigītaṃ sumatibhiḥ // śrīśrivārpaṇam astu // iti śrībhaṭṭajayaṃtakṛtau śrīnyāyamaṃjaryāṃ dvitīyam āhnikaṃ //*

NM 3 [98r–153v] *oṃ svasty astu // upamānānaṃtaraṃ śabdasya vibhāgasūtre nirdeśāt ... kaviraviralaśaktir yukta eveṃdumauliḥ // iti śrījabhaṭṭajayaṃtakṛtau nyāyamaṃjaryāṃ tṛtīyam āhnikaṃ // śrīśirvārpaṇam astu //*

NM 4 [153v–195v] *oṃ svasty astu // evaṃ kṛtakatve varṇānāṃ sādhite sati ... kāryaparād api śabdād vyutpattir bhavaṃtī na vākyārthamātraparyavasāyinī bhavati kiṃ tvekaikapadāvāpo* [195v ends before the end of NM 4 (NM^{Va}, I 693,11); about four folios are missing at the end.]

NM 5 [204r1–237v11] [NM 5 begins on 204r after a gap of about five folios] *-dāyo pi na tadāśrayaḥ tasmāt sarvasādhāraṇam pratipiṃdaparisamāptaṃ* (NM II 16,2) ... *ato vidhisaṃvaṃdhe naña iśyamāṇe etāvān vākyārtho vatiṣṭhate hanana vidhir nā* [NM 5 stops abruptly here (NM^{Va}, II 116,13), were AA 5329 starts]

AA 5329

NM 5 [238r–247v] *-stīti tataś ca hananasya ... tacchabdasya nirastam ity akaluṣaṃ prāmāṇyam asya sthitaṃ // iti śrījabhaṭṭajayaṃtakṛtau nyāyamaṃjaryāṃ pañcamam āhnikaṃ //*

NM 6 [250r–295r] [The beginning of NM 6 (probably two folios) is lost.] *-kṣapaṇadakṣadūṣaṇapātratāṃ pratipadyate / ... siddhyaṃti sarve puruṣārthasārthāḥ // iti bhaṭṭajayaṃtakṛtau nyāyamaṃjaryāṃ ṣaṣṭam āhnikaṃ //*

NM 7 [295v–303v] *oṃ svasty astu // śrīgaṇeśāya namaḥ // evaṃ pramāṇapadārthe parīkṣite ... nūnaṃ ghaṭādyaraṃbhakeṣv avayaveṣu kriyā-* [AA 5329 stops abruptly here (NM^{Va}, II 286,8), where DC 10663 resumes]

DC 10663

NM 7 [304r1–327v5] *jāyate kriyāto vibhāgaḥ vibhāgād dravyāraṃbhakasaṃyogavināśas tadvināśād dravyavināśa iti* (NM^{Va}, II 286,8–9) ... *duḥkhaṃ saṃtyajya niḥśreyasamakhilatayānitam āptuṃ yateta // iti śrījabhaṭṭajayaṃtakṛtau nyāyamaṃjaryāṃ saptamam āhnikaṃ //* [NM 8–12 are missing.]

12.7 Internal divisions of J

NM 1 [1v–39v3] *namaḥ śivāya // namo navasitāsaktacitkriyāśaktisaṃpade ... iti viśeṣyajñānaṃ cākṣuṣam evam idam apīti siddham // bhaṭṭaśrīśaṃkarātmajaśrīcakradharakṛte nyāyamaṃjarīgraṃthibhaṃge prathamam āhnikam // dyaure jagajjalanidhau bhavato jayāmī majjaṃti na smṛtipathapratipannayāpi / sā kāpy acintya caritasya vicitrarūpā śaktir jayaty uḍupakhaṇḍabhṛto bhayasya / ... na hi tryakṣādṛte nyaprabhuḥ //*

NM 2 [39v3–61v3] *oṃ namaḥ śivāya // atathāvivaśvanūpasyeti / saṃśayaviparyayātmakasyety arthaḥ ... kīdṛśī tarhi buddhir ity āha bavati tu matir eṣeti // bhaṭṭaśrīśaṃkarātmajaśrīcakradharakṛte nyāyamaṃjarīgraṃthibhaṃge dvītīyam āhnikam //*

NM 3 [61v4–80v5] *oṃ namaḥ śivāya // lakṣaṇaviniścayārtham iti avyabhicārādiviśiṣṭārthopalabdhijñānakatvaṃ pramāṇalakṣaṇaṃ ... iti bahumānas tadāśrayaṇena / kaviḥ kānte darśanaḥ // bhaṭṭaśrīśaṃkarātmajaśrīcakradharakṛte nyāyamaṃjarīgraṃthibhaṃge tṛtīyam āhnikam // jaṭājūṭabhara(bhrasya)dgaṃ // gāṃbudyanadurddine / ullasac caṃdrakaṃ vaṃde nīlakaṃṭhasya tāṃḍavam //*

NM 4 [81v1–124v5] *oṃ namaḥ śivāya // prakaraṇaṃ (bh)intāhetor iti ... na cirāya na kadācid amākam upayujyata ity artha iti // bhaṭṭaśrīśaṃkarātmajaśrīcakradharakṛte nyāyamaṃjarīgraṃthibhaṃge caturtam āhnikam iti //*

NM 5 [125v1–156r2] *oṃ namaḥ śivāya // unmattāsyonmattasaṃvarṇṇanam iti ... ity āśaṃkyāha śabdasya pratyakṣavad iti // bhaṭṭaśrīśaṃkarātmajacakradharakṛte nyāyamaṃjarīgraṃthibhaṃge paṃcam āhnikam iti //*

NM 6 [156r2–186v3] *oṃ namaḥ śivāya // bījaṃ padārthavākyārthabuddheḥ padavākye / ... bhogī śeṣaḥ tanmataṃ mahābhāṣyaṃ tacchrutena saṅgaśīlā ye bhartṛhariprabhṛtayaḥ āryā iti bhadram // bhaṭṭaśrīśaṃkarātmajacakradharakṛte nyāyamañjarīgranthibhaṅge ṣaṣṭhamāhnikaṃ samāptam // oṃ jayaty ekaśarāghātavidāritapuratrayaḥ / dhanurddharāṇāṃ dhaureya pinākī bhuvanatraye //*

13 The foliation of M

In M, the alphanumerical foliation (see Grünendahl, 2001, xiv,94) is preserved only in few folios:

- 279.3 = *kṛ* = 7
- 271.2 = *ko* = 13
- 267.2 = *kaḥ* = 16
- 263.3 = *khā* = 18
- 261.2 = *khi* = 19
- 259.3 = *khū* = 22
- 255.2 = *khe* = 27
- 255.1 = *kho* = 29
- 251.2 = *khau* = 30
- 211.2 = *ghe* = 59
- 207.3 = *gho* = 61
- 207.2 = *ghau* = 62
- 115.3 = *jo* = 125
- 115.2 = *jau* = 126
- 115.1 = *jaṃ* = 127
- 111.3 = *jaḥ* = 128
- 111.2 = *jha* = 129
- 111.1 = *jhā* = 130
- 107.2 = *jhī* = 132
- 107.1 = *jhu* = 133
- 103.3 = *jhū* = 134
- 95.2 = *jhe* = 139
- 99.1 = *jhai* = 140
- 95.3 = *jho* = 141
- 95.1 = *jhau* = 142

Nonetheless, these are enough to reconstruct the folio numbers of all the extant leaves and fragment of leaves. NM 6 probably begins on folio *ka* and ends at *jhau*. Six leaves are lost. According to Grünendahl, there should be 55 numbers (i.e., the sequence of the vowels) before *ka*, but this scheme cannot be applied to AL 70179B. If, as it is the case, 142 leaves covered NM 6 to NM 12, 55 leaves would not be enough to cover NM 1 to NM 5, a portion of text that it is more than half of the full NM. At the ratio of the extant part, indeed, the first half would have been covered in about 176 leaves. Possibly the count of the first, missing half of AL 70179B, if it existed at all, started from *ka*, as does the second half, and not from the vowels as in the case of Grünendahl's example (partitions with new starts of the foliation are observed also in BHU C-1015 and BORI 390/75–6, see Section 3.4.6).

The following is a reconstruction of the original foliation. The first number refers to the batch of images consulted by me (courtesy Adyar Library, Chennai, and Taishei Shida). Whenever the alphanumeric character is in parenthesis, it was inferred and not anymore visible. The last number is the translation of alphanumeric *akṣara*-s into digits, which I will use in this edition for reference to this manuscript.

NM 6
- (missing) = (*ka*) = 1
- (missing) = (*kā*) = 2
- 131.3 = (*ki*) = 3r
- 130.3 = 3v
- 121.1 = (*kī*) = 4r
- 124.1 = 4v
- 165.3 = (*ku*) = 5r
- 167.3 = 5v
- 283.1 = (*kū*) = 6r
- 282.1 = 6v
- 279.3 = *kṛ* = 7r
- 277.3 = 7v
- 275.3 = (*kṝ*) = 8r
- 273.3 = 8v
- 275.2 = (*kḷ*) = 9r
- 273.2 = 9v
- 275.1 = (*kḹ*) = 10r
- 273.1 = 10v
- 173.2 = (*ke*) = 11r
- 175.2 = 11v (end of NM 6.1)
- 271.3 = (*kai*) = 12
- 271.2 = *ko* = 13
- 271.1 = (*kau*) = 14
- 267.3 = (*kaṃ*) = 15
- 267.2 = *kaḥ* = 16
- 267.1 = (*kha*) = 17
- 263.3 = *khā* = 18
- 261.2 = *khi* = 19
- 279.2 = (*khī*) = 20
- 117.3 = (*khu*) = 21
- 259.3 = *khū* = 22
- 263.1 = (*khṛ*) = 23
- 259.2 = (*khṝ*) = 24
- 259.1 = (*khḷ*) = 25
- 255.3 = (*khḹ*) = 26
- 255.2 = *khe* = 27
- 249.3 = (*khai*) = 28
- 255.1 = *kho* = 29
- 251.2 = *khau* = 30
- 251.1 = (*khaṃ*) = 31
- 227.1 = (*khaḥ*) = 32

NM 7
- 245.3 = (*ga*) = 33
- 247.2 = (*gā*) = 34
- 227.2= (*gi*) = 35
- 227.3= (*gī*) = 36
- 231.1= (*gu*) = 37
- 231.2= (*gū*) = 38
- 231.3 = (*gṛ*) = 39
- 235.1 = (*gṝ*) = 40
- 235.2 = (*gḷ*) = 41
- 235.3 = (*gḹ*) = 42
- 239.1 = (*ge*) = 43
- 239.2 = (*gai*) = 44
- 239.3 = (*go*) = 45
- 243.1 = (*gau*) = 46
- 243.2 = (*gaṃ*) = 47
- 243.3 = (*gaḥ*) = 48
- 247.1 = (*gha*) = 49
- 223.2 = (*ghā*) = 50
- 223.1 = (*ghi*) = 51
- 219.3 = (*ghī*) = 52
- 219.2 = (*ghu*) = 53

NM 8
- 219.1 = (*ghū*) = 54
- 215.3 = (*ghṛ*) = 55
- (missing) = (*ghṝ*) = 56
- 215.2 = (*ghḷ*) = 57
- 211.3 = (*ghḹ*) = 58
- 211.2 = *ghe* = 59
- 211.i = (*ghai*) = 60
- 207.3 = *gho* = 61
- 207.2 = *ghau* = 62
- 207.1 = (*ghaṃ*) = 63
- 203.3 = (*ghaḥ*) = 64
- 203.2 = (*ṅa*) = 65
- (missing) = (*ṅā*) = 66
- 195.3= (*ṅi*) = 67
- 199.1= (*ṅī*) = 68
- 199.2= (*ṅu*) = 69
- 199.3= (*ṅū*) = 70
- 191.3 = (*ṅṛ*) = 71

NM 9
- 195.1 = (*ṅṝ*) = 72
- 203.1 = (*ṅḷ*) = 73
- 195.2 = (*ṅḹ*) = 74
- 191.1 = (*ṅe*) = 75
- 187.3 = (*ṅai*) = 76
- 187.2 = (*ṅo*) = 77
- 187.1 = (*ṅau*) = 78
- 175.3 = (*ṅaṃ*) = 79
- 171.1 = (*ṅaḥ*) = 80
- 179.1 = (*ca*) = 81
- 179.2 = (*cā*) = 82
- 179.3= (*ci*) = 83
- 277.1= (*cī*) = 84
- 279.2= (*cu*) = 85
- 183.2= (*cū*) = 86
- 183.3 = (*cṛ*) = 87
- 171.2 = (*cṝ*) = 88
- 171.3 = (*cḷ*) = 89
- 175.1 = (*cḹ*) = 90
- 167.2 = (*ce*) = 91
- 131.1 = (*cai*) = 92
- 167.1 = (*co*) = 93

NM 10
- 163.3 = (*cau*) = 94
- 163.2 = (*caṃ*) = 95
- 163.1 = (*caḥ*) = 96
- 159.3 = (*cha*) = 97
- 159.2 = (*chā*) = 98
- 159.1= (*chi*) = 99
- 155.3= (*chī*) = 100
- 155.2= (*chu*) = 101
- 155.1= (*chū*) = 102
- 151.3 = (*chṛ*) = 103
- 151.1 = (*chṝ*) = 104
- 147.3 = (*chḷ*) = 105
- 147.2 = (*chḹ*) = 106
- 147.1 = (*che*) = 107

NM 11
- 143.3 = (*chai*) = 108
- 143.2 = (*cho*) = 109
- 143.1 = (*chau*) = 110
- 139.3 = (*chaṃ*) = 111

- 139.2 = (*chaḥ*) = 112
- 139.1 = (*ja*) = 113
- 135.3 = (*jā*) = 114
- (missing)= (*ji*) = 115
- (missing)= (*jī*) = 116
- 133.1= (*ju*) = 117
- 131.2= (*jū*) = 118
- 127.2 = (*jṛ*) = 119
- 127.1 = (*jṝ*) = 120
- 123.3 = (*jḷ*) = 121
- 123.2 = (*jḹ*) = 122
- 119.2 = (*je*) = 123

NM 12

- 119.1 = (*jai*) = 124
- 115.3 = *jo* = 125
- 115.2 = *jau* = 126
- 115.1 = *jaṃ* = 127
- 111.3 = *jaḥ* = 128
- 111.2 = *jha* = 129
- 111.1 = *jhā* = 130
- 107.3 = (*jh*)i = 131
- 107.2 = *jhī* = 132
- 107.1 = *jhu* = 133
- 103.3 = *jhū* = 134
- 103.2 = (*jhṛ*) = 135
- 103.1 = (*jhṝ*) = 136
- 99.3 = (*jhḷ*) = 137
- 99.2 = (*jhḹ*) = 138
- 95.2 = *jhe* = 139
- 99.1 = *jhai* = 140
- 95.3 = *jho* = 141
- 95.1 = *jhau* = 142

14 A bird-eye view of commented sūtra-s

In the following table, the *sūtra*-s commented in the NM are listed. The purpose is to look at the NM from a different perspective, as a commentary of selected *sūtra*-s. Due to the detailed and digressive style of the NM one may indeed lose sight of the relation among the commentary and the commented *Nyāyasūtra*. The numbering of the *sūtra*-s follows the one adopted in NBh^{Tha}.

NM^{Va}	Pre-quote, Sūtra, Post-quote	Type	NS
NM 1			
(I 12.14)	*tatredam ādimaṃ sūtram— "pramāṇa- [...] niḥśreyasādhigamaḥ"*	*uddeśa*	(1.1.1)
(I 31.2)	[...] *idānīm eva vivriyate— "pratyakṣānumānopamānaśabdāḥ pramāṇāni"*	*uddeśa*	(1.1.3)
(I 171.6)	*evaṃ pramāṇānāṃ sāmānyalakṣaṇe vibhāge ca nirṇīte sati adhunā viśeṣalakṣaṇavarṇanāvasara iti* [...] *prathamaṃ pratyakṣasya lakṣaṇaṃ pratipādayitum āha— "indriyārthasannikarṣotpannaṃ jñānam avyapadeśyam avyabhicāri vyavasāyātmakaṃ pratyakṣam"*	*lakṣaṇa*	(1.1.4)
NM 2			
(I 282.6)	*"tatpūrvakaṃ trividham anumānaṃ pūrvavac cheṣavat sāmānyatodṛṣṭaṃ ca" / evaṃ pramāṇajyeṣṭhe 'smin pratyakṣe lakṣite sati / kathyate 'vasaraprāptam anumānasya lakṣaṇam //*	*lakṣaṇa*	(1.1.5)
(I 373.13)	*anumānānantaram upamānaṃ vibhāgasūtre paṭhitam iti tatkrameṇa tasya lakṣaṇam ucyate— "prasiddhasādharmyāt sādhyasādhanam upamānam"*	*lakṣaṇa*	(1.1.6)
NM 3			
(I 396.4)	*upamānānantaraṃ śabdasya vibhāgasūtre nirdeśāt tasya lakṣaṇaṃ pratipādayitum āha— "āptopadeśaḥ śabdaḥ"*	*lakṣaṇa*	(1.1.7)
NM 4			
(I 609.9)	*tasmāt āptoktatvasya siddham āyurvedādau vyāptigrahaṇam / vyāptipradarśanāyaiva sūtrakṛtā— "sa dvividho dṛṣṭādṛṣṭārthatvāt"*	*uddeśa*	(1.1.8)
NM 5			
(II 47.15)	*iha tu "vyaktyākṛtijātayas tu padārthāḥ" iti sūtrakāraḥ pṛthag ākṛtiṃ jāter avocad iti saṃsthānam eva ākṛtim ucyate /*	*lakṣaṇa*	(2.2.66)
NM 7			

NM^Va	Pre-quote, Sūtra, Post-quote	Type	NS
(II 263.3)	*evaṃ pramāṇapadārthe parīkṣite sati yadarthaṃ tatparīkṣaṇaṃ tat prameyam idānīṃ darśayitum āha— "ātmaśarīrendriyārthabuddhimanaḥpravttidoṣapretyabhāvaphaladuḥkhāpavargās tu prameyam"*	*uddeśa*	(1.1.9)
(II 278.6)	*tad āha sūtrakāraḥ— "icchādveṣaprayatnasukhaduḥkhajñānāny ātmano liṅgaṃ"*	*lakṣaṇa*	(1.1.10)
NM 8			
(II 360.3)	*ātmānantaraṃ vibhāgasūtre śarīranirdeśāt tadanukrameṇa tatsvarūpanirūpaṇārtham āha— "ceṣṭendriyārthāśrayaḥ śarīram"*	*lakṣaṇa*	(1.1.11)
(II 365.17)	*"ghrāṇarasanacakṣustvakśrotrāṇīndriyāṇi bhūtebhyaḥ" / atra indriyāṇāṃ viśayopalabdhikāraṇatvaṃ sāmānyalakṣaṇaṃ prasiddham eva /*	*uddeśa*	(1.1.12)
(II 367.12)	*tāni punar indriyāṇāṃ kāraṇāni "pthivy āpas tejo vāyur ākāśam iti bhūtāni" /*	*uddeśa*	(1.1.13)
(II 381.6)	*"gandharasarūpasparśaśabdāḥ pthivyādiguṇās tadarthāḥ" tadarthāḥ ity ata evāpakṛṣya vā prakramād vā arthāḥ iti lakṣyapadaṃ darśayitavyam /*	*uddeśa*	(1.1.14)
(II 386.14)	*"buddhir upalabdhir jñānam ity anarthāntaram" / nanu paryāyoccāraṇam etat / na buddher lakṣaṇābhidhānam /*	*lakṣaṇa*	(1.1.15)
(II 408.5)	*"yugapajjñānānuptattir manaso liṅgam" / manaso yad eva sattve pramāṇaṃ tadgamyatvam evāsya lakṣaṇam /*	*lakṣaṇa*	(1.1.16)
(II 413.2)	*"pravṛttir vāgbuddhiśarīrārambhaḥ" / vāg iti varṇātmakaśabdakāraṇasaṃyogādy ucyate /*	*lakṣaṇa*	(1.1.17)
(II 415.2)	*"pravartanālakṣaṇā doṣāḥ" / pravartanā pravṛttiṃ prati prayojakatā /*	*lakṣaṇa*	(1.1.18)
(II 418.14)	*"punarutpattiḥ pretyabhāvaḥ" / kasyeyaṃ punarutpattir ucyate / ātmanaḥ śarīrasya vā /*	*lakṣaṇa*	(1.1.19)
(II 424.14)	*"pravṛttidoṣajanito 'rthaḥ phalam" / pravṛttidoṣās tu vyākhyātāḥ / tajjanito 'rthaḥ phalam ity ucyate /*	*lakṣaṇa*	(1.1.20)
(II 427.10)	*"bādhanālakṣaṇaṃ duḥkham" / bādhanā pīḍanaṃ santāpanam /*	*lakṣaṇa*	(1.1.21)
NM 9			
(II 430.3)	*evaṃ śarīrādau duḥkhaparyante heye prameye nirṇīte yadartha etadupadeśaḥ yatparam upādeyaṃ prameyaṃ yadarthaḥ śāstrārambhaḥ tam apavargaṃ lakṣayitum āha / "tadatyantavimokṣo 'pavargaḥ"*	*lakṣaṇa*	(1.1.22)
(II 440.3)	*uktam eva bhagavatā sūtrakāreṇa / "duḥkhajanmapravttidoṣamithyājñānānām uttarottarāpāye tadanantarāpāyād apavargaḥ"*	*lakṣaṇa*	(1.1.2)
NM 10			
(II 522.4)	[...] *prathamasūtre ca prameyānantaraṃ saṃśayoddeśāt uddeśānukrameṇa tasya lakṣaṇaṃ pratipādayitum āha / "samānānekadharmopapatter vipratipatter upalabdhyanupalabdhyavyavasthātaś ca viśeṣāpekṣo vimarśaḥ saṃśayaḥ"*	*lakṣaṇa*	(1.1.23)
(II 540.14)	*"yam artham adhiktya pravartate tat prayojanaṃ" yam ity atra deśakālapuruṣadaśābhedabhinnaprayojanaviśeṣavyāptaye vīpsā draṣṭavyā /*	*lakṣaṇa*	(1.1.24)
(II 542.16)	*"laukikaparīkṣakāṇāṃ yasminn arthe buddhisāmyaṃ sa dṛṣṭāntaḥ" laukikaparīkṣakau vādiprativādinau dṛṣṭāntalakṣaṇaprastāvād veditavyau /*	*lakṣaṇa*	(1.1.25)
(II 544.5)	*"tantrādhikaraṇābhyupagamasaṃsthitiḥ siddhāntaḥ" / tantryate 'nena padārthasthitir iti tantraṃ pramāṇam ucyate /*	*lakṣaṇa*	(1.1.26)
(II 545.10)	*tasya svakaṇṭhena vibhāgam āha / "sa caturvidhaḥ sarvatantrapratitantrādhikaraṇābhyupagamasaṃsthityarthāntarabhāvāt"*	*uddeśa*	(1.1.27)
(II 545.15)	*tatra "sarvatantrāviruddhas tantre 'dhikto 'rthaḥ sarvatantrasiddhāntaḥ"*	*lakṣaṇa*	(1.1.28)

NM^{Va}	Pre-quote, Sūtra, Post-quote	Type	NS
(II 546.4)	[missing in NM^{Va}, but present in the NM mss.:] *"samānatantrasiddhaḥ paratantrāsiddhaḥ pratitantrasiddhāntaḥ" tantre adhikṛto 'rtha iti vartate /*	*lakṣaṇa*	(1.1.29)
(II 546.16)	*"yat siddhāv anyaprakaraṇasiddhiḥ so 'dhikaraṇasiddhāntaḥ" prakriyata iti prakaraṇaṃ pakṣa ucyate /*	*lakṣaṇa*	(1.1.30)
(II 548.4)	*"aparīkṣitābhyupagamāt tadviśeṣaparīkṣaṇam abhyupagamasiddhāntaḥ" atra aparīkṣitābhyupagamād iti yathāśrutapañcamīnirdeśam anurudhyamānaḥ pramāṇamūlābhyupagamaviṣayīkṛto 'rthaḥ siddhānta iti [...]*	*lakṣaṇa*	(1.1.31)
(II 552.7)	*tasmāt parārthānumānavākyopapatteḥ tadekadeśāḥ avayavā yuktā iti lakṣyante / "pratijñāhetūdāharaṇopanayanigamanāny avayavāḥ"*	*uddeśa*	(1.1.32)
(II 554.16)	*teṣām / "sādhyanirdeśaḥ pratijñā"*	*lakṣaṇa*	(1.1.33)
(II 559.17)	*evaṃ lakṣaṇako hetur iti tatsvarūpāvadhāraṇaṃ sati tadabhidhāyakaṃ vacanaṃ mukham eva lakṣyate ity arthātmakahetulakṣaṇaṃ tāvad ucyate / "udāharaṇasādharmyāt sādhyasādhanaṃ hetuḥ"*	*lakṣaṇa*	(1.1.34)
(II 564.11)	*"tathā vaidharmyāt" / udāharaṇagrahaṇam anuvartate sādhyasādhanaṃ ca /*	*lakṣaṇa*	(1.1.35)
(II 569.2)	*"sādhyasādharmyāt taddharmabhāvī dṣṭānta udāharaṇam" yathā tatpūrvakam anumānam ity atra pratibandhagrahaṇopāyamātraṃ pratipāditam / iha tu pratibandhasvarūpam udāharaṇasādharmyam uktam /*	*lakṣaṇa*	(1.1.36)
(II 571.4)	*"tadviparyayād vā viparītam" / dṛṣṭānta udāharaṇam iti vartate /*	*lakṣaṇa*	(1.1.37)
(II 574.16)	*"udāharaṇāpekṣas tathety upasaṃhāro na tatheti vā sādhyasyopanayaḥ" / udāharaṇam ātmalābhe apekṣata iti /*	*lakṣaṇa*	(1.1.38)
(II 579.12)	*"hetvapadeśāt pratijñāyāḥ punarvacanaṃ nigamanam" / hetuḥ dṛṣṭāntadharmiṇi nirjñātaśaktiḥ sādhye dharmiṇiy apadiśyate 'neneti hetvapadeśa upanayaḥ /*	*lakṣaṇa*	(1.1.39)
NM 11			
(II 584.3)	*avayavānantaraṃ prathamasūtre tarkasyoddeśāt uddeśānukrameṇa tasya lakṣaṇam āha / "avijñātatattve 'rthe kāraṇopapattitas tattvajñānārtham ūhas tarkaḥ" /*	*lakṣaṇa*	(1.1.40)
(II 592.8)	*tarkānantaraṃ nirṇayo bhavati / paṭhitaś ceti sa lakṣyate / "vimśya pakṣapratipakṣābhyām arthāvadhāraṇaṃ nirṇayaḥ" /*	*lakṣaṇa*	(1.1.41)
(II 596.6)	*nyāyaparīkṣādvārakavastuvicārayogyāḥ kathā vādināṃ bhavanti vādaḥ jalpaḥ vitaṇḍeti / tatra vādas tāvad ucyate / "pramāṇatarkasādhanopālambhaḥ siddhāntāviruddhaḥ pañcāvayavopapannaḥ pakṣapratipakṣaparigraho vādaḥ" /*	*lakṣaṇa*	(1.2.1)
(II 599.20)	*"yathoktopapannaś chalajātinigrahasthānasādhanopālambho jalpaḥ" yathoktopapannagrahaṇena sarvātideśe vādajalpayor aviśeṣa iti śaṅkamānāḥ [...]*	*lakṣaṇa*	(1.2.2)
(II 602.14)	*"sa pratipakṣasthāpanāhīno vitaṇḍā" / sa eva yathoktalakṣaṇakaḥ jalpaḥ vitaṇḍā bhavati /*	*lakṣaṇa*	(1.2.3)
(II 603.13)	*pakṣadharmatvādīni paṃca lakṣaṇāni hetor uktāni / teṣām ekaikāpāyāt paṃcahetvābhāsā bhavantīti tān darśayitum āha "savyabhicāraviruddhaprakaraṇasamasādhyasamakālātītā hetvābhāsāḥ" /*	*uddeśa*	(1.2.4)
(II 605.6–7)	*teṣāṃ savyabhicāras tāvad ucyate "anaikāntikaḥ savyabhicāraḥ" /*	*lakṣaṇa*	(1.2.5)
(II 610.8–9)	*"siddhāntam abhyupetya tadvirodhī viruddhaḥ" / sapakṣavipakṣayoḥ vṛttyavṛttī hetor lakṣaṇam /*	*lakṣaṇa*	(1.2.6)
(II 610.11)	*"yasmāt prakaraṇacintā sa nirṇayārtham apadiṣṭaḥ prakaraṇasamaḥ" / ekaikalakṣaṇāpāyanimittahetvābhāsapaṃcakapratijñānāt asat pratipakṣatvalakṣaṇavaikalyāt kila prakaraṇasamo nāma hetvābhāso vaktavyaḥ /*	*lakṣaṇa*	(1.2.7)

NM^{Va}	Pre-quote, Sūtra, Post-quote	Type	NS
(II 622.11)	"*sādhyāviśiṣṭah sādhyatvāt sādhyasamaḥ*" / *anyataravādiprasiddhaṃ anyataraṃ prati yat sādhayitum upādīyate tat sādhyam* /	*lakṣaṇa*	(1.2.8)
(II 632.13)	"*kālātyayāpadiṣṭaḥ kālātītaḥ*" / *yathāprāptaṃ hetuprayogakālam atītya yo hetur apadiśyate sa kālātyayāpadiṣṭaḥ kālātīta ucyate* /	*lakṣaṇa*	(1.2.9)
(II 635.3)	*tathāpi jalpavitaṇḍe eva teṣāṃ prācuryeṇa kṣetram iti tadaupayikatayā tatsvarūpanirūpaṇaṃ yuktam ity uddeśakrameṇa chalasya tāval lakṣaṇam āha* / "*vacanavighāto 'rthavikalpopapattyā cchalam*" /	*lakṣaṇa*	(1.2.10)
(II 637.6)	*evaṃ sāmānyalakṣaṇam abhidhāya chalasya vibhāgam āha* / "*tat trividhaṃ vākchalaṃ sāmānyacchalam upacāracchalaṃ ca*" /	*uddeśa*	(1.2.11)
(II 637.11)	*atha vibhāgakrameṇa lakṣaṇāny āha / tatra* "*aviśeṣābhihite 'rthe vaktur abhiprāyād arthāntarakalpanā vākchalam*" /	*lakṣaṇa*	(1.2.12)
(II 639.9)	"*sambhavato 'rthasyātisāmānyayogād asambhūtārthakalpanā sāmānyacchalam*" / *ativyapakaṃ sāmānyam atisāmānyam* /	*lakṣaṇa*	(1.2.13)
(II 641.1)	"*dharmavikalpanirdeśe 'rthasadbhāvapratiṣedha upacāracchalam*" / *abhidhānasya dharmaḥ anekaprakāraḥ* /	*lakṣaṇa*	(1.2.14)
(II 642.18)	*evaṃ chalasya viśeṣalakṣaṇāny abhidhāya tatparīkṣārtham ākṣepaṃ karoti* / "*vākcchalam evopacāracchalam tadaviśeṣāt*" /	*parikṣā*	(1.2.15)
(II 643.5)	*atra samādhim āha* / "*na tadarthāntarabhāvāt*" /	*parīkṣā*	(1.2.16)
(II 643.17)	"*aviśeṣe vā kiñcitsādharmyād ekacchalaprasaṅgaḥ*" / (1.2.17) *chalasya dvitvam abhyanujñāya* [...]	*parīkṣā*	
NM 12			
(II 645.3)	*chalānantaraṃ jāter uddeśāt tasyās sāmānyalakṣaṇaṃ tāvad āha* / "*sādharmyavaidharmyābhyāṃ pratyavasthānaṃ jātiḥ*"	*lakṣaṇa*	(1.2.18)
(II 646.10)	*atha bhedavattvāj jāteḥ caturviṃśatidhā vibhāgam āha* / "*sādharmya - vaidharmya - utkarṣa - apakarṣa - varṇya - avarṇya - vikalpa - sādhya - prāpti - aprāpti - prasaṅga - pratidṛṣṭānta - anutpatti - saṃśaya - prakaraṇa - ahetu - arthāpatti - aviśeṣa - upapatti - upalabdhi - anupalabdhi - anitya –nitya - kāryasamāḥ*"	*uddeśa*	(5.1.1)
(II 651.4)	*atha viśeṣalakṣaṇāny āha / tatra* "*sādharmyavaidharmyābhyām upasaṃhāre taddharmaviparyayopapatteḥ sādharmyavaidharmyasamau*"	*lakṣaṇa*	(5.1.2)
(II 652.9)	*atas tad vyutpādanārtham āha* / "*gotvād gosiddhivat tatsiddhiḥ*"	*parīkṣā*	(5.1.3)
(II 653.2)	"*sādhyadṛṣṭāntayor dharmavikalpād ubhayasādhyatvāc cotkarṣāpakarṣavarṇyāvarṇyavikalpasādhyasamāḥ*" *dṛṣṭāntadharmaṃ sādhye dharmiṇi yojayan* [...]	*lakṣaṇa*	(5.1.4)
(II 654.13)	*atra pañcānām uttaram* / "*kiñcitsādharmyād upasaṃhārasiddher vaidharmyād apratiṣedhaḥ*"	*lakṣaṇa*	(5.1.5)
(II 655.2)	*atha ṣaṣṭhasyottaram* / "*sādhyātideśāc ca dṛṣṭāntopapatteḥ*"	*lakṣaṇa*	(5.1.6)
(II 655.9)	"*prāpya sādhyam aprāpya vā hetoḥ prāptyāviśiṣṭatvād aprāptyāsādhakatvāc ca prāptyaprāptisamau*"	*lakṣaṇa*	(5.1.7)
(II 655.17)	*anayor uttaram* / "*ghaṭādiniṣpattidarśanāt pīḍane cābhicārād apratiṣedhaḥ*"	*lakṣaṇa*	(5.1.8)
(II 656.6)	"*dṛṣṭāntasya kāraṇānapadeśāt pratyavasthānāc ca pratidṛṣṭāntena prasaṅgapratidṛṣṭāntasamau*" *atiprasaṅgāpādanena pratyavasthānaṃ prasaṅgasamaḥ pratiṣedhaḥ* /	*lakṣaṇa*	(5.1.9)
(II 657.7)	*atra prasaṅgasamasya tāvad uttaram āha* / "*pradīpopādānaprasaṅgavinivṛttivat tadvinivṛttiḥ*"	*lakṣaṇa*	(5.1.10)
(II 657.15)	*atha pratidṛṣṭāntasamasyottaram* / "*pratidṛṣṭāntahetutve ca nāhetur dṛṣṭāntaḥ*"	*lakṣaṇa*	(5.1.11)
(II 658.7)	"*prāg utpatteḥ kāraṇābhāvād anutpattisamaḥ*" *anutpattyā pratyavasthānam anutpattisamaḥ pratiṣedhaḥ* /	*lakṣaṇa*	(5.1.12)

NM^{Va}	Pre-quote, Sūtra, Post-quote	Type	NS
(II 658.16)	*asyottaram / "tathābhāvād utpannasya kāraṇopapatter na kāraṇapratiṣedhaḥ"*	*lakṣaṇa*	(5.1.13)
(II 659.5)	*"nityānityatva- (nityānityatva-] sāmānyadṛṣṭāntayor aindriyakatve samāne nityānitya-* NBh^{Tha}, 291,3) *sādharmyāt saṃśayaḥ" (saṃśayaḥ] saṃśayasamaḥ* NBh^{Tha}, 291,3)	*lakṣaṇa*	(5.1.14)
(II 659.13)	*asyottaram / "sādharmyāt saṃśaye na saṃśayo vaidharmyād ubhayathā vā saṃśaye 'tyantasaṃśayo nityatvānabhyupagamāc ca sāmānyasyāpratiṣedhaḥ"*	*lakṣaṇa*	(5.1.15)
(II 660.4)	*"ubhayasādharmyāt prakriyāsiddheḥ prakaraṇasamaḥ" pakṣapratipakṣau nirṇayalakṣaṇe vyākhyātau / tāv eva prakaraṇam /*	*lakṣaṇa*	(5.1.16)
(II 661.1)	*atrottaram / "pratipakṣāt prakaraṇasiddheḥ pratiṣedhānupapattiḥ pratipakṣopapatteḥ"*	*lakṣaṇa*	(5.1.17)
(II 661.12)	*"traikalyānupapatter (traikalyānupapatter] traikālyāsiddher* NBh^{Tha}, 293,10) *hetor ahetusamaḥ" kālatrayānupapattyā hetum ākṣipya kriyamāṇaḥ pratiṣedhaḥ ahetusamo bhavati /*	*lakṣaṇa*	(5.1.18)
(II 662.1)	*asyottaram / "na hetutaḥ sādhyasiddhes traikālyāsiddhiḥ"*	*lakṣaṇa*	(5.1.19)
(II 662.11)	*pratiṣedhe ca tulyo 'yam anuyoga ity āha / "pratiṣedhānupapatteś ca pratiṣeddhavyāpratiṣedhaḥ"*	*lakṣaṇa*	(5.1.20)
(II 662.16)	*"arthāpattitaḥ pratipakṣasiddher arthāpattisamaḥ" arthād āpadyate pratipakṣasiddhiḥ* [...] (5.1.21)		
(II 663.4)	*asyottaram / "anuktasyārthād āpatteḥ (anuktasyārthād āpatteḥ] anuktasyārthāpatteḥ* NBh^{Tha}, 295,3) *pakṣahāner upapattiḥ" anupapāditasādhanam* [...] *doṣāntaram āha / "anaikāntikatvāc cārthapatteḥ" (anaikāntikatvāc cārthāpatteḥ] anuktatvād anaikāntikatvāc cārthāpatteḥ* NBh^{Tha}, 295,3–4 (there is thus a *sūtravibhāga* of 5.1.22 in the NM)	*lakṣaṇa*	(5.1.22)
(II 663.17)	*"ekadharmopapatter aviśeṣe sarvāviśeṣaprasaṅgāt sadbhāvopapatter aviśeṣasamaḥ" aviśeṣopapādanena pratyavasthānam aviṣeṣasamaḥ pratiṣedhaḥ /*	*lakṣaṇa*	(5.1.23)
(II 664.5)	*etasyottaram / "kvacit taddharmopapatteḥ kvacic cānupapatteḥ pratiṣedhābhāvaḥ"*	*lakṣaṇa*	(5.1.24)
(II 665.6)	*"ubhayakāraṇopapatter upapattisamaḥ" ubhayakāraṇopapattyā pakṣadvayopapattivarṇanam upapattisamaḥ pratiṣedhaḥ /*	*lakṣaṇa*	(5.1.25)
(II 665.15)	*atrottaram / "upapattikāraṇānujñānād (-kāraṇānujñānād] -kāraṇābhyanujñānād* NBh^{Tha}, 297,9) *apratiṣedhaḥ"*	*lakṣaṇa*	(5.1.26)
(II 666.4)	*"nirdiṣṭakāraṇābhāve 'py upalambhād upalabdhisamaḥ pratiṣedhaḥ" (pratiṣedhaḥ] om.* NBh^{Tha}, 298,3) *nirdiṣṭasya sādhyadharmasiddhikāraṇasyābhāve 'pi sādhyadharmopalabdhyā pratyavasthānam upalabdhisamaḥ pratiṣedhaḥ /*	*lakṣaṇa*	(5.1.27)
(II 666.10)	*asyottaram / "kāraṇāntarād api taddharmopapatter apratiṣedhaḥ"*	*lakṣaṇa*	(5.1.28)
(II 667.12)	*"tadanupalabdher anupalambhād abhāvāsiddhau (abhāvāsiddhau] abhāvasiddhau* NBh^{Tha}, 299,7) *tadviparītopapatter anupalabdhisamaḥ" anupalabdher anupalambhopanyāsena pratyavasthānam anupalabdhisamaḥ pratiṣedhaḥ /*	*lakṣaṇa*	(5.1.29)
(II 668.1)	*asyottaram / "anupalambhātmakatvād anupalabdher ahetuḥ"*	*lakṣaṇa*	(5.1.30)
(II 668.12)	*"jñānavikalpānāṃ ca bhāvābhāvasaṃvedanād adhyātmam" jñānavikalpāḥ pratītiprakārāḥ /*	*lakṣaṇa*	(5.1.31)
(II 669.5)	*"sādharmyāt tulyadharmopapatteḥ sarvānityatvaprasaṅgād anityasamaḥ" sarvabhāvānityatvaprasaṅgena pratyavasthānam anityasamaḥ pratiṣedhaḥ /*	*lakṣaṇa*	(5.1.32)
(II 669.13)	*atrottaram / "sādharmyād apy (apy] om.* NBh^{Tha}, 301,10) *asiddheḥ pratiṣedhāsiddhiḥ pratiṣedhyasādharmyāt"*	*lakṣaṇa*	(5.1.33)

NM^{Va}	Pre-quote, Sūtra, Post-quote	Type	NS
(II 670.1)	*kiṃ ca / "dṛṣṭānte (dṛṣṭānte] dṛṣṭānte ca* NBh^{Tha}, 301,16) *sādhyasādhanabhāvena pratijñātasya (pratijñātasya] prajñātasya* NBh^{Tha}, 301,16) [...] *dharmasya hetutvāt tasya cobhayathābhāvānn aviśeṣaḥ"*	*lakṣaṇa*	(5.1.34)
(II 670.12)	*"nityam anityabhāvād anitye nityatvopapatter nityasamaḥ"*	*lakṣaṇa*	(5.1.35)
(II 671.1)	*asyottaram / "pratiṣedhye nityam anityabhāvād anityatvopapatteḥ (anityatvopapatteḥ] anitye 'nityatvopapatteḥ* NBh^{Tha}, 302,10) *pratiṣedhābhāvaḥ"*	*lakṣaṇa*	(5.1.36)
(II 671.19)	*"prayatnakāryānekatvāt kāryasamaḥ" prayatnakāryanānātvopanyāsena pratyavasthānaṃ kāryasamaḥ pratiṣedhaḥ /*	*lakṣaṇa*	(5.1.37)
(II 672.9)	*atrottaram / "kāryānyatve prayatnāhetutvam anupalabdhikāraṇānupapatteḥ" (kāraṇānupapatteḥ] kāraṇopapatteḥ* NBh^{Tha}, 304,5)	*lakṣaṇa*	(5.1.38)
(II 673.8)	*kathaṃ punaḥ ṣaṭpakṣī pravartata iti / tatpathaṃ darśayitum āha— "pratiṣedhe 'pi samāno doṣaḥ"*	*lakṣaṇa*	(5.1.39)
(II 674.4)	*sa hi caturthapakṣastha evaṃ vadati / "pratiṣedhavipratiṣedhe pratiṣedhadoṣavad doṣaḥ"*	*lakṣaṇa*	(5.1.41)
(II 674.9)	*sā ca "pratiṣedhaṃ sadoṣam abhyupetya pratiṣedhavipratiṣedhe samāno doṣaprasaṅgo matānujñā"*	*lakṣaṇa*	(5.1.42)
(II 675.3)	*tad etad āha / "svapakṣalakṣaṇāpekṣopapattyupasaṃhāre hetunirdeśe parapakṣadoṣābhyupagamāt samāno doṣaḥ" svapakṣaḥ mūlasādhanavādyuktaḥ prayatnānanantarīyakatvād anityaḥ śabdaḥ iti /*	*lakṣaṇa*	(5.1.43)
(II 677.19)	*jātyanantaraṃ nigrahasthānoddeśāt tallakṣaṇapratipādanārtham āha— "vipratipattir apratipattiś ca nigrahasthānaṃ"*	*lakṣaṇa*	(1.2.19)
(II 678.18)	*ata evānantaram āha— "tadvikalpāj jātinigrahasthānabahutvam"*	*lakṣaṇa*	(1.2.20)
(II 679.4)	*taddvāviṃśatidhā vibhajya darśayati— "pratijñāhāniḥ pratijñāntaraṃ pratijñāvirodhaḥ pratijñāsannyāso hetvantaram arthāntaraṃ nirarthakam avijñātārtham apārthakam aprāptakālaṃ nyūnam adhikaṃ punaruktam ananubhāṣaṇam ajñānam apratibhā vikṣepo matānujñā paryanuyojyopekṣaṇaṃ niranuyojyānuyogo 'pasiddhānto hetvābhāsāś ca nigrahasthānāni"*	*uddeśa*	(5.2.1)
(II 681.12)	*evaṃ sāmānyalakṣaṇaṃ vibhāgaṃ cābhidhāya viśeṣalakṣaṇāny āha— "pratidṛṣṭāntadharmābhyanujñā svadṛṣṭānte pratijñāhāniḥ"*	*lakṣaṇa*	(5.2.2)
(II 683.14)	*"pratijñātārthapratiṣedhe dharmavikalpāt tadarthanirdeśaḥ pratijñāntaram" pratijñātārthapratiṣedhe pareṇa kṛte* [...]	*lakṣaṇa*	(5.2.23)
(II 686.5)	*"pratijñāhetvor virodhaḥ prajñāvirodhaḥ"*	*lakṣaṇa*	(5.2.4)
(II 689.11)	*"pakṣapratiṣedhe pratijñātārthāpanayanaṃ pratijñāsannyāsaḥ" pakṣasādhane pareṇa dūṣite* [...]	*lakṣaṇa*	(5.2.5)
(II 690.19)	*"aviśeṣokte hetau pratiṣiddhe viśeṣam icchato hetvantaram" aviśeṣābhihite hetau pratiṣiddhe* [...]	*lakṣaṇa*	(5.2.6)
(II 692.3)	*"prakṛtād arthād apratisambaddhārtham arthāntaram" prakṛtād arthād arthāntaram tadanaupayikam abhidhataḥ arthāntaraṃ nāma* [...]	*lakṣaṇa*	(5.2.7)
(II 693.9)	*"varṇakramanirdeśavan nirarthakam" abhidheyarahitavarṇānupūrvīprayogamātraṃ nirarthakam nāma* [...]	*lakṣaṇa*	(5.2.8)
(II 695.9)	*"pariṣatprativādibhyāṃ trir abhihitam apy avijñātam avijñātārtham" yat sādhanavākyaṃ dūṣaṇavākyaṃ vā* [...] *avijñātārthaṃ nāma* [...]	*lakṣaṇa*	(5.2.9)
(II 696.13)	*"paurvāparyāyogād apratisambaddhārtham apārthakam" pūrvāparāsaṅgata* [...] *apārthakaṃ nāma* [...]	*lakṣaṇa*	(5.2.10)
(II 698.2)	*"avayavaviparyāsavacanam aprāptakālam" pratijñāhetū-* [...] *aprāptakālaṃ nāma* [...]	*lakṣaṇa*	(5.2.11)
(II 699.4)	*"hīnam anyatamenāpy avayavena nyūnam" paṃcāvayave* [...] *nyūnaṃ nāma* [...]	*lakṣaṇa*	(5.2.12)

NM^Va	Pre-quote, Sūtra, Post-quote	Type	NS
(II 699.19)	"*hetūdāharaṇādhikam adhikam*" *ekenaiva hetunā* [...] *adhikaṃ nāma* [...]	*lakṣaṇa*	(5.2.13)
(II 700.18)	"*śabdārthayoḥ punaruccāraṇaṃ punarvacanam* (*punarvacanam*] *punaruktam* NBh^Tha, 5.2.14) *anyatrānuvādāt*" *arthād apannasya* [...] *punaruktaṃ nāma* [...]	*lakṣaṇa*	(5.2.14)
(II 703.16)	"*vijñātasya pariṣadā trir abhihitasyāpy apratyuccāraṇam ananubhāṣaṇam*" *parṣadā viditasya* [...] *ananubhāṣaṇaṃ nāma* [...]	*lakṣaṇa*	(5.2.16)
(II 706.7)	"*avijñātaṃ cājñānam*" *pariṣadā vijñātasyāpi* [...] *ajñānaṃ nāma* [...]	*lakṣaṇa*	(5.2.17)
(II 707.12)	"*uttarasyāpratipattir apratibhā*" *parapakṣe gṛhīte 'pi* [...] *apratibhā nāma* [...]	*lakṣaṇa*	(5.2.18)
(II 708.11)	"*kāryavyāsaṃgāt kathāvicchedo vikṣepaḥ*" *udgrāhaṇikām upagramya vā* [...]	*lakṣaṇa*	(5.2.19)
(II 710.2)	"*svapakṣe doṣābhyupagamāt parapakṣe doṣaprasaṅgo matānujñā*" *svapakṣe parāpāditadoṣam anuddhṛtya* [...] *matānujñā nāma* [...]	*lakṣaṇa*	(5.2.20)
(II 711.2)	"*nigraha* (*nigraha-*] *nigrahasthāna-* NBh^Tha, 5.2.21) *prāptasyānigrahaḥ paryanuyojyopekṣaṇam*" *paryanuyojyo nāma* [...]	*lakṣaṇa*	(5.2.21)
(II 713.4)	"*anigrahasthāne nigrahasthānābhiyogo niranuyojyānuyogaḥ*" *anujjhitayathocitakramaṃ* [...]	*lakṣaṇa*	(5.2.22)
(II 714.15)	"*siddhāntam abhyupetyāniyamāt kathāprasaṅgo 'pasiddhāntaḥ*" *yaḥ kaṃcana* [...] *saḥ apasiddhāntena parājīyate*	*lakṣaṇa*	(5.2.23)
(II 717.6)	"*hetvābhāsāś ca yathoktāḥ*"	*lakṣaṇa*	(5.2.24)

Abbreviations

Abbreviations of primary sources

The following list of abbreviations is meant for quick reference. The full bibliographical data corresponding to these abbreviations can be found in the list of primary sources below.

ĀḌ^{Ra}	*Āgamaḍambara.* Raghavan, V. and A. Thakur (1964).
Bṛh	*Bṛhatī.* Chinnaswami Shastri, A. (1929).
DhV	*Dhvanyāloka.* Durgaprasad, Pandit and Vasudev Lakshman Shastri Pansikar (1928).
GBh^{Sha}	*Nyāyamañjarīgranthibhaṅga.* Shah, Nagin J. (1972).
HNAV	*Harināmāmṛtavyākaraṇa.* Haridas Shastri (1985).
KKS	*Kādambarīkathāsāra.* Durgaprasad, Pandit and Kashinath Pandurang Parab (1888).
MBh	*Mahābhārata.* Sukthankar, Vishnu S. and S.K. Belvalkar (1933–1959).
MSū	*Mīmāṃsāsūtra.* Abhyankar, Kashinath Vasudev and Ganesh Shastri Ambadas Joshi (1970–1974).
NĀ	*Nyāyālaṅkāra.* Thakur, Anantalal and J.S. Jetly (1981).
NBh^{Ja}	*Nyāyabhāṣya.* Tarkapanchanana, Jayanarayana (1864–1865).
NBh^{Tha}	*Nyāyabhāṣya.* Thakur, Anantalal (1997).

NBhū	*Nyāyabhūṣaṇa*. Yogindrananda Svami (1968).
NKa^{Jha}	*Nyāyakalikā*. Jha, Ganganatha (1925).
NKa^{Ka}	*Nyāyakalikā*. Kataoka, Kei (2013).
NKC	*Nyāyakumudacandra*. Mahendra Kumar, Nyaya Shastri (1938–1941).
NM^{Ga}	*Nyāyamañjarī*. Gangadhara Shastri (1895).
NM^{Gau}	*Nyāyamañjarī*. Gaurinatha Shastri (1982–1984).
NM^{KKa}	*Nyāyamañjarī: Vijñānādvaitavāda*. Kataoka, Kei (2003).
NM^{KKb}	*Nyāyamañjarī: Āgamaprāmāṇya*. Kataoka, Kei (2004).
NM^{KKc}	*Nyāyamañjarī: Īśvarasiddhi*. Kataoka, Kei (2005).
NM^{KKd}	*Nyāyamañjarī: Śāstrārambha*. Kataoka, Kei (2007).
NM^{KKe}	*Nyāyamañjarī: Kumārila's Criticism of Apoha*. Kataoka, Kei (2008).
NM^{KKf}	*Nyāyamañjarī: Buddhist Refutation of Kumārila's Criticism of Apoha*. Kataoka, Kei (2009).
NM^{KKg}	*Nyāyamañjarī: Jayanta's View on Jāti and Apoha*. Kataoka, Kei (2010).
NM^{KKh}	*Nyāyamañjarī: the Buddhist Refutation of Jāti*. Kataoka, Kei (2011).
NM^{Ma}	*Nyāyamañjarī*. Shukla, Suryanarayana and A. Madhvacarya Adya (1969–1971).
NM^{Pa}	*Nyāyamañjarī*. Pancanana Tarkavagisha (1939–1941).
NM^{Sha}	*Nyāyamañjarī*. Shah, Nagin J. (1975–1992).
NM^{Shu}	*Nyāyamañjarī*. Shukla, Suryanarayana (1936).
NM^{Va}	*Nyāyamañjarī*. Varadacharya, K.S. (1969-1983).
NSū	*Nyāyasūtra*. Thakur, Anantalal (1997).
NV	*Nyāyavārttika*. Thakur, Anantalal (1997).

NVTP	*Nyāyavārttikatātparyapariśuddhi*. Thakur, Anantalal (1996).
Pā	*Āṣṭādhyāyīsūtrapāṭha*. Prahlad Giri, Svami (1985).
PrP	*Prakaraṇapañcikā*. Subrahmanya Sastri, A. (1961).
PSṬ	*Pramāṇasamuccayaṭīkā*. Steinkellner, Ernst, Helmut Krasser, and Horst Lasic (2005).
RaV	*Raghuvaṃśa*. Kashinath Pandurang Parab (1925).
RT	*Rājataraṅgiṇī*. Stein, Marc Aurel (1989).
ŚBh	*Śābarabhāṣya*. Abhyankar, Kashinath Vasudev and Ganesh Shastri Ambadas Joshi (1970–1974).
ŚKau	*Śabdakaustubha*. Ramakrishna Shastri (1898).
SphS	*Sphoṭasiddhi*. Biardeau, Madeleine (1958).
ŚPr	*Śṛṅgāraprakāśa*. Raghavan, V. (1998).
$\text{ŚV}^{\text{Dvā}}$	Dvārikādāsa, Śāstrī (1978).
ŚV^{Ra}	*Ślokavārttika*. Ramanatha Shastri, S.K. (1971).
SVR	*Syādvādaratnākara*. Ladhaji, Motilal (1926–1927).
ŚVT^{Ra}	*Ślokavārttikatātparyaṭīkā*. Ramanatha Shastri, S.K. (1971).
TB	*Tattvabindu*. Biardeau, Madeleine (1956).
TR	*Tantrarahasya*. Shamasastry, Rudrapatna (1923).
VKG	*Vṛttikāragrantha*. Frauwallner, Erich (1968).
VMBh^{Bha}	*Vyākaraṇamahābhāṣya*. Bhargava, Shastri et al. (1987).
VMBh^{Ki}	*Vyākaraṇamahābhāṣya*. Kielhorn, Franz (1880-1884).
VP^{Iyer}	*Vākyapadīya*. Subramanya Iyer, K.A. (1966-1973).
VP^{Rau}	*Vākyapadīya*. Rau, Wilhelm (1977).

Abbreviations of catalogues

The following list of abbreviations is meant for quick reference. The full bibliographical data corresponding to these catalogues can be found in the list of secondary sources below.

ABC	*An Annotated Bibliography of the Catalogues of Indian Manuscripts.* Janert, Klaus L. (1965).
BBC	*Bibliographic Survey of Indian Manuscript Catalogues.* Biswas, Subhas C. (1998).
Cat. AL 1911	*A Preliminary List of the Saṃskṛt and Prākṛt Manuscripts in the Adyar Library.* Schrader, F. Otto (1911).
Cat. AL 1928	*A Catalogue of the Sanskrit Manuscripts in the Adyar Library.* Chintamani, T.R. (1928).
Cat. AL 1972	*Descriptive Catalogue of Sanskrit Manuscripts.* Aithal, K. Parameswara (1972).
Cat. AS 1957	*A Descriptive Catalogue of the Vernacular Manuscripts in the Collections of the Royal Asiatic Society of Bengal.* Haraprasada Shastri (1957).
Cat. BHU 1971	*Descriptive Catalogue of Sanskrit Manuscripts in Gaekwad Library, Bharat Kala Bhavan Library and Sanskrit Mahavidyalaya Library.* Tripathi, Ram Shankar (1971).
Cat. BORI 1955	*Descriptive Catalogue of the Government Collections of Manuscripts Deposited at the BORI.* Katre, Sumitra Mangesh (1955).
Cat. DC 1888	*A Catalogue of the Collections of Manuscripts deposited in the Deccan College.* Bhandarkar, Shridhar R. (1888).
Cat. GJRI 1967	*Descriptive Catalogue of Sanskrit Manuscripts in Ganganatha Jha Research Institute.* Mishra, Umesha (1967).

Cat. GOL 1922	*Catalogue of Sanskrit Manuscripts in the GOLMy* (1922).
Cat. JJBh 1972	*New Catalogue of Sanskrit and Prakrit Manuscripts. Jesalmer Collection.* Punyavijayiji, Muni Shri (1972).
Cat. LU 1951	*Catalogue of Oriental Manuscripts in the Lucknow University Library.* Prasad, Kali (1951).
Cat. ÖNB 1990	*Katalog der Sanskrit-Handschriften der Österreichischen Nationalbibliothek.* Slaje, Walter (1990).
Cat. Radh. 1871	*Pustakānāṃ Sūcipatram* (1871).
Cat. Report 1875	*Detailed report of a tour in search of Sanskrit mss. made in Kashmir, Rajputana and Central India.* Bühler, Georg (1877).
Cat. SBhL 1962	*A Descriptive Catalogue of Sanskrit Manuscripts Acquired for and Deposited in the Sanskrit University Library (Saraswati Bhavan), Varanasi, During the Years 1791-1950* (1964).
Cat. SC 1902	*List of Sanskrit, Jaina and Hindi Manuscripts. Purchased by Order of Government and Deposited in the Sanskrit College, Benares, during 1897, 1898, 1899, 1900 and 1901* (1902).
Cat. SORL 1989	*A Catalogue of Sanskrit Manuscripts.* Kaul, Sri Kanth and D.N. Yach (1989).
Cat. Stein 1894	*Catalogue of the Sanskrit Manuscripts in the Raghunatha Temple Library of His Highness the Maharaja of Jammu and Kashmir.* Stein, Marc Aurel (1894).
Cat. VOHD 2010	*Verzeichnis der Orientalischen Handschriften in Deutschland. Band II, 17.* Ehlers, Gerhard (1987).
CC	*Catalogus Catalogorum* (1962).
NCC1	*New Catalogus Catalogorum.* Raghavan, V. (1968).
NCC3	*New Catalogus Catalogorum.* Raghavan, V. (1967).

Bibliographical references

Primary sources

Abhyankar, Kashinath Vasudev and Ganesh Shastri Ambadas Joshi, eds. (1970–1974 (2nd ed.)). *Mīmāṃsādarśana*. Ānandāśramasaṃskṛtagranthāvāli 97. Vol. 1: MS 1.1, with Śābarabhāṣya and Prabhābhidhā commentary by Vaidyanath Shastri. Vol. 2: MS 1.2–2.1, with Śābarabhāṣya and Tantravarttika. Vol. 3: MS 2.2–2.4, with Śābarabhāṣya and Tantravarttika. Vol. 4: MS 3.1–3.8, with Śābarabhāṣya and Tantravarttika. Vol. 5: MS 4.1–7.4, with Śābarabhāṣya and Ṭupṭīkā. Vol. 6: MS 8.1–10.8, with Śābarabhāṣya and Ṭupṭīkā. Vol. 7: MS 11.1–12.4, with Śābarabhāṣya and Ṭupṭīkā. 1st ed. 1930–1933. Pune: Anandasrama [**MSū-ŚBh-TV**].

Bhargava, Shastri et al., eds. (1987). *Vyākaraṇamahābhāṣya of Patañjali with Bhāṣyapradīpa of Kaiyaṭa and Uddyota of Nageśa Bhaṭṭa.* Six volumes. 1st ed. Nirnyaya Sagar Press, 1917–1945. Delhi: Chaukhamba Sanskrit Pratishthan [**VMBh^{Bha}**].

Biardeau, Madeleine, ed. (1956). *Le Tattvabindu de Vācaspatimiśra.* Edition critique, traduction et introduction. Pondichéry: Institut Français d'Indologie [**TB**].

— ed. (1958). *La démonstration du sphoṭa par Maṇḍana Miśra. Introduction, traduction et commentaire.* Pondichéry: Institut Français d'Indologie [**SphS**].

Caland, W., ed. (1904–1913). *Baudhāyana Śrauta Sūtra. Belonging to the Taittirīya Saṃhitā.* 2nd ed. 1982 Munshiram Manoharlal, New Delhi. Calcutta: Asiatic Society

Chinnaswami Shastri, A., ed. (1929). *Bṛhatī of Prabhākara Miśra with the commentary Ṛjuvimalā of Śālikanātha Miśra [reaching until ad MS 1.1.32]*. Chowkhambā Sanskrit Series 391. Benares: Vidya Vilas Press [**Bṛh**].

Dezső, Csaba, ed. (2004). "'Much Ado About Religion'. A Critical Edition and Annotated Translation of the Āgamaḍambara, a Satirical Play by the ninth century Kashmirian philosopher Bhaṭṭa Jayanta". Submitted in Hilary Term 2004 for the Degree of Doctor of Philosophy. Available for download at http://www.claysanskritlibrary.org/downloads.php. PhD Thesis. Oxford: Balliol College

Durgaprasad, Pandit and Kashinath Pandurang Parab, eds. (1888). *The Kādambarīkathāsāraḥ of Abhinanda*. Kāvyamālā 11. Bombay: Nirnaya Sagar Press [**KKS**].

Durgaprasad, Pandit and Vasudev Lakshman Shastri Pansikar, eds. (1928). *The Dhvanyāloka of Ānandavardhanāchārya. With the Commentary of Abhinavaguptāchārya*. Kāvyamālā 25. 3rd revised edition. Bombay: Pandurang Jawaji [**DhV**].

Dvārikādāsa, Śāstrī, ed. (1978). *Ślokavārttika of Śrī Kumārila Bhaṭṭa with the Commentary Nyāyaratnākara of Śrī Pārthasārathi Miśra*. Prāchyabhārati Series 10. Varanasi [**ŚV^{Dvā}**].

Dwivedi, Parasa Nath, ed. (2004). *The Kāmasūtra of Śrī Vātsyāyanamuni. With the Commentary Jayamaṅgalā by Śrī Yaśodhara*. Chaukhamba Surbharati Granthamala 299. Edited with Manoramā Hindi Commentary. Varanasi: Chaukhamba Surbharati Prakashan

Frauwallner, Erich, ed. (1968). *Materialien zur ältesten Erkenntnislehre der Karmamīmāṃsā*. Veröffentlichungen der Kommission für Sprachen und Kulturen Süd- und Ostasiens 6. Wien: Österreichische Akademie der Wissenschaften [**VKG**].

Gangadhara Shastri, ed. (1895). *The Nyāyamañjarī of Jayanta Bhaṭṭa*. Vizianagram Sanskrit Series 8. Benares: E.J. Lazarus and Co. [**NM^{Ga}**].

Gaurinatha Shastri, ed. (1982–1984). *Nyāyamañjarī of Jayanta Bhaṭṭa. With the commentary 'Granthibhaṅga' by Cakradhara.* Varanasi: Sampūrṇānanda Saṃskṛta Viśvavidyālaya [NM^Gau].

Haridas Shastri, ed. (1985). *Harināmāmṛtavyākaraṇa of Jīva Gosvāmī.* Vrindaban: Śrī Gadādharagaura Press [**HNAV**].

Jha, Ganganatha, ed. (1925). *The Nyāya Kalikā of Bhaṭṭa Jayanta.* The Princess of Wales Sarasvati Bhavana Texts 17. Printed by the Vidya Vilas Press. Benares: Government Sanskrit Library [NKa^Jha].

Kashinath Pandurang Parab, ed. (1925). *Raghuvaṃśa of Kālidāsa.* With the commentary (the Sañjīvinī) of Mallinātha. Revised by Vasudev Lakshman Shastri Pansikar. 9th revised edition. Bombay: Pandurang Jawaji, NIrnaya Sagar [**RaV**].

Kataoka, Kei, ed. (2003). "Critical Edition of the Vijñānādvaitavāda Section of Bhaṭṭa Jayanta's Nyāyamañjarī". In: *The Memoirs of the Institute of Oriental Culture* 144, pp. 115–155 [NM^KKa].

— ed. (2004). "Critical Edition of the Āgamaprāmāṇya Section of Bhaṭṭa Jayanta's Nyāyamañjarī". In: *The Memoirs of the Institute of Oriental Culture* 146, pp. 131–175 [NM^KKb].

— ed. (2005). "Critical Edition of the Īśvarasiddhi Section of Bhaṭṭa Jayanta's Nyāyamañjarī". In: *The Memoirs of the Institute of Oriental Culture* 148, pp. 79–132 [NM^KKc].

— ed. (2007a). "Critical Edition of the Śāstrārambha Section of Bhaṭṭa Jayanta's Nyāyamañjarī". In: *The Memoirs of the Institute of Oriental Culture* 150, pp. 123–170 [NM^KKd].

— ed. (2008). "A Critical Edition of Bhaṭṭa Jayanta's Nyāyamañjarī: The Section on Kumārila's Refutation of the Apoha Theory". In: *The Memoirs of the Institute of Oriental Culture* 154, pp. 1–31 [NM^KKe].

— ed. (2009). "A Critical Edition of Bhaṭṭa Jayanta's Nyāyamañjarī: The Buddhist Refutation of Kumārila's Criticism of Apoha Theory". In: *The Memoirs of the Institute of Oriental Culture* 156, pp. 1–41 [NM^KKf].

Kataoka, Kei, ed. (2010). "A Critical Edition of Bhaṭṭa Jayanta's Nyāyamañjarī: Jayanta's View on Jāti and Apoha". In: *The Memoirs of the Institute for Advanced Studies on Asia* 158, pp. 61–113 [**NM**[KKg]].

— ed. (2011). "A Critical Edition of Bhaṭṭa Jayanta's Nyāyamañjarī: The Buddhist Refutation of *jāti*". In: *The Memoirs of the Institute for Advanced Studies on Asia* 160, pp. 1–43 [**NM**[KKh]].

— ed. (2013). "A Critical Edition of Bhaṭṭa Jayanta's Nyāyakalikā. First Part". In: *The Memoirs of the Institute for Advanced Studies on Asia* 163, pp. 1–53 [**NKa**[Ka]].

Kielhorn, Franz, ed. (1880-1884). *The Vyākaraṇa-Mahābhāṣya of Patañjali.* 3 vols. Government Central Book Depot [**VMBh**[Ki]].

Ladhaji, Motilal, ed. (1926–1927). *Syādvādaratnākara of Vādidevasūri (śrīmadvādidevasūriviracitaḥ pramāṇanayatattvālokālaṅkāraḥ tadvyākhyā ca syādvādaratnākara).* Ārhatamataprabhākara 4. 5 vols.. Dated Vīrasaṃvat 2453, presumably Śvetambara age (527 CE). Puṇyapatana: Hanuman Printing Press [**SVR**].

Mahendra Kumar, Nyaya Shastri, ed. (1938–1941). *Nyāyakumudacandra of Śrīmat Prabhācandrācārya. A Commentary on Bhaṭṭākalaṅkadevas' Laghīyastraya.* Girgaon, Bombay: Pandit Nathu Ram Premi [**NKC**].

Oka, Krishnaji Govind, ed. (1913). *Amarakośa. The Nâmalingânus'âsana (Amarakosha) of Amarasimha. With the Commentary (Amarakoshodghâtana) of Kshîrasvâmin.* Edited with critical Notes, an Essay on the time of Amarasimha and Kshîrasvâmin, a list of works and authors quoted, glossary of words, etc. etc. Poona: Law Printing Press, D.G. Khandekar

Pancanana Tarkavagisha, ed. (1939–1941). *Nyāyamañjarī of Jayantabhaṭṭa.* Vol. 1. Two volumes. The first volume covers NM 1, the second NM 2. No other volumes were published. Kolkata: Calcutta University Press. Sanskrit text of NM 1 and 2, in Bengali script, with Bengali translation and commentary [**NM**[Pa]].

Prahlad Giri, Svami, ed. (1985). *Aṣṭādhyāyīsūtrapāṭha of Pāṇini.* Varanasi: Kṛṣṇadāsa Academy [**Pā**].

Raghavan, V., ed. (1998). *Śṛṅgāraprakāśa of Bhoja, Part I.* Harvard Oriental Series 53. Cambridge, MA: Department of Sanskrit and Indian Studies, Harvard University [**ŚPr**].

Raghavan, V. and A. Thakur, eds. (1964). *Jayantabhaṭṭakṛtaṃ saṃmatanāṭakāgamāḍambaraṃ nāmarūpakam.* Darbhanga: Mithila Institute [**ĀḌ**^{Ra}].

Ramakrishna Shastri, ed. (1898). *Śabdakaustubha of Bhaṭṭojī Dīkṣita.* Printed in ten fascicles at the Raj-Rajeshwary Press. Varanasi: Chowkhamba [**ŚKau**].

Ramanatha Shastri, S.K., ed. (1971c). *Ślokavārttikavyākhyā Tātparyaṭīkā of Umveka Bhaṭṭa.* Revised by K. Kunjunni Raja and R. Thangaswamy. 1st Ed. 1940. University of Madras [**ŚV-ŚVT**].

Rau, Wilhelm, ed. (1977). *Bhartṛharis Vākyapadīya.* Deutschen Morgenländischen Gesellschaft, Band XLII, 4. Wiesbaden: Franz Steiner [**VP**^{Rau}].

Sarup, Lakshman, ed. (1967). *The Nighaṇṭu and the Nirukta. The Oldest Indian Treatise on Etymology, Philology, and Semantics.* 2nd reprint (1st ed. 1926). Critically edited from original manuscripts and translated for the first time into English, with introduction, exegetical and critical notes, three indexes and eight appendices. Motilal Banarsidass

Shah, Nagin J., ed. (1972). *Cakradhara's Nyāyamañjarīgranthibhaṅga.* Lalbhai Dalpatbhai series, 35. Ahmedabad: L.D. Institute of Indology [**GBh**^{Sha}].

— ed. (1975–1992). *Jayanta Bhaṭṭa's Nyāyamañjarī.* 5 vols. Sanskrit text in Gujarati script, with Gujarati translation. Vol. 1, L.D. Series 48, 1st āhnika: 1975; vol. 2, L.D. series 67, 2nd āhnika: 1978; vol. 3, L.D. series 97, 3rd āhnika: 1984; vol. 4, L.D. series 108, 4th–5th āhnikas: 1989; vol. 5, L.D. series 115, 6th–9th āhnikas: 1992. Ahmedabad: L.D. Institute of Indology [**NM**^{Sha}].

Shamasastry, Rudrapatna, ed. (1923). *Tantrarahasya of Rāmānujācārya.* Baroda: Central Library [**TR**].

Shukla, Suryanarayana, ed. (1936). *Nyāyamañjarī: Gautamasūtratātpāryavivṛti.* 2 vols. Kashi Sanskrit Series, 106. Benares: Jaya Krishna Das Haridas Gupta, Vidya Vilas Press [**NM**$^{\mathbf{Shu}}$].

Shukla, Suryanarayana and A. Madhvacarya Adya, eds. (1969–1971). *The Nyāyamañjarī of Jayanta Bhaṭṭa. With Notes by Pt. Sūryanārāyaṇa Śukla.* 2 vols. Vārāṇasī: Chowkhamba Sanskrit Series Office. Revised version of the 1936 edition by S.N. Śukla [**NM**$^{\mathbf{Ma}}$].

Stein, Marc Aurel, ed. (1989b). *Kalhaṇa's Rājataraṅgiṇī. Chronicle of the Kings of Kaśmīr.* Vol. 3. Sanskrit text with critical notes. 1st ed. 1892. Delhi: Motilal Banarsidass [**RT**].

Steinkellner, Ernst, Helmut Krasser, and Horst Lasic, eds. (2005). *Jinendrabuddhi's Viśalāmalavatī Pramāṇasamuccayaṭīkā. Chapter 1.* Beijing–Vienna: Austrian Academy of Sciences Press [**PSṬ**].

Subrahmanya Sastri, A., ed. (1961). *Prakaraṇa Pañcikā of Śālikanātha Miśra with the Nyāya-Siddhi of Jaipuri Nārāyaṇa Bhaṭṭa.* Darśana Series 4. Benares: Benares Hindu University [**PrP**].

Subramanya Iyer, K.A., ed. (1966-1973). *Vākyapadīya of Bhartṛhari.* Pune: Deccan College [**VP**$^{\mathbf{Iyer}}$].

Sukthankar, Vishnu S. and S.K. Belvalkar, eds. (1933–1959). *The Mahābhārata.* 15 vols. Poona: Bhandarkar Oriental Research Institute [**MBh**].

Tarkapanchanana, Jayanarayana, ed. (1864–1865). *Nyāyadarśana with the Commentary of Vātsyāyana.* Bibliotheca Indica 50. Calcutta: Asiatic Society of Bengal [**NBh**$^{\mathbf{Ja}}$].

Thakur, Anantalal, ed. (1996). *Nyāyavārttikatātparyapariśuddhi of Udayanācārya.* Nyāyacaturgranthika 4. Delhi: Indian Council of Philosophical Research [**NVTP**].

— ed. (1997a). *Gautamīyanyāyadarśana with Bhāṣya of Vātsyāyana.* Nyāyacaturgranthikā 1. For the first chapter, it is the revised edition of the same author's edition of the Nyāyacaturgranthika, Adhyāya 1. Mithila Institute Series Ancient Text 20. Darbhanga 1967. New Delhi: Indian Council of Philosophical Research [**NBh-NSū**].

– ed. (1997c). *Nyāyabhāṣyavārttika of Bhāradvāja Uddyotakara*. Nyāyacaturgranthikā 2. Indian Council of Philosophical Research [**NV**].

Thakur, Anantalal and J.S. Jetly, eds. (1981). *Nyāyālaṅkāra (Pañcaprasthānanyāyamahātarkaviṣamapadavyākhyā). A Commentary on the five classical texts of the Nyāya Philosophy of Abhayatilaka Upādhyāya*. Baroda: Oriental Institute [**NĀ**].

Vaidya, Parashuram Lakshman, ed. (1969–1971). *The Harivaṃśa. Being the Khila or Supplement of the Mahābhārata*. 2 vols. For the first time critically edited. Vol. 1 Critical text, vol. 2 Appendices. Poona: Bhandarkar Oriental Research Institute

Varadacharya, K.S., ed. (1969-1983). *Nyāyamañjarī: with Ṭippaṇī Nyāyasaurabha*. 2 vols. Mysore: Oriental Research Institute [**NM^{Va}**].

Varakale, Vaidyanatha Shastri, ed. (1927). *Vṛttaratnākara of Bhaṭṭa Kedāra*. With a Commentary of Bhaṭṭa Nārāyaṇa, as well as the Śrutabodha, the Chandomañjarī and the Suvṛttatilaka. Varanasi: Chowkhamba

Yogindrananda Svami, ed. (1968). *Nyāyabhūṣaṇa of Bhāsarvajña*. With explanatory gloss in Sanskrit by the editor. Vārāṇasī: Ṣaḍdarśana Prakāśana Pratiṣṭhānam [**NBhū**].

Secondary sources

Aithal, K. Parameswara, ed. (1972). *Descriptive Catalogue of Sanskrit Manuscripts*. Vol. 8. Sāṃkhya, Yoga, Vaiśeṣika and Nyāya. Madras: The Adyar Library and Research Centre [**Cat. AL 1972**].

Aufrecht, Theodor (1962). *Catalogus Catalogorum. An alphabetical register of Sanskrit works and authors*. 2 vols. Wiesbaden: Franz Steiner. 1st ed. 1891, 1896, 1903, in three parts [**CC**].

Author unknown (1902). *List of Sanskrit, Jaina and Hindi Manuscripts. Purchased by Order of Government and Deposited in the Sanskrit College, Benares, during 1897, 1898, 1899, 1900 and 1901*. Allahabad: Government Press, U.P., of Agra and Oudh [**Cat. SC 1902**].

Author unknown (1922). *Catalogue of Sanskrit Manuscripts in the Government Oriental Library of Mysore.* Mysore: Government Branch Press [**Cat. GOL 1922**].

– (1964). *A Descriptive Catalogue of Sanskrit Manuscripts Acquired for and Deposited in the Sanskrit University Library (Saraswati Bhavan), Varanasi, During the Years 1791-1950.* Vol. 8. Nyāya–Vaiśeṣika. Varanasi: Shri Vishveshwara Press, Sanskrit University [**Cat. SBhL 1962**].

Bhandarkar, Shridhar R., ed. (1888). *A Catalogue of the Collections of Manuscripts deposited in the Deccan College.* Bombay: Government Central Press [**Cat. DC 1888**].

Biswas, Subhas C., ed. (1998). *Bibliographic Survey of Indian Manuscript Catalogues. Being a Union List of Manuscript Catalogues.* Delhi: Eastern Book Linkers [**BBC**].

Borsani Scalabrino, Giuseppina (1962). "Il Kādambarīkathāsāra di Abhinanda". In: *Estratto dei Rendiconti, Classe di Lettere, Istituto Lombardo – Accademia di Scienze e Lettere* 96, pp. 133–190

Bühler, Georg (1877). *Detailed report of a tour in search of Sanskrit mss. made in Kashmir, Rajputana and Central India.* Ed. by Georg Bühler. Extra number of the *Journal of the Bombay branch of the Royal Asiatic Society.* Bombay-London: Society's Library, Town hall (Bombay). Trübner & Co. (London) [**Cat. Report 1875**].

Burnell, A.C. (1878). *Elements of South-Indian Paleography from the Fourth to the Seventeenth Century A.D. Being an Introduction to the Study of South-Indian Inscriptions and Mss.* 2nd enlarged and improved edition. London: Trübner & Co., 57 & 59 Ludgate Hill

Cardona, G.R. (1981). *Antropologia della scrittura.* Torino: Loescher

Chintamani, T.R., ed. (1928). *A Catalogue of the Sanskrit Manuscripts in the Adyar Library.* Vol. 2.2. Adyar Library Series. By the Pandits at the Library. Madras: Adyar Library [**Cat. AL 1928**].

Cort, John E. (1998). "Who is a King?" In: *Open Boundaries.* Ed. by John E. Cort. Albany, NY: State University of New York Press, pp. 85–110.

Cunningham, Alexander (1871). *The Ancient Geography of India. The Buddhist Period, Including the Campaigns of Alexander, and the Travels of Hwen-Thsang*. London: Trübner and Co.

D'Arco Avalle, Silvio (2002). *Principi di critica testuale*. Revised 2nd ed.; 1st ed. 1972. Padova: Antenore

Devdutt Shastri, ed. (1992). *The Kāmasūtra of Śrī Vātsyāyanamuni. With the Jayamaṅgalā Sanskrit Commentary of Śrī Yaśodhara*. Chaukhamba Surbharati Granthamala 299. Edited with Hindi Commentary. Varanasi: Chaukhamba Sanskrit Sansthan. 4th edition. 1st ed. 1964

Dezső, Csaba, ed. (2005). *Much ado about religion*. The Clay Sanskrit library. New York: New York University Press. Sanskrit text and translation of Bhaṭṭa Jayanta's *Āgamaḍambara* [**ĀḌ^{De}**].

Dundas, Paul (2002). *The Jains*. 2nd ed. (1st ed. 1992). London and New York: Routledge

Ehlers, Gerhard, ed. (1987). *Verzeichnis der Orientalischen Handschriften in Deutschland. Band II, 17: Indische Handschriften*. Stuttgard: Franz Steiner [**Cat. VOHD 2010**].

Einicke, Katrin (2009). *Korrektur, Differenzierung und Abkürzung in indischen Inschriften und Handschriften*. Abhandlungen für die Kunde des Morgenlandes 68. Wiesbaden: Deutsche Morgenländische Gesellschaft, Harrassowitz Verlag

Esposito, Anna Aurelia (2012). "The South Indian Drama Manuscripts". In: *Aspects of Manuscript Culture in South India*. Ed. by Saraju Rath. Brill's Indological Library 40. Leiden: Brill, pp. 81–98.

Fowler, D.C. (1951). "Contamination in Manuscripts of the A-Text of Piers the Plowman". In: *PMLA (Publications of the Modern Language Association of America)* 4, pp. 495–504

Frauwallner, Erich (1936). "Beiträge zur Geschichte des Nyāya: I. Jayanta und seine Quellen". In: *Wiener Zeitschrift für die Kunde des Morgenlandes* 43, pp. 263–278. Reprinted in *Kleine Schriften*, eds. Gerhard Oberhammer and Ernst Steinkellner, Franz Steiner Verlag Gmbh, Wiesbaden 1982, pp. 145–160.

Garge, Damodar Vishnu (1952). *Citations in Śabara-bhāṣya. A Study.* Deccan College Dissertion Series 8. Pune: Deccan College

Gaskell, Philip (1972). *A New Introduction to Bibliography.* Oxford: Clarendon Press

Graheli, Alessandro (2003). "Teoria dello *sphoṭa* nel sesto *āhnika* della *Nyāyamañjarī* di Jayanta Bhaṭṭa". Tesi di Laurea (MA). Roma: Università degli Studi "Sapienza"

– (2012a). "A Preliminary List and Description of the Nyāyamañjarī Manuscripts". In: *Journal of Indian Philosophy* 40. DOI: 10.1007/s10781-012-9155-2, pp. 317–337

– (2012b). "The choice of the best reading in Jayanta Bhaṭṭa's Nyāyamañjarī". In: *The Study of Asia between Antiquity and Modernity.* Ed. by Elisa Freschi et al. Special issue of RSO (*Rivista degli Studi Orientali*), no. 84. Rome: University of Rome "Sapienza", pp. 107–122.

– (2015a). "Book review: Ehlers, Gerhard: Indische Handschriften Teil 17. Die Śāradā-Handschriften der Sammlung Janert der Staats-bibliothek zu Berlin – Preussischer Kulturbesitz. Stuttgart: Franz Steiner Verlag 2010". In: *Orientalistische Literaturzeitung* 110.2. DOI 10.1515/olzg-2015-0059

– (2015b). "Epistemology of Textual Re-use in the *Nyāyamañjarī*". In: *Journal of Indian Philosophy* 43.2–3. DOI: 10.1007/s10781-014-9234-7

– (forthcoming[a]). "The Editio Princeps of the NBh". In: *Shaping the Sciences of the Past. Proceedings of the SAW–ERC Workshop, Paris, June 17–21 2013.*

– (forthcoming[b]). "The Force of Tātparya: Bhaṭṭa Jayanta and Abhinavagupta". In: *Around Abhinavagupta – Aspects of the Intellectual History of Kashmir from the 9th to the 11th Centuries.* Ed. by Eli Franco and Isabell Ratié. Proceedings of the Abhinavagupta conference, Leipzig 2013. Wien: Verlag der Österreichischen Akademie der Wissenschaften.

Grünendahl, Reinhold (2001). *South Indian Scripts in Sanskrit Manuscripts and Prints.* Wiesbaden: Harassowitz Verlag

Gupta, Brahmānanda (1963). *Die Wahrnehmungslehre in der Nyāyamañjarī.* Walldorf-Hessen: Verlag für Orientkunde Dr. H. Vorndran

Hacker, Paul (1951). "Jayantabhaṭṭa und Vācaspatimiśra, ihre Zeit und ihre Bedeutung für die Chronologie des Vedānta". In: *Beiträge zur indischen Philologie und Altertumskunde.* Alt- und neuindische Studien 7. Hamburg: Cram, de Gruyter. Reprinted in *Kleine Schriften*, ed. Lambert Schmithausen, Franz Steiner Verlag Gmbh, Wiesbaden 1978, pp. 110–119.

Haraprasada Shastri, ed. (1957). *A Descriptive Catalogue of the Vernacular Manuscripts in the Collections of the Royal Asiatic Society of Bengal.* Vol. 11. Revised by N.C. Vedāntatīrtha and C. Cakravarti. Kolkata: Asiatic Society of Bengal [**Cat. AS 1957**].

Hegde, R.D. (1983). "Bhaṭṭa Jayanta". In: *Annals of the Bhandarkar Oriental Research Institute* 64, pp. 1–15

Inglese, Giorgio (1999). *Come si legge un'edizione critica. Elementi di filologia italiana.* Roma: Carocci

Janert, Klaus L. (1965). *An Annotated Bibliography of the Catalogues of Indian Manuscripts.* Ed. by Klaus L. Janert. Wiesbaden: F. Steiner [**ABC**].

Kapadia, H.R. (1937). "Foliation of Jaina Manuscripts and Letter-Numerals". In: *Annals of the Bhandarkar Oriental Research Institute* 18, pp. 171–186

Kataoka, Kei (2007b). "Was Bhaṭṭa Jayanta a Paippalādin?" In: *The Atharvaveda and its Paippalādaśākhā. Historical and Philological Papers on a Vedic Tradition.* Ed. by Arlo Griffiths and Annette Schmiedchen. Geisteskultur Indiens: Texte und Studien 11. Aachen: Shaker Verlag, pp. 319–333.

Katre, Sumitra Mangesh, ed. (1955). *Descriptive Catalogue of the Government Collections of Manuscripts Deposited at the Bhandarkar Oriental Research Institute.* Vol. 9, part 2. Pune: BORI [**Cat. BORI 1955**].

Kaul, Sri Kanth and D.N. Yach, eds. (1989). *A Catalogue of Sanskrit Manuscripts.* Srinagar: The Research and Publication Department, Jammu & Kashmir Government [**Cat. SORL 1989**].

Kavi, M. Ramakrishna (1940). "Bhaṭṭa Jayanta and Yaśovarman of Kashmir". In: *D. R. Bhandarkar Volume*

Maas, Paul (1958). *Textual Criticism.* Tr. by Barbara Fowler from the 2nd German edition (1949) and including changes from the 3rd (1957). Original German edition published in 1927. Oxford: Clarendon Press

Maas, Philipp A. (2009–2010). "Computer Aided Stemmatics – The Case of Fifty–Two Text Versions of Carakasaṃhitā Vimānasthāna 8.67–157". In: *Wiener Zeitschrift für die Kunde Südasiens* 52–53, pp. 63–119

Maddison, David R. and Wayne P. Maddison (2003). *MacClade 4. Version 4.06.* Updates and more information available at http://macclade.org. Sunderland, MA: Sinauer Associates, Inc.

Malato, Enrico (2008). *Lessico filologico. Un approccio alla filologia.* Roma: Salerno Editrice

Marui, Hiroshi (2000). "Some Remarks on Jayanta's Writings: Is Nyāyakalikā his Authentic Work?" In: *The Way to Liberation. Indological Studies in Japan.* Ed. by Sengaku Mayeda. Vol. 1. Delhi: Manohar, pp. 91–106.

– (2008). "On the autorship of the Nyāyakalikā again". In: *Journal of Indian and Buddhist Studies* 56, pp. 27–35

Matilal, Bimal Krishna (1977). *Nyāya-Vaiśeṣika.* A History of Indian Literature 6. Wiesbaden: Otto Harrassowitz

Mishra, Umesha, ed. (1967). *Descriptive Catalogue of Sanskrit Manuscripts in Ganganatha Jha Research Institute.* Vol. 1. Allahabad: Ganganatha Jha Research Institute [**Cat. GJRI 1967**].

Mortara Garavelli, Bice (2007). *Prontuario di punteggiatura.* 1st ed. 2003. Bari: Laterza

Moser, Heike (2012). "From Palmleaves to a Multimedia Databank: A Note on the 'Bhāsa-Project'". In: *Aspects of Manuscript Culture in South India*. Ed. by Saraju Rath. Brill's Indological Library 40. Leiden: Brill, pp. 139–156.

Muroya, Yasutaka (2006). "Some Observations on the Manuscript Transmission of the Nyāyabhāṣya". In: *Journal of Indological Studies* 18, pp. 1–62

— (2009–2010). "A Study on the Marginalia in Some Nyāyamañjarī Manuscripts: The Reconstruction of a Lost Portion of the Nyāyamañjarīgranthibhaṅga". In: *Wiener Zeitschrift für die Kunde Südasiens* 52–53, pp. 213–267

Naik, Bapurao S. (1971). *Typography of Devanagari*. Vol. 3. Revised edition. 1st ed. 1965. xxxi, 421 p. illus. (part fold.), facsims. 22 cm. At head of title: Government of Maharashtra. Vol. I: i–xxxii, 1–324 (history of the script and fonts). Vol. 2: i–xiv, 327–668 (evolution of typesetting and techniques). Vol. 3: 1–38, 113 plates (specimen, fac-similes). Bombay: Directorate of Languages

Nardella, Paola (2006). "Lo status della scienza grammaticale nella Nyāyamañjarī. Edizione e traduzione annotata della terza parte del sesto āhnika." PhD thesis. Roma: Università degli Studi "Sapienza"

Oberhammer, Gerhard (1962). "On the sources in Jayanta Bhaṭṭa and Uddyotakara". In: *Wiener Zeitschrift für die Kunde Süd- und Ostasiens* 6, pp. 91–150

O'Hara, Robert and Peter Robinson (1993). "Computer-Assisted Methods of Stemmatic Analysis". In: *The Canterbury Tales Project*. Ed. by Norman Blake and Peter Robinson. Oxford: Office for Humanities Communication, pp. 53–74.

Pasquali, Giorgio (1988). *Storia della tradizione e critica del testo*. 1st ed. Le Monnier, Firenze 1934. Firenze: Casa editrice Le lettere

Pecchia, Cristina (2009–2010). "Transmission-specific (In)utility, or Dealing with Contamination: Samples from the Textual Tradition of the Carakasaṃhitā". In: *Wiener Zeitschrift für die Kunde Südasiens* 52–53, pp. 121–159

Potter, Karl H., ed. (1977). *Indian Metaphysics and Epistemology: the tradition of Nyāya-Vaiśeṣika up to Gaṅgeśa*. Encyclopedia of Indian Philosophies, vol. 2. Princeton, Delhi: Princeton University Press, Motilal Banarsidass

Prasad, Kali, ed. (1951). *Catalogue of Oriental Manuscripts in the Lucknow University Library.* Lucknow: P.P. Kapur, Ram Kumar Press [**Cat. LU 1951**].

Punyavijayiji, Muni Shri, ed. (1972). *New Catalogue of Sanskrit and Prakrit Manuscripts. Jesalmer Collection.* Ahmedabad: L.D. Institute of Indology [**Cat. JJBh 1972**].

Raghavan, V. (1960). "Why was Jayantabhaṭṭa known as the Vṛttikāra?" In: *Professor P.K. Gode Commemoration Volume.* Ed. by H.L. Hariyappa and Madhukar Mangesh Patkar. Poona Oriental Series 93. Poona: Oriental Book Agency, pp. 173–174.

– ed. (1967). *New Catalogus Catalogorum. An alphabetical register of Sanskrit and allied works and authors (ū-kārtavīrya°).* Vol. 3. Madras: University of Madras [**NCC3**].

– ed. (1968). *New Catalogus Catalogorum. An alphabetical register of Sanskrit and allied works and authors. Revised edition (a).* Vol. 1. Madras: University of Madras. 1st ed. 1949, with a preface by C. Kunhan Raja. This is a revised edition of that first volume of the NCC with an addition of more than 100 pages. [**NCC1**].

– (1978). *Bhoja's Śṛṅgāra Prakāśa.* Study. 3rd revised and enlarged edition. Adyar, Madras: Punarvasu, Vasanta Press, The Theosophical Society

– (1980). *Abhinavagupta and His Works.* Chaukhambha Oriental Research Studies 20. Varanasi: Chaukhambha

Rajaram Shastri (1871). *Pustakānāṃ Sūcipatram.* According to the *Catalogus Catalogorum*, a list of the manuscripts belonging to Radhakrishna Pandit of Lahore. The list is available in Tübingen (Universitätsbibliothek), Berlin (Staatsbibliothek Preußischer Kulturbesitz) and London (India Office, British Library). It was compiled and/or printed in 1871 or before that, according to a hand-written note present on the first page of the Tübingen copy. [**Cat. Radh. 1871**].

Rath, Saraju (2012a). "Aspects of Manuscript Culture in South India". In: *Aspects of Manuscript Culture in South India*. Ed. by Saraju Rath. Brill's Indological Library 40. Leiden: Brill, pp. 187–206.

— ed. (2012b). *Aspects of Manuscript Culture in South India*. Brill's Indological Library 40. Leiden: Brill

Robinson, Peter and Robert O'Hara (1996). "Cladistic Analysis of an Old Norse Manuscript Tradition". In: *Research in Humanities Computing* 4, pp. 115–137

Schrader, F. Otto, ed. (1911). *A Preliminary List of the Saṃskṛt and Prākṛt Manuscripts in the Adyar Library*. Vol. 1. By the Paṇḍits of the Library. Madras: Adyar Library [**Cat. AL 1911**].

Segre, Cesare (1999). *Avviamento all'analisi del testo letterario*. 1st edition 1985. Torino: Einaudi

Slaje, Walter (1986). "Untersuchungen zur Chronologie einiger Nyāya-Philosophen". In: *Studien zur Indologie und Iranistik* 11–12, pp. 245–278

— ed. (1990). *Katalog der Sanskrit-Handschriften der Österreichischen Nationalbibliothek*. Sammlungen Marcus Aurel Stein un Carl Alexander von Hügel. Wien: Verlag der Österreichischen Akademie der Wissenschaften [**Cat. ÖNB 1990**].

— (2012). "Wann, Wo und Weshalb schrieb Bhaṭṭa Jayanta seine 'Blütenrispe am Baum des Nyāya'?" In: *Highland Philology. Results of a Text-Related Kashmir Panel at the 31st DOT, Marburg 2010*. Ed. by Roland Steiner. Halle (Saale): Universitätsverlag Halle-Wittenberg, pp. 121–142.

Speijer, Jacob Samuel (1886). *Sanskrit Syntax*. Leiden: E.J. Brill

Stein, Marc Aurel, ed. (1894). *Catalogue of the Sanskrit Manuscripts in the Raghunatha Temple Library of His Highness the Maharaja of Jammu and Kashmir*. Bombay: Nirnaya Sagar Press [**Cat. Stein 1894**].

— ed. (1989a). *Kalhaṇa's Rājataraṅgiṇī. A Chronicle of the Kings of Kaśmīr*. Vol. 1. Translated, with an introduction, commentary, and appendices. 1st ed. 1900. Delhi: Motilal Banarsidass

Stussi, Alfredo, ed. (1998). *Fondamenti di critica testuale*. Bologna: Il Mulino

Svenbro, Jesper (1995). "La Grecia arcaica e classica: l'invenzione della lettura silenziosa". In: *Storia della lettura*. Ed. by Guglielmo Cavallo and Roger Chartier. With revised bibliography. 1st ed. 1995. Bari: Laterza, pp. 4–36.

Tanselle, G. Thomas (1989). *A Rationale of Text Criticism*. Philadelphia: University of Pennsylvania Press

Tarkavacaspati, Taranatha (1962–1969). *Vācaspatyam: bṛhat saṃskṛtābhidhānam*. 2nd. Varanasi: Chowkhamba

Thakur, Anantalal (1955). "Nyāyamañjarī of Guru Trilocana – A Forgotten Work". In: *Journal of the Bihar Research Society* 41.4, pp. 507–511

Timpanaro, Sebastiano (2003). *La genesi del metodo del Lachmann*. With a Postilla by Elio Montanari. 1st ed. 1963. Torino: UTET

Tripathi, Chandrabhal (1975). *Catalogue of the Jaina Manuscripts at Strasbourg*. Leiden: Brill

Tripathi, Ram Shankar, ed. (1971). *Descriptive Catalogue of Sanskrit Manuscripts in Gaekwad Library, Bharat Kala Bhavan Library and Sanskrit Mahavidyalaya Library*. Varanasi: Banaras Hindu University [**Cat. BHU 1971**].

West, Martin L. (1973). *Textual Criticism and Editorial Technique, applicable to Greek and Latin texts*. Stuttgart: B.G. Teubner

Wieser, Katharina (1991). "Der Sphoṭavāda in Jayantabhaṭṭas Nyāyamañjarī. Übersetzung, Anmerkungen, Analyse". MA thesis. Wien: Universität Wien

Witzel, Michael (1990). "On Indian Historical Writing: the Role of Vaṃśāvalīs". In: *Journal of the Japanese Association of South Asian Studies* 2, pp. 1–57

Index